The Clergy and the Modern Middle East

The Clergy and the Modern Middle East

Shi'i Political Activism in Iran, Iraq and Lebanon

Mohammad R. Kalantari

I.B.TAURIS
LONDON • NEW YORK • OXFORD • NEW DELHI • SYDNEY

I.B. TAURIS
Bloomsbury Publishing Plc
50 Bedford Square, London, WC1B 3DP, UK
1385 Broadway, New York, NY 10018, USA
29 Earlsfort Terrace, Dublin 2, Ireland

BLOOMSBURY, I.B. TAURIS and the I.B. Tauris logo are trademarks of Bloomsbury Publishing Plc

First published in Great Britain 2022
This paperback edition published 2023

Series design by Adriana Brioso
Cover image © Jasmin Merdan/Getty Images

A catalogue record for this book is available from the British Library.

A catalog record for this book is available from the Library of Congress.

ISBN: HB: 978-1-8386-0556-8
PB: 978-0-7556-4487-2
ePDF: 978-1-8386-0559-9
eBook: 978-1-8386-0558-2

Typeset by Deanta Global Publishing Services, Chennai, India

To my parents, Sharbanoo and Mohammad Ali
for teaching me how to love challenges.

Content

List of figures viii
Preface ix

1 Introduction 1
2 Shiʿi clerical authority: Structures and functions 17
3 Shiʿi clergy political activism: A modern history 29
4 Iran 1979: The birth of the mujtahid statesmen 57
5 Iraq 2003: The pragmatic Shiʿi mujtahids 85
6 Lebanon 2006: The networked Shiʿi mujtahids 113
7 The power of Shiʿi clergy's solidarity and the future of the Middle East 151

Glossary 165
Notes 167
Bibliography 211
Index 231

Figures

1.1	The context for Shiʿi clerical elites political activism and quietism	11
4.1	Political activism of mujtahids in modern Iran	84
5.1	Political activism of mujtahids in modern Iraq	109
6.1	Political activism of mujtahids in modern Lebanon	149

Preface

I was doing a PhD in Business at Lancaster University when demonstrations broke out in Iran in 2009 to protest the outcome of the presidential election being held that year. Like many of my peers who had been raised in conservative Iranian families, I would have been expected to remain committed to the political orientation of the Islamic Republic and to seek advice about these events from the Ayatollahs and their families in Iran and throughout the Shiʿi world with whom, through my family, I had previously been in contact. In my religious practice, I was considered to be a follower of Grand Ayatollah Sistani in Iraq. Perhaps it was because of this that many of my friends approached me to ask why the Ayatollah was not supporting the demonstrators in the streets of Tehran who, eventually, began to chant against Grand Ayatollah Khamenei, the supreme leader of Iran.

At that time, Sistani had become popular in Iran. But I had been a follower well before 2009, at a time when not many ordinary Iranians knew him. I vividly remember when, as a devout young follower of the Ayatollah in 1998, my father surprised me with a trip to Sistani's house in Najaf, Iraq. In order that we would not attract suspicion, he asked my younger brother and I to put on the Arab garments, *dishdasha*, which we had bought in Najaf one afternoon. We approached the Ayatollah's house, only yards away from the holy shrine of Imam Ali, knocked at the door and asked the houseboy if the Ayatollah would meet with us. My father had some money – 'religious alms' paid by a few Iranian followers of Ayatollah Sistani – and wanted to pass it to him and get receipts for it. I still can feel how my heart was beating during this meeting of less than 5 minutes I had with him. It is a memory that I will cherish for the rest of my life.

Almost a decade later, the number of Ayatollah Sistani's followers in Iran has grown exponentially; and, in post-Saddam Iraq, he is widely considered to be an important and influential figure. A large number of his followers admired his so-called quietest approach to politics, which represented a contrast to his 'activist' colleagues in Iran. Nevertheless, the 2009 events in Iran was a watershed moment for me in my understanding of the political posture of the Ayatollah and, for that matter, of the Shiʿi clerical milieu. It soon became a personal quest. Is there any strategic difference between the so-called activist and 'quietist' camps within the Shiʿi clergy? When it comes to politics and political participation, is there any doctrinal differences between, say Ayatollah Sistani and Ayatollah Khamenei?

In quest of an answer to this question, I gave up my PhD research at the business school at Lancaster, against the will of my *Bazaari* family, in order to visit libraries across the UK. I started reading about the Shiʿi clerical elites, their history and politics in the Middle East. In this, I was more interested in exploring what outsiders have to say about them. Since the 1950s, dozens of academics and observers, working from different perspectives and across many disciplines, have tried to explain the

Shiʿi clergy. As I engaged in a reading of what had been produced in the West, how observers have tried to categorize the Ayatollahs as 'quietist' and 'activist', especially after the Revolution in Iran, I began to realize that the one voice that was missing was that of the Ayatollahs' themselves.

I had been living among them in Iran. As a kid, I played with the sons of many Ayatollahs who now, themselves, have joined the seminaries in Qum and Najaf and become religious elites. I had the opportunity to frequently sit with them and attend their sermons on different occasions. Yet, what I was reading – some of which was written in great detail and was the result of many years of research – somehow had overlooked a crucial aspect: how the Shiʿi clergy perceive themselves and their surrounding world.

Later, when I joined the University of London as a beginning PhD student in Politics and International Relations, I had a crystal-clear research agenda and question to explore: with respect to political engagement, do Shiʿi clerical elites themselves believe that there are two categorically different positions – 'quietist' and 'activist'? This book is the result of a four-year-long struggle to answer this question based on an exhaustive investigation of primary Shiʿi sources, as well as on scores of in-depth interviews with Shiʿi clerics in Iran, Iraq and Lebanon and those closely associated with them.

This book treats the Shiʿi clergy as a 1100-year-old person, born *c.* 940 CE, with the commencement of the Major Occultation era. Through both contemporary case studies and historical surveys, it sets out to explore how Shiʿi clerics, in their own eyes, adapted themselves to the surrounding environment; and how this adaptability to the changing context enabled the clergy to endure. It focuses on three groundbreaking events in the modern Middle East: the 1979 Islamic Revolution in Iran, the 2003 Iraq War and the 2006 July war in Lebanon. But the book represents a broader biography of the Shiʿi clergy, of their roots and how they have grown and matured, through their experiences over the course of the last eleven centuries. By examining the nature and evolution of a Shiʿi clerical network, the book finds that, far from there being strategic differences between 'quietest' and 'activist' clerics, Shiʿi mujtahid statesmen have matured, from 1979 in Iran to 2003 Iraq, by way of a pragmatism which led to a strong form of transnational and associated whole in Lebanon in 2006.

This book offers an empirically grounded understanding of Shiʿi Islamic clerical elites. It aims to break down the established, and misleading, dichotomization of the Shiʿi clergy into 'quietists' and 'activists'. In doing so, it concludes that there is no meaningful and strategic divergence among Shiʿi clerical elites regarding how they deal with the political leadership of their respective communities. It argues that the decision of Shiʿi clerical elites to become politically active or to stay out of politics depends on their perception of whether a given opportunity structure enables or constrains social mobilization. The study of perception and political opportunities, and the application of the concept of 'perceived opportunities' to case studies has not been extensive. Thus, the framework that the book develops and applies to the Shiʿi clerical elite makes a theoretical contribution by shedding light on what is still a *terra incognita* in the literature on the role of political elites in social movements.

This book finds that, in responding to political events, differences in the postures taken by different clerical elites are attributable not to doctrinal differences but to their differing perceptions of the political opportunity structure which they confront at any given time. Thus, the decision of a Shiʿi cleric to assume a quietist or an activist political posture at a particular time and place depends on the political context and, specifically, (1) the multilevel political opportunity structure which bears on the ability of a clerical elite to mobilize his followers and (2) his perception of that structure.

Nevertheless, as some rightfully point out, an opportunity is only an opportunity if it is perceived to be one by the relevant agents. Thus, effective use of the concept requires consideration of agents' subjective interpretations of political opportunities. One of the key goals of this book, therefore, is to reconstruct the history of Shiʿi political activism based on the perceptions of the clerical elites and to shed further light on how the clergy reads its history.

On the other hand, understanding of clerical perceptions is a key aspect of this book's argument. Every move a Shiʿi cleric makes, every opinion he expresses and every sociopolitical posture he adopts is rooted in principles that he applies to the circumstances he is facing. Indeed, authoritative Shiʿi clerics, Mujtahids, act and live based on their ijtihad. As they claim, during the Occultation era – when the Shiʿi community is deprived of the leadership of the infallible Imam – clerical elites act as general deputies of the Imam. To discover the divine law governing a given circumstance, it is incumbent upon a mujtahid to exert his utmost effort to interpreting fundamental principles in ways that provide an appropriate response to those circumstances. Mujtahids believe that the response they make to changing circumstances based on their ijtihad represents a tactical decision, and not a strategic one that bears on the fundamental principles that are set out in the Quran by the Prophet and the Imams. The ijtihad of a mujtahid is a determining factor in his political positioning in response to given circumstances.

There is a considerable literature on Shiʿi history and politics in Iran, Iraq and Lebanon. There is also a large collection of scholarly works on modern Shiʿi transnationalism in the Middle East. However, our understanding of how the Shiʿi clerical elite perceives its role and engages in politics is, to a large extent, based on secondary sources. This book strives to contribute to our knowledge about the politics of Shiʿi clerical elites by addressing this methodological gap. I was placed in a unique position that enabled me to visit various religious and political figures in Iran, mainly in Tehran and Qum, Iraq, the cities of Najaf and Karbala and, in Lebanon, in Beirut and the south. With both direct and indirect personal recommendations, I was seen by these figures as a member of their rank and file and, hence, was mostly greeted warmly by them. The interviewees ranged from elite informants (e.g., teachers of Shiʿi seminaries, and local politicians) to prominent individuals at the forefront of contemporary Middle Eastern politics. In total, I was able to conduct interviews with sixty individuals. I prepared an initial list of potential interview subjects, based on conversations that ensued from my approach to the highest-ranking Maraji' in Iran and Iraq, and those who were closely associated with them (i.e., their sons, representatives and students). After this initial data collection, I re-evaluated the list and introduced further changes as the interviews proceeded and, upon the recommendations of others, removed some figures from the list, and added others.

As the interviews proceeded, I composed additional questions for subsequent interviewees, both to avoid repetition and to fill the remaining gaps. I started every interview with a broad and open question about whether the interviewee believed that there exists 'two Shiʿisms' among the clergy – one politically quiet and the other active. Their answers to this question were very revealing, not only for how interviewees viewed this dichotomy but also how they related themselves, more broadly, to ongoing political issues and conflicts in the region. In many cases, their responses to this broad opening question turned out to be very elaborate, indicating that the interviewees had done considerable thinking about the political postures taken by the clergy and this assumed schism among Shiʿi clerical elites. Clearly, it is still an ongoing debate among some of them. In all cases, they engaged in a compassionate manner with me and showed a willingness to answer my questions. I felt that they had a keen desire to have their voices heard in 'the west'.

The responses of the group of high-profile individuals who participated in the interviews make an important contribution to our knowledge of the Shiʿi political ascendancy in the contemporary Middle East. They provide insider information on the process of how clerical elites themselves interpret the structure of political opportunities in a given context. Also, they explain the rationale for the political postures adopted by Shiʿi clerical elites, their perceptions of the existing political opportunity structure throughout the history of the sect and, specifically, over the three case studies. The interviews conducted for the purpose of this book were therefore subjective in nature. While this feature of the interviews must be borne in mind throughout, it in no way detracts from the value of the pool of data or the validity of the perspectives it presents. Where necessary, interview data has been checked against other sources, mainly secondary, to further elucidate the objective political opportunity structure which individual interviewees confronted.

* * *

This book, and the personal journey I took to pursue this quest, would not have been possible without the support of many people. I wish to express the deepest gratitude to my academic mentor, Professor Sandra Halperin, who was abundantly helpful and offered treasured assistance, support and guidance. I am indebted to Professor Francis Robinson, Professor Abdulaziz Sachedina and the late Professor Reza Sheikholeslami. Thanks are also extended to Professor Charles Tripp and Dr Laurence Louër for their constructive comments on an early draft of this book.

Of course, I cannot forget friends who went through hard times with me, cheered me on, and celebrated each of my accomplishments: Hussein Rouhani and Muhammad H. Saeed. I am highly indebted to them for their fraternal support.

I especially thank my mother and father, who have taught me much about the mysterious ways of life, how to value life and how to care for others unconditionally. I love them so much, and I would not have made it this far without them. And last but by no means least, I gratefully thank my wife, Leila, whose dedication and love have taken the load off my shoulders over the course of researching and writing this book. I owe Leila for her generosity in not letting her passions and ambitions collide with mine. How thrilled I am that the completion of the research on this book coincided with the birth of our beloved daughter, Asma. There are no words to convey how much I adore their company.

1

Introduction

The clerical authority in Shiʿi Islam has always been intertwined with the politics of the community. For decades, many scholars and observers have been concerned to understand the nature of, and the likely balance of power between, what has been characterized as Shiʿi 'quietism' and 'activism' in the current politics of the Middle East. This book challenges the notion that a meaningful strategic distinction can be defined between these supposed political factions among the Shiʿi clerical elite. Although some clerics did not explicitly reach for political power, and some abstained themselves from interfering in affairs of the rulers, at no time in the history of the faith, the mainstream clerics have been under this illusion that they should be indifferent from sociopolitical affairs of the community and remain apolitical. The distinction between political acquiescence and being apolitical is one underlying theme throughout this book.

The very root of Shiʿi identity was bolstered when in the eyes of his partisans Ali's right of caliphate was usurped by Abu Bakr. Mainstream Shiʿi belief entails that the twelve Imams are the just rulers, and as their general deputies, the clerics have appropriated some of their prerogatives and claimed for similar roles, including protecting the principles of Shiʿism and the community of believers. A high-ranking Shiʿi cleric puts it in the context when asked about whether the clerical elite are politically active or quiet, saying,

> The Prophet has told us that, 'all of you are guardians and are responsible for your wards' . . . so the clergy cannot be apathetic vis-à-vis the Shiʿi community, the Muslim community, and even the whole humanity. With that said, the situation is not always ripe. How come it is not licit for an ill-person to fast, for a cleric who doesn't perceive an appropriate situation, it is to refrain from political engagement. Quietism, in this sense, does not mean indifference; and if somebody says that clerics are not political, he doesn't understand Shiʿi clerical authority altogether.[1]

Notwithstanding for centuries, observers had generally viewed the Twelver Shiʿis[2] as 'moderate' and, relative to other Muslims, politically quiet.[3] As the community was growing, in size and age, it was facing the grievances of the religious leadership vacuum as well as the later emergence of the modernity. This has always been an underlying factor that shapes political postures of the clergy. The need for political engagement became more evident and necessary as the so-called Occultation era of the last Imam prolonged. With the rise of activism on the part of Shiʿi clerics in

Iran, however, scholars began to reconsider Shiʿi political doctrines and to search in them for elements they might have previously overlooked in their understanding of the community. It no longer appeared as quietistic relative to the various other Islamic political ideologies. Since then, this previously 'most moderate' faith has been characterized as a 'revolutionary' and politically 'active' ideology.

The establishment of the Islamic Republic in Iran as well as its broader impact on the Middle East caught observers by surprise. No one expected a revolution in Iran, or at least one led by the religious elites and their followers.[4] The Revolution consequently triggered a wave of scholarly research and writing on the political tendencies of Shiʿi Islam. It also inspired a reassessment of historical events that had been decisive in the evolution of the political activism of the modern Shiʿi clergy.[5] For the clerics themselves, the 1979 Revolution was a watershed moment. Their role in politics was redefined dramatically, for then they succeeded in becoming the backbone of the state in the modern time.

From the very early stages of the Islamic Republic, its religious leadership represented itself as leaders of both the Shiʿi and Sunni masses, and called on them to rise up against their usurper unjust rulers. However, as time went by, the new regime in Iran perceived more as a sectarianized state, which primarily prompted the Shiʿi communities of the region, trying to 'awaken' in them a religio-political identity.[6] For great numbers of Shiʿis in the Middle East, the Islamic Republic provided not only a model for activism but also a source of moral and financial support.[7]

An example is Hezbollah in Lebanon, which was formed in 1982 to represent the underprivileged Shiʿis in the Civil War.[8] The rise of Hezbollah was aided by, and helped to further advance, a decisive shift in Lebanon's sectarian balance of power in favour of the Shiʿi community. In the mid-1980s it became evident to most scholars and analysts that Shiʿis had passed beyond what, in retrospect, appeared to have been a politically quiet phase and, at least for a large fraction of the community, had been converted to a more activist Islam. Yet, given the pace of change in regional politics at that time, there was still no clear understanding of how this transformation had taken place, and how the actors involved interacted to produce this political activism.

The Iraq War in 2003 was another event which, after Iran's 1979 revolution, brought about a change in the balance of sectarian power in favour of Shiʿi Muslims. The ascent of the Shiʿi community in post-Saddam Iraq has raised concerns among many regional and international actors, not least among them the Sunni rulers of the region. More than a decade later, what Vali Nasr noted long ago has been confirmed: that the Middle East which would emerge 'from the crucible of the Iraq war', though it 'might not be more democratic', would 'definitely be more Shiʿi'.[9] The overthrow of Saddam's regime bolstered a Shiʿi political revival in Iraq. For the first time since the foundation of the modern state, the Shiʿa of Iraq was provided with the opportunity to rule. However, this alarmed a group of Sunni leaders in the region. Just a month before the Iraqi National Assembly Election in 2005, King Abdullah of Jordan stated that a 'Shiʿi Crescent' was emerging in the Middle East. He warned that

> [i]f pro-Iran parties or politicians dominate the new Iraqi government, a new crescent of dominant Shiʿi movements or governments stretching from Iran into

> Iraq, Syria and Lebanon could emerge, alter the traditional balance of power between the two main Islamic sects and pose new challenges to U.S. interests and allies.[10]

While the notion of a 'Shiʿi Crescent' is largely meant to serve as a call for Sunni solidarity and vigilance, it does capture a newly emerged political reality in the contemporary Middle East.[11]

The establishment of a Shiʿi government in Iraq also mobilized groups of Shiʿi clerics who, for decades, had remained quiet under the rule of the Baʿath Party. This unexpected activism confronted observers with new queries. Attention has focused, in particular, on the political role of the clergy in Qum and Najaf Seminaries following the war in Iraq. Many have tended to view this political activism as the expression of a distinctive type of Shiʿism, and to seek support for this view in the complexities of the relevant doctrines.[12]

Understanding the role played by the Shiʿi clergy in the political transformations that have taken place in Iran, Iraq and Lebanon during the last four decades requires an exploration of the responsibilities they assume for themselves within their community and how they perceive the world around them. Although Shiʿis comprise about 10–15 per cent of the Muslim World, they represent the majority of the population in the Persian Gulf. However, the internal dynamics of the Shiʿi community appears to be an area about which there is much confusion among scholars and policymakers.

The aim of this book, therefore, is to provide greater clarity about the seeming transformation of Shiʿi politics from the perspective of the clerical elite and, in this way, to contribute to a better understanding of the nature and dynamics of Shiʿi clergy political activism. What does 'political activism' mean here? There is a saying, and a logical principle often used by Shiʿi clerics in their study circles, that 'things are known through their opposites'. To understand activism, one may try to discover what does quietism mean? In his oft-cited work, *Activism and Quietism in Islam*, Michael Cook attests that Islam is a political religion, therefore, 'activism is given in Islam' and it is the quietists 'who have to work to provide themselves with excuses'.[13] Quietism, in this sense, is a position entailing the refusal to rebel, detachment from political engagement and withdrawal from the society.

Reflecting on early Islam and to underpin why different groups and thinkers rejected rebellion, Robert Gleave comes up with three categories: (1) those who viewed the state as legitimate and had no reservations about engaging with it; (2) those who viewed the state as illegitimate, thus refrained to engage with it; and (3) those who viewed the state as illegitimate but would engage with it for strategic reasons.[14] He calls the third category as 'pragmatic quietism' and puts Shiʿis under it. Yet perhaps the very idea of pragmatism acknowledges the active agency of its subject.

Those who do not rebel against the (unjust) state, perhaps because they do not have enough means and power, and get along with it for their strategic prudence, although relatively seem as quiet, but are engaged in a political action – we will read about them in the following chapters. Likes of Ayatollah Khoei in Iraq, who despite being viewed as quiet between 1970 and 1991, in contrast to his colleagues in Iran, was engaged in politics albeit using different methods. In his case, not being overtly active in politics to preserve the Shiʿi community and seminary in Iraq, which were under the siege of Baʿath Party, was the outmost manifestation of political activism. I define political quietism as being apolitical and showing apathy towards the community and the external political threats; all else, throughout this book, is political activism.

In this book, I express a story of Shiʿi clergy and their political engagement in the modern Middle East, as I heard them telling it to me. Without grappling with the narrative of the clergy about its history, it is difficult to reflect accurately on the influence of their involvement in the ongoing affairs. The story of this book is, therefore, a historical one as well. By the same token, the book surveys the history of Shiʿi community and the clergy; yet I do not see it as my task in this book to narrate an exhaustive history of Iran, Iraq and Lebanon, or for that matter the Middle East.

What I hope this book begins to offer is, in general, that the practice of categorizing various actors in the Middle East under the clear-cut groups is anything but illuminating; and more specifically, the Shiʿi clerics, like any other actors in the Middle East, no matter if we label them as quietists or activists, are all politically alert. They will engage in the politics of the community to the extent to protect it and their interests.

Shiʿi clerical political activism

The term 'Shiʿi Activism' emerged in the lexicon of the Middle East studies, only after the 1979 Revolution in Iran. In the last four decades, many have tended to characterize Shiʿi Islam as comprised of two different political factions: 'quietist' and 'activist'. But this distinction misunderstands both Shiʿi political doctrine and the contemporary political history of the Middle East.

Since the Revolution, some take the idea that there is a fundamental difference between two factions within the clergy; this so-called dichotomies are captured by, for example 'Quietism-Activism',[15] 'Quietism-Revolutionary',[16] 'Quietism-Resistance',[17] 'Silent-Speaking'[18] or 'Quietism-Islamism'.[19] This dichotomization of Shiʿi doctrine and practice assumes that 'Quietism' is a deliberate withdrawal from direct involvement in politics, and as a mainstream, is rooted in an orthodox belief in Shiʿi Islam.[20] The proponents of this idea assume that the main duty of the clergy during the Occultation era is to await the re-emergence of the Imam, to stay quiet politically and to avoid active confrontation with the so-called unjust rulers. They, therefore, see clerics of Najaf seminary, such as Ayatollah Khoei (d. 1992) and Ayatollah Sistani (b. 1930), as advocates of a so-called mainstream Shiʿi quietism; and place, figures such as Ayatollah Khomeini (d. 1989) at the other extreme of this dichotomy. To that end, Ernesto Braam suggested a third category of clerical elite, the 'whispering jurisprudent'.[21] And in a further modification of the Quietism–Activism dichotomy, Hamoudi suggested four distinctive Shiʿi doctrinal categories: Islamism, Quietism, semi-Quietism and Ambiguous Liberalism.[22] In his view, Islamist or activist Shiʿi clerics are those who propagate the idea of the Guardianship of the Jurist, *Wilayat e Faqih*, and believe that the government desired by God involves a state ruled by Shiʿi Jurist on the basis of their interpretations of Sharia. Khomeini and Muhammad Baqir Sadr (d. 1980) are two renowned advocates of this view. Quietist Shiʿi clerics, according to Hamoudi, deliberately avoid interfering in politics and the affairs of the state (he names Khoei as an example for this category). Semi-quietist Shiʿi clerics are those who fall between the Islamists and Quietists, as they prefer to choose a more ambiguous position in terms of their political involvement. These semi-quietists neither seek the establishment of a Shiʿi state nor absent themselves from the political scene (Sistani is an example). Finally, ambiguous liberal Shiʿi clergy, such as Muhammad Husayn Fadlallah (d.2010) in Lebanon, believe in a sort of religio-political pluralism that promises a secure coexistence even with non-Muslims 'with whom there are disagreements' as part of 'a Muslim's cultural and human responsibility'.[23]

Yet another group of political commentators have become more interested in studying the clergy political activism since 2003. Although they appreciate that there are different levels of political inclusion for Shiʿi quietists throughout the abode of Islam – from south Pakistan to North Africa, with Iran and Iraq at its very heart – they acknowledge that the 'context' is vital in analysing one's political activism or quietism. Jelle Puelings, for example, advised policymakers to include Shiʿi clergy as one of the main political actors in Middle East as they 'can and will play a role in the socio-political developments of their community, even if they are known to be quietist'.[24] Similarly, many have criticized the normative view of the Najaf Seminary as a politically quiet institution. This view, they argue, led to the belief that the seemingly quiet, or reticent, clerics of Iraq are totally apolitical. Some have argued that the role of Sistani in his second phase of political life since 2003 is a clear indication that clerics, regardless of what political posture they might assume from time to time, should not be ignored as an important factor in the future of the Middle East.[25] Scholars also argue that Shiʿi Islam is, in its very essence, political, and that if some clerics seem more extreme than others, it is because of the context in which they find themselves.[26] A consideration of Shiʿi history throughout the Occultation era leads them to conclude that, whenever conditions have permitted them to do so, Shiʿi clerical elites have exhibited some form of activism, even when they had previously been perceived to be committed to quietism. Contexts which have permitted Shiʿi clerics to engage in political activism include the rise of the Safavid dynasty in 1501 in Iran, the Tobacco Protest of 1890, the Persian Constitutional Revolution in 1905, and the Iraqi Shiʿi revolt against the British Empire in 1920. Examining these events suggests that even if a line can be drawn between Shiʿi quietism and activism, it will be, at best, an ambiguous and unstable one. The proponents of this stream argue that what seems to some to represent two distinctive political factions are really only different tactics clerical elites use either to achieve justice during the Occultation era or to accommodate the community to the rule of *usurpers*.[27] As Sachedina observes, both quietism and activism respond 'to the existence of injustice in the Muslim polity; both are seen as part of the long-term attempt to establish a just polity in historical time; and both are sanctioned in religious texts'.[28]

Therefore, they imply that the distinction between quietism and activism is not based on doctrinal differences, and that the aim of both so-called factions is to protect the community during the era in which it is deprived of an infallible source of leadership; and that, in pursuing this aim, they may take different approaches, sometimes moderate and sometimes more extreme, according to the context. Thus, two main tenets of Shiʿi belief, *taqiyya* and martyrdom, representing quietism and activism respectively, should best be understood as representing *two sides of the same coin*.[29] This implies that the supposed distinction between quietism and activism is based on positions that are closely related to differing contexts.

Some go a step further and focus on how the personality of Shiʿi clerical elites shapes their understanding of their religio-political role. They note that in some cases, under different circumstances, a given Shiʿi figure might act as either a quietist or activist. But rather than positing the existence of two disparate doctrines within Shiʿism, they analyse the personality and political thought of clerical elites to explain these differences. For them, a noteworthy case is Khomeini himself. They acknowledged that Khomeini, known as one of the most active clerics in history, had not been that engaged in political affairs prior to 1960s. At that time, he was just a distinguished teacher of scholarly circles at the seminary in Qum. He was reluctant to interfere in politics at any level. He therefore provides an example of how the practice of quietism and activism can be found to characterize a single Shiʿi figure.[30] The case of Sistani is equally interesting. He has become more actively involved in the politics of the Shiʿi community in Iraq since 2003; but prior to the overthrow of Saddam's regime in Iraq, he had not engaged in a single political activity. Both Khomeini and Sistani moved from a quietist posture towards more activism. There are Shiʿi figures who had reversed political trajectory: from holding an activist posture to a relatively quiet one. Muhammad Husayn Fadlallah, the former spiritual leader of Hezbollah from 1982, and Hossein Ali Montazeri (d. 2009), deputy Supreme Leader of Iran (until 1989), are two notable cases: both gave up direct involvement in politics as they grew older.[31] Evidence of both political quietism and activism in a single Shiʿi cleric raises questions about the very reliability of the 'Quietist-Activist' dichotomy in Shiʿi politics.

Exploring these wide-ranging analytic viewpoints shows that defining two apparent poles within Shiʿism – Quietism and Activism – obscures rather than illuminates the role of the clergy in modern politics of the Middle East. What is proposed and discussed over the last decades, in large parts, have overlooked the broader picture. First, any attempt towards elaborating on clerical authority within Shiʿi Islam should consider the role of ijtihad – the right of personal reasoning and perception for a qualified Shiʿi cleric, a mujtahid. A Shiʿi mujtahid must rely on his personal perceptions when confronted with different circumstances. Since 941 CE – the commencement of Occultation era – the majority of Shiʿi clerics have, to varying degrees, believed in the theory of the Guardianship of the Jurist. Some observe the guardianship as restricted to non-litigious affairs, *al-Umour al-Hesbiah*; others, who appear more activist, hold a more wide-ranging view of guardianship for the jurists and, in some cases, even extend this to his right of Islamic rule. With the contingencies of the modern era, however, the definition of non-litigious affairs needs to be redefined. Therefore, categorizing Shiʿi clerics between proponents and opponents of Guardianship of the Jurist, and to assume that the theory is an extreme Shiʿi political posture held only by activist figures like Khomeini and Muhammad Baqir Sadr does not reflect the historical practices and principles of Shiʿi Islam.[32]

Second, terms such as Quietism, Activism, Islamism and semi-Quietism have generated a great deal of confusion. Different studies, for example, have classified

Sistani as a quietist, or as semi-quietist, or even an active cleric.[33] This shows that the boundaries defining each position are unclear, and those who seek to draw a line between these seemingly different political tendencies have not provided a robust rationale for their arguments. Applying different labels to these various figures does not seem helpful as it causes more confusion than clarification in the study of political Shiʿism.

Third, it seems that different clerics' personal characteristics and their approach to political affairs in the contemporary era have encouraged this dichotomy as they may act differently depending on the circumstances. Studies have built widely different and somewhat confusing understandings of Islamic doctrine and practice, based on these outwardly dissimilar clerical political practices. Neither can Khomeini's opposition to Pahlavi dynasty define Shiʿi Islam as radical and extremist, nor does the quietism of Khoei in delaying with the autocratic regime of Saddam suggest that the mainstream Shiʿism is indeed quietistic and apolitical.

Given the current concerns regarding Shiʿi supremacy in the region, it is an even more pressing need to develop a sound understanding of the circumstances under which the Shiʿi clergy is more likely to engage in politics and social mobilization. To undertake this task, one needs to underpin the likelihood of clerical political postures as political context changes. What comes first for Shiʿi clergy vis-à-vis the community of faithful? How important is it for the clergy to reach for political power? When is it likely for a cleric to engage in politics? And how the clergy as whole, and its different members, evaluate a given circumstance to become actively engaged in politics or to remain quiet? At the time that we are witnessing an overarching sectarian tension across the Middle East, addressing these questions and underpinning how Shiʿi clerical elites, perceive the world, cannot be more vital.

Shiʿi clerical political activism and opportunity structures

As we seek to explain the processes that incline a Shiʿi cleric towards assuming an activist political posture, a number of assumptions and concepts need to be set out and clarified as a prelude to the study. First and foremost, what do we mean by the Shiʿi clerical elite or clergy?[34] What are their interests, and do they constitute a social class?

Historically, during the life of the Prophet, there were group of Muslims who devoted themselves to learning his message and teach it throughout the community.[35] Since then, Muslims from different social backgrounds who became acquainted with the teachings of the Quran, the traditions of the Prophet and his successors have formed the community of religious doctors, the clergy. Their responsibility in general, as the Quran has set forth, is to 'warn others' about the divine rulings and obligations and to protect the citadel of Islam, to safeguard the community of Muslims and the *true message* of Islam.[36] Shiʿi belief entails, however, that the most prestigious clerics are those twelve righteous successors of the Prophet, the infallible Imams. Their responsibility was to preserve the divine knowledge and to transmit it through the community of the faithful.

With the commencement of the Major Occultation, fallible Shiʿi clerics have acted as the Imams' general deputies and, since then, led the community and appropriated almost the same responsibilities. Although their corps have changed over the course of the last eleven centuries, their main responsibility as sociopolitical actors has remained largely intact. From the establishment of Shiʿi Islam until modern times, being a Shiʿi cleric was not considered as an occupation, nor did it confer social privileges. Therefore, Shiʿi clerical elites cannot be considered as forming a social class per se. The Shiʿi clergy, historically, forms a social stratum within the community, whose members are grouped based on shared values and responsibilities, and interact with each other in regard to those so-called divine duties.[37]

Ayatollah Alavi Burujirdi (b. 1954), one of the candidates to hold the leadership of Qum seminary, quotes a *hadith* from the eighth Imam reading as,

> May God have Mercy upon who revives our affairs . . . he who learn our knowledge and teach it to the people. If the people get informed of our knowledge, they would follow us.

He continues the interview, clarifies the clergy's raison d'être, and states:

> Today, we ulama are standard-bearers of this knowledge. And our moves shape over how we would perceive our duty in safeguarding and disseminating this knowledge. Our engagements in politics, or refrainment from it should be observed within this framework therefore; while they cannot be apolitical, politics comes after this important goal.[38]

Nevertheless, the clergy betrays an entropic dynamic: 'the order of the clerical authority is in its disorder.'[39] The power of Shiʿi clerical elites throughout history rests in the extent to which they, as an individual and/or a social status, are able to direct the will of the community of lay followers and mobilize them. To fulfil this preordained role, clerical elites have used different procedures in interacting with their followers – from differing social classes, such as the merchants, landowners, petty bourgeoisie – and with the rulers.

In the face of different circumstances arising during the transitory phase of the Occultation era, clerical elites have been tasked for safeguarding the Shiʿi principles and leading the community.[40] Shiʿi clerical elites are responsible for (1) 'the protection of the citadel of the faith', and (2) engaging in a process of ijtihad (independent reasoning) and remaining vigilant in their practice and deployment of their ijtihad. Therefore, almost all Shiʿi Usuli mujtahids believe that the 'transmitters of the Imams' hadiths', the qualified jurists, have assumed a divine responsibility to lead and safeguard the community based on their ijtihad.[41]

One way to study how a Shiʿi cleric responds to existing sociopolitical circumstances is through employing the concept of 'opportunity structure'. This concept provides a means of explaining, and sometimes predicting, the 'periodicity, style, and content of activist claims' in a political context.[42] Tarrow defines political opportunity structures as 'consistent but not necessarily formal, permanent, or national signals to social or political actors which either encourage or discourage them to use their internal resources to form social movements'.[43]

Political opportunity structure is the 'most widely used concept' in defining the characteristics of the relevant external environment of contentious politics.[44] Although social-movement theorists may not necessarily share a common definition of the concept, the majority of scholars focus on 'the opening and closing of political space and its institutional and substantive location' while studying a social movement.[45] While an 'open opportunity structure' may encourage political actors to engage in collective actions and to form a social movement, a 'closed opportunity structure' impedes the emergence of contentious politics.

Furthermore, a closed and/or opened political opportunity structure as a component of a given political context can involve factors located at multiple levels of analysis. To systematically address these levels, throughout the book I consider the objective political opportunity structure at six interrelated levels of analysis: international, regional, national, societal, bureaucratic and individual. For instance, international relations can influence the openness or closeness of political opportunity structure for a political movement within a given country. At the regional level, for example, throughout the volatile Middle East, political developments in a given country may influence the opportunity structure of a neighbouring country. At the national level, state repression would contribute to a closed political opportunity structure. At the societal level, the sociopolitical structure of a country can contribute to defining the political opportunity structure within which a social movement operates. At the bureaucratic level, coherent organizational structures may be a factor in the opening or closing of a political opportunity structure. And finally at the individual level, the activities of a political leader can shape the political opportunity structure.

The use of the concept of political opportunity structure has been criticized because of the tendency of scholars to emphasize objective political opportunities without reference to perception.[46] The overall argument is that an opportunity is only an opportunity if it is perceived to be one by agents.[47] Thus, effective use of the concept requires a consideration of agents' subjective interpretations of political opportunities. While different dimensions have been attributed to the political opportunity structure within the relevant studies, it seems that recognition of a structure as relatively closed or open is crucial in the formation of social movements. To encourage mobilization, the existing political opportunity structure must be perceived as 'open' by potential actors. However, while political actors act upon their perceptions about the available resources and opportunities, their interpretation 'will not always mirror reality'.[48]

This is where in applying the concept to Shiʿi clerical elites' political postures, their ijtihad comes to play. Among Shiʿi clerics, a perception or interpretation of a situation will necessarily involve their engagement with divine law through ijtihad. Ijtihad is the maximum 'exertion of mental energy' by a mujtahid, to search for and apply the faith's principles for the purpose of discovering the divine law applicable to a given circumstance.[49] Every move a Shiʿi cleric makes, every opinion he expresses and every political posture he adopts is rooted in the principle that he interprets as applicable to the circumstances he is facing. Indeed, a given mujtahid, as the title suggests, acts and lives based on his ijtihad.

Mujtahids believe that during the Occultation era – when the community of the faithful is deprived of infallible leadership – they should act as his general deputies. To discover the divine law governing a given circumstance, it is incumbent upon them, therefore, to exert their utmost effort to interpreting fundamental principles towards providing appropriate responses to those circumstances. Although it is licit for every mujtahid to reason differently from his colleagues responding to a very similar sociopolitical circumstance, this exclusive interpretation of mujtahids' authority, as they have claimed, gives a unique dynamism to Shiʿi clerical elites in their responsibility as leaders of the community.

Mujtahids, duly, are vigilantly aware of their shortcomings, and strive to protect the faith and the integrity of the community, while Shiʿis are inevitably under constant threat during the Occultation era. As deputies of the Imam, and central to fulfilling this responsibility, they sometimes may pursue political activism and mobilize their followers.

The overarching analytical argument of this book is that whether Shiʿi mujtahids adopt an activist or relatively quietist political posture depends on their interpretation of a given political opportunity structure. To this end, the 'context' for Shiʿi clerical activism consists of the interaction between (1) the objective political opportunity structure and (2) the perception of the clergy about that structure. Therefore, different postures taken by clerical elites in different contexts can be shown to be attributable, not to doctrinal differences but, at least in part, to their different perceptions of the political opportunity structure at the time.

This argument evidently challenges the notion that there exists a strategic distinction between 'activism' and 'quietism'. It sees 'quietism' and activism' in their common usage, instead, as tactical political postures. Thus, a Shiʿi mujtahid's seemingly quietist posture in a given context may, in fact, represent the utmost political activism possible at a particular time and place. It may also be part of an activist political strategy. For instance, during the National Movement in Iran, Ayatollah Burujirdi (d.1961), then leader of Qum seminary, assumed a relatively quietistic posture publicly but, as archival materials revealed decades later he was, at the same time, engaged in back-channel negotiations with the royal court and enforced his will.[50]

There has not been extensive study of perception and political opportunities; nor has the concept of perceived opportunities been applied to specific case studies. In this book, using the case of Shiʿi clerical elites and their role in the contemporary politics of the Middle East, I strive to shed some light on what remains a *terra incognita* by exploring the role that perception about whether opportunities enable or constrain social mobilization plays in the decision of Shiʿi clergy to become politically active or to stay out of politics. I argue that the principle that constructs clerical elite authority within the Shiʿi community – the responsibility to preserve the very existence of the faith and its followers – is a strategic and cohesive one. The argument to be developed here is that the decision of the Shiʿi clergy to assume an activist political posture at a given time and place depends on the political context that is: (1) the multilevel political opportunity structure which bears on the ability of clerical elites to mobilize their followers and (2) their perception of that structure. If the context appeared to be permissive, a Shiʿi cleric would be more likely to become

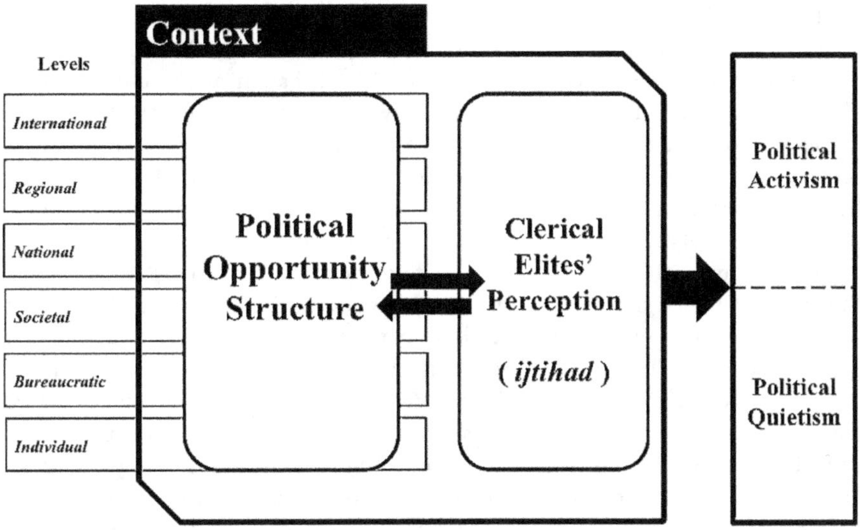

Figure 1.1 The context for Shiʿi clerical elites political activism and quietism.

actively engaged in politics to fulfil his role vis-à-vis the community; otherwise, he would remain politically quiet.

Shiʿi clerics, like any other political actors, might perceive the political opportunity structure as being open or closed and the context, therefore, as either permissive or restrictive. Whenever he perceives an open structure, he will be more likely to engage in politics, either individually or through alliance with his colleagues, and through giving legal opinions or engaging in legal arbitration. However, as Charles Kurzman observes, there is a possibility of a mismatch between the objective political opportunity structure and an actor's perception of it. As he points out, political opportunities are subjective, and actors may either fail to perceive those which might appear objectively to exist, or perceive opportunities where none exist.[51] To fulfil their sociopolitical responsibilities, it is believed that mujtahids have the responsibility of *Qadha*, giving legal opinions in disputes among their Shiʿi followers.[52] Consequently, Shiʿi clerical elites will engage in political activism to secure this task whenever they perceive the political opportunity structure to be open (Figure 1.1).

Four distinctive outcomes are suggested from this analytical framework. Like any other political actor, a cleric cannot seize a political opportunity unless he perceives there to be an opportunity; thus

- if there exists a relatively open political opportunity structure, and the mujtahid has an accurate perception of it, he will become activist;
- if he misperceives it, he will remain quiet and miss the opportunity;
- if the opportunity structure is relatively closed, and the mujtahid perceives it accurately, he will remain quiet; and finally,
- if they misperceive it, he will be active, but cannot orchestrate a successful mobilization.[53]

Modern Shiʿi history provides examples of all four contexts and outcomes. As I note later, the Islamic Revolution of Iran, the expanding role of Shiʿi clergy in post-Saddam Iraq and the Shiʿi ascendance in post-2006 Lebanon, all represent examples of the first outcome: the political opportunity was relatively open, the Shiʿi clergy perceived it accurately, and this produced a permissive context for their becoming actively engaged in politics. An example of the second outcome is the 1991 Shiʿi Uprising in Iraq, which illustrates a circumstance in which the political opportunity structure was relatively open, but the clergy missed the opportunity due to its misperception. At the time, that Iraqis were ready to actively oppose the regime of Saddam, but the clerical leadership in Najaf was unwilling to take action, and its delay to act led to a government crackdown of the popular uprising. Another notable case in recent Shiʿi history demonstrates the third context. In this case, the activism of the Shiʿi clerical elite during the Persian Constitutional Revolution (1906–11) was one in which the political opportunity structure was closed but the clergy perceived it open, inaccurately. And finally, the fourth outcome, where the Shiʿi clergy accurately perceived that the opportunity structure was closed and, thus, remained quiet, is represented by the routine practice of clerical elites during the pre-modern history of Shiʿism.

In exercising their ijtihad, Shiʿi mujtahids may perceive a given structure to be open and/or closed for engaging in contentious politics. Considering the interaction between the existing political opportunity structure and clerical elite interpretations of that structure throughout history, therefore, provides us a better and more thorough understanding of Shiʿi clerical political activism.

Shiʿi clerical political activism in Iran, Iraq and Lebanon

On 3 January 2020, at the direction of President Donald Trump, and Iranian Army General, Qasem Soleimani, and a group of his Iraqi hosts were killed in an airstrike. What was lost in the heat of the moment was an unprecedented letter of Sistani, the leader of Najaf seminary in Iraq, addressed to Khamenei. It read as,

> The news of the martyrdom of the distinguished General, Hajj Qasem Soleimani (may Allah's mercy be upon him) brought deep sorrow and sadness. The extraordinary role he played during these many years in the fight against the ISIS agents in Iraq and his numerous services are unforgettable.I would like to express condolences on the heartrending loss of the eminent martyr to you, to his respected children, his other relatives, and all the dignified Iranians . . . . I ask Allah, the Exalted, to elevate his rank in the Heavens to the highest degree, and to bestow patience and rewards on his family.[54]

In investigating the political role that the clergy played in the Shiʿi ascendancy in 1979 Iran, 2003 Iraq and 2006 Lebanon, we try to shed light, as well, on the power that they, as political actors, have for mobilizing their followers. This book focuses on three cases of Shiʿi clerical elite political engagement in the contemporary Middle East – three examples of transformative events in which the Shiʿi clerical elite played an important political role. In the wake of 11 February 1979, mass protests against what, at that time, was generally held to be one of the most stable states in the Middle East[55] enabled a wide variety of opponents of the Iranian regime to overthrow the Persian monarchy. Although various groups with different ideologies and political views played an active role in the fall of the regime, it was Shiʿi elites, with their vigorous social networks and charismatic leadership that played the most crucial role in mobilizing urban mass resistance against the Shah. The mujtahid statesmen were born after Iran officially became the first Shiʿi state of the modern Middle East, when an absolute majority of Iranians voted in favour of establishing an Islamic Republic in a referendum in April 1979.

The second event which contributed importantly to the current Shiʿi ascendancy in the region is 2003 Iraq War. The US-led war and its aftermath remains the focus of an ongoing controversy. The parliamentary elections held in 2005 under the transitional law established following the invasion brought Iraqi Shiʿis to power after centuries of being ruled by Sunni Muslims. The leaders of Najaf seminary and, particularly, Sistani's edict calling for 'one man, one vote' on the eve of the election, played an undeniable role in bringing about the triumph for the Shiʿi community.[56] Amid huge numbers of casualties, sectarian violence and civil war, the Shiʿis of Iraq were provided with an opportunity to form the first Shiʿi government in the Arab world. Thirty years after the Revolution, the clergy mastered in capturing the political power through a pragmatic means.

The third case to be explored is the war of 2006 between Lebanon's Shiʿi Hezbollah, and Israel. Hezbollah is a social and political party that enjoys huge mass support in Lebanon, especially among the Shiʿi community.[57] In July 2006, Hezbollah's paramilitary forces fired rockets across Israel's northern border, killing three soldiers and capturing two. They demanded the release of four Lebanese prisoners held by Israel in exchange for the two captured Israeli soldiers.[58] Israel blamed the Lebanese government for this incident; and, despite Prime Minister Fouad Siniora's denial of Lebanese government responsibility, Israel launched airstrikes that targeted not only Hezbollah's Southern Lebanese strongholds but also Lebanon's civilian infrastructure.[59] After thirty-three days of constant attacks, and without having achieved its planned objectives, Israel accepted a ceasefire. Although Lebanon sustained considerable casualties and damage, Hezbollah and its secretary general, Hassan Nasrallah, claimed victory for themselves. Since Israel had failed to achieve its stated goals, made earlier by Prime Minister Olmert, this represented the first defeat of the Israeli army in a fight with a neighbouring Muslim state.

These cases – the establishment of the Islamic Republic of Iran in 1979, Iraq War in 2003 and the Israel-Hezbollah war in 2006 – allow us to explore both the political opportunity structures that the clergy confronted at these specific times and places, and how the perception, ijtihad, of individual Shiʿi figures led to them taking an activist political posture in response to unfolding circumstances.

The political opportunity structures that the clerical leadership faced in each of these cases were multi-levelled, and the development of both structures, and of the clergy perceptions of them, occurred over the course of the modern history of the countries concerned. The political opportunity structure of Iran in 1979, along with the perception of the Shiʿi clergy at the time, the political context of the Islamic Revolution, were shaped throughout the decades following the Persian Constitutional Revolution of 1905. The 1920 Iraqi Revolt influenced the post-2003 Shiʿi ascendancy in Iraq. The activities of Musa Sadr beginning in 1958 provided a foundation for the Shiʿi hegemony achieved in post-2006 Lebanon. Consequently, a substantial part of the narrative of each case study is devoted to explaining factors that had been developing throughout the modern history of Iran, Iraq and Lebanon, and that contributed to the objective political opportunity structures that existed at the time of these events. To understand the political postures that Shiʿi clerics assumed in each of these cases, the history of these events must also be read from their point of view. In sum, how the modern history of Iran, Iraq and Lebanon shaped the objective political opportunity structure in each of the specific events that constitute cases of Shiʿi clerical elite political engagement, and how they were seen through the eyes of involved Shiʿi clerics, are of central importance in explaining the three cases.

On the other hand, these three cases have much in common. First, in all cases Shiʿi clerics were relatively active in mobilizing the community. Second, in Iran and Iraq, Shiʿis constituted the absolute majority of the population and in Lebanon they constituted the most populous sect. Approximately 92 per cent of Iran's population are Shiʿis; they constitute about 60 per cent of Iraq's population and more than one-third of Lebanon's population.[60] Third, in all cases, and in contrast to their Sunni counterparts, Shiʿi clerical elites enjoyed a degree of autonomy from the state. Shiʿi clerical elites are supported by funds from their followers, especially wealthy merchants. Consequently, with the exception of a few brief historical periods, their authority has remained rooted more in their popular constituency than in the state's support. Shiʿi clerical elites in Iran of 1979, Iraq in 2003 and Lebanon in 2006 were all independent of formal state power, thus providing them with greater freedom of action.

Despite these similarities, the three cases also exhibit differences. The political opportunity structures in Iran, Iraq and Lebanon differed and so, therefore, did the context in which the events that each case highlights unfolded. Although, international and regional factors in all three countries overlap to some extent, national, societal, bureaucratic and individual factors comprising the political opportunity structures varied considerably. For example, three distinctive national-level factors shaped the political opportunity structures in each case: nationalist sentiments in Iran,[61] tribal social fabric of Iraq[62] and confessionalism in Lebanon.[63] Different political opportunity structures distinguish each of these cases from the others and, together, make these case studies individually unique, yet collectively comprehensive. These three cases have not only undeniably influenced the politics of the contemporary Middle East but, given their common features and different political opportunity structures, they offer an opportunity to analyse the factors which shaped the course of Shiʿi clerical elite political activism in different contexts. Each is intended to show how different Shiʿi elite figures, with different perceptions of the existing political opportunity structure, conducted themselves.

Demystifying the role of Shiʿi clerics in politics of the modern Middle East

This book is divided into two parts. Part I takes up to define principles of political Shiʿism and the consolidation of the clergy from early ages to the early modern era. Part II focuses on three case studies of Shiʿi clerical political activism in modern Iran, Iraq and Lebanon. It tries to tell a story of the clergy through their own narrative; how they led the revolution in Iran, what was their role in years prior to the ousting of Saddam in Iraq, and how they succeeded in mobilizing the underprivileged Shiʿi community in Lebanon to the extent that they could stand against the most formidable army of the Middle East, Israel.

The relevant context of clerical activism in the Middle East consists of the political opportunity structure that existed at the time and the perceptions that Shiʿi clergy had of that structure. To understand the perceptions of key clerical elites involved in these events, this book draws on three distinct, yet collectively comprehensive, data sources: historic archives, original manifestos and interviews with elite Shiʿi clerics. Discussion of perceptions of clerical elites who confronted challenges in the earlier history of Iran, Iraq and Lebanon – in the Persian Constitutional Revolution, the great Iraqi revolt against British Occupation in 1920, and the Lebanese civil war – draws on material in historic archives, including personal letters, formal telegraph messages and newspaper reports. I also consulted public manifestos of the groups involved in the Islamic Revolution of Iran, the formation of the Shiʿi government in post-Saddam Iraq and the Shiʿi parties, Hezbollah and AMAL in Lebanon.

The pool of interviewees ranged from elite informants (e.g. teachers of Shiʿi seminaries, and local politicians) to prominent individuals at the forefront of contemporary Middle Eastern politics (e.g. Ayatollah Sistani in Najaf, and former President Hashemi Rafsanjani of Iran).

The responses of the high-profile individuals with whom I conducted interviews constitute an original contribution to our knowledge of Shiʿi political activism and to the current Shiʿi political ascendancy in the Middle East. They provide insider information about the political postures assumed by clerical elites in relation to key events in the contemporary history of the region. Overall, the interviewees reveal clerical elite perceptions of different political opportunity structures, both at key points in the history of the community and with respect to the three cases that are the focus of this book, and the processes through which they interpreted them.

Chapter 2 provides an understanding of Shiʿi jurisprudence and the sociopolitical role of the clerical elite. It reviews arguments concerning clerical authority prior and during the Occultation era, and the function of ijtihad as a means of inferring religious law from the Shiʿi principles. It also defines the institution of Shiʿi clerical authority, *marjaʿiyya*. The chapter continues to discuss the factors that influence the process of ijtihad by mujtahids, and how this, in different contexts, pushes them to hold distinct political postures.

Chapter 3 presents a brief historic overview of the role of the Shiʿi clerical elite in politics and their interactions with governments, especially after the establishment of the Shiʿi Safavid dynasty in Persia. It clarifies the main variables which the argument of this book employs to explain when the clergy is likely to be more or less active in politics: the interaction of different objective political structures with different mujtahids' perceptions. It traces a turning point in the history of Shiʿi politics, the rise of Safavid Persia and offers a novel reading of the posture of the Shiʿi clerical elite during the Persian Constitutional Revolution (between 1906 and 1911), which marked the emergence of Shiʿi clerical activism in the contemporary Middle East.

Part II takes up on the Shiʿi clerical activism in the contemporary Middle East. In an overlaying fashion, the next three chapters focus on Iran of 1979, Iraq of 2003 and Lebanon of 2006. Chapter 4 explores Shiʿi activism which led to the Islamic Revolution of Iran. It begins with a discussion of the sociopolitical context of the post-Constitutional Revolution and then examines the role played by Ayatollah Burujirdi in the institutionalization of the Qum seminary and the political posture that he adopted while he was the sole Shiʿi marja' of the time. Finally, it reviews the rise of Ayatollah Khomeini as the most active religious figures of the time and the role of the Shiʿi clergy in establishing the Islamic Republic of Iran.

Chapter 5 lays down the clerical activities which led to political ascent of Shiʿis in post-Saddam Iraq. It starts by tracing the background of the events that are the focus of this chapter: the role of Najaf seminary and its mujtahids within the Shiʿi world, the leadership of the clerical elite in the 1920 revolt in Iraq, why in its aftermath, the Shiʿis of Iraq felt swindled, and how this resentment within the community surfaced almost nine decades later; the political postures of Ayatollah Muhsin Al-Hakim (d. 1970) and of Muhammad Baqir Sadr prior to and after the rise of the Baʿath Party in the late 1960s; incidents that occurred during the Shiʿi uprising against Saddam's regime in 1991, and the role of Ayatollah Khoei in that uprising. With this as a background, it then explores the role of Shiʿi elites in post-Baʿth Iraq, with a focus on Ayatollah Sistani's activities and his pragmatic approach to politics.

Chapter 6 goes through an overview of the Shiʿi community in Lebanon and how, in the mid-twentieth century a reformist Shiʿi cleric, Imam Musa Sadr (disappeared in 1978) laid the foundation for the later transformation of what was then a fragmented community, the place of the Shiʿi in the politics of the country, and the series of activities beginning in the 1980s that led to the foundation of Hezbollah. It then moves to a discussion of regional, the threat of Israel and of Shiʿi commitments to the Islamic Republic of Iran, and the impact of these factors on Lebanese internal and external policies. Finally, it focuses on the role of Shiʿi clerics in the events of 2006, and the Hezbollah–Israel war.

The epilogue to the book, Chapter 7, collates the findings of this study, current Shiʿi political doctrines in the Middle East, the sociopolitical revival of Shiʿi hegemony in the region and how the clergy sees itself within broader politics of the modern Middle East.

2

Shiʿi clerical authority

Structures and functions

Monotheism, prophecy, resurrection, justice and the Imamate are five principles of Shiʿi Islam. Monotheism is the belief that God is the ONE who is self-sufficient, needless and that nothing is equal or comparable to him. Shiʿis believe that individuals have infinite necessities and, thus, are obliged to be part of a community, hence, social life requires people to fulfil a set of responsibilities. For the community of believers, it is inevitable, therefore, to go beyond mundane rules and regulations; after all, as the mainstream Shiʿis belief entails, some of these rights and responsibilities are divine. This is where the necessity of just and infallible legislation appears in Shiʿism. They argue that to lead the community of believers towards its true salvation, a divine authority is needed. God, therefore, has bestowed such authority to his prophets, of whom Muhammad is the seal and the last one.

Shiʿis also believe that, as God is the most ultimate and the complete creator, he is the source of justice. According to this belief, there should, therefore, be another world in which individuals are rewarded or punished. This is how Shiʿis justify the need for the resurrection and the Judgement Day. Finally, they believe that, as it is impossible for the Prophet to leave humanity abandoned without a leader, there is a necessity for divinely guided leaders, who are called Imams. Therefore, as Allah has ultimate authority over all humans, he would assert this authority through his prophets. After Muhammad sealed the prophecy, the infallible Imams have become responsible to lead humanity.

What are the specific roles of the Prophet and the infallible Imams during their lifetimes in regard to humanity? And what if they are unable to accomplish these roles within the particular circumstances they might be facing? What if their followers do not have direct access to infallible Imams that will define their responsibilities? Are there any alternatives, though fallible, to handle the roles of the Imams when they are out of reach? To answer these questions, Shiʿi principles provide a series of explanations that eventually consolidated clerical authority among the community of believers.

The 'Imamate' and the 'Occultation' are the two main beliefs among Shiʿi Muslims. The former belief entails that after the death of the Prophet, the newborn Islamic community was still in need of leadership. Although the Prophet had delivered some preliminary Islamic principles, how to implement them was still unclear. The period of divine legislation, *tashrī'*, therefore, should be extended beyond the life of the Prophet. To this end, he assigned the role of leadership of the community to his legitimate successor, Ali Ibn Abu Talib, as one of his last divine duties, Shi'is believe. In support of this belief, they point to this Quranic verse:

> O' Messenger, announce that which has been revealed to you from your Lord [the succession of Ali], and if you do not, then you have not conveyed Allah's message completely.[1]

In the eyes of Shi'is, the majority of Muslims chose to disobey the Prophet's wishes that they acknowledge Ali as his legitimate successor. Consequently, concurrent with the death of the Prophet, Shi'is were forced into a marginal position within the community and they have practised remonstrance against the majority of Sunnis ever since. Although Ali and his sons were put aside by the ruling caliphs, they still had the responsibility to construe and convey the divine message until the promised day when the last Imam will re-emerge. This is where the 'Occultation' discourse appears in Shi'i Islam.

The belief in the occultation of the twelfth Imam entails that with the rise of threats to the life of the last infallible descendant of Ali, he disappeared in 874 CE. Mainstream Shi'is believe that he will re-emerge in the future in order to fill the world with justice and crown the suppressed humans who are the heirs of God on the Earth. This constitutes the Messianic posture embedded in Shi'i Islam, which represents the most influential factor in the faith's sociopolitical engagements during the last eleven centuries.[2]

According to the Shi'i belief, the last infallible Imam introduced deputies to lead the community during the Occultation era. These deputies are either 'specific', those explicitly named by the Imam himself, or 'general', those recognized by the Imam implicitly. The General Deputies of the Imam during the Occultation era are those clerical elites capable of extracting religious laws from the tenets of the faith in relation to occurring circumstances. The infallible Imams had already laid down for them a series of prerequisites for holders of this position. During the pre-Occultation era, the Imams accomplished the role of delivering the divine message; and it is the responsibility of their righteous deputies to pursue their mission further, to propagate the principles and to preserve the community, while the last of them is absent from the scene. This is the framework constructed by the Imams for their followers. Consequently, the most significant responsibility of the Shi'i elite is to preserve the community and its principles, in different arising circumstances, until the day that the conditions become permissive for the re-emergence of the last Imam.

This reading of the Imamate and the occultation in Shi'i mainstream beliefs to a great extent guarantees that the community of the believers is capable of becoming dynamically adapted to the fast pace of sociopolitical changes. To this end, the sociopolitical posture of the Shi'i elite and the behaviour of the laity throughout history can be understood through the prism of these two fundamental beliefs. In order to describe the roots and structures of the Shi'i clerical elite authority, using the primary sources, this chapter considers two distinctive periods in the history of Shi'i Islam: the era of the Prophet and the infallible Imams, and the Occultation era. The chapter probes the Prophet and his infallible successors' sociopolitical responsibilities to deliver and institutionalize the divine message according to Shiʿi beliefs. Next, it emphasizes the formation and consolidation of Shiʿi jurisprudence in regard to its clerical authority during the Occultation era. It also suggests a redefinition of the 'Marja'iyya' in order to resolve some ambiguities surrounding clerical authority in Shiʿi Islam.

Early Shiʿi political doctrines

This period starts with the establishment of the first Islamic state by the Prophet Muhammad in Medina in 620 and terminates with the start of the last Shiʿi Imam's Major Occultation in 941. According to Shiʿi beliefs, during this era Muslims had access to the infallible leaders, either directly or through specific deputies. According to Shiʿi belief, true Islam started to flourish through the rule of the Prophet and was developed and established by the endeavours of his twelve infallible successors.[3]

After thirteen years of propagating Islam, the restrictive context of Mecca made it impossible for the Prophet to fulfil his responsibilities properly. Thus, he accepted an invitation made by the tribes of Yathreb (later known as Medina), and he migrated there and formed the first Islamic state. Henceforth, the responsibilities of the Prophet vis-à-vis the Muslim community were extended to three distinctive functions: the revelation of the divine message exactly as it had been related to him, the establishment and rule over the Islamic government, and the issuing of legal judgements for his followers.

The first and most important role of the Prophet was to deliver the divine message; he was the last messenger to receive the will of God through the revelation and had the duty to lead humanity towards felicity.[4] The second role of the Prophet, which materialized after his settlement in Medina, was to establish a government based on the divine rules of Islam. The fact that the tribes' sheikhs and inhabitants of the city had greeted him with open arms provided him with an opportunity to publicize Islam more easily at the time.[5] The last, but not least, of the Prophet's roles was to legislate for and arbitrate among Muslims. This was the authority that God had assigned to him, as it is believed that only divine laws may deflect humans from obstinacy.[6]

Although the Prophet has delivered the divine message, he did not have time to thoroughly expand and compile it during his lifetime. Moreover, the life of the Islamic state hardly exceeded ten years, and Muslims were unfamiliar with the principles of Islamic rule and legislation. At the time he died, the common belief was that, without a competent leader, the new community would go astray. Thus, the main question was over a successor who could take on the roles performed by the Prophet. In seeking an answer to this question, Muslims divided into two camps: the majority, later to be known as 'Sunnis', believed that representatives from the community should elect the successor or 'caliph', and the minority 'Shiʿis' believed that the Prophet had answered this vital question during his lifetime and had named Ali Ibn Abu Talib, his son-in-law, as his righteous successor.[7]

Mainstream Shiʿi belief entails that the Prophet's caliph should be free from sin, as his major role is to lead the community based on divine will. This marked a period of consolidation of Imamate discourse. The Imamate in Shiʿi Islam mainly rests on the idea of the permanent need for a divinely guided Imam to act as the authoritative teacher of mankind in all religious matters. The Imam thus is 'the only legitimate successor of the Prophet. . . . Whoever obeyed the Imam was a true believer, and whoever opposed or rejected him, an infidel'.[8] Thus, the infallible Imams' responsibilities are exactly the same as those of the Prophet, with a single difference: they are not God's messengers, and only exist to protect and interpret the message that the Prophet has already delivered.[9]

Likewise, the infallible Imams are the most competent to perform the role of judicial authority. As the most complete available informants of the divine will, they are righteous substitutes for the Prophet in arbitrating justly among Muslims. The logical corollary to these roles is that Imams become the most competent individuals to rule the Muslim community; however, depending on the opportunity structure they face, they may not be able to assert this divinely assigned responsibility.

Mainstream Shiʿi belief holds that infallible Imams have the right, bequeathed by the divine source, to rule, whether or not the context provides them with the opportunity to establish their reign on the earth. On the day of the Prophet's death, Ali, the legitimate successor, according to Shiʿis, was deprived of the Caliphate position. Instead, Abu Bakr (d. 634) became the Prophet's first caliph, with the result that Ali was cut off from public affairs and retreated to his house for the next twenty-five years. Umar Ibn al-Khattab (d. 644) and Uthman Ibn Affan became the second and third caliphs.[10] When Uthman passed away in 656, some Muslims who owed their allegiance to Ali asked him to become the fourth caliph. Although he rejected the offer initially, he eventually agreed to become the caliph, as the popular will left him with no other choice. Later, he narrated the incident personally and stated,

> If people had not come to me and supporters had not exhausted the argument and if there had been no pledge of Allah with the learned to the effect that they should not acquiesce in the gluttony of the oppressor and the hunger of the oppressed, I would have cast the rope of Caliphate on its own shoulders and would have given the last one the same treatment as to the first one. Then you would have seen that, in my view, this world of yours is no better than the sneezing of a goat.[11]

This statement shows that, while Shiʿis believe in the right of infallible Imams to rule, the support of the community has an undeniable influence in institutionalizing this position. It confirms that the desire of the Imam to form a government was secondary to his divine duty, to safeguard the divine message and the community of believers.

Ali's caliphate lasted about five years. His son, Hassan, ascended to power in 661. Like his father, Hassan, he was opposed by, and continued to fight with, the Ummayad, Muawiyah (d. 680), the rebellious governor of Syria. However, betrayed by a group of his army's commanders, Hassan eventually was forced to sign a peace treaty with Muawiyah. He handed the caliphate post to Muawiyah after just six months of being in office. With the conclusion of this treaty, this Shiʿi Second Imam migrated to Medina and resigned from politics. He remained 'quiet' for the rest of his life. Hassan's younger brother, Husayn, became the third Shiʿi Imam. He was loyal to the terms of his late brother's treaty with Muawiyah, and thus remained relatively quiet. Nonetheless, when Muawiyah appointed his own son, Yazid, as the heir to the caliphate, breaching the terms of the treaty, Husayn could not remain indifferent. Responding to the request of Iraqi Muslims, Husayn migrated to Kufa with the aim of revitalizing the religion of his grandfather. On the way to Kufa, on Ashura of 680 the army of Yazid attacked Husayn and his companions at Karbala, and brutally massacred them.

After the ruthless death of Husayn, the third Shi'i Imam, his son, Ali Ibn al-Husayn, succeeded him as the new Imam. The strict surveillance by Umayyads over the activities of the Imam and his Shi'i followers compelled them to completely retire from public life thoroughly. The life of the fifth Shi'i Imam, Muhammad Ibn Ali, occurred simultaneously with a series of Muslim civil wars that made the Umayyad Caliphs weaker than ever. Consequently, the door was left open for the Imam and his followers to establish teaching circles in Medina in order to propagate Shi'i principles. This era was monumentally important in the history of the Shi'i faith. It was the first time since the time of the abdication of the Caliphate by the Second Imam that Shi'is had an opportunity to consolidate the divine message through the teachings of the infallible Imam. It was during this era that the theory of the Imamate was principally framed.[12] The situation became even more favourable for the Shi'is during the life of the sixth Imam, Ja'far Ibn Muhammad.[13] During the era of his Imamate, the Shi'i principles were institutionalized and he started to spread and to develop them throughout the known world. He instructed more than 4,000 pious students and, making the most out of the permissive opportunity structure existing at the time, encouraged them to disseminate the divine message throughout the community.[14] Nevertheless, the last years of his life were concurrent with the consolidation of the Sunni Abbasids, who had been succeeded by the Umayyads. After Ja'far Ibn Muhammad passed away, his son, Musa Ibn Ja'far, received the Imamate. By that time, the Abbasid caliphate had established its reign and had started to control the activities of the Shi'is in order to diminish their potential threats. Consequently, the seventh Imam was put in the Caliphate jail for most of his life.

The Shi'i principles had been already transplanted into the community through the teachings and activities of the previous Imams, and their students and disciples had migrated all over the Islamic world. Yet the followers' direct access to the infallible Imam was under the strict control of Abbasid caliphs. Over such contingencies, the Shi'is of Iraq, Hejaz and Iran were required to refer to someone in order to ask their religious questions and duties. This, perhaps, was the very first stage of the initiation of the Shi'i Marja'iyya as the authority of religious reference in the history of the faith. The Imams' companions were among the earliest elite figures that became the references for Shi'i laity – substitutes responsible for leading the community when the infallible Imams were not accessible to lay followers.[15]

The Abbasid caliph, al-Ma'mun, harshened the situation for the Shi'i and forced the eighth Imam to migrate from Medina to Tus, in Iran. He also made the eighth Imam agree to become the heir to the throne, because he hoped to attract popular support and strengthen his shaky caliphate at the time. However, he had no other choice but to kill the Imam in 818 CE. The ninth Shi'i Imam, Muhammad Ibn Ali, remained under the strict surveillance of the Abbasid as well. The level of the Abbasid's oppressions towards Shiʿi Imams increased even more during the era of Ali Ibn Muhammad, the tenth Imam, to an extent that they kept him under house arrest during his lifetime. His son, Hassan Ibn Ali, the eleventh Shiʿi Imam, never had the opportunity to exit the military base of Abbasid in Samarra through his whole life. According to Shiʿi beliefs, these harsh strategies and intolerable suppressions eventually led the twelfth Imam, Hujjat Ibn al-Hassan, to be occulted from the scene.

However, by 874 CE, over the activities of the previous Imams and their pious disciples, the Shiʿi community became ready, to some extent, to deal with the new circumstances. After the faith's tenets were institutionalized by the teachings of the fifth and the sixth Imams, the community was more reliant on their trustworthy companions and disciples, as direct access to the next Imams was severely limited and controlled. The success of the previous Imams became more evident, as the eleventh Imam had the greatest number of specific deputies all over the Islamic world. It shows that, just years before the occultation, the Imams had laid the cornerstone of Shiʿi principles and their followers were taught how to exploit them in upcoming events in order the preserve the faith and further develop it.

The belief that the twelfth Imam, Mahdi, is alive but has been occulted, and that the establishment of the 'just Islamic order' is awaiting his re-emergence is central to Shiʿi faith.[16] According to this belief, he had a minor occultation that lasted sixty-nine years and terminated in 941; since then, he is passing the Major Occultation. The majority of Shiʿis believe that, during the minor occultation, the Imam had appointed 'the Four Specific Deputies' to mediate between the Imam and his followers concerning Shiʿi religious and social affairs.[17] The specific deputies were assigned to handle two of the Imam's responsibilities: the interpretation of the divine message and judicial arbitration among the community.[18]

It seems that the former period was aimed to prepare the Shiʿi community more than ever for the Major Occultation period as Ali Ibn Muhammad al-Samarri (d. 941), the last of the four deputies, claimed to have received a letter from the Imam, which reads as follows:

> May Allah grant the great reward to your Muslim brothers in mourning of your death; you will pass away in six days. Order everything and do not appoint any successor for yourself as the Major Occultation period has been already started.... As Allah wishes, I will re-emerge after a long period when the Earth is filled by oppression and brutality.... Be aware that anyone who claims that he has seen me or come directly on my behalf is a liar and calumniator.[19]

Although the notion of the Imam's specific deputies that was originated in the time of the Fifth Imam was terminated by the death of al-Samarri, years earlier, the twelfth Imam clarified the Shiʿi duty over his Major Occultation. He stated the following:

> When I will remerge? It is upon the will of Allah, and you should be aware that whoever determines the time for that is a deluder . . . and in the upcoming incidents, refer to those who narrate our traditions; they are my proof to you as I am the proof of Allah to them.[20]

Shi'is believe that the narrators of the Imams' traditions are his general deputies – the Shi'i clerical elites, who are competent enough to induce religious law from the principle sources: Quran and utterances of the infallible Imams, *Hadiths*. Therefore, with the commencement of the Major Occultation era, while the Shi'i laity would be deprived of direct access to the infallible Imam, the authority of leading the community would go the clerical elite until the re-emergence of the Imam.

The abandoned Ummah: Shi'i clerical authority and the Occultation era

The Prophet delivered the divine message, and the infallible Imams laid down the Shi'i principles through interpreting that message. Nevertheless, a series of incidents caused the occultation of the last Imam and materialized the Messianic thought in Shi'i Islam.

Shi'is principally believe that the Imam will 'emerge' rather than will 'be presented' or come back in the future.[21] Thus, Shi'i doctrine is believed to be innately dynamic. The fact that the infallible Imam has been always present on the Earth implies that, over time, as the context changes, Shi'i doctrine should adapt itself to the given circumstances. Nevertheless, the question still remains of who has the responsibility to act on his behalf during the Occultation era? And what is the driving force behind this sort of dynamism? Based on numerous and trusted traditions, Shi'is believe that the authority would be vested in those qualified clerical elite, who will lead the laity until the 'promised day' when the Imam will re-emerge.

As mentioned earlier, the community was awaiting commencement of the occultation of their last Imam, based on the traditions of the Prophet and previous Imams. With regard to the responsibilities of the clerical elite, Prophet Muhammad had acknowledged a special role for the scholars.[22] The infallible Imams have also confirmed the issue in greater detail. During the Imamate of the Sixth Shi'i Imam, a group of elites formed the closest circle of the Shi'i propagation office. Upon the confirmations of the infallible Imams, those pious disciples were responsible to give legal opinions, called *ifta*, and to arbitrate among laity based on the just legal regulations of the Shi'i principles. Thus, the Imams had focused on instructing the principles to those elite and permitted them to deduce religious law in upcoming circumstances.[23] The mainstream Shi'i belief is that Imams depicted the situation of the Occultation era and stated,

> If the Shi'i Ulama – who invite people to Allah, who are proofs to Allah, and who are the protectors of the people against the Evil – would not survive during the occultation of the last Imam, people have no alternative but to become apostate from Islam and to go astray. Indeed, they will capture the hearts of true believers, and they are the true servants to Allah.[24]

Whenever the Imams have been asked how the Shi'i laity will survive during the Occultation era, when the community has no direct access to the infallible Imam, the answer was that the laity should refer to the Shi'i clerical elite. Hence, the Shi'i religious elite has been nominated as the secondary expositor of the divine law after the Prophet and the infallible Imams. Nonetheless, because the clerical elite could not be infallible, infallible Imams have laid down sets of prerequisites for the laity to consider while following these general deputies.[25] According to this, since the dawn of the Major Occultation, the qualified Shiʿi elite has started to publish numerous treatises and books that answer the laities' inquiries in order to keep the community as vivid as possible.

With the rise of the Shiʿi Buyids in mid-900, just years after the commencement of the Major Occultation era, the clerical elite had been offered the opportunity to disperse and to develop the Imam's will throughout the Islamic world.[26] In order to adapt the principles to the contingencies of the Occultation era, the Shiʿi elite was to exert ijtihad. The term is derived from the root *J-H-D* in Arabic, which literally means 'the utmost striving and exertion in doing an action'. Technically, the term has two totally different meanings in Islamic jurisprudences.

The first meaning, which is held by the majority of Sunni religious elite, interprets ijtihad as a personal reasoning, or *ra'y*, in deducting an Islamic law.[27] The second meaning is held by Shiʿi mujtahids, who forbid the application of ijtihad in the sense of personal reasoning to the religious law. Al-Sharif al-Murtada, who is one of the proponents of this stream, explains that 'ijtihad [according to the belief of Abu Hanifa's followers] is seeking for an overriding opinion in issues that have no evident indicators; yet the dubious supposition, *zann*, does not have any place in Islamic jurisprudence and a jurist is not allowed to establish his opinion based on this'.[28] In this regard, the Shiʿi clerical elite interprets the ijtihad as a process of signifying 'the application by a jurist of all his faculties to the consideration of the authorities of law with a view to finding out what, in all probability, is the law'.[29] This legitimate sense of ijtihad is the action, which has been practiced since the era of the Prophet and his infallible successors to their particular students and disciples and is still common among the qualified elite, mujtahids.

Although exerting ijtihad had been common among the Shiʿi religious elite since the era of the infallible Imams, it was Allameh Hilli (1250–1325) who labelled the process and redefined it retrospectively. His endeavours heralded an evolutionary turning point in Shiʿi jurisprudence. Hilli's reading of the process of ijtihad, which has prevailed among Shiʿi jurisprudence since then, is principally different from that of the Sunni Schools, especially *the Hanafis*. At the time Hilli was living, Shiʿi jurisprudence had become so pervasive that a restating of the ijtihad, a mechanism of clerical elites' perception, was necessary. Since then, jurisprudence has become the most noteworthy driving power of the Shiʿi dynamism utilized by the clerical elite.

A Shiʿi cleric aiming to become a mujtahid must be able to deduce the religious law from the faith's principles; and for this he must have some qualifications and comprehensively studied religious courses. Shiʿi believers are divided into two groups: they are either mujtahids, who personally strive to resolve the legal Islamic legal questions, or they are ordinary laymen, who should seek the assistance of a mujtahid. Therefore, ijtihad adds two corollaries to Shiʿi jurisprudence: it establishes a group of Shiʿi clerical elites, the mujtahids, and it also recommends the laity to follow the verdict of a special religious elite. It is from this that the concept of Taqlid, and the office of Marja'iyya, the highest-ranking position among Shi'i clerical elites, have been moulded.

The formation and consolidation of the office of Shi'i Marja'iyya

The third evolutionary phase of Shi'i jurisprudence in regard to its clerical authority was initiated by the endeavours of Sheikh Murtada Ansari (1781–1864). Following the crackdown of the internal scholastic oppositions, the Usuli School had been restored once again in Najaf seminary during the nineteenth century. Moreover, with the introduction of peace treaty between Ottomans and Persians, streams of Iranian pilgrims to Najaf and Karbala had developed the economy of the holy cities and their religious schools. Under such circumstances, Sheikh Ansari became the leader of the seminary, following the death Sheikh Muhammad Hassan Najafi (1785–1849), and became known as the first Shi'i Marja' Taqlid.[30]

The role of Sheikh Ansari in institutionalizing the concept of Taqlid and developing the extent of Shi'i jurisprudence is undeniable. He has been so central to the concept of Shi'i Marja'iyya that the characteristics of a Shi'i Marja' Taqlid are defined by his personal characteristics and manners; he was well known to be most pious, knowledgeable and dissociated from earthly matters.[31] A Marja' Taqlid, a position that originated mainly during the era of the Sheikh, is believed to be held by the most righteous mujtahid of the time. It makes clear who, among all other mujtahids, is more capable of becoming the supreme exemplar, and thus the virtuous religious reference for ordinary Shi'i laymen.

The practice of Taqlid was initiated at the time of the Sheikh and, respectively, each Shi'i believer has three alternatives to practicing the Ancillaries of the faith. These range from praying to Jihad.[32] He should be either a mujtahid himself, capable of inferring the law from the principles personally or, if he is not, he should follow a Marja' Taqlid's verdicts in religious matters; finally, if he is not a mujtahid and would not like to follow any Marja', he 'should act on such precaution which should assure him that he has fulfilled his religious obligation'.[33] The rationale behind the Taqlid is evident: not every single Shi'i layman has the time to spend years in religious lectures to become an expert in religious principles. Quran justifies this in the following statement:

> It is not possible for the believers to go forth all together. Why, then, does not a party from every section of them go forth, that they may become well versed in religion, and that they may warn their people when they return to them, so that they may guard against evil?[34]

Nevertheless, the word 'Taqlid' has not only been misunderstood by some Western scholars, but some Shi'i secular scholars have also misinterpret the term, at least technically. The mainstream literature has mistranslated the term 'Taqlid' to mean 'imitation' or 'emulation'.[35] It believes the term to mean 'imitation', in the sense of a person observing an action and replicating it exactly; which is the sort of behaviour that a monkey would be expected do.[36]

This fundamentally differs from how the Shiʿi clergy define the term technically. '*Taqlid*' from the infinitive of '*Qal-la-dah*' basically refers to throwing '*Qiladah*', a necklace or, more precisely, a dog's leash on somebody's neck. Consequently, the act of Taqlid in the Shiʿi Ancillaries is not tantamount to a blind mimicking of whatever a learned jurist does or says, which is illicit principally.[37] It instead metaphorically means that a Shiʿi laymen can throw a leash on the neck of one of the most righteous mujtahids and follow him in order to have less responsibility and more peace of mind when it comes to practising the complexities of his faith.[38] It is like assigning one's religious accountability to his Marja' Taqlid. Subsequently, Marja' Taqlid can be more properly translated as the 'supreme religious reference' in English.

Among the most crucial factors for a mujtahid to attain the support of his fellows and gather a group of followers are the time and the place he is living in. In fact, in the case of Sheikh Ansari himself, who is the first fully fledged Shiʿi Marja', these factors played an extremely important role. Prior to his era, following a 'sole Marja' Taqlid' was not a routine among the Shiʿi laity;[39] most commonly, the lay Shiʿi Muslims had been used to following a local Marja'. Yet it seems that the Marja'iyya of the Sheikh, throughout the Shiʿi world, owed partially to the auspicious circumstances he was living in. A major case in point was the development of communication technology concurrent with his rise as the leader of Najaf seminary. The telegraph lines had just been introduced in the region, a communication medium which years later played a central role in broadcasting the clerical elite's messages from Iraq to followers residing in Iran. Another influential factor was the financial development of the Najaf seminary at the time. Iraq is the host to a handful of Shiʿi holy cities; the money that is brought annually by millions of pilgrims has an undeniable impact on the economy of the country. In the post-Safavid era,[40] the Shiʿi clerical elite has relied on religious taxes received from their followers to finance the seminaries and their objectives.[41]

It was in the era of Sheikh Ansari that, with the advance of the communication developments, the Shiʿi laity started to send their religious taxes directly to their Marja' Taqlid, and the Sheikh distributed the funds among religious students who were at the seminary. Following the activities of the Sheikh, the Maraji' who succeeded him have continued to ensure that an extensive share of the religious taxes is distributed among seminary students.

Since the mid-nineteenth century, in contrast to its Sunni counterparts, the Shiʿi clerical authority has become independent of state powers, relying on the religious taxes of the laity. The position of Marja' Taqlid has been detached from any worldly funds by its definition; thus it is more capable of attaining the trust of his followers to receive their religious taxes and to distribute these among fellow religious students properly. Therefore, if religious taxpayers perceive that their Marja' has lost his qualifications, they would not support him financially. In losing this support, he would inevitably lose his position.

Moreover, as the recommendations of just and well-informed mujtahids in introducing a Marja' is crucial, there are some other control mechanisms over the activities of Marja'iyya. This has formed an enduring monitoring over each Shiʿi Marja'

Taqlid from the very first day he joins the seminary as an ordinary religious student up until the time he holds office as the highest clerical authority within the community.

During the Major Occultation era, hundreds of mujtahids have become Marja' Taqlid. There were some periods when Shiʿi Muslims from all around the world referred to a 'sole' Marja' Taqlid (e.g. the Era of Sheikh Murtada Ansari); there were also some periods in Shiʿi history when numbers of qualified mujtahids have held the position, all at the same time. Yet they consistently respect each other's opinions on religious matters. A dispute over a religious or social case among Marja' Taqlid is similar to the dispute of two physicians over a medical case. As the Shiʿi principles are surrounded by divine and moral messages, there is no room for different Maraji' to fight over their personal desires.

Nevertheless, the institution of Shiʿi Marja'iyya has been advanced through positive competition towards the objective of developing the most compatible reading of the principles to the context. Consequently, Maraji' may always offer a critical review of each other's legal opinions in a constructive atmosphere. However, if in exceptional cases a Marja' passes this framework, he may naturally endanger his own credibility and his support among his fellows. Ultimately, the point of views taken by different Maraji' over a given structure are absolutely contingent on their very personal perception on how to preserve the principles of the Shiʿi Islam at the time. In other words, the strategy and main goal for each Shiʿi Marja' or the general body of Shiʿi clerical authority are identical, although Maraji' may differ in the tactics that they adopt.

* * *

Based on Shiʿi primary sources, this chapter presented a more precise understanding of Shiʿi clerical authority by exploring the faith's principles and the role of qualified clerical elites during the Occultation era. It has discussed how it is incumbent for a Shiʿi mujtahid to lead the community through the exercise of his ijtihad and this is influenced by his perception of a given opportunity structure.

To lead the community and to protect the citadel of the faith during the Occultation era, the Shiʿi clerical elite may engage in political actions. Yet, what does 'political' mean in the eyes of the Shiʿi clergy? In general, politics encompasses practices that reproduce and transform the social relations. In this sense, and as it will be elaborated in next chapters, Shiʿi clerical elites are among the most significant political actors of their relevant communities and throughout history have strived to transform social relations whenever necessary to advance the goals they have for the community.

Politics may be exploited in different ways here. It is, first, used to refer to the level of divine politics. About this level, mujtahids are explicit as to what politics entails. However, reviewing the political postures held by the clergy throughout Shiʿi history, it is clear that, in some cases, it is also used to refer to the more mundane and pragmatic level of politics, including how clerical elites engage with secular authorities and with their followers (e.g. in the case of the mujtahids and the Safavid formation), how they work to obtain funding and strategies and manoeuvre with respect to these things (e.g. the Tobacco Revolt in Persia).

Addressing high-profile Friday prayer Imams in Tehran, Imam Khomeini defined politics as the practice whose aim is 'to guide the community . . . to consider all interests of the human and the society and to lead them towards what is good for them'.[42] With this end in mind, Shi'i clerical elites are aware that any state under the rule of a fallible figure during the Major Occultation era is not ideal. A state monitored and guided by the mujtahid, however, is the best alternative for surviving the period when, deprived of access to the infallible source of leadership, the survival of the community is under constant threat.

At this 'divine' level of politics, the clergy is considered more righteous than the secular ruler, as it not only considers the mundane affairs of the community but also reflects, as they govern, the rule of God. In the eyes of clerical elites, during the Occultation era, it is the preservation of the faith and community that constitute the authentic principles of Shi'i Islam. Shi'i clergy, to this end, is the bearer of these principles, and it is its responsibility to deduce the most appropriate action compatible with a given context. Yet to fulfil its responsibility, it may engage in various political manoeuvres, not necessarily at the level of divine politics. This was the case, especially in more recent centuries, when nation-states and a sense of nationalism was emerging throughout the Islamic abode. In seizing the most from the existing political opportunity structure, the clergy may engage in alliances with secular states, and with other communal groups, to advance its goals. A notable example of such a practice is the alliance between Grand Ayatollah Burujirdi and the Shah of Iran against the Communist Tudeh Party in the 1950s (see Chapter 4). In a given context, the clergy, as the fallible political actor may, in the name of religion, engage in another, more mundane level of politics. To retain their autonomy from the state, the clerical elite may consider seeking the assistance of specific social classes (e.g. wealthy landowners and merchants).

To understand Shi'i political postures held by the clerical elite, one should study his perceptions and interpretations of the situation he is facing. As is shown through this chapter, the authority of Shi'i clergy has not been dependent on any source of routine power, yet at the same time gains its credibility through the support of the Shi'i public. This is one of the most significant points that the current literature fails to address properly. Understanding how the Shi'i clerical elite perceives the political opportunity and acts accordingly is an area in the current literature that needs to be addressed in more detail. One can only hope for a better understanding of this quasi-federal structure and the possibility of a closer interfaith association among different Shi'i communities in the region. In order to do so, the following chapters try to examine the Shi'i clerical elite's activities throughout the history up until the contemporary era.

3

Shiʿi clergy political activism

A modern history

Politics constitutes the backbone of Shiʿi Islam and its clerical authority. This chapter tries to reconstruct Shiʿi clerical history in order to probe their political postures in more detail. Using Shiʿi sources, the aim here is to explore how, between the tenth and twentieth centuries, Shiʿi clerical elites facing different political opportunity structures developed their ijtihad and assumed different political postures.

Arguably, even during the lifetime of the Prophet, the partisans of Ali (Shiʿis) developed a unique political posture that became consolidated around the charisma of the Prophet's son-in-law. When Abu Bakr became the first caliph in 632 CE, Ali and his devoted partisans ultimately chose not to challenge the caliph, and stayed out of politics. However, the seemingly quietist posture that Ali and his companions adopted was conditional. Ali clarified this in a public address after the appointment of Uthman in 644, in which he stated the following:

> You have certainly known that I am the most rightful of all others for the Caliphate. To Allah, as long as the affairs of Muslims remain intact and there is no oppression in it save on myself, I shall remain quiet, seeking reward for it [from God] and keeping aloof from its attractions and allurements for which you aspire.[1]

Here, Ali accentuates that remaining politically quite in some circumstances could be a religious duty. This implies the culture of expectation among followers of Ali in the immediate aftermath of the Prophet's death. The line of Shiʿi Infallible Imams who followed this path in their political lives and their specific and general deputies have made this their practice during the Occultation era. This distinctive political doctrine was put into practice by the Shiʿi Imams during the early stages of the foundation of the Muslim Empire in the seventh century in the aftermath of the epic battle of Karbala, when the Imams' doctrine did not permit the taking of military action against the caliphate or other routine powers.

This seemingly quietist posture in no way implies that Shiʿi Imams became apathetic towards political affairs. Despite their belief that Islamic rule was their divine right and that the caliphs were unjust rulers, they became involved in politics only covertly and only at times it was necessary in order to protect the Shiʿi community's interests.

A means of advancing this mission was to encourage their pious companions to collaborate with unjust rulers in favour of the community. One of the most renowned examples of this strategy was the case of Ali Ibn Yaqteen, the devoted companion of the seventh Shiʿi Imam who became chancellor to the Abbasid caliph.[2] While collaborating with an unjust ruler is forbidden in Shiʿi Islam, at times such involvement becomes licit. For instance, when the life of a Shiʿi is endangered, it becomes obligatory for other Shiʿi Muslims to cooperate with rulers, when they are confident such cooperation will prevent further threats.[3]

Shiʿi clerical elites, the general deputies of the infallible Imams during the Occultation era, adhered to a similar political practice. However, the implications of this doctrine have varied from time to time as a result of the existence of differing political opportunity structures. This chapter starts by delving into the early history of Shiʿi clergy in the aftermath of the commencement of Major Occultation. During this period, while Shiʿi clerical elites were aware that their interpretations of a given opportunity structure were fallible, they believed it was still incumbent upon them to issue a judgement in order to lead their laity followers.[4] Thus, the discrepancies in political postures of different clerics throughout Shiʿi history are tactical, based on differences in their perception of a given context and on how they could fulfil their divine responsibility to the best of their abilities. Even before the rise of the Safavid dynasty in the sixteenth century, when Shiʿi Islam became the state religion in Persia, the Shiʿi elites, though deprived of an infallible leader, were presented with unique opportunities to propagate their faith.

Concurrent with the commencement of the Major Occultation, the Shiʿi Buyid dynasty (934–1062) launched a rebellion against the Abbasid caliphate, the pivot of Sunni Islam at the time, and succeeded in destroying its political supremacy. This provided an opportunity for Shiʿi clerical elites to propagate their thought with more freedom. Although numerous books and treatises had been produced during the period, little had been written on Shiʿi politics and social affairs, as clerics and their followers did not expect that the Occultation of the Imam would last for long. Hence, most of the judgements issued by clerics concerned jurisprudential questions, as responses to political inquiries, they believed, could await the day when the Imam would reappear and establish the last state.

With the fall of Baghdad, the Abbasids' capital, in 1256, Shiʿis were once again provided with perceivably an open political opportunity structure. Shiʿi clergy exploited this opportunity to become politically active for several reasons. First, the Occultation of the Imam, the ultimate just ruler, had reached its 300th anniversary, and his general deputies were facing numerous inquiries from lay followers regarding the political affairs at the time.[5] Second, when the Mongols invaded the Islamic world in the thirteenth century, their rule did not distinguish between Sunni and Shiʿi sects. Consequently, during the reign of the Mongol Ilkhanids in Persia, and with the absence of Sunni hegemony, Shiʿi clerical elites perceived the political opportunity structure to be permissive, and rejectionist Sufi and Shiʿi movements emerged in Persia and Iraq. This was the context within which the rise of the Safavids took place.

The chapter goes on to probe the political activism of the Shiʿi clerical elite throughout the Safavid era. In 1501, Ismail established the Safavid dynasty with the support of his Sufi devotees. Given the popularity of Shi'i Islam among the Persians, Ismail was inspired to declare it to be the state religion in order to unite different parts of the country. The establishment of the Safavid dynasty caused a wave of immigration of Shi'i clerical elites to Persia from all around the Islamic world. However, the Shi'i clergy had to await the reign of Ismail's son, Shah Tahmasb, before it was able to institutionalize its authority and initiate a scholastic movement in Safavid Persia. Because they provided the Safavids with religious legitimacy, clerical elites were enabled to form a prestigious social stratum and to share power with the monarchs. For more than two centuries of the Safavid rule, Shi'i clerical elites were provided with a unique political opportunity to develop their ijtihad concerning the sociopolitical affairs of the Shi'i community. During this era, they succeeded in compiling thousands of books and treatises, and established numerous seminaries to nurture future clerical elites. This glorious era came to an end, however, with the fall of Isfahan to Sunni Afghans and the subsequent rise of the Afsharids in 1736. Thus, two centuries after the Safavids had provided a safe haven for Shi'i clerical elites seeking to launch political movements, the political opportunity structure in Persia became relatively closed, and, pushed out of politics in Persia, they then migrated to the holy cities of Iraq.

Nonetheless, the social status that the clerical elites had achieved in Safavid Persia had succeeded in entrenching their authority in the Shi'i world at the time. Therefore, when the Qajars ascended to power in Persia, they sought the Shi'i clerical elite's support for their rule. After a short period of decline, the Shi'i mujtahids once again returned to the forefront of the politics. This time, however, with the rising influence of the West and of non-Muslim communities, and the strengthening of colonial powers in the region, Shi'i activism was pursued to achieve different goals from those of the previous eras. Not only did the Qajar monarchy support the Shi'i clerical elite in exchange for their legitimization of Qajar rule in Persia, the clergy also succeeded in mobilizing the masses against the so-called 'infidel' powers during the Russo-Persian Wars of the nineteenth century. This association between the monarchy and the clergy sometimes became strained, however and, especially, when the actions of the Qajars clashed with the interests of the religious elites and their followers. This occurred, for instance, in the Tobacco Protest of the 1890s and in the Persian Constitutional Revolution in the early twentieth century.

The early mujtahids

With the commencement of the Occultation era, and in the absence of an infallible source of religio-political leadership, Shi'i clerics, the narrators of the Imam's traditions, assumed the central role of leading the community. However, at that time, the abode of Islam was mainly under the rule of the Sunni Abbasids. Given this political structure, Shi'i clerics saw their responsibility as safeguarding the essential principles of the faith through their teachings and by the production of ijtihad. At the same time, perhaps because they hoped that the Occultation of the infallible Imam would not last long, the majority of religious elites remained politically quiet. The perceptions of Shi'i clerical elites concerning the political opportunity structure at the time were shaped by these assumptions.

Subsequent to the commencement of the Major Occultation era, the Shiʿi Buyids ascended to power. In contrast to their predecessors in Persia, the Buyids defied the Abbasids, descended on Baghdad in 945, and brought the caliph under their tutelage. Their authority over Persia and Iraq coincided with Shiʿi rule in Egypt (the Fatimids), Syria (the Hamdanids) and Yemen (the Zaidis).[6] However, Shiʿis were still evidently threatened by the well-established Sunni hegemony throughout the Islamic world; thus, it was impossible to fully consolidate Shiʿi political power at the time. The Buyids, therefore strove to retain their popular constituency during their reign by preserving the Abbasid caliphs in Baghdad and, in that way, maintaining the balance between Shiʿi and Sunni communities.

The timing of the 'Shiʿi golden century' could not have been better for the religious elites. Perceiving an open political opportunity structure, Shiʿi clerical elites started the process of consolidating the tenets of the faith in response to the discontent of the Occultation era. Muhammad Ibn 'Ali Ibn Babawaih Qummi (923–91), *Sheikh al-Saduq*, was among the forerunners of this scholastic movement. Settled in Rey, just miles from the Shiʿi stronghold of Qum, he managed to compile hundreds of books and treatises under the benevolent rules of the Buyids.

During the same period, Al-Sharif al-Murtada (965–1044), wrote an independent treatise on politics, *Mas'alah fi al-Amal ma'a al-Sultan*, in which he states that, under some circumstances, Shiʿis may collaborate with an unjust ruler. He says that, in reality, the collaborator in this case is 'acting on behalf of the infallible Imams [just rulers]', as he is obeying their commands.[7] Henceforth, Al-Sharif al-Murtada's verdict, which was a relative breakthrough at the time, had gained the support of a majority of clerical elites.[8]

The demise of the Abbasids also provided an opportunity for Shiʿi elites to collaborate with the state and to mediate its attitude towards the Shiʿi community. Their efforts bore fruit in 1180, when the Sunni Abbasid caliph, al-Nasir, openly bestowed his patronage to Shiʿi Islam.[9]

Occurring simultaneously with this was the beginning of the Mongol campaign in Middle Asia. Genghis's descendants furthered the Mongol advance in the Islamic world and, in the mid-thirteenth century, established the Ilkhanid dynasty in Persia and Iraq. Without the least compassion towards Sunni, Shiʿi or any other sect or ideology, the Mongols had just one principle: to conquer the land through mass destruction and to show the utmost brutality. Nevertheless, as long as enmity existed between the Sunni caliph and the Mongols, the political opportunity structure was relatively favourable for the Shiʿi minority that under the changing balance of power was able to assert itself. This change would ultimately substitute an oppressive Sunni rule with the rule of the more flexible Ilkhanids. Three major Shiʿi personalities were involved in this shift of power: Nasir al-Din Tusi, previously under the service of the Ismailis, Ibn Alqami, the minister of Abbasids in Baghdad, and Sayyid Ibn Tawus, the distinguished Shiʿi cleric of Hilla.[10]

The fall of the Abbasids to the Mongols provided the Shiʿi clergy an unsurpassed opportunity to become actively involved in politics. Concurrent with the outbreak of Genghis's campaign against the Khawrazmid, and drifting from place to place like many other Muslim scholars, Nasir al-Din Tusi finally took refuge with the Ismailis of Quhistan in 1227. But with the Mongol siege of the Ismaili fortress, Tusi recommended that the Ismaili ruler, Rukn al-Dawlah Khourshah, surrender to Hulagu in order to reduce the number of casualties.[11]

The reason Tusi was willing to collaborate with the advancing Mongols had to do with his 'ijtihad', which can be extracted from one of his most renowned books, *The Nasirean Ethics*, or *Akhlāq-e Nāṣerī*. In this book, he writes that 'humans are civic in their nature' and that, to 'manage their social life, they are in need of a structured system', the politics through which the elites could restore the rights of the laity.[12] He expressed the belief that a society has one of two forms: it is either 'complete' or 'incomplete'. He argued that it is incumbent for everyone, lay or elite, to fully exploit his capabilities towards transforming an incomplete society into a complete one. Tusi offered his services to Hulagu willing to establish the complete society he had sought, just as he had done previously when he had joined the then-formidable Ismailis.

Another Shi'i cleric who witnessed the fall of Baghdad and became involved in the politics of the post-Abbasid era was Ibn Tawus (1193–1266). Previously, the Abbasid caliphs had offered Ibn Tawus the opportunity to serve at the court. Yet, his ascetic personality barred him from collaborating in the earthly matters that arose under the unjust rule of the caliphate. He justifies his political posture in a letter to his son:

> When the caliph became disappointed with my response to his several attempts, he sent one of my dearer friends, who asked me: 'How can you refuse to work with the caliph, while Sayyid Razi and Sayyid Murtada had done otherwise?' I replied that they both were living at the time of Shi'i Buyids, who were preoccupied with the caliph and subjugated the caliphate; thereby, by accepting the position, they could proceed with their divine intentions.[13]

Despite this, after the conquest of Baghdad, Ibn Tawus accepted the position of Neqabat (*Head of Sayyids*). Etan Kohlberg observes that after Hulagu entered Baghdad, he ordered all Muslim scholars to form a convention to issue a fatwa on the question of who is better: 'a just infidel ruler or an unjust Muslim ruler?' The first one who confirmed in writing and granted a privilege to the former over the latter option was Ibn Tawus, whose recommendation was then followed by the rest of the Shi'i elite.[14] Consequently, Ibn Tawus's *ijtiahd* confirms that when it comes to choosing between justice and faith, he preferred the former.[15]

Ultimately the prudential activities of Tusi, Ibn Alqami, and Ibn Tawus helped to ensure that the Shi'i community, Islamic libraries and schools, and several towns and cities remained intact in spite of the Mongols' destructive campaigns. With the fall of the formidable Ismaili fortresses and the Abbasid caliphs, and the establishment of the religiously neutral Ilkhanids in Persia and Iraq, a promising era began for the Shi'i community. Moreover, since the Sunni Abbasids were considered to be enemies of the Ilkhanid dynasty, Shi'i scholars had more political opportunities than their Sunni counterparts during the early rules of Mongols.

Ilkhanids were religiously tolerant. In 1295, however, Ghazan converted to Islam and required his court and the majority of Mongols who were in Iran to embrace Islam.[16] Uljeitu, Ghazan's successor, ascended the throne in 1304. His rule in Persia marked an important turning point for the Shiʿi community and enabled their clerical elite an opportunity to consolidate their authority to the favour of their followers. Though at the time Persia had a Sunni majority, Uljeitu converted to Shiʿi Islam and gave orders for the name of Imam Ali and his sons to be invoked in sermons. In 1309, just fifty years after the fall of Baghdad, Uljeitu ordered coins to be inscribed with the name of Imam Ali and declared Shiʿi Islam to be the religion of his state.[17]

In a surviving treatise, addressing the Sunni community, Uljeitu defends his conversion as follows:

> Whoever is wise enough understands that [my conversion to Shiʿi Islam], is rooted in embracing the most righteous path in order to please the Prophet. I trust that I will be rewarded for this move. Therefore, anyone who accepts this will prosper in front of God and there will not be any duress on those who do not agree with this. The sermon and the coin inscription, however, are the ruler's right and should be under my name. Therefore, I order to call and inscribe the glorious name of Amir al-Mu'minin, Ali, and his infallible sons, prior to my name.[18]

With Shiʿi Islam established as the official religion of the state for the first time since the caliphate of Imam Ali, Uljeitu invited Shiʿi scholars from all around the Islamic world to come to Persia and propagate the faith's principles.

The most prominent Shiʿi personality who accepted the royal invitation and attended to the Ilkhalid court was Allameh Hilli (1250–325). He played a pivotal role in establishing Shiʿi Islam in Persia during the auspicious rule of Uljeitu, by instructing in portable Shiʿi schools. With the support of the ruler, Shiʿi scholars, at the individual level, succeeded in influencing the sociopolitical structure in favour of the community throughout Persia and Iraq.

After the death of Uljeitu, the authority of the Ilkhanids became enfeebled in Persia, and opposition movements raised the flag of independence in every corner of the country. Shiʿi clerical activities during the reign of Uljeitu had influenced most of these movements.[19] One of these opposition movements was formed by Sarbadars of Sabzevar, a group of militant Sufi dervishes and yeomen who had ruled in Khorasan for almost fifty years until 1386.[20]

Although it is dubious that Sarbadars were a purely Shiʿi movement from the outset, it is evident that, during the last stages of their reign, popular pressure pushed their rulers to patronize the faith. A letter written by the Sarbadar ruler, Ali Mua'yyid, to Shahid Awwal (1334–85), is noteworthy with regard to this development. Ali Mua'yyid invited the Shahid to migrate to Sabzevar to lead the community, telling him, 'We are concerned that our homeland will be subject to the wrath of God due to the lack of a leader and guidance.'[21] Although Shahid Awwal, who was preoccupied with establishing a seminary in Jabal Amil (Lebanon) at the time, did not agree to move to Sabzevar, he wrote one of the most famous Shiʿi books, *al-Lum'ah al-Dimashqiya*, as a response to the Sarbadar ruler. He was the second supreme Shiʿi mujtahid, after Allameh Hilli, to become involved in politics and was one of the foremost Shi'i political theologians during the period.

Concurrent with the Sarbadars and the establishment of the Timurid dynasty in Eastern Persia,[22] various Sufi orders were active throughout the Islamic world. Among these was the Zahediyeh Sufi order, located in northern Persia, which enjoyed huge popular support due to the charisma of their late spiritual leader, Sheikh Zahed Gilani, and the Sheikh's son-in-law, Sheikh Safi al-Din Ardabili. With the rising popularity of Shi'i Islam throughout Persia and eastern Anatolia, Sheikh Safi's descendants and their followers succeeded in establishing the Safavid dynasty and in declaring Shi'i Islam as the official religion of the dynasty in 1501.

Five centuries after the Occultation of the last Imam, the community was provided with an opportunity to enjoy greater freedom and to eradicate the power of Sunni rulers in Persia. Throughout this period, the Shi'i clergy, as the general deputies of the infallible Imam, led the laity and strove to protect the community. However, the rise of Shi'i Buyids (934 CE), the fall of the Sunni Abbasid Caliphate (1258 CE), and the rule of Shi'i Ilkhanid (1308–16) made the most important contribution to enabling the Shi'i clerical elite to exert their sociopolitical responsibilities. These structural turning points also allowed them to develop their ijtihad in regard to the relationship between religion and politics. They were pushed to utilize its power in order to find out how they might participate in the political affairs of their community in order to fulfil the role accorded to them by the infallible Imams. And eventually, through the activities they pursued over the course of the 560 years that had passed since the commencement of the Occultation era, the people of Persia were ready to embrace Shi'i Islam. This also influenced the Safavid rulers, who made Shi'i Islam the official religion of their rule in order to unite the various parts of the country around a common belief.

The establishment of the Shi'i Safavid dynasty in Persia is one of the most significant events in the shaping of political Shi'i Islam in the modern era. The Safavid dynasty provided Shi'i clerical elites with a relatively open political opportunity structure for propagating their views and institutionalizing Shi'i Islam in Persia. The Shi'i clerics, who had been invited to share authority with the Safavid rulers, were presented with a unique opportunity to develop their ijtihad with respect to political questions. It was during this period that the foundations of the Shi'i clerical elite's modern activism were established. There was a group of Shi'i clerical elites who preferred not to become involved in politics; but though they remained politically quiet, their teaching at seminaries supported their politically active colleagues.

With the dissolution of the Abbasids, the popularity of Sufism and Shi'i Islam increased and, throughout Iraq, eastern Anatolia and Persia, it remained at its peak level for centuries. This can be seen with respect to several sociopolitical movements that were active from the thirteenth to fifteenth centuries in the region. With the demise of the formidable pivot of Sunni orthodoxy in Baghdad, the Shi'i clergy became more active, and their rapprochements with different Sufi orders finally redounded to their benefit.[23] In 1501, Ismail, who was fourteen years old at the time, established the Safavid dynasty with the support of his Sufi devotees[24] and declared Shi'i Islam to be the religion of his state.[25] Perhaps the main factor leading to the establishment of an official Shi'i dynasty in Persia was the popularity of the faith among the Persians, at a time in which the country was sandwiched between two formidable Sunni ruling groups – the Ottoman Turks and the Uzbeks. The result was the increased popularity of Shiʿism among the majority of Persians, who were nominally Sunnis – at least in major cities – but were extremely sympathetic to Shiʿi Islam. This later led to the swift institutionalization of Ismail's reign.

The official establishment of the Shiʿi dynasty received tremendous support from the majority of Shiʿi religious elites, from Persia to Jabal Amil in Lebanon.[26] Protected by the safe haven provided by the newly established state, religious elites were able to freely propagate their opinions. However, their political involvement and influence, vis-à-vis the state varied from time to time over the course of the ensuing two centuries.

The Shiʿi clerical hierocracy was constructed within the context provided by the Safavids as well as by the earlier Shiʿi mujtahids whose actions served as a forerunner to it by their pursuit of solutions that involved compromise with monarchs and sharing of power with the state. In the early years of Safavid rule, the ruler's authority was comprised of tribal Sufism and extreme Shiʿi Islam.[27] When Ismail was crowned in Tabriz, he was accounted as a God in the eyes of his pious followers. Minorsky quotes a Venetian merchant present in Tabriz at the time as saying that Shah Ismail 'is loved and reverenced by his people as God and especially by his soldiers, many of whom enter into battle without armor expecting their master to watch over them in the fight'.[28] But the Safavids further incited the Persians by inventing a family tree that allowed them to claim legitimacy through direct descent from the seventh Shiʿi Imam.[29] It was in such circumstances that Ismail began to establish his reign and found a dynasty which was to rule throughout Persia for more than two centuries. His was the longest lasting Persian state to exist in the post-Islamic era, since 637 CE. To unite the Persian territories, Ismail began a series of conquests right after ascending to the throne in 1501. He succeeded in conquering Iraq in 1508. When he seized authority over Khorasan from the Sunni Uzbeks in 1510, he summoned the Shiʿi clergy, Arabs, Persians and other notables to Herat to celebrate the victory.[30] However, at least until the Battle of Chaldiran, in 1514, Shiʿi clerical elites did not exercise much influence over political affairs. His revolutionary activities in Persia were facilitated by his personal charisma and the power of the sword of his Sufi devotees.

Ismail's defeat at Chaldiran gradually evaporated his charisma among his subjects. He was not this divinely inspired and protected ruler anymore; and as his young dynasty found itself in dire need of an alternative source of legitimacy, the Shiʿi clergy seized the opportunity. Consequently, what was to become a long-lasting connection between Safavid monarchs and Shiʿi religious elites was established. As a result of this, a trend of Shiʿi ijtihad started to develop, mainly through the initiatives of Jabal Amili (Lebanese) scholars. A number of these mujtahids travelled to Persia where they were granted official positions in the state apparatus (e.g. Sheikh al-Islam), while some preferred to remain in Jabal Amil and support the Safavids remotely.

The relationship between the Shiʿi clergy and the Safavids had its ups and downs over the course of some 200 years, although, in general, both parties benefited from it. The support of clerical elites provided rulers with the legitimacy they needed among the community and the leverage they needed to advance their doctrines against hostile Sunni neighbouring states. At the same time, the rise of the Safavids offered opportunities for the Shiʿi clerical elite to propagate the faith's principles and to strengthen its foundations.

Among the most notable forerunners of this auspicious association was Nur-al-Din Abu al-Ḥasan Ali Ibn Ḥussein Ibn Abd-al-ʿĀli, known as Mohaqeq al-Karaki (1464–533). Born in the suburbs of Baalbek in Lebanon, al-Karaki belonged to the Jabal Amil Shiʿi school of thought, which had been founded by Shahid Awwal decades earlier.[31] In 1509, he was stationed in Najaf, when the city was conquered by Safavid troops.[32]

A year later, al-Karaki, along with scores of other Shiʿi clerics, travelled to Persia for the first time and stayed in Khorasan for almost two years. During this period, he took advantage of the existing political opportunities to propagate his ijtihad by writing a series of treatises and books.[33] Through the pages of those treatises, al-Karaki attempted to define a new role for the Shiʿi clerical elite and its sociopolitical status within the community. Around 1511, al-Karaki wrote one of his first famous treatises in support of Ismail's order on the ritual cursing of Sunni Caliphs.[34] It was in the introduction to this treatise that, for the first time, al-Karaki addressed the Safavid rule as the 'supreme, impressive, honourable, Musawi, and expressed the hope that God Almighty might prolong its victory and empowerments'.[35] In 1515, following his return to Najaf, al-Karaki wrote another influential treatise on Friday prayers, in which he defined his view of the role of the Imam's general deputies.[36] He claimed that, during the Occultation era, a fully qualified jurist could lead the Friday Prayer as the infallible Imam's deputy and on his behalf.[37] Nonetheless, it was only during the rule of Ismail's successor that al-Karaki was provided an opportunity to put this view in practice.[38]

Shah Tahmasb ascended to the throne in 1524, when he was only ten years old, and after Ismail's charisma and support had declined. His fifty-two-year-long reign represented one of the most fruitful periods for the consolidation of Shiʿi clerical authority. He paved the path for a group of Arab Shiʿi clerics, including al-Karaki, to develop their ijtihad with the full support of the court.

Consequently, while Ismail's reign was the era of the establishment of the Shiʿi Safavids, Tahmasb's rule promised an era of Shiʿi consolidation throughout Persia. His most important contribution, during the reign of the young king, to the status of the Shiʿi clergy occurred when, during a visit to Iraq in 1528, he issued a decree stating that opposition to al-Karaki, the deputy of the infallible Imam, is equal to idolatry.[39]

Al-Karaki travelled to Iran for the second time, and this time with a greater authority. When he entered the capital, Qazvin, the Shah addressed him and said: 'Today you, as the deputy of the Imam, are more righteous to rule; I am carrying out your orders on your behalf, as one of your humble agents.'[40] The majority of al-Karaki's activities during this era were focused on issuing religious verdicts, which ranged from forbidding wine drinking to teaching Shiʿi jurisprudence. In acknowledgement of his pragmatic approach and achievements, the historian Rumlu declared that he was the most politically influential Shiʿi cleric since Nasir al-Din Tusi.[41]

Al-Karaki was in Persia for only three years during Tahmasb's reign. But the teachings of the school that he founded at that time remained predominant in the country for decades as a result of the activities of his family, students and Arab colleagues who migrated to Persia after he had. Indeed, he had established the cornerstone of a structure that provided his descendants with opportunities to pursue the further strengthening of the clerical sociopolitical authority. It should be noted that this extended well beyond the activities of the clerics who migrated to Persia and held high-ranking positions in Safavid courts.

Some Shiʿi clerics remained in their hometowns in Iraq and Lebanon and never visited Persia; yet they supported the Shiʿi state and aligned themselves with their colleagues who had migrated to Persia. Al-Shahid al-Thāni (1506–58) and Muqaddas al-Ardabili (d. 1585) were among this group of clerical elites. While the former was settled in Jabal Amil, which was at the time under the authority of the Sunni Ottomans, the latter resided in Najaf and never visited the Safavid capital. Nevertheless, both supported Safavid rule and produced verdicts that strengthened the state's Shiʿi base. For both, perhaps the reason, which recurred in many other cases throughout Shiʿi history, was to protect the seminaries of their towns of residence and to foster the next generation of clerics.

Al-Shahid al-Thāni never left Jabal Amil for Persia, but was teacher to a number of clerics who later held positions in Safavids courts. He further developed the judgements of al-Karaki concerning the Friday Prayer, clarifying his ijtihad and perception concerning the support of the Shiʿi state during the Occultation era. In contrast to his predecessor, who believed that the Friday Prayer was optional, Al-Shahid al-Thāni was the among the first Shiʿi mujtahids who ruled that conducting Friday prayers should be obligatory. He observed that Shiʿis had not conducted the Friday Prayer throughout history because of the necessity, at times, to conceal their faith. But because, as he stated, 'the excuse is withdrawn in this era', he argued that everyone should strive to fulfil this religious practice routinely.[42] In the same clause, he implicitly endorsed the rise of the Shiʿi dynasty as a favourable development for the community.

The teachings of Muqaddas al-Ardabili, who exhibited a more apolitical personality and saintly conduct, also supported the rise of the Safavids. Although he never visited Persia, it seems that there was a mutually respectful relationship between him and the monarch.[43] He clearly states that any form of government during the Occultation era, including that of the Safavids, is unjust, although he prescribes active involvement in their court with the aim of protecting Shiʿi Islam against its enemies. After reciting the Quranic verse of 'And do not incline toward those who do wrong, lest you be touched by the Fire',[44] Muqaddas justifies cooperation with (unjust) Safavid rulers and states:

> If someone agrees to the survival of a Shiʿi or non-Shiʿi regime, because its unjust ruler likes the believers and hence protects their interests and faith, and prevents the domination of their enemies, this verse does not apply to him.[45]

These remarks from al-Ardabili clearly show that although he had reservations about the rule of Shiʿi Safavids, he preferred them to the Ottomans and Uzbeks.

With the clergy perception of the opportunity structure as being favourable, the Amili Shiʿi mujtahids and their students focused on propagating their judgements, building religious schools with royal financial support, and strengthening their social base by filling religious positions like leading prayers, *Pishnamazi*, in major mosques. Their authority had reached such a level in less than fifty years after al-Karaki that they could have easily overthrown the monarch's power.[46]

However, the rise of Shah Abbas resulted in restraint of mujtahids' authority. This eventually led to an internal schism among the Shi'i clergy, the subsequent rise of anti-mujtahids Akhbāris and the end of clerical activism for the coming century.

In 1587, after almost a decade of disorder throughout the Safavid realm, Abbas ascended the throne. His reign was among the most important in that era of Persian history and shaped the early socioeconomic structure of the country during subsequent centuries.[47] Iskandar Beg Turkaman notes that he individually monitored every single affair of politics and religion and was 'the moderator of the religion and the state's affairs, and the developer of the people and kingdom's arrangements'.[48]

Notwithstanding the mutual respect that existed between the monarch and these religious figures, the power of clerical elites and their engagements in politics was restrained during this era. In contrast to Tahmasb's, during Abbas's reign, it was the Shi'i clerical elite who became the monarch's agents at the royal court.[49] Beyond this, the clergy still retained the privileges of the Awqaf that the king had allocated for religious affairs.[50] Impediments to the rising authority of Shi'i clerical elites, who had no other alternative under the arbitrary rule of Shah Abbas, along with the decay of ijtihad among the renowned Shi'i mujtahids of the time, resulted in the rise of a religious scholastic movement known as Akhbārism or 'Islamic Scripturalism'.[51] Generally opposing the ijtihad and the role of Shi'i mujtahids in any social affairs, the movement was begun under the leadership of Mulla Muhammad Amin Astarabadi (d. 1627), who resided in Hijaz. Astarabadi was an astute Shi'i scholar who harshly attacked Usulis like Sheikh Mufid, Sheikh Tusi and Allameh Hilli, and accused them of deviation from the path of the Prophet and the Imams.[52] He believed that instead of conducting ijtihad, which derived from Sunni jurisprudence, Shi'i scholars should rely on the traditions of the Prophet and the Imams as the most important source of Islamic law.[53]

Astarabadi's reservations soon found traction among people in Persia, Bahrain and Iraq, initiating a dark age of Usuli mujtahids beginning in the early seventeenth century. The dynamism of the Shi'i Usuli School, which was anchored to the power of ijtihad, was displaced by the dogmatic Akhbāri School, which focuses mainly on the literal exegesis of traditions. Although Akhbārism was a setback for Shi'i scholarship,[54] it had one main advantage: it inaugurated a mass collection of Shi'i traditions with the support of Safavid monarchs. A case in point is the *Biḥār al-Anwār*, consisting of thousands of Shi'i traditions, compiled by Muhammad Baqir Majlesi (1616–98).[55] He was among those Shi'i clerics who enjoyed popularity among the community and enforced his will on the rule of Shah Sultan Hussein, the last Safavid ruler.

In 1722, Isfahan surrendered in the face of a revolt of Afghan Ghalzais, and soon, Shah Sultan Hussein abdicated the throne in favour of Mahmud Afghan.[56] The new Afghan rulers revealed extreme hatred for the Shi'is and Persians when they categorized and prioritized the inhabitants of his rule into seven distinct classes: Sunni Ghalzais, Armenians, Sunni Dargaznis, Multan Indians, Zoroastrians, Jews and Shi'i Persians.[57] It seemed the permissive context of Shi'i activism was soon to be ended by the fall of the Safavids; however, the foundations that had been laid down by the activities of the Shi'i clerical elites and their entourages throughout Persia, and the popularity of the Shi'i Safavid rulers, who were believed to be the descendants of the infallible Imams, were strong enough to withstand the enmity of the Sunni Afghan invaders. As a matter of fact, eventually an Afsharid commander, Nader, enjoying the charisma of a Safavid prince, Tahmasb II, was able to reunite Persia and expel the Afghan invaders after seven years of occupation.

The Safavids had come to the power in Persia by fashioning their doctrines to those of Shiʿi Islam. At the time, Shah Ismail announced that Shiʿi Islam was to be the religion of his newly established state, and a powerful sense of pro-Shiʿi Islam was felt throughout Persia. The establishment of the Shiʿi dynasty at a time in which the Islamic abode was under the influence of the formidable Sunni Ottoman Empire provided an opportunity for Shiʿi scholars to develop a new ijtihad in order to make the most of an opportunity structure that was favourable to their goals.

Throughout the Safavid era, there were some Shiʿi clerics who, based on their interpretations of the existing political opportunity structure, migrated to Persia to become actively involved in the politics of the monarchy, while the rest of the scholars, those who did not leave their hometowns and were seemingly proponents of political quietism, did not do anything to undermine the Shiʿi state. In general, it can be said, then, that the Shiʿi clergy of the time worked to make the most out of the open opportunity structure and to institutionalize their authority throughout the community. Although their authority had been subjected to various upheavals during the two centuries of Safavid Persia, in general, the Shiʿi religious elite achieved an unsurpassed position, one which laid a foundation for the performance of their sociopolitical roles over the subsequent centuries and up until the contemporary era.

Mujtahids in the aftermath of the Shiʿi Safavid dynasty

Following the fall of Isfahan in 1722 to the Sunni Ghalzais, the Shiʿi clerical supremacy in Persia faced a decade of stagnation. The historical irony was that thousands of Shiʿi scholars and notable families fled to the holy cities of Iraq and took refuge among the Ottomans, despite their former enmity. The process of mass migration continued even after Nader liberated Persia from the Afghans and founded the Afsharid dynasty in 1736. On 22 January of that year, Nader, who triumphantly defeated the Afghans, had pushed back the Ottoman and Russian forces. Having restored Persian sovereignty once again, he ordered all notables to be gathered in Mughan Plain to decide the future of the country.[58] After a month, he conditionally agreed to found a new dynasty, which would be called the Afsharids. The most significant of the conditions that he set force, was the abolition of Shiʿi Islam as the official religion of Persia. Addressing the gathering, he said: 'Previously, Sunni Islam had been practiced throughout Persia. It was the Safavids who abandoned our ancestors' religion, in favour of their own state interests, and thus substituted Shiʿi Islam and caused degeneracy herein and shed blood.'[59]

He then asked the notables to think over his conditions and to express their opinion. The only opposition came from Mirza Abdul Hassan Mullabashi, a famous cleric who was later executed in Mughan to signal Nader's stance against the Shiʿi hegemony in Persia. This sent a strong message to the Shiʿi clergy that there would not be any opportunity for political activism, at least not while Nader held office. Nader went even further by confiscating all Awqaf from the clerics in favour of his army and moving the capital from Isfahan to Mashahd, which showed the utmost departure from the Safavids' politics.[60]

Nevertheless, it has not been clearly understood whether Nader was a despot and brutal ruler, or if he was a benevolent Muslim who sought to dedicate his efforts to uniting different Islamic sects.[61] In the last stages of his reign, a twofold reality became more evident than ever: while the seeds of Shiʿi Islam that had been planted during the reign of the Safavids were flourishing among the majority of Persians,[62] which, in a sense, transformed the state-clergy relationship to a laity-clergy relationship. In other words, the Persians showed patronage towards Shiʿi Islam and the clerical elites were still benefiting from this.

When Nader was killed in 1747, Persia once again went through anarchy. Eventually in 1750, Karim Khan established the Zand dynasty and named Shiraz as the capital of his new rule. As one of the most well reputed kings of Persian history, he left Khurasan to the family of Nader, for his honour, and allocated a pension to Ismail III until his death. This also indicates how, more than a half a century since the fall of the Safavids, the surviving members of the dynasty remained popular in the eyes of Persians. The fate of Karim Khan's dynasty, however, did not follow the same path. Some years after his death, Agha Muhammad Khan Qajar killed the last Zand king, Lotf Ali Khan, in 1794, two years before Qajar's coronation in Tehran, the capital of his new dynasty.

The ascension of Agha Muhammad Khan to the throne inaugurated a new period of Shiʿi political activism. This time, however, contrary to the Safavid era, the Shiʿi clerical elite did not only have the experience of establishing relationships with the state, but also had been of enjoying great popular support, which provided a new constituency for them. The establishment of Qajar dynasty was also coincided with the resurge of Usuli mujtahids, whose popularity had been overshadowed by their Akhbāri rivals since the mid-seventeenth century.[63]

In such circumstances, Agha Muhammad Khan became the new monarch and swore to protect Shiʿi Islam. In contrast to the Safavids, the Qajars did not have the advantage of having a prestigious background. Thus, the new monarch tended to incline towards Shiʿi clerics as a means of consolidating the legitimacy of his rule. This set in place the foundation of a benign and respectful relationship between Qajar rulers and Shiʿi clerical elites who, at the time, were enjoying an ever-increasing popularity among their lay followers in Persia and in the holy cities of Iraq. This, again, provided a political opportunity for the Shiʿi clergy. Qajar Persia witnessed three major incidents which involved the active engagement and pivotal role of Shiʿi clerical elites in politics: The Russo-Persian Wars, the Tobacco Protest and the Persian Constitutional Revolution.

The Russo-Persian Wars: The Jihadi mujtahids

The history of Russo-Persian conflicts goes back to 1722, at the time of both the fall of the Safavids and the rise of Peter the Great in Russia. The founder of the Russian

Empire wished to prevent the growth of influence of his rivals, the Ottomans, in the Caspian and South Caucasus. In his will, Peter advised his successors that, to rule the world, 'they must hasten the downfall of Persia, push on to the Persian Gulf'.[64] It was in this context that Georgia and the Caucasus became the frontlines of a Russo-Persian conflict. In 1723, when Persia was under the occupation of Afghans, a handful of Persian provinces were annexed to Russia. However, in 1735, Russia returned them to Persia in order to gain Persian support for a war with the Ottomans. This by no means brought to an end the Russian grand ambition of vanquishing Persian authority in the region. Over the succeeding centuries, whenever an opportunity became available, Russia tried to pursue the will of Peter the Great and to enforce its hegemony in Persia.

Russian supremacy was diminished in the Southern Caucasus and Georgia with the rise of Agha Muhammad Khan and his expedition against the ruler of Tbilisi in 1795. Later on, in 1804, the Russians invaded the region during the reign of Fatah Ali Shah in Persia, and this led to a protracted war between the two countries. At the time, two other major powers, Britain and France, were actively influencing the situation to their own advantage, mainly at the cost of Persia.[65] Nine years on, and despite the resistance of Persians under the leadership of Abbas Mirza, the Persians were forced to sign the Treaty of Gulistan (1813). This outcome was a great disappointment for the Persians, and it represented a strong threat to Qajar legitimacy. Consequently, the Shah and Abbas Mirza sought to attract the support of the Shiʿi clergy as a means of reversing the precariousness of their rule and restoring their lost dignity.[66]

The Shiʿi clergy had been involved in the Russo-Persian war years earlier, when Abbas Mirza sent envoys to Iraq and to Qum, Kashan and Isfahan in Persia, with the request that Jihad decrees be issued against the 'infidel' Russian invaders. This confirms the popularity of the religious elite at the time of early Qajar rule. Sheikh Ja'far Najafi, known as Kashif al-Ghita (1743–812), was among those high-ranking clerics who accepted the royal envoys and issued a Jihad decree against the Russian forces.[67] He expressed the view that

> [it] is obligatory for every Muslim who wishes to obey the Prophet and infallible Imams to follow the Shah's order in war with enemies of God . . . . Everyone should obey the verdicts of those who appointed the ruler as the protector of the nation from calamities [Shiʿi Ulama], therefore any objection to the ruler ['s request of Jihad] is equal to God's opposition and deserves his wrath and punishment.[68]

Kashif al-Ghita, in a clear expression of his political views concerning the rule of the Qajar Shah, asked his followers to go to war with the 'enemies of God', meaning the Russians, in order to protect the Islamic abode from outsiders' threats. His call, which was supported by the majority of his colleagues, marked the start of clerical activism in the post-Safavid era, after almost a century during which the Shiʿi clergy had preferred to remain out of direct engagement in politics. The Shiʿi clergy had asked to exploit its capabilities to mobilize the masses in support of the state and the campaign against the Russians. As general deputies of the Imam, the clerical elites supported the Qajars as a means of protecting the Islamic abode.

The clerical elite's mobilization of Persian Shiʿis played a more significant role in the second war with the Russians.[69] The war broke out in May 1826 and, this time, Shiʿi clerics from all around the Islamic world became directly involved in the war. They not only issued Jihad decrees, but some members of the Shiʿi clergy also joined the army and personally engaged in warfare.[70]

Among these was Sayyid Muhammad Mujahed, one of the most renowned clerics of the time.[71] This ultimately provided the Qajar court a chance to advance its military campaign and liberate almost all occupied territory under the Gulistan within the first month of the war. However, soon the course of events turned against the Persians. Their early victories were followed by serious defeats on several fronts. This led to a continuing conflict between Abbas Mirza and the religious leadership.[72] To show their resentment at the state's negative propaganda, Sayyid Muhammad and his religious entourages left the front in September 1826. Following this, the Persian army suffered a series of defeats, and Persia was obliged to sign the disadvantageous Treaty of Turkmenchay in February 1828.[73]

The clergy was blamed for this misfortune. The Qajar court claimed that the second war had been triggered by the will of clerics and neither the Shah nor Abbas Mirza had favoured the new campaign against Russia from the outset.[74] Although the Shiʿi clerics had supported the Jihad against Russia after receiving a green light from the Qajar court, the outcome of the war delivered a severe blow to their status among the Shiʿi community compared to the blow suffered by other involved parties. The majority of clerics had misperceived the political opportunity, and thus bitterly stayed out of politics during the coming decades, which was the second major defeat to their social status after the rise of Nader Shah.[75] In the succeeding decades, the Shiʿi clergy, who felt manipulated by the Qajars during the war with the Russians, tried to become more focused on teaching students and sending them to different cities to propagate the Shiʿi principles, and in this way, strengthen their authority among Shiʿis.[76]

The rise of Sheikh Murtada Ansari (1781–864) in Najaf, the first sole Shiʿi Marja' of the Occultation era, occurred subsequently, as the region was going through dramatic changes. It was during Ansari's leadership that a telegraph line connected Persia, home to the majority of Shiʿi Muslims, to Iraq, where the most notable Shiʿi clerics resided. This contributed to the centralization of Shiʿi Marja'yya and created a sense of there being a more coherent transnational network among various members of the clergy. This also provided a major source of religious taxes for leaders of the seminary. It also strengthened the relationship between the clerical elite and their followers, a factor that played a major role in the Tobacco Protest of 1890 and later during the Persian Constitutional Revolution of 1905.

The tobacco revolt: A case of Shiʿi transnationalism

Sixty years since the Shiʿi clerics' direct participation in the Russo-Persian Wars, a group of clerics, interpreting the existing political opportunity structure as relatively open, decided to become more active and to strengthen their authority through supporting the Persian merchant class. At the time, the clerical elite network had been established among various personalities residing in Persia and in the holy cities in Iraq who had been in direct contact with each other. Newspapers and presses had been established throughout the region and a sense of popular awareness, due to changes associated with modernism, had advanced among the laity and elites. These all made Shiʿi clerical elites at that time one of the most influential social strata. Eventually, the clergy made an alliance with the merchant class and, together, the two played a pivotal role in the social movements against the state in what later coalesced in, and became known as, the Tobacco Protest.

Naser al-Din Shah, the fourth Qajar Monarch, ascended the throne in 1848. His reign was concurrent with the introduction of European modernism in the region. He was the first Qajar ruler who was forced to introduce reformist measures in order to bring about advances in the country. However, historical evidence suggests that, throughout his reign, he acted indecisively and at times contrary to popular interests.[77]

During his third visit to the West in April 1889, the Shah granted to Major Gerald Talbot the monopoly right of Persian tobacco business for fifty years.[78] In March 20, 1890, while visiting Tehran, Major Talbot finalized and signed the agreement with the government and started to work out the preliminary arrangements for the new business inside the country.

This not only raised Russian objections but further prompted civil protest on the part of an alliance of Persian merchants and Shiʿi clerical elites.[79] Although the local merchants were among the earliest opponents of the concession, due to the unstructured nature of their activities, they were incapable of mobilizing the masses to advance their objectives. Consequently, they had to ask Shiʿi clerical elites to form an alliance in order to mobilize the masses. Shiʿi clerical elites, themselves, had already been threatened by the mass immigration of the company's foreign cadres, which endangered to introduce a new culture into Persia's conservative society.[80] Furthermore, the merchant class was traditionally among the key financial sponsors of the Shiʿi clergy, and any threat to their interests would ultimately impact the financial health of the clerical elites. Therefore, an alliance was formed between the merchants and clerical elites against the terms of the monopoly concession.

The first city that experienced popular convulsions was Shiraz, which produced the greatest amount of tobacco. In April 1891, the leading mujtahid of the city, Sayyid Ali Akbar Fal-Asiri, expressed his resentment of the terms of the concession and asked his followers to rise against it, saying,

> O' Men, you should move to not wear the ladies' robes! I have a sword and two drops of blood and I will tear up the belly of any foreigner who would like to enter Shiraz for monopoly of tobacco.[81]

The harsh opposition of the clergy against the concession disturbed the government, which had not taken the merchants' objections seriously until then, and it took steps to involve itself in the affair and calm the protests. The mujtahid of Shiraz, Fal-Asiri, was deported to Iraq overnight.

The news of Shiraz and what the government had done to Fal-Asiri was soon reached by the Grand Marja' of the time, Mirza Muhammad Hassan Shirazi (1814–96), who resided in Samarra in Iraq. The Marja' then sent a telegram to Naser al-Din Shah and advised him not to act against the Quran. In a telegram, dated 28 July 1891, he addressed the Shah as follows:

> Even though I have ever asked nothing from your Majesty so far, upon the receipt of a series of letters and based on what I have heard from informants, I have to remind you that to permit the foreigners to interfere in the internal affairs, their authority over Muslims' community by operating banks, tobacco, railways, etc. is contrary to the explicit text of the Quran and the divine honour, humiliates the government's independence, disrupts the community's order, and causes distress to the nation.[82]

The tone of the letter clearly shows that, at that early stage, the Shi'i Marja' was hoping to resolve the turmoil through peaceful means and without engaging in any contentious politics. However, the state was not in a mood to accept popular demands. Thus eventually, the contention reached Tabriz. In the summer of 1891, the people of Azerbaijan, led by merchants and the famous cleric, Mirza Jawad mujtahid Tabrizi, marched in protest against the concession. The protesters' resentments in the city went beyond the control of even the clerical leadership. The government reacted by suspending the concession's activities in Azerbaijan, a setback that worked in favour of the protesters.[83]

The uprising in Isfahan caused a breakthrough for anti-state movements. Following the leadership of the mujtahid of the city, Agha Najafi Isfahani (1846–1914), people decided to impose a boycott on the consumption of tobacco. Religious elites of the city issued a decree that tobacco was unclean and that any sort of transactions with foreigners was illicit.[84] Unrest increased in the city: the merchants boycotted the tobacco business, coffeehouses shut down and smokers smashed water pipes in streets. Later, a harsher threatening telegram was sent to the people of Isfahan from the royal court, ordering the clerical elites and their followers to resume the tobacco consumption.[85] Although the state's iron fist did not inhibit the clerical elites, merchants and people from exercising their civil rights, it made Agha Munir al-Din Isfahani, another renowned Shi'i scholar of Isfahan, leave the city for Samarra in Iraq, where Mirza Shirazi was residing at the time.

Subsequently, the Mirza, sent his second telegram to Naser al-Din Shah. The Shah and his circle of ministers, led by Amin al-Sultan, and caught between the popular protests from one side and threats from the British company on the other, chose not to respond to the cleric's demands.[86] At the time, the nature of the domestic turmoil which had initially been violent but had calmed down considerably, gave the state confidence that it could manage the protesters and accede to the demands of the Régie. However, the protest in the capital turned events in favour of the protesters and pushed the government to review its policies.

In early December 1891, a rumour circulated in the streets of the capital indicating that the Mirza Shirazi had responded to Mirza Hassan Ashtiani, the leading mujtahid of Tehran, and had boycotted the consumption of tobacco. The text of his letter, which does not exceed two sentences, breathed new life into the protests against granting a tobacco monopoly to the Company. The letter read as follows:

> In the name of God, the compassionate the merciful; as of today, the consumption of tobacco in any form is tantamount to war against the Imam of the Age.[87]

The letter implied that, as long as the concession remained, protesters from different social classes and the religious elite would continue their resistance. It was a clear sign considering the existing political opportunity, and the clerical elite perceived that its role was to become actively engaged in politics in fulfilment of its divinely assigned responsibilities.

On the next day, thousands of copies of the Mirza's fatwa were sent to different cities and caused social uprisings throughout the country. The fatwa had been issued by the right person and at the right time. Soon, an effective alignment was formed among the clergy, merchants, and the laity who had been threatened by the concession, and who now had obtained the spiritual leadership of the sole Shiʿi Marja' against the state.

This new phase of the popular protest, with the support of the Mirza's fatwa, seemed more durable, and it forced the Shah to reconsider the agreement with the British company. At a meeting between the chancellor and a group of Tehran's notables, the government withdrew the internal rights of the company, hoping to calm the protests and nullify the fatwa. Nonetheless, the new telegram of Mirza Shirazi, indicating euphoria at the recent developments, caused the government to crack down on the Tobacco Protest. The officials' acknowledgement of Mirza Shirazi's active role further developed popular contention and made the opposition more united and more determined to push for its objectives.

On 3 January 1892, Naser al-Din Shah sent an envoy to Mirza Hassan Ashtiani ordering him 'to either smoke tobacco at the pulpit of the mosque or to leave Tehran at once'.[88] The decision of Ashtiani to leave Tehran rather than to disobey Mirza Shirazi's fatwa pushed the capital to the verge of a revolution. Upon receiving the news, thousands of people demonstrated at the house of the mujtahid of the city and headed towards the Shah's palace, chanting against him. With the intervention of the palace's guards, scores of protesters were killed and wounded, but their actions demonstrated their sincere determination to the Shah himself and to the remnants of the concession's supporters.[89] By nightfall, the Shah and his entourage were reluctantly beginning to consider the means of paying compensation to the British company. Two days later, the government of Persia officially withdrew the concession.[90] On 26 January 1892, Mirza Shirazi's telegram was sent to Tehran indicating the re-legalization of tobacco consumption.

During the Tobacco Protest, from April 1891 until January 1892, Shiʿi clerical elites in general had acted as mediators between the laity and their followers, especially the merchant class, and the state. Although at the outset the protests were ignited by the Persian merchant class,[91] their uprising gained attraction among the masses only after the Shiʿi clergy had agreed to utilize its influences against the concession. It was indeed the popular constituency of Shiʿi clerics that helped the protest to reach its objectives. Those

Shiʿi clerics who became actively engaged in politics during the turmoil had perceived the political opportunity structure to be relatively favourable. After all, the main alibi for their activism was to protect the benefits of their followers and allies against the domination of outsiders over the Islamic abodes. On another level, the clerical elites also succeeded in deploying what was, at least in embryonic form at the time, a transnational network that extended throughout Persia and the holy cities of Iraq at the time. When they perceived the political opportunity structure to be relatively open, the Shiʿi clergy seized its advantages and played a determinative political role. During the later Constitutional Revolution, however, the clerical elite's activism did not lead to a similarly favourable outcome, as the secular counterparts to that revolution were eventually able to hijack the social movement that had been set in motion by the Shiʿi clergy.[92]

Mujtahids and the Persian Constitutional Revolution: Disparate or deceived?

Shiʿi clerical elites, who had lost a portion of their popular support during the Russo-Persian Wars, perceived and seized a political opportunity during the later nineteenth century when they enjoyed great popular support in the aftermath of the Tobacco Protest. By then, Shiʿi clerical authority was consolidated among the laity, and the clergy's successful support of the merchant class during the protest had attracted other social classes' attention to the potential of the Shiʿi clerical elite. A group from among the secular intelligentsia, therefore, attempted to conclude an alliance with the clergy when a wave of constitutionalism became pervasive throughout the country. This promised a new political opportunity structure which, once again, pushed the clerics to the forefront of the political scene during what became a Constitutional Revolution in Persia in the early twentieth century.

An alliance between religious and secular elites at the time constituted the leadership of the Revolution. Yet, the course of events and the outcome of the revolution were by no means what the religious elite had predicted. The consequences of the revolution showed that Shiʿi clerical elites had misperceived the nature of the political opportunity structure and, thus, their political activism undermined their authority among their followers. When the dust of the revolution settled, the Shiʿi clergy, as a social group within the community, had lost a great deal of its popular support, and were confronted with a closed opportunity structure for years to come.

The long reign of Naser al-Din Shah came to an end when he was assassinated in 1896. He was succeeded by Mozaffar al-Din Shah, his ill and weak-willed son. His rule coincided with a wave of civil demands by Persians and the new intelligentsia which looked towards the western European democracies as their ideals. Although the wave of liberalism had started during the last years of Naser al-Din Shah, the evolving international, regional and national structures promised to produce new political opportunities for the clerical elites in Persia in the early twentieth century.[93]

The concept of a limited monarchy, initially, had been introduced by secular elites who had observed democratic developments in the West. However, they were unable to gain the support of the masses, who were mostly religious and illiterate at the time, for this goal. They, therefore, sought the support of Shiʿi clerics, who had greater popularity, and who had shown their capabilities during the Tobacco Protest. In a letter written during the reign of Naser al-Din Shah, Mirza Agha Khan Kermani (1854–97) expresses to Mirza Malkam Khan that perhaps the intelligentsia would reach their goals sooner if they sought 'limited assistance from the Mullahs'.[94]

However, clerical elites did not have a clear understanding of the concept of constitutionalism at the time. The clerical elite's political activism during the Persian Constitutional Revolution was like playing on a football pitch without knowing where the goalpost was set. This crucial weakness eventually showed itself to be the clerical elite's Achilles heel. Following the Revolution, the renowned Shiʿi mujtahid of Tehran, Sheikh Fazlollah Noori, was executed (in 1909), Sayyid Abdullah Behbahani was assassinated (in 1910), and Akhund Khorasani, the Shiʿi Marja' of Najaf, reportedly was poisoned (in 1911). The post-Revolution age became, for Shiʿi clerics, a dark time which, for decades, they engaged in no overt political activism.

In March 1905, commemorating Ashura, a group of people and religious students marched through the streets of Tehran after listening to Sayyid Abdullah Behbahani harshly attack the behaviour of foreign officers.[95] Soon, an alignment was formed between Behbahani and Sayyid Muhammad Tabatabai, another leading mujtahid of Tehran. From that date, these two, referred to as the 'Two Sayyids', (*Sayyidain*), represented the constitutionalist religious elites of Tehran during the Persian Constitutional Revolution.

Another anti-state protest broke out in December 1905, when the governor of Tehran, 'Ala al-Dowleh, publicly bastinadoed a group of esteemed merchants of the city for not lowering the price of sugar. This incident, akin to what had happened earlier during the Tobacco Protest, led to the conclusion of another alliance between the religious elite and the merchant class against the Shah, his chancellor, and the governor of Tehran. On 13 December 1905, a large group of clerics and religious students, led by the Two Sayyids, left the city, taking sanctuary in the holy shrine of Shah Abd al-Azim in Rey.[96] After days of negotiations between the refugees and the state's representatives, the Ottoman ambassador to Tehran was asked to act as an intermediary and convey the protesters' demands to the Shah and his chancellor. Among a series of preliminary demands, such as the dismissal of the governor of Tehran and Mr Naus, the Belgian custom officer, the religious elite added one more demand: the establishment of a 'house of justice' that would assess the people's petitions and complaints and act on them fairly and with equality.[97] Eventually, Mozaffar al-Din Shah accepted their demands and asked clerical elites and their followers to return to the capital in early 1906. In his royal decree, the Shah addressed his chancellor as follows:

> As I repeatedly have stated my true personal intentions about this matter, and as the foundation of the official house of justice for executing the Islamic law and the social welfare are among the most important tasks, I give order for the establishment of such a legal body to define and to implement Sharia rules throughout the country.[98]

The royal recognition of the refugees' demands was a triumph for the religious elite, although it did not fulfil the goals of the secular constitutionalists, who believed at the time that they could ask for more.[99]

When the reformist clerical elite became disappointed by the failure of the Shah to fulfil his promises, they organized another agitation against the government of Ein al-Dowleh (d. 1927) in the summer of 1906. This time, the Sayyidain sought the assistance of the leading mujtahid of Tehran, Sheikh Fazlollah Noori, who had a close relationship with the chancellor.[100] This led, in July 1906, to the formation of an association between the clergy and the secular constitutionalists. The main group of clerics left Tehran to take refuge in the holy city of Qum, and the other constitutionalists took sanctuary in the British Embassy in Tehran, where they believed was a safe place. They increased the extent of their civil demands. This time, the clerical elite's opposition was more solid than the one earlier during the minor migration, as they were enjoying the support of Sheikh Fazlollah, who, at the time, had a close relationship with the grand Maraji' of Najaf, Akhund Khorasani and Sayyid Kadhem Yazdi.[101] A few days later, the secular constitutionalists called for the establishment of a *National Assembly* instead of a house of justice.[102]

Hoping to ease the turmoil, the Shah, who was seriously ill at the time, agreed to endorse the establishment of a constitution. The first decree, dated 5 August 1906, addressed the chancellor and ordered the swift 'establishment of an assembly of representative of the Qajar princes, the religious and secular elite, landowners, and merchants in Tehran to consult and to assist the reform process which would benefit both the government and the nation of Persia'.[103]This decree, however, was not recognized by the constitutionalists because of its vagueness and failure to mention the will of the masses. Consequently, Mozaffar al-Din Shah issued a second decree two days later, which read as follows:

> To complete our previous decree, dated 5 August 1906, we give an order for the establishing of the Majlis based on what we have already promised. After the election of the representatives, we will sign the presented articles of the constitution that will aim to restore the nation's rights and to implement the sacred law of Sharia law.[104]

This letter was communicated to the clerical elites stationed at Qum. However, the secular constitutionalists who mainly took refuge in Tehran and had the support of the British Chargé d'Affairs opposed the second royal letter and asked that both previous decrees be combined into a third one and that 'Islamic Assembly' be changed to 'National Assembly'. On 9 August 1906, the third royal decree was read to those who had taken sanctuary in the British Embassy in Tehran. In this third decree, the Shah ordered the establishment of a 'National Assembly'. Following that, the letter of the clerical elite was read to other constitutionalists, who were then asked to leave the Embassy as their goals had been 'fulfilled' by the government.[105]

Two months later, the first Assembly opened in Tehran. On 30 December 1906, just a few days prior to his death, Mozaffar al-Din Shah was fortunate in being able to engrave his name in the history of Persia by signing the first Persian Fundamental Law. His autocratic and Russophile son, Muhammad Ali, ascended the throne in January 1907. From the earliest days of his reign, Muhammad Ali Shah showed his opposition to the constitution and the Assembly by not inviting any of its members to his coronation ceremony. Nonetheless, the members of the assembly were busy working on the ratification of the constitution's amendments, later to be known as the Supplementary Fundamental Law of Persia. Since the ratification of the amendment, the constitutionalist religious elites in Tehran had been united in their activities. Nevertheless, witnessing the fanatical actions of secular parliamentary members, the clergy leadership in Tehran formed two distinctive camps: one led by the Sayyidain, who had agreed to the constitution that had been established, and the other led by Sheikh Fazlollah Noori, who mistrusted the initial goal of the secular constitutionalists.

In addition to the daily editorials written by modernist secular constitutionalists against the religious camp, Sheikh Fazlollah was opposed to some articles of the draft Supplementary Fundamental Law which he considered to be anti-Islamic. He thus became actively involved in trying to prevent their ratification at the Assembly's court.[106] At the same time, he proposed that an article be added to the Supplementary Fundamental Law, indicating that each parliamentary act should be observed by a group of appointed mujtahids before ratification in order to check whether it was consistent with Sharia laws. There were discussions in April 1907 among parliamentary members, accompanied by the *Sayyidain* and Sheikh Fazlollah Noori, about the article that Sheikh Fazlollah had proposed.[107] Although Noori enjoyed the full support of his high-ranking colleagues in Najaf at the time, a minority faction of the Assembly led by Sayyid Hassan Taqizadeh began to attack him and the other religious figures around him.[108]

Despite these contentions, the determined Sheikh Fazlollah continued his activities, which led to the ratification of Article II of the Supplementary Fundamental Law. This article, passed by members of the Assembly, states the following:

> At no time must any legal enactment of the Sacred National Consultative Assembly, established by the favour and assistance of His Holiness the Imam of the Age, the favour of His Majesty the Shah of Islam, the care of the Proofs of Islam, and the whole people of the Persian nation, be at variance with the sacred principles of Islam or the laws established by His Holiness the Best of Mankind. It is hereby declared that it is for the Ulama to determine whether such laws as may be proposed are or are not conformable to the principles of Islam; and it is therefore officially enacted that there shall at all times exist a committee composed of not less than five mujtahids or other devout theologians, cognizant also of the requirements of the age in this manner.[109]

The ratification of this article represented progress for Sheikh Fazlollah and his companions. The clerical elite believed that having such an article would secure their interests in the new regime and would also guarantee the rule of Sharia in Persia. Consequently, and putting tactical differences aside, the Sayyidain met with Sheikh Fazlollah Noori in June 1907 and orally agreed to respect their mutual interests in any future activities.[110] While the Sayyidain guaranteed that the Assembly's laws 'would always be compatible with the law of Sharia', Sheikh Fazlollah promised to stop opposing the Assembly and not to organize any rally against it. However, the course of events, which were mainly under the direct influence of secular figures inside the Assembly and was supported by their propaganda machine, seemed completely out of the Sayyidain's hands. The upcoming events proved that secular constitutionalists had promised something to the clerical elite and, nonetheless, were covertly doing something else. With the establishment of the constitution, the constitutionalist religious elite had no further use for their previous secular allies, who were working to develop the country along the lines of western European models. Thus, the objectives of the secular constitutionalists could not be aligned with that of any member of the Shi'i clerical elite and would basically undermine the principles of Shi'i Islam.

The posture of the secular constitutionalists became threatening enough for the Sheikh and his followers, who at the time were known as the proponents of a constitution in accordance with the shari'a, *Mashruteh Mashrue'*, to take sanctuary in the Rey on 21 June 1907.[111] From this date on, the determined Sheikh Fazlollah found a pulpit to express his views of the ongoing events. His stirring speeches, which were opposed to the secular constitution and emphasized the Islamic nature of the country, filled the news headlines throughout Persia and reached the Shi'i clergy in Najaf. In one of their proclamations, which was issued during their stay in Rey, the Islamic Constitutionalists replied to their secular opponents as follows:

> We clearly announce to all the Muslim people of Persia that, today, the National Assembly does not have a denier, neither from the mujtahids nor from any other groups. Therefore, if some jealous and ill-minded figures accused Sheikh Fazlollah of not recognizing the National Assembly, it is a lie, a lie . . . . As his eminence once mentioned, especially in his speech last Friday: I am not ruling out the very existence of the National Assembly, and even I believe that I have entered to this prior to anyone else; I was the one who brought all other Ulama, who were residing in Iraq and other countries and had been quiet about this issue, to support this popular movement . . . . My initial intentions and goals have not been changed since then. I clearly declare to all of you, and publish it to those who are not present here: I want that National Assembly that the majority of Muslims are demanding. The one that is founded on the principles of Islam, that is not against the Quran, and that does not pass any law that might contradict the principles of the sacred J'afari faith.[112]

In the hindsight, in comparison with his constitutionalist colleagues, Sheikh Fazlollah Noori's perceptions about what was going on at the time and the movement's deviations from its initial Islamic goals were more accurate and would serve the clerical authority among the followers more appropriately. His advantage over those high-ranking constitutionalist clerics in Najaf was that he could monitor the covert actions of secular figures closely while he was in Tehran. In Noori's opinion, the rule of the autocrat Muhammad Ali Shah was more preferable to that of the secular constitutionalists.[113] After all, the activities of Sheikh Fazlollah in Rey and his treatises, which were produced by his companions during the time they take refuge in the holy shrine of Shah Abd al-Azim, marked a significant turning point in the divergence of perceptions among the religious elites during the constitutional movement in Persia and Iraq. This was a disparity that everyone could have predicted would occurr sooner or later, as the Shiʿi clerical elite had entered the constitutional movement based on loosely defined goals. Kasravi clearly states this when he acknowledges their leading role in the Persian Constitutional Revolution, but also states that, at the same time, they 'did not understand the constitution, as they were later to see it'.[114]

Concurrent with these tensions, the political opportunity structure was going through dramatic changes.[115] In Tehran, Amin al-Sultan, the renowned chancellor of Qajar, who had benign relationships with both religious camps, was assassinated in front of the Assembly. This, along with further guarantees by the Assembly to consider Islamic law before their decisions, led to the end of the Islamic Constitutionalists' sanctuary and their return to the capital in September 1907.[116]

On 23 June 1908, upon his failed assassination plot, Muhammad Ali Shah ordered the bombardment of the National Assembly. Subsequently, a group of constitutionalists were hanged. Some took refuge in the British Embassy in Tehran, and others, including the Sayyidain, were expelled from the capital. A period of the 'sole autocratic rule of the Shah' commenced. With the Sheikh Fazlollah Noori preferring to stay quiet, along with the banishment of the Sayyidain from Tehran, the religious leadership of the constitutional movement was placed on the shoulders of the religious elite of Najaf during this period. The Shah had made a strategic mistake by seeking assistance from the foreign Russian forces. This left the clerics of Najaf with no option but to immediately condemn Muhammad Ali Shah. At the time, they were not only worried about the Shah's autocracy, but were also alarmed about the threat of foreign sovereignty over the Islamic land of Persia. Therefore, when the Shah sent a letter to clerical elites in Najaf stating that he had shut down the National Assembly because he feared that its activities would diminish the sacred religion of the Prophet, the Shiʿi clergy responded,

> Your Highness must consider thoroughly what has been done to your nation and state. You, as a Muslim ruler, should not have used your position to dismantle the principles of Islam . . . God willing you will stop undermining the religion and the nation, and thus will prevent us taking further action.[117]

The respectful tone of the telegraph clearly indicates that, as early as July 1908, even the constitutionalist clergy of Najaf were hoping to ease the upheavals by peaceful means. Yet the course of future incidents forced them to abandon this path. It seemed that the political divergence of the Shiʿi clerics reached its peak during this period: while those residing in Najaf, frustrated by the despotic actions of the Shah, issued a fatwa indicating that the struggle to restore the constitution was equal to taking part in 'Jihad alongside the Imam of the Age',[118] Sheikh Fazlollah Noori, freed from the radical activities of the suppressed Assembly, issued a decree that confirmed that a 'constitution [as of what we have seen], is incompatible with Islam from many facets'.[119] These declarations clearly show that the Shiʿi clerical elite had different perceptions concerning the basic meaning of the concept of a constitution. In the eyes of constitutionalist clerics stationed in Najaf at the time, the new regime was more of a 'limited monarchy' – one that would respect the sociopolitical role of the clergy and perhaps decrease the state's authority in their favour. Yet the principles of constitutionalism, as the secular intelligentsia was demanding at the time and at least in eyes of Sheikh Fazlollah, would consequently decrease the role of Shari'a and would propagate concepts like freedom and gender equality, in evident contrast of the Shiʿi jurisprudence. This is why, after a while, the Sheikh became the staunch adversary of the type of constitutionalism going on the ground.

From June until July 1908, which was known as the 'Minor Autocracy' period, the Assembly was shut down and the two camps of the religious elite – those supporting and those opposing the constitution based on their very different perceptions – produced a series of treatises. Perhaps the most renowned book in support of the constitution is one written by Mirza Muhammad Husayn Naʿini, the disciple of Akhund Khorsani, entitled *Tanbīh al-ummah wa-tanzīh al-millah*. To argue that constitutional monarchy is preferable to autocratic monarchy, and hence would be more suitable for the Muslim community during the Occultation era, Naʿini categorized states into three types: the government of the infallible Imam, the autocratic monarchy and the constitutional monarchy. He stated that autocratic unjust rule encompasses three expropriations of the rights of God, infallible Imam, and the Nation, while constitutional monarchy would only infringe upon the right of the infallible Imam to rule; hence the latter is to be preferred over the former during the absence of the Imam.[120]

Meanwhile, Muhammad Ali Shah was under constant internal and external pressures initiated through the active engagement of the constitutionalist elite of Najaf. The clerics stationed in Iraq at the time sent a handful of telegraphs to foreign governments, especially the Muslim Ottomans, demanding their political assistance to restore the constitution in Persia. Furthermore, they issued a fatwa addressing all Muslims, asking them to boycott the despotic rule of Muhammad Ali Shah and to not pay their taxes to the government.

On 9 May 1909, the Shah agreed to issue a decree and to restore the constitution within two months. However, it was too late, and the Nationalist forces triumphantly entered the capital in July, just days earlier than the date of a promised election. The Shah, fearing for his life, took sanctuary in the Russian Embassy. The conquest of Tehran by the constitutionalist forces could not be promising for the Shiʿi clerical elite, especially when the life of Sheikh Fazlollah Noori and his companions were under serious threat. Eventually, the constitutionalist court sentenced the Sheikh to death by hanging on 31 July 1909. When he was preparing to be executed, he addressed the crowd:

> God Almighty, you are my witness that, in these last minutes of my life, once again, I remind these people that the founders of this regime [the constitutional government] are infidels who have deceived the nation; this regime is fundamentally against Islam.[121]

The Sheikh's destiny, which was exceptional throughout Shiʿi history, made other members of the clergy, who had been manipulated by other political actors, reconsider their political postures. As soon as the news reached Najaf, Akhund Khorasani sent a telegram to the constitutionalists, who were governing the city, and ordered them to safeguard the life of Sheikh Fazlollah. However, the telegram only became public after the Sheikh's execution. By killing one of the most famous mujtahids of the time, the secular constitutionalists sent a concise and clear message that they would not tolerate any opposition to their intention, even if it came from their former allies.

Throughout the Constitutional Revolution, all members of the Shiʿi clergy had been actively involved in politics. Since the early stages of the incident, some Shiʿi clerics were aligned with secular constitutionalists, while some had concerns about the upheavals that were going on. The former group of religious elites succeeded in securing the support of Akhund Khorasani and his companions in Najaf, while the latter group of clerics, led by Sheikh Fazlollah, was soon to find out that the intentions of the secular constitutionalists were not compatible with the principles of Shiʿi Islam.

After the fall of Tehran, Akhund Khorsani and other so-called 'constitutionalist clerics' and their laity followers were pushed more towards the Sheikh's judgements. Thus, the secular constitutionalists got the upper hand in seizing the political opportunity structure, while the majority of Shiʿi clerics were baffled about the outcome of their endeavours. In the eyes of the Shiʿi clerical elites, especially those supporting the constitutionalist camp, they had been manipulated by secular forces during the turmoil. Therefore, the Constitutional Revolution left a wound on the body of Shiʿi religious elites, and this wound took some seven decades to be healed. Once Imam Khomeini, addressing a group of Shiʿi clerics, stated: 'You should take lessons from history and must not let outsiders propagate evil temptations among your ranks, as they had done during the Constitutional Revolution.'[122]

* * *

This chapter briefly examined the historical trajectory of the Shiʿi clerical elite's political activism as it related to their perceptions about the political opportunity structures they confronted since the commencement of the Major Occultation era.

Since 941, the Shiʿi laity has been deprived of divine and infallible leadership, and the clerical elite became responsible for leading the community until the promised day when the Imam will re-emerge. This constitutes the Shiʿi Occultation discourse which is promoted by all members of the clerical elite. Seemingly different political tendencies exhibited by different Shiʿi clerics throughout history could be seen as a result of their perceptions about the political opportunity structure that they confront, and their implications for how they fulfil their sociopolitical responsibilities vis-à-vis their relevant communities. Thus, the political activism and/or quietism of the Shiʿi clergy in a given context represent more of a tactical disparity than a strategic one.

Concurrent with the Occultation of the last Imam, Shiʿi clerics, his general deputies, who at the time did not expect the era to take long, devoted their activities to answering the inquiries of the laity in ways that were compatible with the changing contexts in which they found themselves. Therefore, their early ijtihad did not encompass political affairs at all. Taking advantage of the empowerment they experienced under the Shiʿi Buyid dynasty, Shiʿi personalities of the early ages strived to compile books and treatises to propagate the tenets of the faith in a way that responded to the community's emerging questions. Politically, they became less active, at least overtly, among the circles of their students and schools to undertake this responsibility.

Four centuries after the commencement of the Occultation era, with the development of Shiʿi ijtihad and emergence of more active personalities, the reign of the Sunni Abbasid caliph came to an end. This favourable opportunity structure led groups of Shiʿi clerics to assume an activist posture to protect the community. This new trend, along with the further development of Persian interests in Shiʿi Islam, helped the Safavids to establish their dynasty in 1501. This heralded a period within which Shiʿi clerics from all around the world either exercised political activism or supported their colleagues while praying for the triumph of the new Shiʿi dynasty.

The open structure for the Shiʿi clerical elite's political activism reached its peak with the consolidation of Safavid rule in Persia. Although some members of the Shiʿi clergy who were seemingly quiet did not partake in the routine politics of the era, none opposed the activism of their fellow clerics. Yet, with changes in the political opportunity structure, and to the dismay of Shiʿi religious elites, an internal schism occurred and the static Akhbāri School marginalized the Usuli mujtahids in the mid-Safavid era. Subsequently for a century to come, Shiʿi clerics were barred from political involvement. This coincided with the fall of the Safavids and emergence of Nader Shah Afshar, who decreased state support for Shiʿi clerics and made them seek refuge in the holy cities of Iraq, to quietly pursue their routine activities. The first setback for the Shiʿi clergy in the aftermath of Safavids, however, turned out to be in their favour eventually. It was as a result of this setback that clerical elites were forced to think about alternative sources of financing, and it thus led to the consolidation of a valuable social base among the Shiʿi laities. Henceforth, they became independent of the state and received their legitimacy, along with financial support, from the people. This change made the Qajar rulers seek the assistance of clerical elites in establishing their rule in Persia, and in mobilizing the masses to participate in war with Russian forces during the early nineteenth century.

The second political impediment for Shiʿi clerics came after the conclusion of the Turkmenchay Treaty, when the state propaganda machine blamed the miseries of war on the clerical leadership. This again caused the religious elite to abandon activism. Decades later, they played an active role during the Tobacco Protest in Persia and made the monarchy and the British reconsider their policies in favour of Shiʿi clerics, their allies and their followers. The structured activities of the Shiʿi clerical elite at the time were partly owed to the formation of the basic transnational network they had succeeded in shaping. The triumph of the Shiʿi religious elite camp during the Revolt pushed them once again to the forefront of politics during the Persian Constitutional Revolution. Yet, their political activism this time cost them a great deal in regard to their authority and their popular constituency. They basically lost the game to the contingencies of the modern context, their misperceptions and internal schisms. When the dust of the Revolution settled, all members of the clerical elite, ranging from those who had approved the secular constitutionalist to those who had opposed the mainstream revolutionaries, found out that the outcome would be inconsistent with Shiʿi principles or with the will of clerical elites. Therefore, the last experience of political activism for the clerical elite in pre-contemporary history taught them that, to achieve success, they have to thoroughly consider their perceptions of the existing structure of political opportunities and wait for a more permissive context.

4

Iran 1979

The birth of the mujtahid statesmen

The previous chapter presented a brief historic review of premodern Shiʿi political thought. The aim was to explore how the Shiʿi clergy responded to the political opportunity structure that was available to them through the prism of their personal perceptions. This and the next two chapters focus on the activities of Shiʿi clerical elites in modern Iran, Iraq and Lebanon.

The Shiʿi political revival in the region during the last century had its roots both in the Persian Constitutional Revolution of 1905–7 and the uprisings against British and French imperialism in Iraq and Lebanon. The increasingly pervasive Shiʿi political supremacy we are witnessing throughout the Middle East today is the result of a political transformation that, within specific contexts, has been relatively developed by Shiʿi clerical leadership in conformity with their perceptions and political postures over the last century. This chapter employs political opportunity theory to explain how Shiʿi clerical activism led to the establishment of the Islamic Republic of Iran.[1]

The establishment of the Islamic Republic of Iran in 1979 marked the beginning of a period in the modern political history of the Middle East during which the Shiʿi clergy, seizing the opportunities that this pivotal event afforded, introduced a model of Shiʿi government based on the theory of the 'Guardianship of the Jurist'.[2] The movement which developed around the leadership of Ayatollah Khomeini, and which led the overthrow of the Pahlavi monarchy in Iran, emerged from the perceptions and experiences that the Shiʿi clerical elite had accumulated throughout the centuries of the Occultation era that began in the tenth century. This was evident in the aftermath of its establishment in February 1979, that the Islamic Republic of Iran was supported by a great number of Shiʿi clerics. The new government was centred on the rule of the Shiʿi clergy, and it emerged because of the relatively open political opportunity structure that its leadership had correctly perceived and had acted on at the time.

As previously discussed, after the Occultation era commenced and deprived the Shiʿi community of an infallible source of leadership, qualified Shiʿi clerics, acting as the general deputies of the Imam, assumed leadership of the community. At the time of the emergence of the Shiʿi Safavid dynasty in the sixteenth century, the Shiʿi clerical elite had increased their involvement in politics, with some Shiʿi figures becoming associated with the ruling monarchs. They were, thus, provided with an unsurpassed opportunity to promote Shiʿi doctrines. Henceforth, a majority of the religious elite constituted, either directly or indirectly, the backbone of government and exercised an active leadership role in the community and in protecting the principles of the faith. Their role in the establishment of a constitutional monarchy in Persia in 1906 heralded a turning point in Shiʿi modern political doctrine. However, the outcome of that revolution was not favourable for the majority of the Shiʿi clergy, and during the decades that followed, they were forced to abandon politics.

Clerical elites believed that they had become involved with the Constitutional Revolution to protect the citadel of Shiʿi principles and to support the will of their followers by confining the monarch's power and establishing an assembly.[3] Taking the opportunity structure into account, at the time Shiʿi clerics were generally connected with the majority of the population and succeeded in mobilizing the masses against the arbitrary Qajar rulers. Since the sixteenth century, they had succeeded in establishing a more personal, one-to-one relationship with various members of the laity by engaging in every possible aspect of the laity's routine life, ranging from providing education and conducting marriage ceremonies to managing funerals. Although they did not want to establish an Islamic state ruled by a Shiʿi cleric – perhaps because they did not perceive the political opportunity structure to be open at the time – they sought to require the state to respect the clergy's sociopolitical role.

The course that events took, however, moved against the will of high-ranking Shiʿi clerics. Though they undoubtedly had played a role in mobilizing the masses, due to the clear mismatch between the political opportunity structure that existed at the time and the perception of that structure on the part of the constitutionalist clergy, the clergy eventually lost the game to other actors and were pushed out of the politics. The execution of a leading mujtahid of Tehran, Sheikh Fazlollah Noori, had the utmost negative effect on Shiʿi clerical authority at the close of the Constitutional Revolution. This huge blow to their popular status ultimately decreased the political activism of the clerical elite for decades.

The post-Constitutional Revolution era in Persia coincided with social, economic and political disarray. Ahmad Shah Qajar, who succeeded his father in 1909, was unable to restore central governmental authority throughout the country as, just a few days after his coronation at the age of eighteen in July 1914, Persia became a backyard to the belligerents of the Great War. At the end of the First World War, the writ of Ahmad Shah's government hardly extended beyond the capital city of Tehran and a few other big cities. It was provincial with tribal chiefs holding actual authority throughout Persia. With the collapse of Tsarist Russia, which had been the power in Persia since the Treaty of Turkmenchay (1828), Britain became the most powerful political player in Persia. According to an Anglo-Persian Agreement – signed between the Prime Minister Vosuq al-Dowleh and the British Chargé d'Affaires, Sir Percy Cox, on 9 August 1919 – Persia was nominally independent, but its military and financial affairs were subject to British tutelage.[4]

Internal political turmoil in Persia between proponents and opponents of the 1919 Agreement, and the emergence of rebel groups throughout the country to the dismay of the young monarch, urged concrete initiatives to sustain the integrity of the country. Persia was desperately in need of a saviour who could prevent the country's disintegration and also, satisfy British political goals. It was in this context that Reza Khan, a mid-ranking Cossack officer at the time who seemed equipped to play this role, seized power in a bloodless coup on 22 February 1921.

The rise of Reza Khan on the Persian political scene occurred during the early stages of the establishment of Qum seminary by Ayatollah Hairi. A power vacuum in Persia during the early 1920s, at the time when Iraq and Najaf seminary were under British occupation, provided an opportunity that enabled the Shiʿi clergy to strengthen the religious centre in Qum, under the leadership of Hairi.

The leadership of Hairi, who accurately perceiving the closed opportunity structure was politically quiet, constitutes the first phase of the Shiʿi political trajectory in modern Persia. His life in Qum as the Shiʿi Marja' coincided with the rise of Reza Shah and his introduction of a modernization–secularization campaign throughout the country. Indeed, it was the Ayatollah's providence that sustained the very fragile foundation of the Qum seminary against the later repressions of the Pahlavi rule. Consequently, his successors, who inherited the leadership of the seminary after he passed away in 1937, did not attempt to pursue any form of political contention, despite concerns about the initiatives of Reza Shah.

Amid the Second World War, in September 1941, Reza Shah stepped down from the power and his son, Muhammad Reza, ascended to the throne. The reign of the young monarch inaugurated an interregnum era in which a relatively open opportunity structure emerged at the political scene of the country. The leadership of Qum seminary, at the time, was in the hands of three Shiʿi figures, known as *Maraji' Tholath*,[5] struggling to manage the financial shortcomings of the centre. Then the charismatic Marja', Ayatollah Burujirdi, moved from local seminary of Broujerd in west Iran to Qum, and assumed the seminary's leadership in 1946. Under his watch, a new spirit invigorated the life of the city's seminary and the clergy in Iran. Although not all members of the clergy in Iran were in favour of Burujirdi's political posture at the time, he had managed to maintain a unique engagement with the monarch, a coexistence that, although it had gone through a series of upheavals, was also based on mutual respect and understanding.

Just after Burujirdi passed away, Muhammad Reza Shah initiated a series of socioeconomic development schemes undeterred by the potential opposition of the deceased Ayatollah. Yet, when in early 1963, the details of the so-called White Revolution were publicly announced, it drew the condemnation of the Shiʿi clergy of Qum. At the time, the political opportunity structure was far more open to the religious elites than in the 1920s when Reza Shah had started his modernization–secularization programmes. By 1963, and as a result of the activities of Hairi and Burujirdi, the Qum seminary was strong enough to denounce state activities that were considered threatening to Shiʿi clerical authority. Nine renowned clerics of the seminary, among them the sixty-two-year-old Khomeini, condemned the referendum in an open letter and encouraged the authorities to respect Islam and to honour the Constitution.[6] The clash with the clergy heated up in the following months until eventually, in June 1963, Khomeini was arrested in Qum and transferred to Tehran.

On 5 June 1963, there was a mass demonstration of Iranians in opposition to Ayatollah's being taken into custody that provided a shocking reaction to the ruling apparatus. It heralded the rise of a sociopolitical movement formed around the religious elites, although one that required further development in order to be able to achieve a tangible victory. A year later, when Khomeini was expelled to Turkey, he and his entourage had succeeded in consolidating their anti-state activities. While his proponents were forming a covert, informal network in Iran, Khomeini started to mature his political doctrine in Najaf addressing the contingencies of the modern developments. Throughout the years between 1963 and 1979, other members of the clergy were politically active, albeit in a more discrete manner. Various Shiʿi figures, as one of the many political actors at the time, responding to the opportunities afforded by the structure, though sometimes with different tactics, were actively engaged in Iranian politics and in the condemnation of the Pahlavi's policies.

In early 1979, these activities culminated in the overthrow of the monarchy in Iran and, eventually, to the favour of the clergy, in the consolidation of an Islamic Republic. How was this powerful association formed among various members of the Shiʿi clerical elite in Iran? How did religious elites succeed in seizing the advantages offered by the political opportunity structure? Was there a meaningful disagreement among the top echelons of the religious leadership throughout the revolutionary phase? This chapter addresses these questions by probing the role of the context – the political opportunity structure at the time in Iran from the Constitutional Revolution until the establishment of the Islamic Republic, and clerical elite perception of concerning.

The rise of the Pahlavi and the Iranian mujtahids

Persia was undergoing dramatic sociopolitical changes at the midst of the Pahlavi rise. Political activism on the part of the Shiʿi clergy during this period was much influenced by the post-constitutionalism context. Reflecting on their vain experience, they chose to stay out of politics for the time being. Instead, as Reza Shah was consolidating his reign, circles of Shiʿi clerics, gathered around Ayatollah Hairi, were working on establishing the Qum seminary. Here, we seek to explain the political posture assumed by the clerical leadership during this period, through an examination of the political opportunity structure that confronted the generation of Qum seminary's cadre and their perception of it.

Persia, under the reign of Ahmad Shah Qajar, was in absolute chaos, and was nowhere close to adopting the principles of democratic parliamentary rule.[7] Concurrently, in early twentieth century, the pace of international changes was speeding up. The 1917 Bolshevik Revolution had wiped out the Tsarist Russian hegemony in Persia, and the British were seeking to reinforce their influence in the East by means of their proposed 1919 Anglo-Persian Agreement. Disenchanted over the fate of the agreement, a number of British authorities were cultivating this idea of a coup to unseat Ahmad Shah Qajar. Meanwhile, a group of mostly urban middle-class Persian constitutionalists, frustrated by Qajars incompetency to rule, sought for an alternative. For them, the chaotic post-constitutional Persia was in desperate need of an 'enlightened despot' capable of transforming the underprivileged and fragmented country into a united one.[8]

Reza Khan happened to be the shining star, corresponding to the concern of both groups at the time. He was provided an opportunity to lead the country through the 1920s, and to revitalize Persia along with modernization programmes. However, as with all Persian rulers in the post-Safavid era, he had to develop a framework for dealing with the religious elite. This became even more important when, just four years prior to the establishment of the Pahlavi dynasty, Hairi had established the seminary in Qum in 1921. The relationship between Reza Shah and the clergy at the early stages of his rule was overshadowed by the restoration of the seminary. This, consequently, defined the structural political opportunity presented to the Shiʿi clerical elite at the time.

The state–clergy relationship under Reza Shah can be traced through three distinct periods. First was the pre-Pahlavi dynasty period, between 1921 and 1925, during which Reza Khan was generally obedient to the clerical leadership. During this period, he competed with Ahmad Shah Qajar to form alliances with the religious elite.[9] In the second period, from 1925 to 1927, Reza Khan ascended the throne and, confident of his position, let his relations with the Shiʿi clerical leadership sour. Finally, during the third period, from 1927 until the last days of Reza Shah's reign, there was a growing enmity between the state and the religious elite.

In 1921, Ayatollah Hairi, a prominent student of Mirza Shirazi, the leader of the Tobacco Revolt, arrived in the holy city of Qum near Tehran to reinstate the city's dormant seminary.[10] Born in 1859, Hairi personally witnessed the political transformations in Persia and Iraq during the early twentieth century. With the fall of Ottomans in sight and the political structure in Iraq undergoing dramatic changes, he committed himself to strengthening clerical authority in neighbouring Persia, where the majority of the Shiʿi population resided. In pursuit of this goal, he undertook to do whatever he found to be necessary and, in the given circumstances, viable. With the establishment of Pahlavi's rule, however, Shiʿi clergy activities became restrained in Persia. Consequently, Hairi chose to focus on his school rather than to interfere in political state affairs, perceiving an unfavourable context.[11] The course of later events proved this to have been a providential choice, as this politically quiescence posture ultimately worked to the benefit of the seminary, clergy and their followers.

About the same time the Ayatollah settled in Qum, Reza Khan (later known as Reza Shah) emerged on Persia's political scene. Reza Khan was a pious Shiʿi and a man of integrity, and he came to be regarded by the religious elites as a person capable of protecting the community. It was on this understanding that his relationship with the religious leadership developed in Persia. A key turning point in the relationship between Reza Khan and the clerics, nonetheless, occurred, following the commencement of the Republican Movement by his supporters in Persia.[12]

Reza Khan viewed Republicanism as similar to what Mustafa Kemal had established in neighbouring Turkey, and as a means of abolishing the Qajar dynasty and ascending the throne.[13] Promoting this scenario, he eventually faced formidable opposition from merchants, some members of Parliament and the clerical apparatus. Perhaps the most influential and active of his opponents was Sayyid Hassan Modarres (1870–1937), a cleric member of Parliament. The debate in Persia about Republicanism exacerbated the political turmoil in the country and led Reza Khan to seek assistance from high-ranking Maraji', including two Grand Ayatollahs, Muhammad Husayn Na'ini (1861–1936) and Abu al-Hasan Isfahani (1860–1946), both of whom had temporarily migrated from Najaf and were in Qum at the time.[14]

The two Grand Ayatollahs had previously sought sanctuary and support from the seemingly religious Reza Khan against occupying British forces in Iraq. In the view of the mainstream clergy at the time, the abolition of the Islamic Ottoman Caliphate by Kemal Ataturk had forged an identification of Republicanism with secularism. The Shi'i clergy had traditionally been more confident with a monarchical form of government, a system that they believed would be more likely to respect their sociopolitical role than one associated with the new concept of 'republic'. Therefore, after meeting with Reza Khan, the leadership of Qum seminary issued a signed statement and public declaration of their opposition to the Republican Movement.[15] On that same day, Reza Khan proclaimed that upon the request of the Shi'i ulama and to 'preserve the majesty of Islam and the independence of Persia',[16] an idea of republicanism should be abandoned in the country.[17] Eventually, in October 1925, Majlis voted to abolish Qajar dynasty and named Reza Khan as the new monarch. By vote of the Constituent Assembly, on 15 December 1925, Reza Shah, the founder of what would become the Pahlavi dynasty, took the oath to 'uphold the Fundamental Laws of Constitution, to support the Shi'i faith, and to devote himself to Iran's independence'.[18]

He had managed to attain implicit, although conditional, support from the Shi'i clergy in Najaf. However, Hairi did not reply to the court's invitation either to participate personally or to send an envoy to Reza Shah's coronation ceremony. Shortly after the establishment of the new dynasty, in August 1927, a state announcement appeared in the press, indicating,

> Some people have tried to provoke division and discord throughout the country in the name of preserving religion . . . . Nobody is entitled to independently preach 'Forbidding the Evil' with justification of the religious propagation; otherwise he is worthy of the utmost punishment.[19]

The wordings and implications of the announcement clearly challenged the clerical authority. Furthermore, it signalled the emergence of a newly restrictive political structure. Then came the ratification of the Compulsory Conscription in 1926, which enforced the youths, including those who wished to study at religious seminaries, to participate in military service. Resented from new state initiatives, Aqa Nur Allah Najafi,[20] the renowned mujtahid of Isfahan called for a mass demonstration and asked his fellow colleagues to migrate and take sanctuary at the holy city of Qum. Responding to his call, hundreds of clerics from all around the country convened in Qum by later 1927. The demonstrators' ultimate goal was to force Reza Shah to either abide by his constitutional duties, most notably his oath of protecting Shi'i Islam, or abdicate, the later disclosed archives reveal.[21] In a private meeting with his trusted circle, Aqa Nur Allah explicitly states,

> This improvident, impious servant of foreigners [Reza Shah] is basically incapable of rule. We should force him to abdicate, which is an easy task. We must push this donkey down, as we had already raised it up![22]

In this, it appears that Aqa Nur Allah had perceived there to be an opportunity to ensure that the Shah would fulfil his duty to respect the clerical authority. As the size of the dissenting clerics' gathering was growing, Reza Shah sent his envoys to meet with Aqa Nur Allah, to broker a deal. Amid the negotiation with the state's envoys, in January 1928, Aqa Nur Allah passed away mysteriously, leaving his companions no alternative but to give up pursuing their demands.

Consequently, one of the last Shiʿi clerical movements opposed to Reza Shah's rule was stalled just when it appeared to be making progress towards achievement of its goals. Henceforth, Reza Shah would become more vigilant in guarding against the orchestration of any movement that might threaten his reign, especially one led by religious figures. Hairi's political posture, held over the accurate perception of the unfavourable structure, had tightened hands of Reza Shah to challenge his leadership of the seminary. Evidences indicate that the Ayatollah's main concern, at the time, was the destiny of his newborn seminary. Therefore, he not only remained politically quiet, but also advised his circles of students to follow suit.

Nonetheless, a critical moment to provoke Hairi's opposition occurred in March 1928. During a visit to the Shiʿi Holy Shrine in Qum, Reza Shah's wife and daughters were confronted and openly disparaged by a high-ranking disciple of Hairi, Sheikh Muhammad Taqi Bafqi, for their inappropriate attires. In hours, Reza Shah arrived from Tehran, entered Qum and beat the Sheikh inside the holy shrine.[23] Qum was thrown into turmoil in response to what was perceived to be an outrageous act on the part of the monarch. For its part, the state was prepared to crack down on any sort of protest. Nevertheless, the Hairi issued a declaration stating, 'Any talk around the incident of Hajj Sheikh Muhammad Taqi is against the sacred law of Islam and is religiously illicit.'[24] His posture, although seemingly passive, was designed to ensure that the seminary would be protected from Reza Shah's iron fist and his authorities' repression. He remained quiet at the time because he believed that the aggravation that the Shah would threaten the very existence of Shiʿi Islam in Persia.[25]

The Qum incident, nonetheless, was perceived by the clergy as disloyalty on the part of Reza Shah to their sacred beliefs. They and their followers perceived that the structure for social activities under the Pahlavi rule was one of the most restrictive they had ever faced. Thus, as the leader of the community, Hairi chose to remain politically quiet and to devote his life, instead, to religious teaching and to developing the seminary.

Reza Shah's socioeconomic initiatives and modernization reforms began in 1927. Over the coming years, the government's modernization of the economic, juridical and educational systems undermined the clerical authority, which was going to discharge from numerous social activities.[26] While these initiatives were being established throughout the country under the 'iron fist of Reza Shah', the clergy, who were mainly under the influence of Hairi's leadership, pursued a doctrine of not interfering in politics and, in this way, tried to protect their community of followers, to preserve the citadel of Shiʿi Islam in Iran under Pahlavi rule.

However, there took place another clash between the Shiʿi religious elite and the state following the return of the Shah from a visit to Turkey in 1936. In January of that year, the royal family appeared in public unveiled for the first time in the history of modern Iran.[27] The government then promulgated the law of 'Women's Emancipation', by which no Iranian women should wear a veil, or *chadur*, in public.[28] Years earlier, in 1928, the government had ratified the 'Dress Unification' law, requiring Persians to observe uniformity of dress. Although Shiʿi clerics were, with some conditions, exempt from the law,[29] life for religious students became miserable.[30]

With this, religious students, some were already resented of Hairi's quiescence, became more critical of this political posture. Despite this, the position Hairi maintained – that his disciples must tolerate pressures from state activities and wait for the time when Qum seminary would become formidable enough to stand up against the arbitrary rule – was generally trusted. He exhorted students to focus on studying and not to bother with what the state was doing with regard to their religious attire. He urged that they remain quiet 'even', he said, 'if they take off my own turban'.[31] The new law regarding women, however, was considered a serious challenge to Islamic principles. As perhaps the government had anticipated, it was not only controversial throughout Persia's conservative community but also invited the clergy opposition.

Persians became divided between the supporters of the law, mainly secular modernists, and its opponents, the Shiʿi clerics and their followers. The holy cities of Qum and Mashhad were in greater turmoil than anywhere else, due to the great influence of religious elites. On 3 July 1935, and for the first time, Hairi sent a personal telegram from Qum to Reza Shah, which read as follows:

> To Your Majesty, May God Almighty perpetuate your reign. It is clear that I always have desired the prosperity of the Imperial government. Nonetheless, I must note that current affairs are in evident opposition to the Sharia Law and the sacred beliefs of Shiʿi Islam, a cause for concern for all Muslims. Indeed, as one of the pious patrons of Islam, it is your responsibility to resolve the issue . . . . I hope that by your immediate act, you will relieve my concerns and those of all the Shiʿi of Iran.[32]

The tone of the letter clearly shows that Hairi was trying to fulfil his role as the leader of his religious followers, and yet show respect for the state and prevent further tension at the same time. However, Reza Shah issued a discourteous reply to the telegram, demonstrating to the Ayatollah, once more, that religious leadership did not carry weight in Reza Shah's reign. Instead of the Shah, against the respectful protocol, the prime minister had signed the responding telegram, advising the seminary leader not to trust 'the rumours' and implicitly threatening him with state prosecution should he choose to do otherwise.[33]

The demonstrations were agitating faster in Mashhad, however. There, the prominent Marja', Sayyid Husayn Qummi (d. 1947) addressed his followers who were gathered in opposition and stated,

> Islam needs devotees and Muslims should rise [against this law], and I am ready to devote myself to this cause.[34]

Qummi's reaction was more contentious than that of Hairi. He, at the time his colleague had no choice but to remain quiet in Qum, considered the new law in opposition to

Islam and decided to challenge the Shah and his apparatus. Consequently, Qummi, who had until then stayed out of politics, decided to go to Tehran and personally discuss the concerns of the religious elite and their followers with Reza Shah. On 1 July 1954, the Ayatollah arrived in Tehran and stayed at the neighbouring city of Rey. Concerned over the prospects of a popular uprising, the government cordoned off the place of his sitting and put the Ayatollah under house arrest.[35] His followers in Mashhad, however, in protest against his arrest, took sanctuary in the Gowharshad Mosque next to the Imam Reza Holy Shrine. After four days of protests, with crowds chanting that 'the Shah is a new Yazid . . . Imam Husayn protect us from this Evil Shah', state forces opened fire on the crowds and hundreds were killed and wounded.[36] Later on, Qummi was expelled to Iraq, where he remained until his death.

The message of the Gowharshad crackdown was clear for the religious leadership: the Shah would not tolerate any opposition to its modernization programmes. To this end, to protect the community and their authority, the clergy had no option but to abstain itself from political affairs. This was the posture that was adopted by Hairi until he passed away in January 1937, just months after the Gowharshad Revolt.

Upon the death of the Ayatollah, the government issued a proclamation permitting only one ceremony to be held in Qum and forbade commemoration of his death in any other cities. Reza Shah had already weakened the Shiʿi establishment in Iran, and his schemes undermined the clerical authority. During the last three years of Hairi's life, to his and their followers' chagrin, Reza Shah banned veiling, wearing turbans for the religious students, and outlawed public procession of Shiʿi rituals and gatherings, *majalis*. Decades later, in one of his speeches as the supreme leader of the newly established Islamic Republic, Khomeini recalled this period and mentioned it to be 'darkest era, the seminary has ever seen'.[37]

Following Hairi's will, the leadership of the Qum seminary was inherited by two of his prominent disciples: Sadr al-Din Sadr and Hujjat Kuh Kamarei. His successors assumed a very similar political posture to that of their predecessor, as the context would not permit them to do otherwise. They managed to minimize the seminary's encounters with the state until September 1941, when Anglo-Soviet forces removed Reza Shah from the throne in favour of his young son, Muhammad Reza Pahlavi.

In 1941, the twenty years during which Reza Shah had been the face of Iran came to an end and it appeared that this would put an end to the restrictions against the clerics' sociopolitical activities too. The reign of the first Pahlavi would be among the most repressive periods for Shiʿi clergy in the history of Iran. As described above, the rule of Reza Shah coincided with the early stages of the foundation of the Qum seminary under the leadership of Hairi Yazdi. His leadership period was among the most politically quiet eras in Shiʿi history. Nevertheless, in evaluating the context and the political posture of Hairi, it can now be concluded that he assumed this posture in order to protect the very existence of Shiʿi clerical authority and to preserve the community with a minimum of loss throughout a critical period in its history. Thus, though this tactic was sometimes criticized by groups of his colleagues,[38] the majority of the clergy supported his political posture. As his reign continued, and as Reza Shah became a quintessential dictator, the Ayatollah and his followers dedicated themselves to more indirect forms of political involvement in order to strengthen the fragile foundations of the seminary and its, then, small number of members. They had to await a more permissive context.

The interregnum era, and the permissive context for clerical activism

With the abdication of Reza Shah in September 1941, his twenty-two-year-old son, Muhammad Reza, ascended the throne. For the religious elite who had witnessed two decades of Reza Shah's repressions against the clergy in Iran, this was perceived as establishing a political opportunity structure that would be favourable for once again restoring their authority. The greater freedom afforded by the combination of the ineffectiveness of the young Shah, the dismantling of the armed forces, and the occupation of Iran by Allied forces, permitted different ideological currents within the country to emerge and to seek popular support. Concurrent with the coronation of the new Shah, and inspired by the Soviet Union, the Tudeh Party of Iran was established and, having succeeded in gaining the support of a group of leftist intelligentsia, soon became one of the main political players in modern Iran.[39] There also emerged nationalist movements, whose members were mainly the remainders of those who had been active during the Constitutional Revolution who sought to seize the maximum advantage offered by the political opportunities offered by this political interregnum.

Perceiving there to be an open political opportunity structure, the clergy, for its part, sought to reinforce the foundations of the seminary in Qum. During the subsequent decades, the state–clergy relationship went through two distinctive periods. First was concurrent with the leadership of Ayatollah Burujirdi, who happened to become the last Shiʿi Marjaʾ of history, following by the post-Burujirdi era, which lasted until the Islamic Revolution in 1979. While the former is seen as a period of consolidation for Shiʿi clerical authority in Iran, the latter period was one in which Shiʿi clerics succeeded in developing their political postures concerning Islamic government and the establishment of the first Shiʿi state in the modern Middle East. Movement towards these ends was undeniably initiated at the time, Burujirdi entered the city of Qum to assume the leadership of its seminary.

With the death of its founder, Ayatollah Hairi, and over the repressions of Reza Shah's rule, the Qum seminary was nothing but the name by early 1940s. Yet, with the formidable Reza Shah out of the scene, the clergy, once again, sought to strengthen and to re-institutionalize their authority. Comparing with Najaf seminary in Iraq which was the main recipient of the religious taxes, the seminary in Qum was struggling to manage its routine activities, due to financial shortcomings. The trio Marajiʾ, who were collectively leading the seminary, therefore, came to an understanding that they should reach for a unique personality famous and charismatic enough to fill the position of its late founder. A candidate that came to the fore through their endeavours, over the recommendation of Khomeini,[40] then a teacher in Qum, was Ayatollah Muhammad Husayn Burujirdi, who had been residing in the local seminary of the city of Broujerd for last thirty-four years.[41]

Two main Shiʿi Maraji' of Najaf Seminary – Isfahani and Qummi – passed away within months of Burujirdi's arrival in Qum, providing him with a great opportunity to operate as the sole Marja' of the Shiʿi world. For the next decade, Qum seminary became the most important Shiʿi centre in the world. During the fifteen years of his Marja'iyya, Burujirdi managed to establish a constructive rapport with Muhammad Reza Shah. The Burujirdi era might be seen as representing one of the most respective periods that clergy-state has ever been overseen since the Safavids.

Burujirdi's leadership of the seminary coincided with a series of sociopolitical upheavals in Iran. However, the Ayatollah, who had personally witnessed the defeat of the clergy during the Constitutional Revolution, managed to contain the potential threats to his authority.[42] He personally witnessed how the interest of the clergy had been undermined as a result of their basing their activism on inaccurate perceptions during the Persian Constitutional Revolution. Therefore, he had become cautious in his evaluation of the political opportunities that existed for political activism. As he stated repeatedly on various occasions, 'the Constitutional Revolution in Iran taught me not to be involved in political affairs if I do not have a clear idea of their origins and outcomes'.[43]

Therefore, responding to the national, regional and international incidents – ranging from the formation of the National Movement in Iran to the Arab–Israeli conflict in the Middle East – the Ayatollah adhered to a singular doctrine: whenever he personally perceived that the political opportunity was open and his word was effective, he assumed an activist posture and communicated a clear message to the state; otherwise, he tried to stay out of politics and to instead focus on routine affairs of the seminary.

While leading the religious community, the Ayatollah confronted challenges, which included societal encounters in which, for example, he had to take a position against his fellow Ayatollah, Kashani, and the relatively extremist Shiʿi group of *Fadaian-e-Islam*. On the other hand, in dealing with the Shah, the bipartite soon came to this understanding that while the clergy would not interfere in routine political affairs of the state, it expected the authorities to leave religious affairs to the clerical elite. Overall, the Ayatollah was successful to overrun his posture throughout the community of his fellow colleagues and their followers. Nevertheless, one of the most critical periods, within which his leadership and political posture were out to the test, occurred between 1949 and 1953, when a group of clerics joined the anti-imperialist cause of the National Movement.

Mujtahids and the Iranian national movement: A case of a missed opportunity?

With the removal of Reza Shah's iron first, various movements sought to mobilize social bases and to make strategic alliances which would enable them to seek their political cause. In the 1940s, Iran, number of political groups, with anti-imperialist posture, were focusing on nationalizing the oil industry. In this, nationalists and members of religious elites found a common denominator to merge their causes under the umbrella of the so-called Iran National Movement.

Like their secular nationalist partners, the religious faction of this movement represented a wide array of actors. These ranged from the leader of seminary, Burujirdi, who preferred to remain an observer of the political process (and who was harshly criticized by some of his colleagues for not being actively involved in politics), to the radical Fadaian-e-Islam, whose members believed that the political opportunity structure was sufficiently open to permit the establishment of an Islamic government. Ultimately, the outcome of the movement proved that the providence of the former's posture supersedes that of the latter.

Fadaian-e-Islam, *the devotees of Islam*, was an extremist Islamic group active in Iran for almost a decade between 1945 and 1955. Their leader, Sayyid Mojtaba Mir-Lowhi, known as Navvab Safavi, was in his early twenties when he left Najaf for Iran, mainly to contest what was perceived as the threat of secular intelligentsia.[44]

In early 1946, an open letter, later known as 'the declaration of the Religion and Revenge', was published by Fadaian-e-Islam stating:

> We are alive and the revengeful God is alert. The blood of the deprived has long been dripping from the fingers of the selfish voluptuous people, who are hiding, each with a different name and in a different colour, behind the black curtains of oppression, thievery, and crime. Once in a while the divine retribution puts them in their place, yet the rest would not learn the lesson . . . we are free and alert, believers in God and fearless.[45]

The wording of this letter shows that the group, hoping to make the most out of existing opportunities, was on the verge of launching a revolution in Iran. Subsequent history showed that they were prepared to be as extreme as possible in order to eradicate all obstacles in the way of achieving their goal, which was the establishment of an Islamic state in Iran. Ten days later, Husayn Imami, a member of Fadaian, assassinated Kasravi in Tehran. The incident made Navvab Safavi, a young cleric in his twenties at the time, one of the most famous figures in Qum and Najaf.[46]

Navvab's extremism at the time, however, was not fully embraced by the clerical leadership of Qum. Yet, eventually they managed to reach out for Ayatollah Kashani's support. Sayyid Abu al-Qasim Kashani (1882–1962) was another student of Akhund Khorasani, famous for his anti-British postures.[47] He was among the most politically active clerics in the late 1940s.[48] His blunt rejection of the policies of foreigners and of the Iranians authorities during the 1940s matched that of Navvab's.[49] Consequently, Kashani and Navvab's enemies were the same, and these enemies were threatened by the revenge of Fadaian's supporters.

Moreover, in February 1949, Muhammad Reza Shah got an alibi to clamp down on dissident groups, ranging from the Communist Tudeh Party to religious groups close to Kashani. A would-be assassin shot the Shah while visiting the University of Tehran, but failed to kill him. In the aftermath of this assassination attempt, the Shah, making the most of the public sympathy this had generated, began to expand his authority. Subsequently, the leftist Tudeh Party was banned, and its leaders were put in prison.

Ayatollah Kashani, who was accused of having a relationship with the assassin, was imprisoned in Qazvin, from where he was sent to exile[50] in Lebanon.[51]

Concerned about the re-emergence of another ruler like Reza Shah, Burujirdi sent a telegram to the Shah in which he disassociated himself from the incident and expressed his wishes for the health of the monarch.[52] In his eyes, the threat represented by the Shah's regime for the Shiʿi community and its clerical authority was at the time far less than that of the Communist Tudeh Party. Following this, the Qum seminary leadership issued a proclamation that read as follows:

> Those who wear the cleric habits, either residing in Qum seminary or other religious seminaries, are not allowed to interfere in political affairs or be manipulated by the political parties and, for its part, the Qum seminary does not recognize them and would not provide them with sanctuary. As the seminary clearly has shown since its establishment by Grand Ayatollah Hairi, it is pure from all political affairs and would not pollute itself with political conflicts and interventions.[53]

The position Burujirdi assumed indicated that any sort of overt political contention with the state would be costly to the seminary and the clerical authority at that critical context. His interpretation of the political opportunity structure at the time was completely different from that of Kashani. Nevertheless, with Fadaian's radical interpretation of political Islam, once again, as in the Constitutional Revolution, members of the Shiʿi clergy in Iran seemingly diverged with regard to their positions vis-à-vis the state.

In October 1949, a group of nationalist Iranians led by Muhammad Mosaddeq (1882–1967) issued a declaration demanding free parliamentary elections and calling for a general strike.[54] On the day of the strike, demonstrators moved quietly towards the royal palace while in front of them, marched Mosaddeq and Husayn Imami, a renowned member of Fadaian-e-Islam.[55] This implicitly signalled that an alliance had been formed among Mosaddeq's nationalist camp (later to be members of what was to be known as the National Front),[56] the exiled Kashani and Navvab Safavi's Fadaian. This represented a strategic alignment between elites who would ultimately work together towards bringing about the nationalization of the Iranian oil industry in March 1951.[57]

All the pieces of the puzzle of the movement for the nationalization of the oil industry were falling into place. With Mosaddeq and Kashani in the Parliament, and the implicit support of clerical elites in Qum, the only obstacle remaining was the premiership of the former armed forces commander, General Haj Ali Razmara.[58] He had been appointed as prime minister in order to ratify the supplementary oil agreement. However, during his short-lived administration, he was subjected to harsh, orchestrated attacks by the opposition, who were seeking the nationalization of the oil industry.

Notwithstanding, the radical Fadaian-e-Islam once again came to the aid of the National Front and, on 7 March 1951, assassinated the prime minister Razmara.[59] Navvab Safavi, who had been acknowledged as the executive arm of the nationalists by then, also issued a declaration on behalf of his group and addressing the Shah, 'the son of Pahlavi', threatened his 'illegitimate regime' with further hostile retaliations if the assassin, a member of Fadaian, was not 'freed with full respect'.[60]

The Maraji' of Qum, also, had supported the oil industry nationalization, either explicitly by sponsoring Kashani, or implicitly through back-channel discussion conducted by Burujirdi with the Shah.[61] Nevertheless, signs of the internal schism in the movement appeared as soon as Mosaddeq assumed the premiership. It seemed that each faction, which had different goals for joining the movement, was rushing to get the upper hand over the others.

Fadaian-e-Islam, who believed that they had an undeniable share in this triumph, passed a letter to the prime minister demanding the application of Islamic law throughout the country.[62] Mosaddeq not only refused to give in to this petition but also imprisoned Navvab Safavi. This marked the alienation of Navvab and Fadaian with other groups of nationalist fronts.[63]

Apparently concerned about covert actions of the British against his government, Mosaddeq offered his resignation to the Shah in July 1952 and was immediately succeeded by Ahmad Qavam. The new prime minister, who enjoyed the support of the royal court and of Britain, issued a public declaration threatening the opposition front with harsh reprisals.[64]

At this point, Kashani, perceiving the imminent threat to his vision, tactically came out in support for Mosaddeq, issued a proclamation which reads as follows:

> Ahmad Qavam must know that, in a country whose suffering citizens have already exerted themselves from the dictatorship eventually after years of miseries, he cannot suppress the freedom of thought and threaten people with mass executions . . . . I publicly declare to all my Muslim brothers to partake in this sacred Jihad and, for the last time, prove to the allies of colonialism in Iran that they have no chance of ever re-establishing their power.[65]

The clash between the supporters of the National Movement and the government of Qavam resulted in tens of casualties in the revolt on 21 July 1952. By evening that day, Qavam resigned and the Shah reinstated the premiership of Mosaddeq. The demonstrators felt even more triumphant when, during the coming days, the International Court of Justice voted in support of Iran against British claims.[66]

Nevertheless, the schism between Ayatollah Kashani and Mosaddeq was about to come to the surface following the nomination of the new cabinet. Mosaddeq initiated a series of military and judicial reforms in favour of the Premier's office, dissolved the senate and made the Parliament dependent on a quorum.[67] Consequently, for the Shah, all he had done to assume greater authority for himself over the course of the previous decade was diminished within months. Turning away from his previous allies, especially Kashani's religious base, in order to consolidate his reforms, Mosaddeq was perceivably moved towards the Tudeh Party. This was a political manoeuvre that would cost him the trust of the majority of the Shi'i clerical elite, who until then had remained politically quiet. Events eventually reached the point that on 19 August 1953, and in the face of a US–British coup against his government, Mosaddeq had minimal popular support and was forced to resign and end his political life forever. The success of the coup marked the end of the National Movement in Iran and resulted in the marginalization of its constituent factions in the politics of the country.[68]

On the other hand, the mainstream Shiʿi clerical elite did survive the turmoil, thanks to Burujirdi's more accurate perception of the political opportunity structure, and the political posture he assumed as a result.[69] Following the coup, and in contrast to the bitter experience of the Constitutional Revolution, the Shiʿi clergy, under the leadership of Burujirdi, succeeded in preserving theirs authority and even in developing it further. Throughout the movement, despite the hostile political confrontation of Fadaian-e-Islam with the state and the Shah, both Burujirdi and Kashani had striven to protect the integrity of the country and the Constitution. Although they had differences in their perception of the nature of the existing political opportunity structure, which was in best a tactical disparity, their main objective was to preserve the Shiʿi foundations of Iran and their clerical authority. Evidences prove that despite some differences, the overall relationship between these two religious leaders was based on a common Shiʿi framework and both had learned similar lessons from the experience of the Constitutional Revolution, particularly the lesson that they must not publicly oppose each other's activities.[70]

Following the coup, Burujirdi, who had remained quiet throughout these events, sent a telegram to the Shah offering his blessings and expressing the wish that his return to Iran would result in the 'reform of the previous corruption, the glory of Islam, and the welfare of Muslims'.[71] The Ayatollah's perception of the opportunity structure during the time that Iran was under pressure from foreign forces led him to support a state that was considered to be an Islamic one.[72]

The state–clergy relationship was developing to the mutual interests of both during the post-coup era. Both parties had found out that if they could not overrule the other, they could profit from engaging in a respectful association based on give-and-take pragmatic scheme. The Ayatollah did not interfere directly in the politics of the state and, in turn, he was free from state intrusion into religious affairs.[73] This non-threatening relationship was favourable to the propagation of the faith and fostered the development of Burujirdi's comprehensive, transnational vision. During his leadership of the Shiʿi community, he initiated reforms that resulted in a revival of the authority of the clerical elite in later decades. The population of religious students in Qum increased dramatically from about 100 at the time that Hairi passed away to about 5,000 students under the leadership of Burujirdi.[74]

In general, throughout the political trajectory of the Qum seminary, as the context evolved, the previous quiescent phase under the leadership of Hairi was transformed into a quasi-active one under the authority of Burujirdi. Consequently, in 1961, when Burujirdi passed away, various members of the Shiʿi clergy were then able to exert their authority throughout the community just as they were about to play a more critical role in the politics of Iran. As the Shah was celebrating his twentieth year in power, clerical elites were ready to perform their sociopolitical role in a way that was more compatible with the contingencies of the contemporary era. Nevertheless, they were in need of a solid political *doctrine* and a charismatic leader to promote the will of the mainstream religious elite. This contributed to producing a political opportunity structure that shaped the political postures of the Shiʿi clerical elite in Iran until the establishment of the Islamic Republic.

Burujirdi's inheritors and the modern Iran

The death of Burujirdi in 1961 concurred with the consolidation of the Shah's authority in Iran. To fulfil his mission, as he later claimed, the Shah enforced a series of programmes, and initiated the so-called White Revolution almost immediately. The initiatives, however, agitated the opposition of different groups, among them the clergy in Iran. It was in the context of this opposition to the White Revolution that Ayatollah Khomeini was singled out as the new face of the Iranian Shiʿi clerical elite.

In the period between 1961 and 1979, clerics in Iran were more politically active than clerics had been as any time since the commencement of the Occultation era. The new political structure activated a reformist group of religious elites that the initiatives of the two deceased leaders of the seminary, Hairi and Burujirdi, had fostered. They were ready to actively partake in politics according to the will of their affiliates. They succeeded in forming a transnational network of their colleagues, extending from Iran to Iraq and Lebanon, in order to pursue their objectives at the time. It was through this established network that, in the early 1970s, the political posture of Khomeini, based on his perception of the political opportunity structure offered to him, and with the support of other members of the Shiʿi clergy, led to the establishment of the first Shiʿi state in the Middle East.

The 1963 Uprising: The formation of revolutionary Shiʿism in Iran

The death of the last sole Shiʿi Marjaʿ, and the discontent of the modernism for the clergy, made some reformist religious elite to think over redefinition of the position of Marj'iyya as well as the emerging responsibilities of the clergy.[75]

The core viewpoint of these groups was that the role of the Shiʿi clerics and the Marja'iyya in the new context goes beyond the merely religious affairs of the community and extends to sociopolitical concerns, as well. Retrospectively, the state was seeking an alternative Marjaʿ, who would be less likely to interfere in internal affairs.[76] To his reign's favour, the Shah was looking for a more passive and quietist clerical leadership, and perhaps was more eager to strengthen the Najaf seminary at the cost of the ever-rising school in Qum.[77]

In early October 1962, Iranian authorities announced the details of the reform program. The 'White Revolution' was aimed to fulfil the socioeconomic 'demands of the public' through six initial points: land reform, the nationalization of forests, the privatization of public factories, the institution of profit-sharing schemes for workers in industry, women's suffrage and the formation of the literacy corps.[78] Hours after the news reached Qum, Khomeini, Golpayegani, Shariatmadari and Morteza Hairi convened an extraordinary meeting and decided to each send a telegram to the Shah and inform him of the religious authorities' concerns over the initial plan.[79] In their telegrams, all mujtahids, in solidarity, respectfully addressed the Shah and asked him to revise the bill in a way that would not contradict the Islamic principle and the

Constitution; they specifically requested the state to abstain from the new electoral law that would allow the non-Muslims to vote and be elected in parliamentary elections.[80] A week later, the Shah responded to the telegrams and, while ensuring the clerics that he would 'let the government know their concerns', he also advised the correspondents to 'pay more attention to the situation of other Islamic nations' and the contingencies of the new world.[81]

Thwarted by Shah's reaction, next time, mujtahids sent telegrams to the prime minister, albeit with less precaution. Khomeini's telegram, which was sent to Alam on 20 October 1962, reads as follows:

> Over the long recess of the parliament, it seems that the government is considering some programs that contradict the divine law and clearly are against the Fundamental Law . . . the women's right to enter the parliament and other provincial councils contravenes the indisputable laws of Islam, the interpretation of which, according to the articles of the [Supplementary] Fundamental Law, is given over to the Shiʿi jurists, and no one else has the right to interfere . . . . Likewise, the abrogation of the qualification that electors and candidates must be Muslim, which is stipulated by the Fundamental Law, and replacing the policy of swearing the oath on the Holy Qur'an to one that stipulates swearing on a 'holy book', are an infringement of the said law, are precarious for Islam and the independence of the country . . . . Now that His Majesty has referred the ulama to the government, it is expected that, in compliance with the undisputable laws of Islam and the country, this matter be resolved as soon as possible . . . . In closing, I would like to remind you that the ulama of Iran and the Shiʿi seminaries will not remain quiet on matters that breach the Sharia Law.[82]

Khomeini's wordings imply that although he had perceived a threat to the clerical authority impeded in these initiatives, he was willing to ease the tension with the authorities through peaceful measurements. Like him, other members of the clergy in Qum, Tehran, Mashhad, and even Najaf sent similar telegrams to the government.[83] Thus, over the collective actions of the Shiʿi clerical elite, and their threat of orchestrating a popular uprising, the government issued a declaration of the withdrawal of the six-point bill.[84]

Despite this seemingly tactical setback, in one of his public addresses, Shah harshly attacked the 'black reactionary agents', and asked Iranians to vote in favour of the programme in upcoming referendum.[85] His message to the clergy was sound and clear: he would fight them to the expense of his rule.[86] For their part, clerics unanimously boycotted the referendum to show their resentments over the initiatives; yet, the authorities declared that more than 99 per cent voted in favour of the reforms over the referendum of 26 January 1963.

Posting against what they perceived as a rigged referendum, clerical leadership in Qum issued a signed declaration, and once again declared that the whole programme is 'anti-Islamic' and 'anti-Constitutional'. The nine mujtahids who signed the declaration stated,

> The clerical authority, despite of all the pressures and humiliations that the state intends to make on it, considers its religious and moral duty to draw the people's

> attention to the benefits and disadvantages of this programme. . . . The people of Iran are against these initiatives and had showed their objections earlier, when the state repressions were lesser . . . although the government had agreed to give up the bill, now with its established domination over the will of the people, which has been reached by the imprisonment and torture of various religious and clerical classes, it has initiated the programme that's sequel will hurt Islam and the Muslims . . . . May God wake our government up and offer his mercy over our people and the Islamic nation.[87]

For his part, the Shah responded to the religious elite almost a month later, and said,

> I have seen and heard that some who are like depressed snakes have immersed in their own dirt . . . like louses, which face the rays of the sun gradually, finding out how unfortunate they are . . . would these sordid and vile elements not awake from their sleep of ignorance, the fist of justice, like thunder, will be struck at their head in whatever cloth they are, perhaps to terminate their filthy and shameful life.[88]

Following the Shah's speech, on 22 March 1963, scores of SAVAK agents stormed into the Feyzieh seminary school in Qum and assaulted the gathering.[89]The incident proved that state repression towards the religious community had fortified, and that the more than ever powerful Shah was not willing to compromise with the clergy. Shah had already succeeded in dismantling the leftist and nationalist opposition groups, and there was only the Islamic opposition to handle. For the clerics witnessing the Feyzieh crackdown, it was as if a new Reza Shah had come out of his son, Muhammad Reza. The Shah showed his determination that he would fight against what he believed as a reactionary religious authority until they accept to abstain themselves from state affairs. The political opportunity structure was going to be the closest for the clerical activism, since Muhammad Reza ascended to the throne. The context had transformed during the last three decades. As the later incidents unfold, Shiʿi clerics, however, were not going to remain quiet, as they had done during Reza Shah's rule.[90]

Nevertheless, in Iran, clerics were preparing themselves for the mourning month of Muharram to shout their opposition against the state on the pulpits and throughout all gatherings. The promised day arrived on Ashura of 1963, when Khomeini reached the podium at Feyzieh School and made his revealing speech against the government, its pro-western policies, and offensive statements against the ulama; addressing the Shah, he stated,

> Your Highness! You are being deluded. I wouldn't like to see everyone rejoice if your departure was arranged . . . . I don't want you to end up like your father. Don't aggravate the people so. Don't oppose the clergy so . . . the ulama and the religious scholars of Islam, are they really defiled animals? Do the people see them in this light? If so, why do people kiss their hands? . . . Sir, I hope to God that this is not what you mean. God forbid that you were referring to the ulama when you said the

> black reactionaries . . . . You are now forty-three years old; learn at least something from your father's fate . . . listen to what the clerical elites have to say, as they are those who seek the welfare of the country and the people . . . . Both our country and our religion are in jeopardy . . . . Indeed, you must do something to change this situation. You are being blamed for everything. You don't realise that on the day when a true outburst occurs, not one of these so-called friends of yours will want to know you . . . . We are full of regret and sorrow. We truly regret the situation in which Iran finds itself. We regret the state of our ruined country, of this cabinet and of those running our government.[91]

Following this speech, on 5 June, Khomeini was arrested in Qum and sent to Tehran. The news of his imprisonment led to outbreaks of insurrection in different cities of Iran. The authorities acted harshly and finally surmounted the turmoil with hundreds of casualties.[92] The June 1963 uprising, which was the most serious threat to the Shah's reign since 1953, crystalized the opposition groups and undermined the monarchy.[93] The incident often is regarded as the beginning of the Shiʿi political activism that eventually resulted in the Islamic Revolution.

The political posture of the leader: The Ayatollah on the path to becoming the Imam

In the aftermath of the June 1963 uprising, Khomeini was singled out among his other colleagues as the most politically active cleric. Born in 1902 as Rouhalla Musawi, he lost his father to a group of bandits when he was less than one-year old. The young Rouhalla became one of the disciples of Ayatollah Hairi in Arak and accompanied him in re-establishing the seminary in Qum, later on. While sitting at jurisprudence lectures of Hairi, he also showed a remarkable interest in Islamic philosophy and Gnosticism, modules that were not taught in routine curriculum of seminaries at the time.[94] His later ascendance to one of the most active Shiʿi clerics in history, was much owed to how he shaped his political doctrine, using a combination of jurisprudence, philosophy and Gnosticism over the decades to come.[95]

In June 1963, Khomeini was going to present his novel ijtihad about the role that a Shiʿi clergyman should hold in the sociopolitical affairs of the community, given the context he encounters. In this, he had the support of his colleagues at the time. In protest to his custody and the crackdown of the mass demonstrations of June 1963, a large group of Shiʿi figures and Maraji' gathered in Tehran and summoned numerous meetings to find out how to respond to the state.[96] Their arbitration paid off, and authorities released Khomeini from the prison, yet put him under house arrest in Tehran.[97]

Meanwhile, Alam was replaced by Hasanali Mansour, who sought to make a compromising deal with the clergy.[98] On 5 April 1964, the new prime minister delivered a speech in which he stated: 'Islam is one the most pioneering and remarkable religions of the world and the clerics should be respected. I have the duty to deliver the utmost compassion of His Majesty to them.'[99] On the following day, Khomeini was freed to go to Qum.

Khomeini, however, became even more critical of the monarchy as soon as he arrived to Qum.[100] When in October 1964, Majles passed the capitulation bill, granting political immunity to American nationals in Iran, Khomeini made one the most vehement speeches of his political life against the government and stated,

> They have sold us, they have sold our independence . . . . If some Americans servant, some Americans cook, assassinates your Marja' Taqlid in the middle of the bazaar, or runs over him, the Iranian police do not have the right to apprehend him.

He then harshly criticized the government's strategy in restraining the clergy's involvement in sociopolitical affairs:

> [The government] has come to understand well that, if the religious leaders have influence, they will not permit any government to do whatever it would like, whatever is against the interests of the nation. If the religious leaders have influence, they will not permit the Parliament to come to such a miserable state as this. They will strike this government in the mouth. They will strike this Parliament in the mouth and chase these deputies out of both its houses.
>
> So, the influence of the religious leaders is harmful to the nation? No, it is a threat to you, detrimental to you traitors, not to the nation. You have realized that, as long as the influence of the religious leaders exists, you cannot do everything you want to do, commit all the crimes you want, so you wish to destroy their influence. You thought you could cause dissension among the religious leaders with your intrigues, but you will be dead before your dream can come true. You will never be able to do it. The religious leaders are united.

He went on, and also cautioned the religious group about the ongoing circumstances, and declared,

> Once again, I esteem all religious leaders; I kiss the hands of all the religious leaders. I kiss hands of the religious students.
>
> Gentlemen, I warn you of danger. Iranian army, I warn you of danger. Iranian politicians, I warn you of danger. Iranian merchants, I warn you of danger. The ulama of Iran, Maraji' of Islam, I warn you of danger . . . . It is a dangerous situation; there are issues kept under cover that we know nothing about.

He also condemned the political posture that was assumed by some of his fellows at the time:

> Should I not be saying this? Those gentlemen who had said that we must hold our tongues and not utter a sound – do they still say the same thing on this occasion?

> Are we to keep quiet again and not say a word? They sell us and still we are to keep silence? They sell our Qur'an and still we should hold our tongues? By God, one who does not cry out in protest and does not express his outrage commits a sin.

In closing, for the first time he implicitly presented his ijtihad regarding the authority of Shiʿi jurists in politics and, while accusing the members of the Parliament and the senate who had enacted the capitulation bill, announced,

> Those old men in the Senate are traitors, and all those in the lower house who voted in favour of this affair are traitors. They are not our representatives. The whole world must know that they are not the representatives of Iran. Alternatively, suppose they are; now I dismiss them. They are dismissed from their posts and all the bills they have passed up until now are invalid . . . . From the very beginning of the constitutional period in Iran according to the text of the law, according to Article II of the Supplementary Constitutional Law, no law is valid unless the mujtahids exercise a supervisory role in the parliament. Which mujtahid is supervising the parliament now? They have to destroy the influence of the clergymen! If there were five clerics in this parliament, if there was only one clergyman in this parliament, he would punch them in the mouth! He would not allow this bill to be enacted.[101]

His monumental speech, as a whole, confirms that, as early as 1964, the Ayatollah was determined to consolidate the sociopolitical role of the clergy in Iran. He was keen to diminish any threat against clerical authority, and in this he also sought the assistance of his fellow colleagues to reconsider their roles and to reformulate their postures vis-à-vis the opportunity structure. His statement also showed that if the Fundamental Law of Iran had been deployed precisely, and the role of clergy as per the Fundamental Law had been acknowledged, perhaps they were willing to offer their concessions to the constitutional monarchy rather than seeking for contentious politics. Shah and the state authorities, however, missed this opportunity to compromise with Khomeini and his entourages at the time.

Other Maraji' of Qum followed Khomeini in holding a gathering to show their opposition to the bill known. In one case, addressing his followers who had gathered at his home, Shariatmadari condemned the members of Parliament and the senate for enacting the bill. Although the majority of the Shiʿi clerical elite had unanimously positioned themselves against the bill, the wording of Khomieni's statement was far stronger than that of his fellows.[102] As his anti-state activities perceivably were going out of control, Khomeini was sent to exile in Turkey on 4 November 1964.

Khomeini's expulsion from Iran heralded a new phase in the movement of Shiʿi clergy against the regime of the Shah. The course of future events proved that he by no means mitigated his political activities while he was in exile; rather, he managed to strengthen a transnational network of active religious elites throughout the region in Iran, Iraq and Lebanon to pursue the objective of establishing the Islamic government.[103] A network comprising various social groups loyal to the religious elite and their cause. While Khomeini was in exile, this network managed to broadcast his revolutionary ideas to the most remote towns all around the country.

Performative theory: The modernized guardianship of the jurist

In early September 1965, Khomeini left Turkey for Najaf, where he spent the next thirteen years. His life in Najaf had the paramount influence of shaping the ideological backbone of the Shiʿi revolution that he later led in 1979. During those years, free from the state repressions, perhaps partially due to Iran–Iraq enmity at the time, Khomeini seized the opportunity to further foster his doctrine. His reading from Shiʿi political thoughts, and the so-called reserved role for the clergy during the Occultation, opened the gate for his ijtihad of dismantling the monarchy in Iran, making the most out of the political opportunity structure.

Furthermore, the years in Najaf contributed to the consolidation of the Shiʿi clerical elite's movement in Iran in various ways: it helped the remaining clerical elite and the pious religious students in Iran to work in clandestine groups to further their cause while the state was deluded about the abolition power of religious forces, and it facilitated the Ayatollah's network in Iraq and Lebanon to activate itself under the safe haven provided to them by the socialist government of Iraq, which was hostile to the Iranian monarchy at the time.

The Iranian government hoped that, once in Najaf, the scholarship of other clerics of the seminary would overshadow Khomeini; hence, his political activism would diminish gradually. Nonetheless, it was Khomeini himself who masterfully turned the table and formed his doctrine, making the most out of the Najaf school of thought. He was offered an opportunity to review the path he had taken and to crystalize the route he must take to achieve his goals. To this extent, the Najaf seminary and its leadership, Ayatollah Muhsin Al-Hakim, played a significant role. Perhaps the most important lesson he learned by being in Najaf was that context and full fledge popular support have a great influence on the success of Shiʿi political activism.[104]

Since his arrival in Najaf, Khomeini started to teach in the city's seminary, and groups of students from Iran, Iraq and other countries attended his lectures.[105] It was in early 1970, that he commenced the discussion over the 'guardianship of the jurist' in his lectures, and presented his political posture about the role that the clergy should play in the modern time. His argument not only explicitly called for eradicating the Pahlavi monarchy but also proposed a clear-cut establishment of a Shiʿi state as an alternative that could be followed.[106]

In his book *The Islamic Government*, which is composed of his lectures, Khomeini clearly states that the 'governance of the [qualified] jurist is a subject that in itself elicits immediate assent' and should be pursued to protect the very foundations of Shiʿi Islam.[107] He then argues that to perform the divine responsibilities – including *Ifta* and *Qadha* – in this modern time, Shiʿi mujtahids should enjoy 'an executive power' which could be achieved by establishing an Islamic government. To this end, he states,

> Since the commencement of the Minor Occultation down to the contemporary era – a period of more than twelve centuries that may continue for hundreds of millennia if it is not appropriate for the Occulted Imam to manifest himself – is it proper that the laws of Islam be cast aside and remain unexecuted, so that everyone acts as he pleases, and anarchy prevails . . . . Both law and reason require that we not permit governments to retain this non-Islamic character.[108]

Upon stating the core of his opinion about the Shiʿi clerical elite's authority over the community, he then called for his colleagues to revitalize their capabilities, 'collectively and individually', to implement the laws of Islam by establishing an Islamic government.[109]

Therefore, for the first time in the history of Shiʿi Islam, a clerical leader, active and charismatic enough to ask for mass mobilization, appeared to have a tangible doctrine that would require the religious elite to rule based on the accurate perception about the political opportunity structure. To materialize the Ayatollah's political posture in Iran, the Shiʿi clergy needed to wait for an appropriate point in time when the political opportunity structure and the popular will could facilitate their activism. Less than a decade since Khomeini conducted his lectures, the international, regional and national opportunity structure reached a salient point in Iran.

The power of mujtahids' solidarity in Iran

By the mid-1970s, the regime of Iran had encountered a series of oppositions of various sociopolitical groups ranging from religious groups, mainly under the leadership of the clergy, to leftist parties. Within the opposition, however, the religious elite had the advantage to seize the most out of the political opportunity in Iran at the time. The death of Khomeini's eldest son, Sayyid Mostafa, in Najaf was a turning point that pulled the clergy to the forefront of the revolution leadership. The incident heralded a series of uprisings against the state that eventually led to the overthrown of the monarchy and the establishment of the Islamic Republic in Iran.

To consolidate their authority, the various members of the clergy in the region revitalized their networks and aligned their political postures to that of the opportunity structure in order to mobilize their followers at the time. Among them, the Maraji' of Qum supported the anti-Pahlavi movement, and their exiled colleague, all through the last fifteen years and especially from October 1977 to February 1979. This period, of about one year, which resulted in the triumph of the revolution in Iran, perhaps marked the highest level of the clerical elite's political activism in the history of Islam.

More than half a century since its reestablishment by Ayatollah Hairi, over the activities of its next leader, Ayatollah Burujirdi, the Qum seminary had reached an unsurpassed sociopolitical status in the 1970s. It had played a crucial role during the 1963 uprising and, after the expulsion of Khomeini from Iran, his colleagues Ayatollahs Marashi Najafi, Shariatmadari and Golpayegani were in charge of leading the centre in Iran.[110] Along with these high-ranking Maraji', there were also numerous clerics who had formed a robust network to prevail the Shiʿi political doctrine throughout the most remote towns and to mobilize the laity against the regime.

In the victory of the Islamic Revolution, the Shiʿi Marja'iyya of Iran had supported the sociopolitical posture of Khomeini by directing the community while he was in exile. Although with different perceptions about the political opportunity structure, each of the high-ranking Maraji' of Qum had his share in the dismantling of the monarchy and establishment of the Islamic Republic of Iran.

Ayatollah Sayyid Shahab al-Din Marashi Najafi was born in 1897 in Najaf. Later, he decided to reside in Qum and to teach at its seminary. Upon the death of Burujirdi, Marashi became known as one of the three leaders of the seminary; and by the rise of anti-state demonstrations in 1963, he supported the popular movement by issuing several declarations.[111] However, his support did not go beyond issuing declaration as well as encouraging his students to take part in guiding the demonstrators. After the establishment of the Islamic Republic, Marashi Najafi remained among the most famous Marja' of Qum and supported full-fledged the leadership of Khomeini and his successor, Khamenei.[112]

Another high-ranking Marja' who was in Qum during the formation of the religious anti-regime movement, from 1963 to 1979, was Ayatollah Muhammad Reza Golpayegani. He had been among those Hairi's students who migrated with him from Arak to Qum. During Burujirdi's term, Golpayegani was among the most renowned clerics of the seminary and, in 1961, he agreed to pay half of the religious students' stipends, while his other colleague, Ayatollah Shariatmadari was paying the other half. When he held the Marja'iyya position, he was in full affiliation with other active clerics of the post-Burujirdi era. However, reviewing the political trajectory of his life, he became seemingly quiet in the aftermath of the March 1963 Feyzieh School incident until the last months preceding the revolution. Over these almost fourteen years, nonetheless, he issued a series of declarations condemning some of the states' policies.[113] Perceiving the context as unfavourable for activism, he remained relatively quiet. In general, Golpayegani did not believe in the 'absolute' guardianship of the jurist. Nevertheless, when it comes to the leadership of the lay followers, he, like the majority of Shiʿi high-ranking Maraji', reserved an undisputable right for the clergy. To this end, he stated: 'even lay Muslims cannot be dismissed of the politics of the Islamic state, let alone the clerics, who are the general deputies of the Occulted Imam.'[114]

The last renowned Shiʿi Marja' residing in Qum through the formation of the Islamic Revolution of Iran was Ayatollah Kazem Shariatmadari. As an Azeri Marja', he was enjoying a great popular status among the Azeri Shiʿi followers and a greater sum of the religious taxes than most of his colleagues.[115] During the course of fifteen years ending with the Islamic Revolution, perhaps the most significant input of the Ayatollah to strengthen the Shiʿi political revival in Iran was the establishment of the *Dar al-Tabligh al-Islami* in early 1960s.[116]

On 1 May 1964, deploying his followers' endowments, Shariatmadari established the Islamic Institute in Qum with the goal of reforming the education system of the seminary.[117] Soon, scores of modernist clerics filled his institute. It was through the initiatives of the institute that the first clergy-run magazine of Iran, *Maktab-e Islam*, was published to bridge the gap between the laity commoners and teachers of the seminary.[118] Shariatmadari had been politically active since he became the Marja', albeit at a more moderate pace than Khomeini. A brief comparison of his anti-state declarations' wordings with those of Khomeni's during the 1963–79 period clearly confirms that, while both leaders reserved an undeniable right for clerical activism, perhaps due to their innate personal characteristics, their political postures become seemingly different. Nevertheless, the course of historical incidents and the manoeuvres of the Ayatollah vis-à-vis the political opportunity structure in Iran, put him among the most politically active Shiʿi elite of all time. While Khomeini was in exile, Shariatmadari had remained seemingly quiet and engaged with authorities to safeguard the community via backchannel routes. Yet, as early as 1978, he along with other members of the Maraji' of Qum supported the popular opposition to the end of establishing the aim of establishing the will of the religious revolutionaries.

The Qum seminary had become the centre point of Shiʿi political activism by the eve of the Islamic Revolution in Iran. Through the activities of Hairi and Burujirdi, the seminary had reached a prestigious sociopolitical status among the Shiʿi laity by 1961. It was in the aftermath of Burujirdi's leadership that his inheritors started a phase of political activism in Iran to seize the most out of the political opportunity structure. While Khomeini was in exile, his other colleagues tried to shape the backbone of the revolution by strengthening the network of the seminary and promoting its authority throughout the country. To this end, when the political opportunity was perceivably favourable for the establishment of the Islamic Revolution, the majority of the clergy formed a solid association and led the religious revolutionaries to topple the unjust rule of Pahlavi and to establish the Islamic government in Iran.

The establishment of the Islamic Republic

The level of clerical elite political activism in Iran during the 1970s was evidently influenced by perceivably the open opportunity structure. Throughout history, there were numerous Shiʿi clerics capable of mobilizing their followers towards their politically activated causes; some had tried to establish the Islamic rule, yet, mostly because of the mismatch between structural and perceived political opportunities, they failed to institutionalize their posture. In February 1979, however, the Shiʿi clergy succeeded in seizing the most out of the international, regional and national opportunity structure to its favour. All the required factors for their political activism in Iran converged at the point that hastened the fall of the monarchy and the establishment of the first clergy-led state of the modern Middle East.

The decisive turning point for the clergy alignment towards mobilizing the anti-state movement was the death of Khomeini's son, Sayyid Mostafa, on 23 October 1977. The various religious and secular opposition groups tried to use the incident as an alibi to coalesce their forces. It seems that the period of quiescence preparation for the religious forces, which commenced in June 1963, had reached the point that promised a trend of solid activism against the monarchy. Numerous gatherings were held throughout the country to express the community's condolences to the Khomeini, who was serving his exile in Najaf.[119]

To further diminish the role of Khomeini and his politically active network, SAVAK published a discourteous editorial in *Ettelaat Daily* in January 1978. Trying to exclude the activities of the Ayatollah from those of other high-ranking clerics in Iran, the author reviewed an inauspicious alliance that had formed between the 'black' and 'red' colonialism, referring to rough religious elements and the leftists, over the June 1963 uprising against the White Revolution of Shah. He had gone on and accused Khomeini of being a British agent.[120]

Once again, in resemblance to the 1963 uprising, the people of Qum filled the streets and showed their resentment towards the slanderous editorial. The clash between the state forces and demonstrators resulted in several killed and wounded. The incident of Qum initiated a series of chain mourning gatherings – every forty days – in Tabriz, Yazd and throughout the country.[121] The perceived political opportunity had been changed by the clergy and their lay followers.[122]The country was pushed to all-out chaos by August 1978, when Jafar Sharif Emami, known for his affinity with the clergy of Qum, was asked to form a new cabinet. Nevertheless, the course of the revolution had reached a point of no return on 9 September 1978, when the army opened fire on the people in Tehran and killed scores of them and marked the 'Black Friday' of the Iranian Revolution.[123] The incident made the religious forces form different camps to set up a robust association of quarrelling with the state and planning for an interim government, seizing the most out of the available political opportunity.

In early October 1978, over the request of the Iranian authorities, Khomeini was expelled from Iraq to France. He had been, perhaps mistakenly, offered another unique opportunity to broadcast his opinions throughout the world using the news agencies platform available in France. Back in Iran, as the popular contentions were fuelling in streets, Muhammad Reza Shah decided to appear on the National TV and to personally ask the protesters, and the clergy for a compromise. He addressed the protesters,

> I, as your King, have sworn to protect the country's territorial integrity, national unity, and Shiʿi Islam . . . . I also heard the message of your revolution . . . . Here, I ask the Grand Ayatollahs and the prestigious scholars, who are the religious and spiritual leaders of the people, and the guardians of Islam and especially the Shiʿi faith, to protect this only Shiʿi state of the world, by guiding the protestors to calm down.[124]

The speech, however, was too little too late. On 13 January, Khomeini ordered the formation of a new paramount body, the Revolutionary Council, to work on the post-Shah era.[125] Three days later, Muhammad Reza Pahlavi left Iran for good.

The monarchy was without a monarch, and revolutionaries were counting seconds for the return of their charismatic leader from the exile. On 1 February 1979, Khomeini returned to Iran and was warmly greeted by mass demonstrators in Tehran. Three days after, the Revolutionary Council recommended Mehdi Bazargan to become the prime minister of Iran's interim government. In his decree to the revolution's new prime minister, Khomeini states:

> Upon the proposition of the Revolutionary Council and based on my canonical and legal authority, originated from the vote of the overwhelming majority of

> Iranians for leadership of the movement . . . because of my trust in your sincere faith in the holy tenets of Islam as well as my awareness of your Islamic and national endeavours, I hereby appoint you to form the interim government to attend the affairs of the country, especially with regard to conducting referendum and referring to the votes of the people about changing the political system of the country to the Islamic Republic.[126]

His first official announcement, as the leader of the revolution in Iran, was a manifestation of his ijtihad, which had been fostered during the last fifteen years. He not only recognized the role of the popular support but also mentioned that the leadership of the community is a divinely assigned responsibility for the Shiʿi clergy. According to the will of the revolutionaries and Khomeini's supporters, the army signed a neutrality declaration on early 12 February 1979, and marked the abolishment of the monarchy.

With the triumph of the revolution and establishment of Iran's interim government under the premiership of Bazargan and supervision of the Revolutionary Council, Khomeini left Tehran to reside in Qum and to teach at the seminary in March 1979.[127] The last sequence of the Shiʿi clerical elite's political solidarity was the series of meetings in which the four Marja' of Qum participated to monitor the activities of the Revolutionary government and to institutionalize the Shiʿi tenets in the Islamic Republic. After fourteen centuries, the Shiʿi clergy had managed to seize the opportunity and establish the rule.

* * *

The course of seven decades of the Shiʿi clerical activism in Iran – from the Constitutional Revolution to the establishment of the Islamic Republic – has witnessed the emergence of various figures, who positioned differently in perceiving the opportunity structure (Figure 4.1 depicts an illustrative trajectory of Shiʿi clerical elite activism in modern Iran). Some remained quiet and some were extremely active, but all performed in a way to protect the community and to further their cause. During the last chapter of the era (1963–79), however, the circle of high-ranking clergy worked together to form an association that would make them powerful enough to consolidate their sociopolitical objectives and seize the most out of the political opportunity structure.

During the early stages of the post-Constitutional Revolution, the context was by no means permissive for any sort of clerical political activism. Members of the clergy in Iran not only had relatively lost popular support, but they personally were frustrated by the revolution's outcome. Therefore, considering the political opportunity structure, Hairi decided to remain quiet and work on institutionalizing the new seminary in Qum. Later, as the structure was changed, Burujirdi strived to further develop the authority of the seminary leadership. The unfolded events proved that his political posture, in retaining benign relations with the state authorities, was more accurate than other members of the clergy, including Kashani and Navvab Safavi.

In 1961, however, the popular status of the seminary was ever rising due to the activities of its deceased leader. It was then that a politically active figure, Khomeini, orchestrated a social movement against the monarchy. With him expelled from Iran to

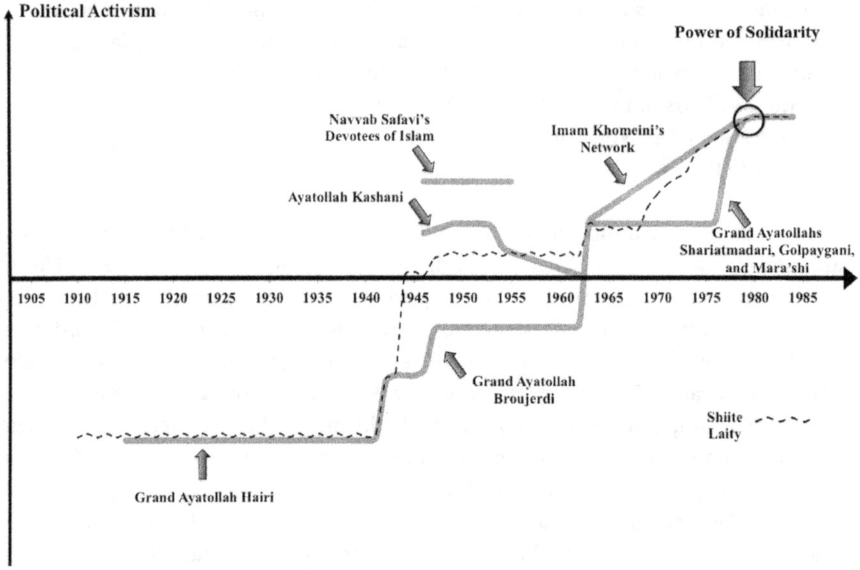

Figure 4.1 Political activism of mujtahids in modern Iran.

work on his thoughts in Najaf, his entourages in Iran shaped a competent network to propagate the Ayatollah's messages.

Other high-ranking Maraji' residing in Qum at the time were actively involved in politics, although with more discretion. Eventually, in early 1978, the political opportunity structure became favourable to strike the final play of political contention. Through a course of almost one year, all members of the clergy in Iran, Iraq and Lebanon formed a solid transnational network to consolidate the power of the clerical elite and dismantled the Iranian monarchy to establish the Islamic Republic under leadership of their charismatic colleague.

5

Iraq 2003

The pragmatic Shiʿi mujtahids

This chapter explores the current Shiʿi political ascent in Iraq through an examination of the perception of Shiʿi clergy over the political opportunity structure in modern Iraq, the context that has shaped their political postures. The Shiʿi community constructs the Arab identity of Iraq. Arab Shiʿis constitute about 60 per cent of the country's population, with Sunni Kurds and Sunni Arab religio-ethnic groups each accounting for around one-fifth of the population.[1] Despite this, the Shiʿi community has always been seen, by Ottoman and subsequent governments, as an Iranian fifth column within the country.

Concurrent with the Muslim conquest of Iraq in 638, Shiʿi communities emerged in the area. At that time, the Second Caliph appointed Salman the Persian, one of Ali's close disciples, as governor of the city of al-Mada'in who implanted the first Shiʿi community in Iraq. Later, Imam Ali, as the Fourth Caliph, moved to Iraq and named Kufa as the capital of his caliphate. Since then, Shiʿi Islam has been thoroughly intertwined with Iraq. The establishment of the Shiʿi seminary of Najaf in the eleventh century by Sheikh al-Tusi was a watershed in the development of Shiʿi Islam in Iraq.[2] For centuries and until the mid-twentieth century, when Hairi and Burujirdi restored the seminary of Qum in Iran, Najaf was the most important Shiʿi scholarly centre in the world. With the rise of Shiʿi Safavid in Persia, neighbouring the Sunni Ottomans, authority over the area was exchanged between the two empires four times, resulting in further pressure on the Shiʿi community there until, with the Treaty of Zahab in 1639, Iraq was placed under Ottoman rule and remained there until the dissolution of the Turkish dynasty.[3]

The re-empowerment of Shiʿi authority in Iraq during the eighteenth century was, to some extent, owing to the hostile attitude of Nader Shah towards the Shiʿi clergy in Iran. Settled in the holy cities of Najaf and Karbala, Shiʿi clerical elites, who had passed the permissive context of the Safavid age, were forced to seek support from the laity and became independent of the state. This transformational move later provided them with an unparalleled opportunity in the early nineteenth century and boosted the authority of the clerical elite throughout the Shiʿi world. Their leadership through the Russo-Persian Wars, Tobacco Revolt and Persian Constitutional Revolution in the following century were all the result of such a shift.

Inasmuch as the Najaf, Karbala and Samarra Shiʿi leadership were actively involved in the politics of Iran, they remained quiet with regard to the politics of Iraq due to the close political opportunity structure, partially imposed by the Ottomans' restraining policies.[4] With Ottoman rule about to be dismantled in the region, Shiʿi leadership of Iraq, for the first time in its modern history, perceived a favourable opportunity structure and became actively engaged in domestic politics and fought against the foreign British forces to protect one of the main abodes of Shiʿi Islam during the Great War. This course of resistance against British forces lasted until 1921, when Faisal I, a Sunni and non-Iraqi national, was nominated as king of Iraq. Frustrated by the outcome of their political activities, the Shiʿi clergy in Iraq were pushed aside from the routine politics of the country for the coming decades. During this interregnum period for political activism in Iraq, it became the Qum seminary's responsibility to assume the role of leadership throughout the Shiʿi world.

The abolition of the Hashemite Monarchy in Iraq in 1958 heralded a new era in which the Shiʿi clerical elite was able to revive itself and become, once again, actively involved in the politics of the then newborn Republic of Iraq. From 1958 until today, various religio-political movements, under the leadership of Shiʿi clerics, have been playing prominent roles in the politics of Iraq and competing to represent the will of the Shiʿi population. These movements experienced the permissive context during the Arif Brothers' governments, from 1963 to 1968, as well as the repressions of the Baʿth administration, yet managed to survive and their authority prevails in today's Iraq.[5] During this period, numerous Shiʿi clerics have emerged in the political mise-en-scène of modern Iraq, each presenting a relatively unique posture responding to the political structure, aiming to protect the Shiʿi community and to preserve the tenet of Shiʿi Islam. During the last half a century, Shiʿis and other Iraqis have had to deal with the establishment of the 'Republic of Fear' by Baʿthist proponents and the rise of Saddam's arbitrary rule.[6] Under the utmost political pressure throughout the period of Iraqi dictatorship, the Shiʿi leadership was responsible for leading a community facing three devastating wars and numerous failed coups and uprisings. In the aftermath of these upheavals, which resulted in millions of casualties, came the political ascent of the Shiʿi majority in post-2003 Iraq, a sociopolitical status that is partly owed to the solidarity of Shiʿi clerical elites during these years.

To explain the process behind the current Shiʿi political ascent in Iraq, this chapter describes the political activities of Shiʿi clerical elites and their perceptions about the opportunity structures of the country's modern history since 1920. It considers the political engagements of the Shiʿi community during the first decades of the twentieth century when Iraq emerged as a new state in the modern Middle East. This section investigates the role of the clerical elites, and their perceptions over the political opportunity structure during the war with foreign British forces, which resulted in their political postures in the 1920 Iraqi revolt, and in the midst of the formation of the Hashemite Monarchy in Iraq. It goes on by reviewing the context of the Republic of Iraq, and the political activities of some Shiʿi religious elites in Iraq, Grand Ayatollah Muhsin Al-Hakim and Ayatollah Muhammad Baqir Sadr, as well as the revival of Shiʿi political activism in the aftermath of the Iraqi monarchy. It also examines the relatively restrictive political structure of the country during the rise of the Baʿath party in Iraq and explains the postures of Shiʿi clerical elites during the war with Iran. More precisely, it probes the role that the Shiʿi leadership of Najaf, under the initiatives of the Grand Ayatollah Abu al-Qasim Khoei, in protecting the seminary through a very critical era. The remainder of the chapter draws attention to the solidarity of the country's Shiʿi clerical elites under the Marja'iyya of Grand Ayatollah Ali Sistani, the process that resulted in the political ascent of the Shiʿi community in today's Iraq.

From Ottoman to independent Iraq: Iranian mujtahids and Iraqi politics

The Shiʿi clergy of Najaf played a prominent role in leading the Persian Constitutional Revolution in early twentieth century. Thus, inasmuch as the outcome of the revolution was considered a setback for the religious leadership, the clerics of Iraq, along with their colleagues in Iran, were pushed out of political affairs, and preferred to reconsider their political postures. Yet, with the outbreak of the Mesopotamia Campaign during the First World War, and the occupation of Iraq by the British forces, the Shiʿi clerical elites who perceived a great threat to the Shiʿi leadership were inevitably involved in defending the abode of Islam. For nine years, during which Ottoman Iraq was under British occupation, the majority of Shiʿi clerical elites were actively involved in the politics of the country. Their activism, however, yielded little for them; for, in August 1921, under the auspices of Britain, the Iraqi monarchy was established and Faisal, a non-Iraqi and Sunni son of the Sharif, became the new king. The Iraqi Shiʿi movement of 1914–20 had, under the leadership of the clerical elites, fought with foreign occupiers and even succeeded in establishing a short-lived local Shiʿi state. However, facing the restrictive political opportunity structure caused by the dissolution of the Ottomans and the British Mandate in Iraq, the Shiʿi clergy gave up politics and claimed that it was adhering to what seemed a greater mission: protecting the holy cities in Iraq and their Shiʿi seminaries. Consequently, although the first two decades of the twentieth century had witnessed considerable political activism on the part of the Shiʿi clerical elites in Iraq, during Iraq's monarchial era, which ended in 1958, the clerical elites remained quiet.

The Shiʿi clergy in Iran and Iraq, at the outset of the First World War, did not exhibit any sort of sectarian political activism. They seemed to recover from the experience of the Constitutional Revolution, and, in order to reassess their capabilities for mass mobilization, they took more time to reconsider their postures.[7] With the death of Akhund Khorasani in 1911, clerical leadership of the Iraqi Shiʿi community had been transferred to Ayatollah Sayyid Muhammad Kazem Yazdi, who had seemingly been less active during the Persian Constitutional Revolution. Nevertheless, when in 1914 the British forces invaded Iraq, he and his entourage refused to backstab the Sunni Ottomans. Against all the odds, Yazdi issued a Fatwa of Jihad and even sent his son to the front to fight with 'non-Muslim' British forces.[8]

Despite the initial victories, due to a series of events, at regional and national levels, the schism became evident within the Ottoman–Iraqi alliance.[9] In March 1917, British forces entered Baghdad, ending Ottoman rule in Iraq forever.

A week after the conquest, the British commissioner in Iraq issued a bilingual proclamation to the Arab people of Mesopotamia, extending his hand towards the people of Iraq against the Ottoman government.[10] However, the evident inconsistencies in British leadership over the occupied territories,[11] coupled with the expulsion of Ottomans from Iraq, provided the Shiʿi clerical elites, among the main political actors at the time, with a permissive opportunity structure to mobilize their followers towards the independence cause.[12]

Two years after the Mesopotamia Campaign, not all parts of Iraq were under British tutelage. The holy city of Najaf, for instance, was still under the control of its Shiʿi inhabitants. The war between Najafis and British forces broke out later that year. This caused the 1918 'Uprising of Najaf', in which Iraqis rose to protect the city from British occupation.[13] Throughout the conflict, two Najafi notables, Sayyid Muhammad Bahr al-Ulum and Sheikh Muhammad Jawad Jazaeri, formed 'The Islamic Revival Society' to pursue their political objectives in a more structured way.[14] The foundation of the Society was, indeed, the first explicit Islamic action of the Shiʿi community towards claiming independence in Iraq. Nevertheless, it was eventually weakened by an internal schism, thus losing the support of the seminary's leadership. In March 1918, the hardliner faction of the Society stormed the residence of the British attaché in Najaf and assassinated him.[15] This led to the city being besieged by British forces. Eventually, after more than forty days, and with the rise of an internal schism among the Shiʿi community of the city, the siege was lifted, British troops entered Najaf, rounded up hundreds of rebels, expelled dozens to India and executed scores of them in retaliation.[16]

In the aftermath of the Najaf Uprising, Britain sought to consolidate a master strategy for its presence in Iraq considering the changing political equations in the region.[17] Consequently, Arnold Wilson, the British Civil Commissioner in Baghdad, strived to institutionalize the British Mandate for Iraq asking for the support of Iraqi notables.[18] In the midst of these developments, Grand Ayatollah Yazdi passed away in April 1919 and Ayatollah Muhammad Taqi Shirazi inherited the clerical leadership. His political leadership of the community within the chaotic situation of the time enabled the Shiʿis of Iraq to play a pivotal role in the 1920 revolt against the British Mandate.

The 1920 Uprising in Iraq: Active mujtahids, failed revolt

The 1920 revolt against the British presence in Iraq was a nationwide struggle for the freedom and independence of the country, and it constituted the very foundations of today's Iraq. For the Shiʿi community in Iraq, which played an unsurpassed role in the revolt, it represents the most significant incident for Iraqi unity, though its outcome never served the Shiʿi community as they had expected.[19] Although short-lived and limited to a defined territory, it was during the revolt that the Shiʿi clerical elites succeeded in founding the first Islamic state of the twentieth century, under the leadership of Muhammad Taqi Shirazi.

In May 1920, a group of Shiʿi clerics, notables and tribal chiefs gathered in the house of Muhammad Taqi Shirazi in Karbala to decide how to respond to the changing political structure.[20] They agreed to work on awakening Iraqis to break Britain's hold over Iraq; if the British forces resisted, then their intention was to mobilize their followers to confront the occupiers with arms.[21] Therefore, as a first step, the Grand Ayatollah issued an open letter, addressing his 'Iraqi Brothers' in which he stated:

> Be informed that your brothers in Baghdad, Kazimayn, Najaf, Karbala and other regions have come to a joint decision to demonstrate peacefully to demand their civil rights. Their righteous demands are basically the independence of Iraq based on the formation of a just Islamic rule. Hence, it is your duty to send your representatives to Baghdad, maintaining peace and order, and trying to prevent an internal schism. I also advise you to respect all opinions throughout this grand Jihad.[22]

His proclamation issued in early 1920 shows that he believed that, at the time, the Shiʿi leadership should establish an Islamic state in Iraq and considered this to be a righteous demand. Yet later, when British officers did not respect this demand, an armed revolt was launched in Baghdad. Consequently, Shirazi issued a fatwa that read as follows:

> [i]t is the duty of Iraqis to plea for their rights. In demanding them, they should maintain peace and order. Were the British to prevent them from obtaining their rights it is legitimate to make use of defensive force.[23]

Mahdi Khalesi of Kazimayn and Shariat Isfahani of Najaf, two distinguished clerics of Iraq, welcomed his fatwa. Subsequently, the urban populations of these holy cities, supported by the Shiʿi tribal fighters, joined the revolt against the British.[24]

By July 1920, various British bases in the mid- and lower Euphrates had been liberated by the revolutionary forces.[25] However, to the dismay of revolutionaries, Shirazi passed away in August. Grand Ayatollah Shariat Isfahani succeeded him and the leadership of the Shiʿi revolt against British forces transferred from Karbala to Najaf. Although the Grand Ayatollah pursued the cause of his predecessor, the revolution was reaching its demise. In late August, British troops were called from India, Iran and Britain to crack down on the revolutionary bases in Iraq. By November 1920, the armed revolt of the Iraqi people against British forces was crushed and the belligerent parties agreed a ceasefire.[26]

The engagement of the Shiʿi community in the 1920 revolt brought it nothing but despair. The deaths of the Shiʿi clerical leaders, who had led the community through independence, for a short period, were a drastic blow to the consistency of activism carried out by Shiʿi clerical elites at the time. Each of the leaders resided in different cities; therefore, political leadership was handed from Karbala to Najaf and, with the death Grand Ayatollah Sharia' Isfahani in December 1920, to Kazimayn, where Sheikh Mahdi Khalesi resided. This further weakened the Shiʿi clerical elite-laity political leadership while they were fighting with British forces and eventually caused their defeat.

In November 1920, and to consolidate the British Mandate in Iraq and contain any further popular revolt, Sir Percy Cox, popular among Iraqis, persuaded Abd

Al-Rahman Al-Kailani, to form a council of ministers under British supervision.[27] It was under the auspices of this political structure that Iraq became an independent Arab monarchy.

For almost a decade, the Shiʿi clerical leadership in Iraq had been actively engaged in the politics of the country and strived to gain independence from British rule and to establish an Islamic state. Their political leadership during the occupation of Iraq had extended beyond the Shiʿi community, and in some cases, prevailed in other communities. Abdul-Aziz Al-Badri, an Iraqi Sunni Mufti, confirms this, saying: 'in post-Ottoman Iraq, Shiʿi clergy of Najaf, Karbala, Baghdad, Samarra, and Kazimayn mobilised Iraqis against the British occupation through issuing fatwas and indeed it was those verdicts that made the Iraqi tribes fight against the British forces in order to liberate Iraq from the filth of colonialism and infidelity.'[28] This, however, resulted in resentment towards Shiʿi authority by British policymakers in Iraq. Gertrude Bell, the oriental secretary to the British commissioner in Mesopotamia, expressed this resentment in a letter to her father:

> I don't for a moment doubt that the final authority must be in the hands of the Sunnis, in spite of their numerical inferiority; otherwise you will have a mujtahid-run, theocratic state, which is the very devil.[29]

It was in such a circumstance that political opportunities for Shiʿi activism were diminishing in Iraq at the time. On the other hand, the cost of the British presence in Iraq was increasing and London was being harshly criticized for its post-First World War policies in the region.[30] To discuss a more stable solution to the future of the ex-Ottoman territories, the Cairo Conference was called in March 1921. It was during the conference that Britain decided to support the establishment of an Arab monarchy in Iraq under the rule of Faisal, son of Husayn Ibn Ali, the Sharif of Mecca, and, as a Hashemite, a descendent of the Prophet.[31]

Responding to the outcome of the conference, the Shiʿi leadership of Najaf and Kazimayn took two different stances with regard to the nomination of Faisal. While Grand Ayatollahs Isfahani and Naʿini of Najaf opposed any government established under the tutelage of Britain, Sheikh Mahdi Khalesi and Sayyid Muhammad Sadr of Kazimayn welcomed the decision of the Cairo Conference.[32] Faisal became King Faisal I of Iraq in August 1921, the first monarch of the newborn Iraqi state.

A clash between the Shiʿi clerical leadership and the state broke with the spread of news concerning the terms of an Anglo-Iraqi Treaty during the summer of 1922.[33] The Treaty embodied almost the same issues that the British had aimed to achieve with the Iranian government three years before, and would place Iraq's financial, military and foreign affairs under close British supervision. In order to ratify the Treaty, and Iraqi Constituent Assembly had to be established.[34] This provided the Shiʿi clerical elites with an alibi to confront Faisal and his government, as they believed the pre-agreed conditions of their support, to oust British supremacy in Iraq, had been breached.

In November 1922, Khalesi, Isfahani and Naʿini issued a series of fatwas against Muslims who wished to participate in the upcoming Constituent Assembly Election.[35] To counter Shiʿi clerical anti-monarchical activities, the cabinet of Prime Minster Abd al-Muḥsin Saʿdun (1922–9) passed a bill, allowing the government to 'deport foreign nationals' who engaged in anti-state activities.[36] Considering that the majority of the Shiʿi clergy in Iraq at the time were originally Persians, the bill represented a declaration of war against Shiʿi clergy in the holy cities. On 25 June 1923, Khalesi along with his sons and nephew were expelled from Iraq to the Hejaz and later resided in Iran based on the government's initiatives. Subsequently, the rest of the Shiʿi clerical elites, and most notably, Isfahani and Naʿini were, humiliatingly, deported to Qum.[37] The government was then able to carry on with its plans without the concern of meaningful opposition from the Shiʿi community. The Constituent Assembly was established in March 1924 and it later ratified the Anglo-Iraqi Treaty, as well as the Fundamental Law of Monarchial Iraq.[38]

The main concern of Shiʿi clerics, who had been expelled to Iran, was the destiny of the seminary of Najaf. Without their leadership of the seminary and allocation of religious taxes among prospective students, the seminary's survival was cast into doubt.[39] On the other hand, for Faisal and his reign to endure robustly, he had to reach an agreement with the Shiʿi clergy, who still held sway over a large popular constituency encompassing much of Iraq's population at the time. This mutual interest resulted in a series of covert negotiations between Faisal's envoy and the expelled Shiʿi elites in Iran during which the latter promised not to interfere in internal Iraqi politics if the government let them return to Najaf.[40] Eventually, the Shiʿi clerical elites chose to protect the 1000-year-old seminary by returning to Iraq, rather than remaining politically active while far away. The political opportunity structure in Iraq at that time gave them no other alternative but to choose to stay out of politics for the coming decade and await a more permissive context. Subsequent history would show that an opportunity for the Shiʿi clerical elites to return to the front lines of politics in Iraq would not occur for more than three decades.

Over a decade between 1914 and 1924, the Shiʿi clerical elites strived to consolidate the right of the Iraqi population in facing foreign British forces. Through the movement of Jihad that took place while Iraq had still been nominally under Ottoman rule, to the Najaf uprising, and finally the 1920 revolt, where Iraqis rose up as one nation, the clerical leadership had been at the forefront of the Iraq political scene. Nevertheless, the course of structural political opportunity, the deaths of the strong leaders and internal schism over the future of the newborn country, were all factors that imposed detrimental blows on their political movement. By April 1924, when Shiʿi clerical elites returned to Iraq, the foundation of the monarchy had been consolidated thanks to British policies, and the context was as restrictive as possible for Shiʿi political engagement. Throughout most of the Hashemite rule in Iraq, the Shiʿi clergy stayed relatively quiet waiting for a more permissive context.

The Republic of Iraq: A permissive context for Shiʿi political movements

Throughout the Hashemite period in Iraq, which lasted for more than three decades, the Shiʿi clergy refrained from political activism. However, the sociopolitical structure of the Shiʿi community in Iraq had been undergoing a great transformation, with the rise of rural–urban migration and the introduction of modern schools. The shortage of Shiʿi clerical elites in responding to those changes was inevitably causing a gap for Shiʿi laity.[41] For thousands of Iraqi Shiʿis, communism and Arab Nationalism were more promising ideologies for elevating their social status. On the other hand, and due to the strong sense of tribalism in Iraq, the Shiʿi community was less likely to show any sort of political activism based on an 'explicit Shiʿi agenda'.[42] This would ultimately close the political opportunity structure for Shiʿi clerical elites in Iraq and restrain them from overt political activism throughout the second half of the twentieth century.

The defeat of those Shiʿi clerics, who had perceived the political opportunity structure open for activism in post-1958 Iraq, had its main root in this void between the Shiʿi elites and laity, an 'ever-lasting' restrictive structure at a societal level. With the establishment of the Republic of Iraq in 1958, the Shiʿi clerical leadership perceived an opportunity for political activism. Over the coming decade, during which Iraq went through three coups, the Shiʿi clerical elites constantly worked towards institutionalizing its authority throughout the community and the country. By the time of the rise of Baʿth to power in 1968, this ascending trend towards political activism was terminated and the Shiʿi clerics in Iraq were gradually pushed towards quiescence. Nevertheless, it was in July 1958, during the change in the political opportunity structure in Iraq over the fall of the monarchy, that Shiʿi clerics decided to get involved in the politics of the country once again with a view to fulfilling the causes of the community.

At the time, a group of Iraqi officers, under the leadership of Abd al-Karim Qasim, attempted a military coup against the government, overthrew the monarchy and announced a Republic in Iraq on 14 July 1958. The rise of Qasim, whose mother was a Shia, and his anti-sectarianism policies, provided the Shiʿis with an open political opportunity to restore their social status and to become active in the politics of the country. At the same time, the clergy in Najaf perceived a threat from communist–Marxist affiliates who shared power with Qasim.[43] Later in 1958, a group of renowned Shiʿi clerics established the 'Ulama Association', *Jamaʿat al-Ulama*, aiming to elevate the sociopolitical consciousness of the Shiʿi community in contrast to other appealing ideologies.[44]

The establishment of the Association under the auspices of the Grand Ayatollah Muhsin Al-Hakim, and the direct participation of renowned Shiʿi personalities, was a response to the growing influence of communist and pan-Arabist ideologies among the Shiʿi laity in Iraq, which had been changing the structure in dismay at the religious camp of the time. Throughout its activities, the association and its members strived to present an argument for Shiʿi politics to conform to the contingencies of the context and the modern world. Therefore, it is fair to call Al-Hakim, the prestigious Arab leader of the seminary, a revitalizer of modern Shiʿi political activism in Iraq.

An Arab mujtahid: The political posture(s) of Muhsin Al-Hakim

Born into a prestigious family in Najaf in 1889, Muhsin Al-Hakim was the son of Sayyid Mahdi, the renowned leader in the south of Lebanon.[45] In his twenties, he sat in on lectures by Akhund Khorasani and Sayyid Muhammad Said Habubi (d. 1915), one of the religious leaders of the Jihad movement against the British invasion. Muhsin Al-Hakim, in his early twenties at the time, fought with the foreigners alongside other Shi'i clerics at the front. With the death of Abu al-Hasan Isfahani in 1946, Al-Hakim became the leader of the Najaf seminary, while at the same time, Grand Ayatollah Burujirdi had been just appointed to take charge of the Qum seminary in Iran. Nonetheless, his leadership, his sons' and students' legacies from Shi'i political movements in Iraq have prevailed until today. He personally witnessed Ottoman Iraq, the British Mandate, the Hashemite Monarchy and the governments of Qasim, the Arif Brothers and the Ba'thists in the Republic of Iraq. Therefore, assessing his political trajectory, shaped by his perceptions of the political opportunities presented to him, would provide an incomparable case through which to study the activism of Shi'i clerical elites in the modern history of Iraq. At an individual level, he himself influenced the opportunity structure in Iraq, as he was the only *Arab* Shi'i cleric who held the position of Marja'iyya on the eve of the rise of pan-Arabism throughout the Middle East. None of his mostly Iranian predecessors and successors during the contemporary era has had such an impact on the Iraqi context.

With the death of Grand Ayatollah Isfahani, the Shi'i Marja'iyya was moved to Iran. With the rise of Burujirdi in Qum, Al-Hakim concentrated his activities on teaching and fostering students in the Najaf seminary.[46] During the reign of the Hashemites, Al-Hakim and his colleagues in Iraq managed to mitigate the relationship with the state by staying out of politics. It was as a consequence of their activities that the number of religious students in Iraq rose dramatically.[47] Indeed these were the Iraqi, Iranian, Lebanese, Afghani, Pakistani and Indian students who shaped the cadres of Shi'i political movements at the dusk of the Hashemite rule and the establishment of the Republic in Iraq.

The fall of the monarchy in Iraq and the rise of Qasim provided an opportunity for the Shi'i religious leadership in Iraq to come out from its cocoon and become more politically active. At the same time, the threats of communism and pan-Arabism were at their height, with the abolition of the Islamic monarchy. Alike relatively underprivileged Shi'i communities in other Arab countries, the Shi'i laity in Iraq were mostly recruited by the communist parties hoping to elevate their social status at the time.[48]

To kill two birds with one stone, with the approval of Grand Ayatollah Al-Hakim, a group of Shi'i activists in Najaf founded the 'Ulama Association', as the first step towards the mostly religious revival of the community in the Republic of Iraq. However, the permissive context for Shi'i activism and their benign relationship with Qasim terminated very soon, when he introduced socioeconomic reforms in September 1958.[49] To the dismay of the Shi'i clergy, Qasim's administration passed the Personal Status Law. The new initiative was intended to give Iraqi women equal rights with men in social and individual matters. This threatened the religious authorities and, for them, was a sign of the rising power of communism in Iraq.[50]

A group of deprived Iraqis welcomed Qasim and his reforms as a shimmering light after decades of darkness, and, as such, were more aligned to the state than the religious authorities; the political opportunity structure was, thus restrictive on a societal level. It appears that the Shiʿi leadership of Najaf was listened to more by the Sunni laity than by their own community.[51] A clear indication of this was the formation of the 'Islamic Party' in February 1960, when this *Sunni* political party introduced the *Shiʿi* Grand Ayatollah Muhsin Al-Hakim as their spiritual leader.[52] The moment at which Al-Hakim became directly involved in the politics of Iraq came just days after the formation of the Sunni Islamic Party. To prevent more members of the laity from joining the Communist Party, which was perceivably a great threat to Shiʿi authority, the Grand Ayatollah issued a breakthrough fatwa on 12 February 1960 and branded communism tantamount to 'infidelity' and 'Atheism'.[53] For the next three years, the political activities of the Shiʿi clerical elites were aligned with those of anti-state secular and nationalist movements.[54]

Qasim's government was toppled in early 1963 by the Baʿthist-nationalist coup and Abdul Salam Arif seized the presidency. Although the short-lived government of Qasim provided the Shiʿi clerical elites and their followers with a more favourable opportunity structure to elevate their social status, its affiliation to communism made religious groups take a position against it.[55] After all, the history of Shiʿi Islam had proved that political triumph comes only after the protection of Islamic principles for every Shiʿi religious leader, among whom Muhsin Al-Hakim was not an exception.

With the demise of the more secular Qasim, the government of Aref ascended to power and, due to his sectarian tendencies, the repression against Shiʿi communities increased.[56]Albeit for obvious reasons, at the outset, President Arif tried to mitigate the relationship with state-Shiʿi clerical elites by sending his envoys to meet with Al-Hakim in 1964. It was at this point that the Grand Ayatollah advised the new administration to be loyal to 'what Iraqis' were demanding. He also recommended the government and stated:

> Previously I had warned some Iraqi rulers, whom God punished very harshly, that Iraqis are Muslims and would not surrender to anything except an Islamic regime . . . opposing their beliefs would further fuel tensions between the people and the government. Therefore, it is for the government to respect the popular will by passing laws in conformity with Islamic principles, for we will use all of our strength to defend our religion and causes.[57]

Al-Hakim's political stance at the time was aimed at preserving the Islamic face of Iraq. For some time, the state also acted accordingly; for example, it abolished the Personal Status Law. However, again the clash between Shiʿi clerical leadership and the government broke out, when President Arif labelled the Shiʿis as communists, *Shuyu'i* and further restrained the financial sources of the Shiʿi clergy by nationalizing the business and trading sectors in Iraq.[58] Simultaneously, to protect the Shiʿi community, some family members and students of Al-Hakim were working on advancing their sociopolitical cause in a more covert manner.

With the death of Abdul Salam Arif and succession of his brother Abdul Rahman, once again the political opportunity structure became favourable for the Shiʿi clergy in Iraq and Al-Hakim, who had held the most significant Shiʿi leadership position in the world since the death of Burujirdi in Iran. In his message after the death of Abdul Salam, Al-Hakim proposed the formation of 'a governing council', *Majlis al-Siyadah*. In response to his initiatives, Iraq would be governed under the authority of a non-sectarian council comprised of three distinct members: a Sunni Arab, a Shiʿi Arab, and a Kurd.[59] Although, his plan did not gain a hold in Iraq at the time, during the next two years, the clerical leadership of Najaf was provided with the most permissive context for political activism towards consolidating Al-Hakim's political posture at least among the Shiʿi community. Therefore, the era is known as the golden age of Shiʿi political activism in Iraq since its independence.[60]

In July 1968, the Baʿthists seized power in Iraq for the second time, this time to remain in power for a longer period. The first two years of the Baʿth government ran concurrently with the last years of Grand Ayatollah Al-Hakim's leadership of the Najaf seminary. The new regime implemented an exclusivist mode of government in Iraq, which did not tolerate even the smallest contention. At the time, the Shiʿi religio-political movements were among the foremost internal threats to the authority of the new regime. Therefore, confrontation with the state-Shiʿi clergy broke out in the very earliest days.[61]

After months of tension between the regime and the Najaf seminary over the blatant actions against Shiʿi clerical authority in Iraq, the Baʿthists issued a warrant against the son of the Grand Ayatollah, Sayyid Mahdi Al-Hakim, and charged him with treason over his alleged covert relationship with Israel, the Kurdish opposition and Iran.[62] Within days, the close circle of the Grand Ayatollah left the country fearing further prosecutions by the repressions of the regime against the Shiʿi activist. For the Grand Ayatollah, however, he chose to migrate to the neighbouring city of Kufa, where he remained politically quiet for the rest of his life.

The political trajectory of Grand Ayatollah Muhsin Al-Hakim in Iraq exemplifies a unique case in the activism of the Shiʿi clergy in the modern history of the Middle East. His activities with regard to the political structure of Iraq, from time to time and in various circumstances, explain how perception of clerics influences and also is influenced by the change in political opportunity structure, and ultimately may lead to the rise and/or demise of political activism among the Shiʿi clergy. With the abolition of the monarchy in 1958, the new phase of the Grand Ayatollah's political activism had been initiated and throughout the following decade it had ebbed and flowed. As the repressions of the Baʿthist state provided close political opportunity, the Grand Ayatollah presented the most politically quiet phase of his life.

When Al-Hakim passed away in June 1970, the Baʿath Party further restricted the Shiʿi clergy by eliminating those clerics who had been politically active. Therefore, to protect the Shiʿi community in Iraq and the very foundation of the Najaf seminary, the clergy, most notably Grand Ayatollah Abu al-Qasim Khoei, chose to become politically quiet. Some younger clerics, though, had different perceptions about the political opportunity structure and held more active posture. Among this younger group was Ayatollah Muhammad Baqir Sadr, an ardent student of Al-Hakim and Khoei, who paid a high personal price for his activism at the time.

Shiʿi activism and its mission in Iraq: The case of Muhamamd Baqir Sadr

Ayatollah Muhammad Baqir Sadr was born in 1935 in Kazimayn to one of the most prestigious Shiʿi families. He is perhaps among the most predominant activist clerics of the contemporary era, a figure who exhibits Shiʿi transnationalism by himself. His novel jurisprudential ideas about the role of Shiʿi clerical elites in politics were seen over writing the constitution of the first Shiʿi state of the World, the Islamic Republic of Iran.[63] He was among the most distinguished active cleric in modern Iraq, founding member of the Islamic Dawa Party, who also built a strong connection with Shiʿi movements in Lebanon, and supported his cousin, Imam Musa Sadr, in his activities there.[64] In other words, he can be named as the central individual to be directly involved in contemporary Shiʿi revival in the Middle East.

Nevertheless, what singles him out as one of the most reformist and brilliant clerics in modern history within the Shiʿi world is his distinctive ijtihad towards political roles, his belief that a religious elite should face up to modern developments. His political trajectory, from 1958 to 1980, encompasses four distinct phases: from 1958 to 1960, as a young Shiʿi cleric, he was affiliated to the Ulama Association and wrote editorials for the al-Adwa journal; at the same time, he, along with other reformist colleagues, founded the Islamic Dawa Party, in response to the perceived open political structure provided by the rise of the Qasim administration; the third phase commenced in 1964 when he cut direct relations with the Dawa over the recommendation of the Grand Ayatollah Al-Hakim to work on his Marja'iyya; and finally, the last phase of his life began at the same time as the rise of Shiʿi revolutionaries in Iran in 1978, when he decided to stand against the repressions of the Baʿth regime supporting the Islamic Revolution in Iran.

'Our Mission' (*Resalatuna*) is the title of the book compiled from weekly editorials he wrote for the Ulama Association, *al-Adwa*, as early as June 1960.[65] In the foreword of this treatise, he identified preconditions for mobilizing the laity, Shiʿi and Sunni, as follows:

> Every community to be mobilised needs an enriched school [of thought] at its disposal. Nonetheless, to revolutionise the community, it needs, not only a doctrinal school, but to understand it thoroughly and also to have a robust faith in it. . . . [W] ere these three conditions to emerge in one community, that community becomes capable of achieving a true revival and can initiate a transformation based on the nature of its doctrine.[66]

In his opinion, Islam provided succinct politics; however, the Muslim community had neither understood its foundations nor had it believed in its capabilities to elevate its sociopolitical status. Sadr believed that the mission of the clerical elites, in any given circumstances was to work on the two latter conditions in order to mobilize the community to revitalize opposition to their miserable situation. Thus, his activities over the next two decades, as a renowned member of the Shiʿi clergy of Iraq, were devoted to building such a structure.

With the establishment of the Republic in Iraq, communist and Arab Nationalist parties got an opportunity to promote their ideologies. Responding to their threat, Sadr concentrated on showing the Muslim laity that not only could these political movements not provide them with a concrete ideology but also that Islam and its principles were what they should be seeking the salvation through. His two main treatises, 'Our Philosophy', *Falsafatuna*, and 'Our Economy', *Iqtisaduna*, were written in the years 1959–61 aiming to show that Islam had a more precise response for the community than any other ideologies which had.[67] He declared his position clearly when he stated:

> Since the establishment of the dominion of the imperialist powers over the Islamic world, Islam has lost its function as the basis of the social order, and essentially alien principles, such as capitalist democracy and Marxist socialism, have taken its place. In addition to having begun to determine the outward development of Muslim society, these ideologies have had an adverse effect on the development of Muslim thought, in the sense that many Muslims have lost the ability to conceive of Islam as the all-embracing spiritual foundation of their lives. In this situation, mere reform or correction is not sufficient, and the various un-Islamic social orders and their ideological principles must be replaced by the principles of Islam, and the achievement of this goal is a revolutionary task.[68]

For him to consolidate his position, a medium was needed, and the Ulama Association, which had been founded by traditional Shiʿi clerics, was clearly not capable enough at the time. Consequently, with the aid of a group of young and reformist clerics, Sadr established a more politically constructed party, the Islamic Dawa, *Hizb al-Dawa al-Islamiyya*, around 1958 in Najaf.[69] The goal of Dawa's founders at the time was to organize, to mobilize and to lead the laity, in order to establish a government based on Islamic values.[70] Making the most of the in-hand opportunity structure, they sought to fill the gap between Shiʿi clerical elites, their political postures and the community that had been largely absorbed by other rival camps in the Iraq of the early 1960s.

The establishment of Dawa and its subsequent activities had the support of Al-Hakim, then the highest-ranking Marja', and it soon got a grip on the Shiʿi youth in Iraq.[71] The popularity of the party triggered opposition to its spiritual leader, Muhammad Baqir Sadr, as well.[72] With opposition stirred up against the party, to ensure the conformity of the seminary and the religious dignity of Sadr, Grand Ayatollah Al-Hakim advised him to resign from the party while continuing to support it indirectly.[73] Since then, the third phase of Sadr's religio-political trajectory commenced during which he concentrated on teaching in the seminary, developing his political thoughts, and becoming the ideologue of Shiʿi activism albeit this time in a discreet manner.

Sadr had confined himself in the seminary, taught jurisprudence and developed his circle of followers and students until 1970. With the death of Al-Hakim, Sadr supported the Marja'yya of his other teacher, Grand Ayatollah Abu al-Qasim Khoei. Nonetheless, he sought transformational ijtihad in defining the position, in conformity with the contingencies of the modern context. At just about the same period, a group of his colleagues in Qum were asking for similar shifts vis-à-vis the position.[74] They were asking, based on Sadr's ijtihad, if a Shiʿi Marja' would like to lead the community in the modern world; this supreme position would have to be reformulated from its individual subjective form to become a more comprehensive and objective, structured aim, *Maudhuwya*.[75]

In other words, Sadr's ijtihad, influenced by his perception of the political opportunity structure and the contingencies of the modern world, demands a horizontal reshape of the Marja'iyya position. He believed that it is impossible for one cleric to fulfil all the requirements of the position, be it in terms of religious, social or political leadership of the community. Therefore, he declared his own Marja'iyya in 1972, to complement the responsibilities of other Marja' towards presenting what he mentions as the 'proper' and the 'righteous' Marja'iyya, *Saliha wa Rashida*.[76] There was another reason for Sadr to give up the party. At the time, he reached the conclusion that for his political ijtihad to prevail he should pursue the path of becoming a Shiʿi Marja'. Becoming a Marja', the highest possible religious position in the community would have provided Sadr with an opportunity, at a bureaucratic level, to make his stance widespread among Shiʿis globally, and would also secure him from state prosecution.

In February 1977, during a ritual walk of Iraqi Shiʿis from Najaf to Karbala in commemoration of the *Arbaeen* of Imam Husayn, a clash broke out with government forces. Groups of pilgrims turned into angry demonstrators, and an uprising formed against the regime.[77] Although *the Shiʿi Intifada* of 1977 initially surprised the state, by sending armed forces to Najaf and Karbala, Baʿthists ousted the demonstrators, killed many and sentenced thousands. In the aftermath of the uprising, Muhammad Baqir Sadr was called to Baghdad for a further inquiry. In the eyes of the regime's security apparatus, it was Sadr and his entourage who mobilized the masses against the government. Therefore, from this time on, the Baʿthists sought an opportunity to restrain him and any other religious opposition forces who might trigger a threat to the government of Baghdad.[78]

From February 1977 onwards, the state repression against Muhammad Baqir Sadr's activities was agitated. The Islamic Revolution in Iran heralded more direct confrontation between Sadr and the Baʿthists in Iraq. For him, the triumph of Shiʿi revolutionaries in Iran under the leadership of Imam Khomeini was the realization of a dream. As he confirmed just days after the establishment of the Islamic Republic in Iran:

> The only thing I have sought in my life is to make the establishment of an Islamic government on earth possible. Since it has been formed in Iran under the leadership of Imam [Khomeini] it makes no difference to me whether I am alive or dead because the dream I wanted to attain and the hope I wanted to achieve have come true, thanks to God.[79]

Therefore, while he congratulated the Shiʿis of Iran on their victory against the secular rule of the Shah,[80] he recommended that the Iraqis support their coreligionists and pursue the same mission in their own country.[81]

In a treatise he sent to Iran after the revolution, to be considered in the drafting of the Islamic Constitution,[82] he accentuated the sociopolitical role of Shiʿi clerics and declared:

> The Muslim and triumphant people of Iran have succeeded in deposing the evil regimes forever . . . . It is because they have been adhered themselves to the Shiʿi Marja'iyya earlier than any other nation . . . . The establishment of an Islamic Republic has not only revived the Iranians but also, in this dark era, has shed a saving light on the Islamic community throughout the world.[83]

His unreserved support for the Iranian Revolution's leadership, along with his bold approach to the establishment of the Islamic state, provided Sadr with a new nickname, 'Iraq's Khomeini'.[84] To prevent the imitation of circumstances in Iran, the Baʿthist regime in Iraq found a way of prosecuting him. In order to fulfil a long-due promise, the Ayatollah was sent to Baghdad on 5 April 1980, only days after the Islamic referendum in Iran. Four days later, Muhammad Baqir Sadr's dead body was presented to his family in Najaf, to be buried overnight.[85]

The short, forty-six-year life of Mohamamd Baqir Sadr, in the midst of a formative period, his political posture and his unique ijtihad was fruitful for Shiʿi political activism in the Middle East. Over his life, with the aid of his colleagues and students, he succeeded in presenting a sample conceptual framework for Shiʿis in Iraq, Iran and Lebanon. Although he has not lived enough to witness the ascendance of Iraqi Shiʿi communities, it became the duty of his followers[86] to institutionalize his political ijtihad in the future Iraq. The Shiʿis of Iraq and their clerical leadership, however, had to deal with the arbitrary rule of Saddam for the following decades.

Baʿthist Iraq, a closed structure, and Khoei's political posture

During the thirty-five years of Baʿth rule in Iraq, the Shiʿi religious and political movements faced the utmost repression as a result of state policies. During the two earliest years of Baʿthist rule in Iraq, Muhsin Al-Hakim was forced to give up his social activities and to quietly take refuge in his house in Kufa. After the death of Al-Hakim in 1970, Grand Ayatollah Khoei, who accurately perceived the political opportunity structure to be closed, the restrictive context, remained politically quiet, aiming to protect the Najaf seminary and the very foundations of the Shiʿi establishment in Iraq from the threat of Baʿthist repressions. Those who, contrary to Khoei's perception, became engaged in politics, like Muhammad Baqir Sadr, were brutally annihilated by the regime.

Baʿth arbitrary rule reached its peak after Saddam Hussein ascended to power. Shiʿis were among those religio-ethnic groups who suffered the most due to the policies of the regime,[87] especially considering the outbreak of the war with Shiʿi Iran. Over the eight years of warfare, Shiʿi clerical elites in Iraq remained politically quiet; they neither supported the Iraqi army nor positioned themselves against the Islamic government of Iran. Taking the objective political opportunity structure of Iraq at the time into account, this stance was the optimum alternative to protecting the community. Covertly retaining their association with their fellow Iranians was the best they could do to show their dismay, though implicitly, with Iraq's policies during one of the longest wars in the modern world.

Nevertheless, an opportunity to reiterate their political activism once again was provided to them in the aftermath of the Gulf War in March 1991. The Shiʿis of Iraq reached the point of establishing a short-lived local government in southern Iraq, supported by the Shiʿi clerical elite of Najaf.[88] Yet, due to the closed political opportunity structure, especially at international and regional levels, and due to some internal inconsistencies, the uprising failed and Saddam's regime swiftly cracked down on it. The incident, however, indicated that the Shiʿi clerical elites had never been apolitical, and their tactical quiescence during Saddam's rule was due to the restrictive context, which had crippled any sense of activism. Just months after the failed uprising, Khoei passed away and his student, Grand Ayatollah Ali Sistani became the leader of the seminary. The political opportunity structure, however, had become more closed in post-Gulf War Iraq. Entangled by international sanctions, Iraqis and the Shiʿi religious leadership were counting the days down until they perceived an opportunity. In such a dark era, Sistani had remained under house arrest, and the routine activities of the seminary reached their lowest point since its establishment in the eleventh century. In post-March 2003, with Saddam out of Iraq's political picture, with the dramatic change in the political opportunity structure, the Shiʿi community and its religious leadership succeeded in reaching power and becoming active once again after decades.[89] Making the most of the favourable opportunity structure provided to them, Shiʿi clerical elites and their laity followers strived to elevate their sociopolitical status in Iraq, taking their demographic share into account.

About the same time as the Baʿath Party came to power in Iraq, Grand Ayatollah Abu al-Qasim Khoei became the leader of the Najaf seminary in 1970. Born in the Iranian city of Khoi in 1899, he moved to Najaf in his early youth and remained there for the rest of his life. Over seventy years of teaching at the Najaf seminary, he succeeded in fostering thousands of pious students and became known as 'the most revered Shiʿi Jurist of the Occultation era'.[90] While he was known as the most apolitical cleric of modern times in the West,[91] his political posture during the 1963 Uprising in Iran, the Iran–Iraq War and the 1991 Uprising in Iraq should be reassessed to get a more accurate picture of how he perceived modern politics. During the 1963 Iranian uprising, Khoei was perhaps the most active Shiʿi cleric supporting his fellow Iranians from Najaf and condemning the regime of Pahlavi, in some cases being even harsher than Khomeini himself.[92] In his message sent to his colleagues in Iran, he clearly advised them to lead the people through the course of 'Jihad' against the oppressors, when he stated:

> It is an honor for me to sacrifice my negligible blood to the path of God in order to protect the religion and Quran and to abolish the despots. Because living under the oppressors and enemies of Islam is tantamount to death and even worse . . . .

> Today, in this holy Jihad, there is a great burden on the shoulders of Iranians and the religious leaders of this movement, and it is hoped that they will be able to bear this responsibility in full . . . . The victory for the Iranians is possible only if they follow their distinguished religious leaders and become united under their flag.[93]

He was also one of the most active supporters of Grand Ayatollah Khomeini during his exile in Najaf, forging a close relationship that lasted until the date the leader of the Islamic Revolution went back to Iran.[94] Yet all this activist posture seemingly came to an end when he encountered the unfavourable opportunity structure of Iraq under the rule of the Baʿath Party.

When he became the leader of the seminary in 1970, the Grand Ayatollah mainly devoted his life to protecting the scholastic nature of the centre and to probing the affairs of religious students. He correctly perceived the political opportunity structure to be closed for political contention. He, personally, had seen the disloyalty of the Shiʿi laymen to his predecessor, Al-Hakim, and was well aware of the Baʿthist's anti-clergy policies. Therefore, his perception over the political opportunity structure made the Grand Ayatollah hold a quietist posture at the time.[95] To this end, what made Khomeini lead the revolution in Iran and what pushed Khoei to remain politically quiet in Iraq under the Baʿth regime was more the result of the different structures of political opportunity in the two countries, than of advocating two different versions of Shiʿi Islam. The life of the Grand Ayatollah, especially while he held the Marja'iyya position at Najaf, is thus known to have been led during one of the most politically quiet eras in the history of the Shiʿi community. After all, he was responsible for preserving the very foundation of Shiʿi Islam in Iraq while the country was going through the most critical incidents, among which the war with Iran was a case in point.

The Iran–Iraq War: Shiʿism, Arabism and Iraqism

One of the longest wars in modern history broke out between Saddam's Iraq and the Islamic Republic of Iran in September 1980.[96] The war resulted in the engagement of almost half of the entire Shiʿi population of the world and proved to be a devastating era. It had no winner, but provided much misery for the Shiʿi communities in the two countries.[97] On the Iranian side, almost all Shiʿi clerical elites supported a defensive Jihad against the Iraqi invasion. At the other side, none of the leading Shiʿi clerics in Iraq condemned their Iranian coreligionists during the course of the war. After all, they could not blatantly condemn a state that was run by a fellow Shiʿi cleric, which would be seen as a threat to the clerical authority in the eyes of the laity and outsiders. Nevertheless, groups of Iraqi Shiʿis fought for their country for various reasons.[98] The course of the conflict is characterized strategically into two distinctive periods: from September 1980 until the Spring of 1982 during which Iraq had the upper hand on the ground and managed to occupy vast territories from Iran; and from the liberation of Khorramshahr in May 1982 until the ceasefire on 20 July 1988, when the Iraqi army was mostly holding a defensive position. Accordingly, the exceptional war propaganda machines of the belligerents divided into two ideological stances. While, during the former period, the Iraqi government anchored its strategy on promoting Arabism to attract Arab citizens from Southwestern Iran, during the second phase, Tehran sought to grasp the support of Shiʿi communities in southern Iraq. Notwithstanding, after eight years of prolonged war, both sides failed to achieve their ultimate goals.[99]

In April 1980, Saddam Hussein gave a speech in the city of Nineveh and accused the leaders of the Islamic Republic of repressing Iranians and threatening neighbouring Arab countries. He continued by saying that Iranian leaders should acknowledge Arab citizens' right of autonomy and should know that 'those who are in Arabistan [Khuzestan] are Arab, and the blood in their veins is Arab'. He then addressed the Arab citizens of Iran, emphasizing the Baʿthist ideology, and stated:

> [t]he Arab homeland must have one territory, and the Arab people must be one nation. It must follow the principles that unite the Arabs and not the path that divides them into shares among covetous states.[100]

For the following two years, this exclusivist reading of Arabism and Iraqi nationalism formed the backbone of Baghdad's rhetoric.[101] To this end, the Baʿth regime of Iraq initiated an Arab–Persian war of words with their counterparts in Iran hoping to attract the support of the Arab rulers of the region.[102]

In September 1980, appearing on national television, Saddam declared an all-out invasion of Iranian territories. In this, he had believed that with the fall of the Islamic Republic not only would there be a demise in the threat of 'export of revolution' to the Iraqi Shiʿi community but also that he would become the one and only respected Arab leader in the world.[103] At the same time, the Shiʿi leadership in Iran managed to utilize a spiritual and national rhetoric to mobilize Iranians to defend the country's territorial integrity against the invasion. The initial position of Khomeini facing the invasion was a continuation of the stance he had prior to the Islamic Revolution. In his first speech after the start of the conflict he addressed Iranians and Iraqis, as follows:

> Throughout the period that we were involved in the movement in Iran, we always had almost nothing by way of forces and weapons of war in comparison to the now-defunct Shah's army.... In a war, power does not lie in numbers. What is important is one's power of thought; that same power which, by relying on God in the early days of Islam, enabled a small force to overpower large armies and throw them into disarray .... For whom do the other armies, etc. fight? The Iraqi army fights for Saddam Hussein. Which sane person will give his life for Saddam? Our soldiers have a good reason: they say that they will go to God if they get killed. Such morale is the most important factor. This kind of spirit stems from a devout belief that a person getting killed is actually a victory in that he will go to rest in God's protection.

He continued with a harsh criticism of the Baʿth government and stated:

> This man [Saddam] resorts to various lies. He claims to be an Arab. Not so, he is an American [stooge]. He and his regime are not Arabs as Arabs are Muslim. They

> now claim to follow Islam. The people of Iraq should take note of the fact that this war is one between Islam and heresy. It is incumbent on all Muslims to defend Islam. Granting the impossibility of this man prevailing over Iran and destroying the Islamic Republic, the repercussions of this world will be felt in all the Muslim countries.[104]

Khomeini's political ijtihad at the time was focused on intensifying Islamic beliefs of the citizens of both countries against the secular regime of Iraq. Although no other Arab countries, except Libya and Syria, supported Iran throughout the conflict, the religious stance of Khomeini was a weighty resource, an equivalent to which Saddam lacked throughout the war. To this end, none of the Shiʿi elites residing in Iraq supported the Baʿth cause and, although they were under harsh repression within the state, they even covertly supported the Iranians by allowing the expenditure of the religious taxes in of the interests of Iranian soldiers.[105]

Khomeini's discourse of Jihad and Martyrdom during the war was also received warmly by groups of Iraqis. Among them were the Supreme Council for Islamic Revolution in Iraq and the Islamic Action Organisation; both had been founded and led by exiled Iraqi Shiʿi clerics.[106]

During the course of the eight years of war between Iran and Iraq, both Saddam's Arabism and Khomeini's Shiʿism had taken hold, though partially. The result of the devastating war, however, proved that none had triumphed over the other in the end. Neither had Saddam succeeded in conquering the hearts of the Arab-Iranians in his favour, nor had the Islamic Republic caused an all-out Shiʿi uprising against the Baʿth regime. Nevertheless, the political postures of the Shiʿi clergy in Iran and Iraq were relatively aligned during the warfare. While the religious elites in Iran were actively engaged in the war, their Iraqi colleagues supported the Shiʿi cause covertly, due to the closed political opportunity structure of Iraq. Some years later when, for a short time, they perceived a shift in political opportunity, the clerics in Iraq played a crucial role during the 1991 uprising.

The 1991 Uprising: Broken promises and missed opportunities

Frustrated about trying to achieve his preset goals in the war with Iran, Saddam Hussein engaged in another devastating conflict with Kuwait. In August 1990, Iraqi troops invaded Kuwait and, after two days, Saddam declared Kuwait to be the nineteenth province of the Republic of Iraq and assigned Iraqi de facto governors for the 'Provisional Government of Free Kuwait'.[107]After months, when international arbitrations had failed, the First Gulf War between Iraq and US-led coalition forces broke out in early 1991,[108] a war that eventually led to the defeat of Iraq. What was imposed on Iraqis in the aftermath of the conflict, taking the future international sanctions into consideration, was even more caustic than the regime they had endured during the war with Iran. However, the ever-weakening nature of Saddam's apparatus after the war provided a seemingly open political opportunity structure to the Shiʿis of the south and Kurds in northern provinces of Iraq to rise against the government of Baghdad. The 1991 Iraqi uprising, though it was initially, absolutely popular, without a meaningful elite leadership, was a case with utmost significance in the contemporary history of Iraq, especially in study of clerical activism. Though Iraqi Republican Guards cracked down the popular uprising harshly, the religious elite of Najaf, led by Grand Ayatollah Khoei, succeeded in establishing a short-lived Islamic government. The unfolding incidents, and the role that the Shiʿi clergy played during the 1991 uprising, questions the very foundations of the argument that asserts that the Najaf seminary was a politically quiet centre.

Triggered by the speech given by President Bush in mid-February 1991, resentful Iraqis perceived an opportunity to mobilize their resources wishing to topple Saddam.[109] Subsequently, in early March 1991, an Iraqi tank officer showed his hatred of the government's policies by firing a shell through a portrait of Saddam in Basra. Soon the Shiʿis of Basra, Nasiriya and Karbala spilled out onto the streets, stormed the state buildings and marched in popular uprising. A week later, the Kurds of the northern provinces joined the uprising, and within days, popular forces took the control of fourteen out of Iraq's eighteen provinces.[110]

On 4 March, the movement succeeded in getting control of Najaf. This prompted the religious elites and tribal chiefs of the city to gather in the house of Grand Ayatollah Khoei to discuss the ongoing events. Consequently, for the first time since he was appointed leader of the seminary, Khoei perceived an open opportunity to engage in politics. The first step for the clergy was to control the popular movement. Thus, the Grand Ayatollah issued a letter, dated 5 March 1991, addressed to his 'dear faithful children', and advised them to respect 'Islamic values', to 'bury corpses' and to 'distribute food' fairly among the poor. However, a second letter issued by Khoei two days later bore a more authoritative tone. In it, he appointed an executive committee[111] to act as a point of reference during the 'transition period'. His letter read, as follows:

> These days, as the country is witnessing critical circumstances; thus the order should be preserved, security restored, the situation should be normalized, and an appropriate management of popular interest should be achieved.... Consequently, the public interest urges us to assign a committee responsible for monitoring affairs in a way that its decisions would be tantamount to my wish.... Therefore, I appoint number of renowned scholars whose providence and efficiency are trusted by me.... It is incumbent to my faithful children to obey and to pay attention to their orders and to support them in fulfilling their role.

The main difference between the two letters rests in their distinctive addressees: while the first letter relates to the affairs of the city of Najaf, the second letter addresses a broader, national spectrum.[112] The role he and his close companions played during the turmoil placed the Shiʿi Marjaʿiyya of Iraq solidly at the forefront of the popular uprising against the regime of Saddam.[113]

The events, however, soon turned against the revolutionaries, especially when the international support they had sought, never came to their help. In mid-March, feeling betrayed by the Bush administration and acknowledging their misperceptions over the political opportunity, the revolutionaries were subject to harsh attacks from the state air force and artillery shelling. The loyal Baʿth forces cracked popular resistance with tanks bearing placards saying, 'No Shiʿi [in Iraq] from this day on', and by the last week in March, the Shiʿi uprising in the south had been fully swept from the streets.[114]

Scholars have suggested various reasons for the failing of the popular uprising in 1991 in Iraq.[115] Nevertheless, the focal point of the Shiʿi uprising's collapse resides in the misperceptions of the religious leadership about the political opportunity structure. To this end, the structure reflected the community's situation in the midst of the Islamic Revolution in Iran; the positions of the elites and laity had been swapped. In 1979, the religious leadership of Najaf, under the initiatives of Muhammad Baqir Sadr, became engaged in politics aiming to topple the Baʿth, yet it could not attract popular support. During the 1991 Shiʿi Uprising of the south, the people filled the streets chanting against Saddam and his Baʿth apparatus, yet the clerical leadership, which had lost its faith in popular loyalty, was incapable of mobilizing and organizing the revolt in a timely manner. In both cases, the failure of political activism rests with the mismatch of structural and perceived political opportunity in Iraq.

The power of Mujtahids' solidarity in Iraq

The defeat of the popular uprising promised an even more unfavourable opportunity structure for Iraqis, including the Shiʿi community and its clerical elites. Concurrently, there were severe sanctions imposed on Saddam's regime by the international community. The regime of Baghdad had lost its regional allies, as well, in the aftermath of the Gulf War. For the Shiʿi community, an even darker decade of miseries was still to come.

In less than a year since the uprising, Grand Ayatollah Khoei passed away, in August 1992. Among his few disciples who were in Najaf at the time, the seminary leadership and Marja'iyya was received by Grand Ayatollah Ali Sistani, then at his early sixties. Sistani was born in the holy city of Mashhad in Iran in August 1930 to a clerical family. He migrated to Najaf in 1951 to pursue his religious study and resided there until now. While he was in Najaf, he attended the lectures of a group of Shiʿi Maraji' at the seminary, including Khoei. Nevertheless, when the Baʿth repression against the seminary was intensified in the 1980s, Sistani was among those few Iranian clerics who managed to stay at the seminary and became one of the members of the entourage closest to Grand Ayatollah Khoei. In the later years of Khoei's life, the question of his successor and the destiny of the seminary after his death came to the fore. The seminary was witnessing a critical circumstance, and the regime of Baghdad had not only confined its activities through expulsion of thousands of non-Iraqi students and teachers, but had also cut most of its relations with other Shiʿi centres throughout the world, most notably the Qum seminary. To this end, Khoei asked Sistani to conduct prayers on his behalf in al-Khadra Mosque in the late 1980s; this was a gesture that, to some extent, clarified his decision over the future leadership of the seminary. When Khoei passed away, it was Sistani who led the prayer for the deceased Marja' and managed the small gathering at the funeral.

By late 1992, Grand Ayatollah Sistani announced his Marja'iyya and came to be known as the leader of the Najaf Seminary. Nevertheless, the context for the Shiʿi community in Iraq was as restrictive as ever. In 1993, Saddam ordered the closure of al-Khadra Mosque in Najaf, and Sistani was virtually forced into a house arrest. Concurrently the regime was looking to support another Marja', preferably a non-Persian figure. Ayatollah Muhammad Muhammad Sadeq Sadr (1943–1999) seemed a likely alternative at the time. He was cousin and a close student of Muhammad Baqir Sadr. He had also attended the lectures of Imam Khomeini during the 1970s.[116] Nevertheless, his Arab ethnic background made Sadr II[117] the most plausible figure, in eyes of the regime, which had started propaganda against the non-Iraqi Shiʿi leadership, 'the deviant' foreigner's agents, in the aftermath of the 1991 uprising.[118] Therefore, a period of benign relations formed between Sadr II and the regime of Baghdad.

At the outset, Ayatollah Sadr perceived an open political opportunity to advance his mission throughout the country. Saddam, defeated in the Gulf War and under crippling international sanctions, on the other hand, was willing to mitigate the state relations with the Shiʿi community. Sadr was invited to conduct Friday Prayer sermons in Kufa by the government, a medium through which he could broadcast his opinions.[119] Appealing to middle-class Iraqis, and specifically tribesmen, soon the Ayatollah received a considerable constituency among the laity in Iraq.[120] His perception about the political opportunity structure at the time made him hold a quasi-activist posture in comparison with the Najaf leadership. To this end, the two camps had tactical differences in interpretation of the political structure. His activism in Iraq at the time reached the point at which he formed an 'informal Sharia court' run by his deputies throughout the country.[121]

Nevertheless, the honeymoon between the state and the Sadr II movement had terminated by the late 1990s. With the rising popularity of Ayatollah Sadr, the administration in Baghdad perceived a threat to its authority. This led to a period of tension between the state and the Ayatollah's followers. On his part, Sadr was unsuccessful in changing the perception of other clerical elites in Iraq about the structure. He stood alone among the group of clergy, those whom he called the advocates of 'silent jurisprudent' at the time.[122] Eventually, the activism of Ayatollah Muhammad Muhammad Sadeq Sadr cost him his life in early 1999.

With the assassination of Muhammad Muhammad Sadeq Sadr, the regime once again proved that it did not accept even a small amount of political activism on the part of the Shiʿi clergy in Iraq. The political activism of Sadr II was also seen to result from his misperception of the political opportunity structure. Some scholars, nevertheless, accused other Shiʿi figures of misperception and of not supporting the activism of Muhammad Sadeq Sadr, hence, they missed the open political opportunity structure.[123]

Whether the Grand Ayatollah was responsible for the misperception, or it was on the part of other Shiʿi leaders, or even both, what is clear is that the context was restrictive for Shiʿi activism at the time. The most important reason for such an unfavourable structure was indeed the policies of the Iraqi state. It became evident for the Shiʿi clergy that while Saddam is in power, the idea of political activism was nothing but wishful thinking. Therefore, from 1999, while the Shiʿi clerical elites in Iraq remained as quiet as ever, it was the responsibility of those Shiʿi actors who were in exile to strive to topple the Baʿth regime in Iraq. A powerful association was formed in this situation. The responsibility of the Najaf clerical leadership, especially Grand Ayatollah Sistani, was to protect the seminary and the community by remaining in Iraq. At the same time, a handful of Shiʿi figures in exile, among them Ayatollahs Muhammad Baqir Al-Hakim (1939–2003) and Muhammad Bahr al-Ulloum (1927–2015), were trying to deploy all available means against the regime of Saddam.[124]

Ayatollah Muhammad Baqir Al-Hakim was son of the great Marjaʾ of the Najaf seminary, Muhsin Al-Hakim, and a close disciple of Muhammad Baqir Sadr, who cofounded the Islamic Dawa Party in 1959. With the rise of state repression against Shiʿi clerics in Iraq, Al-Hakim chose to flee from Iraq and was stationed in Qum from 1979. Regionally, the establishment of the Islamic Republic of Iran did strengthen the activities and foundations of Iraqi Shiʿi organizations, which were mainly operative outside Iraq from the early 1980s. Some Shiʿi parties like Islamic Dawa and the Islamic Action Organisation, formed in Karbala by members of the Shirazi family and under the leadership of Muhammad Taqi Modarresi, had been established earlier in Iraq.[125] In 1982, Muhammad Baqir Al-Hakim also founded the Supreme Council for Islamic Revolution in Iraq. The SCIRI, under his leadership, played an unsurpassed role among Iraqi opposition groups and enjoyed the support of the leadership of the Islamic Republic of Iran.[126] During almost two decades in exile, Muhammad Baqir Al-Hakim was known as the most famous of the clergy among Iraqi opposition groups. The Badr Brigades, the military corps of SCIRI also positioned the Ayatollah and his party among the most active powers within the group of Shiʿis of Iraq who have fought against the regime in Iraq since.[127]

Another Shiʿi cleric who was active against Saddam in the late 1990s was Ayatollah Muhammad Bahr al-Ullom. Born into a prestigious Shiʿi family and a close companion of Muhammad Baqir Sadr in the Dawa Party, Bahr al-Ullom, along with some other politicians, established the Iraqi National Congress in 1992 with a mission to overthrow the regime of Saddam Hussein.[128] One of the main founding members of the Congress was Ahmad Chalabi, an Iraqi Shiʿi politician who was active in the early twenty-first century in lobbying against the Baʿth regime. The Iraqi oppositions groups succeeded in ratifying the Iraq Liberation Act in 1998.[129] The act, passed by the US congress and signed into law by President Clinton, provided a political opportunity at an international level for those opposition groups trying to get rid of Saddam in Iraq.

A pragmatic mujtahid: Sistani and post-Saddam Iraq

Eventually, with the commencement of President Bush's administration, and aligned with his doctrine of a 'War on terror' drafted in the post-9/11 era, a coalition of international forces, led by the United States and Britain, invaded Iraq in March 2003. Within less than 3 weeks, the Baʿth apparatus collapsed in Iraq, Saddam fled only to be captured nine months later, and the coalition forces created the provisional authority in April 2003 to deal with executive, legislative and judicial affairs in Iraq during the interim phase.[130] To proceed with the routine politics, CPA established the Iraqi Governing Council with twenty-four members mainly from Iraqi opposition groups; thirteen members were Shiʿis and Ayatollah Muhammad Bahr al-Ulloum was nominated as the council's first president in July 2003.[131]

After more than eight decades, since the establishment of Iraq, the Shiʿi community and its leadership was provided with an open structure to become actively engaged in politics and to elevate their sociopolitical status throughout the country. With the arbitrary regime of Saddam out of the picture, Shiʿi clerics and politicians were joined in a powerful association to represent their relevant communities. In the early stages, the Marja'iyya, and especially Grand Ayatollah Sistani, supported more active figures indirectly through their fatwas and blessings. Yet, with the assassination of Muhammad Baqir Al-Hakim in August 2003, the role of Sistani became more important in the politics of post-Saddam Iraq. The political structure in Iraq had changed to become open for his activism. In response to the questions in the *Washington Post* in June 2003, Grand Ayatollah mentioned that in post-Saddam Iraq '[clerics] are provided with favorable circumstances to fulfill their responsibilities, to educate people, to settle the ongoing disputes among people of Iraq, and to become active to the interest of Iraqis religion and worldly matters'.[132]

To this end, the Grand Ayatollah's pragmatic approach was developed in order to institutionalize the role of Marja'iyya and the Shiʿi clergy in the sociopolitical affairs of post-Saddam Iraq. His stance against the coalition authorities demanding a general election and numerous fatwas asking for all Iraqi unity made him one of the most influential leaders of the contemporary era. Just months after the abolition of Saddam's regime in Iraq, Sistani issued a fatwa, which read as follows:

> These occupiers do not have the authority to appoint the members of the constitution writing council. There is no guarantee that this council will produce a constitution that responds to the paramount interests of the Iraqi people and expresses its national identity of which Islam and noble social values are basic components . . . there must be general elections in which each eligible Iraqi can choose his representative in a constituent assembly for writing the constitution. This is to be followed by a general referendum on the constitution approved by the constituent assembly. All believers must demand the realization of this important issue and participate in completing the task in the best manner.[133]

Making the most of the open political opportunity structure, and perceiving it accurately, Sistani played an important role in the process that led to the 2005 general election in Iraq; and through this process, he always insisted on the importance of Islamic values in a future government of Iraq. Sistani believed that a democratic Iraq would necessitate direct popular election and asked for a one-man-one-vote formula.[134] Taking the Shiʿi population in Iraq into the account, Sistani's active role during the interim phase provided the Shiʿi community with great opportunity. With the initial boycott of some Sunni parties, the majority of the assembly's seats were reserved for Shiʿis.[135]

The post of premiership, with the utmost executive authority, is reserved for Shiʿis in Iraq. Making the most of the open political opportunity structure, through accurate perception, the Shiʿi clergy in Iraq mobilized the laity in institutionalizing the sociopolitical rights of the community. The activist stance taken by the Shiʿi leadership and the powerful association they formed through the interim phase provided the Shiʿi community with a unique status since the establishment of the country. The ascent of the Shiʿi majority in Iraq has an undeniable relationship with the rise of Shiʿis throughout the region; as Vali Nasr correctly indicates, the 'Middle East that will emerge from the crucible of the Iraq war may not be more democratic, but it will definitely be more Shiʿi'.[136]

* * *

With the importance of the role of the Najaf seminary, Iraq could fairly be called the main cradle of Shiʿi clergy throughout the world. Nevertheless, since its establishment, except for a short period during the Safavids, the seminary has mostly been under the rule of non-Shiʿi governments. This has, inevitably, made the clerical elites residing in Iraq more inclined towards holding a quietist posture in terms of facing the political opportunity structure. However, there have been some historical snapshots within which the Shiʿi clergy in Iraq perceived an open political opportunity structure and became politically active to fulfil their responsibilities vis-à-vis the community (see Figure 5.1 for an illustrative trajectory of Shiʿi clerical elites' activism in modern Iraq).

The British Mesopotamia Campaign during the First World War was an instance of this political activism. Perceiving the threat of foreign occupation, the Shiʿi clergy engaged in politics and led the community into resisting the British forces in 1915. However, to the disadvantage of the Shiʿi majority in Iraq, the British Mandate

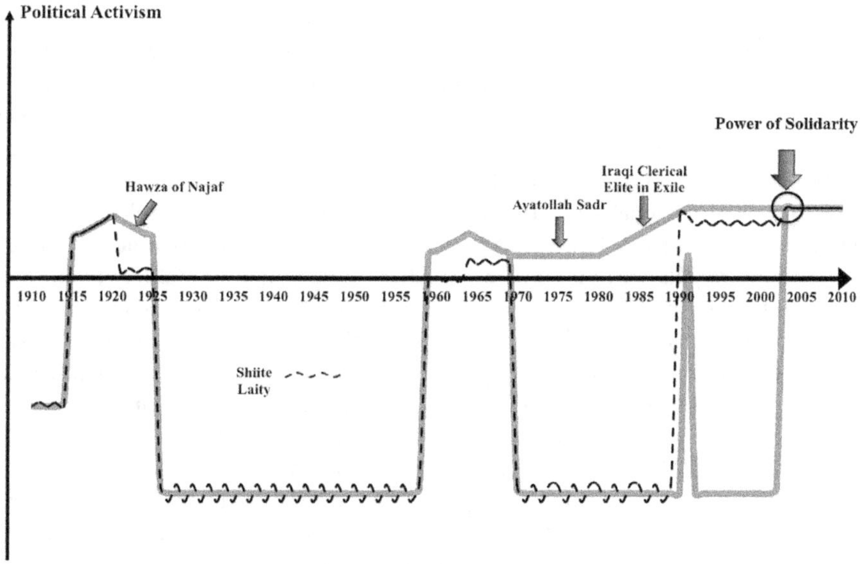

Figure 5.1 Political activism of mujtahids in modern Iraq.

established the Iraqi monarchy. Over more than three decades, Shiʿi clerics in Iraq preferred to stay out of politics and to focus on strengthening the status of the Najaf seminary. At the same time, in neighbouring Iran, the Qum seminary was becoming more important in terms of Shiʿi clergy leadership globally.

With the abolition of the Hashemite Monarchy in Iraq, the Shiʿi clerical elites in Iraq perceived a relatively open political opportunity to become active. This is when Shiʿi movements, like the Islamic Dawa, with the support of the Najaf Marja'iyya emerged onto the political scene in Iraq. For a decade, a group of Shiʿi clerics was offered favourable circumstances for broadcasting their opinions concerning the sociopolitical affairs of the community. The spiritual leadership of Grand Ayatollah Muhsin Al-Hakim, and unique ijtihad of Muhammad Baqir Sadr were two important clerical engagements in Shiʿi politics in Iraq at the time. Nonetheless, with the rise of Baʿthists in Iraq and the state repressions of the Shiʿi clergy, the political opportunity structure became once unfavourable for clerical activism. Concurrently, the establishment of the Islamic Republic in Iran intensified the hostility of the state against the Shiʿi community, which had been alarmed by the rise of their coreligionists in neighbouring country. This eventually led to the annihilation of Muhammad Baqir Sadr by Saddam's regime in 1980.

The Iran–Iraq War (1980–8) put the Shiʿi leadership residing in Najaf into an even more unfavourable position in terms of opportunity structure for political activism. The accurate perception of Grand Ayatollah Khoei, then the leader of the Najaf seminary, made him remain politically quiet hoping to preserve the very existence of the Shiʿi centre in Iraq, confronted with the arbitrary rule of Saddam.

Iraqis' miseries were increased when, after signing a ceasefire with Iran, the government of Baghdad occupied Kuwait and later engaged in the Gulf War in the early 1990s. Defeated in the war, the Shiʿis and Kurds in Iraq orchestrated a popular uprising in March 1991 against the regime of Saddam. For the Shiʿi clerical leadership, which had previously felt abandoned by the masses, they misperceived the relatively open opportunity and delayed in becoming active. This misperception was eventually considered to be one of the main reasons for the failure of the uprising.[137] The death of the prestigious Khoei in 1992 took place at a most critical time for the Shiʿi community.

By this time, at an international level, Iraq was under the most crippling financial sanctions. At a regional level, the majority of countries felt resentful of Saddam's administration and saw him as a threat to regional instability. At a national level, the Iraqis were polarized into different political camps. At a societal level, Shiʿis felt betrayed by the United States, which did not support them during the uprising, and they were under severe state repression. The Shiʿi seminary, at bureaucratic level, was virtually dismantled and mosques were closed by official order. And finally, at an individual level, there was seemingly a divergence of opinions between Grand Ayatollah Muhammad Muhammad Sadeq Sadr and the mainstream of the Shiʿi Marja'iyya in Najaf over the political posture the Shiʿi clergy should take.

In such a context, interpreting the political opportunity as open, Grand Ayatollah Sadr initiated the Sadr II movement and became relatively active in politics. Nonetheless, he failed to mobilize the laity against Saddam's regime, perhaps at least partially due to the lack of alignment with other elites at the time, and he was assassinated in 1999. On the other hand, the clergy of Najaf, under the leadership of Grand Ayatollah Sistani, remained politically quiet, as they perceived the political opportunity structure to be closed. The upcoming events proved that the judgement of the latter group over the political structure was more accurate than that of Sadr's. At the same time, those Shiʿi groups who had fled the country initiated a process of lobbying with international and regional powers to topple the Baʿth regime in Iraq.

The war on terror campaign, provided a political opportunity for the Shiʿi leadership and Operation Iraqi Freedom, aiming to overthrow Saddam Hussein, began on 20 March 2003. With the abolition of the Baʿth regime in Iraq, the Shiʿi clergy perceived an open opportunity structure and became active in post-2003 Iraq. The clerical leadership succeeded in seizing an opportunity in favour of the Iraqi Shiʿis and the community was rewarded with the highest sociopolitical status in the current era; this was the status they had waited for since the establishment of the country.

6

Lebanon 2006

The networked Shiʿi mujtahids

The last two chapters discussed how the activities of Shiʿi clerical elites, shaped by their perceptions about the political opportunity structure – the context – led to the formation of the first Shiʿi state in Iran and the ascent of the Shiʿi majority in Iraq. The aim of this chapter is to evaluate the trajectory of the activism of Shiʿi clerical elites in Lebanon over the last five decades. The Lebanese Shiʿi community tends to be misunderstood, not only by outsiders but also by other Shiʿi communities in the Middle East. One reason for this is the complicated politics of Lebanon, and especially its sectarian heterogeneity. An account of Lebanese politics becomes even more complex when the unique Shiʿi personalities, whose actions have influenced the community since the mid-twentieth century, are added to the analysis. In order to describe the process that has transformed the ever-quiescent Shiʿi minority in Lebanon into one of the most politically active communities in the region, this chapter will scrutinize the post-Ottoman roots of the sect and will trace its various political movements up until Hezbollah's War with Israel in 2006.

The main aim of this chapter is to depict the elements of opportunity structure at international, regional and national levels, which have ultimately shaped today's Lebanon and have shaped today's Shiʿi community. It starts by covering the period from the late Ottoman, Mandate Lebanon, and to the establishment of the Republic in Lebanon. To underpin the relevant structural political opportunities that have influenced Shiʿi activism in Lebanon, it goes through the foundation of sectarianism in the late nineteenth century and the geographical diffusion of Lebanese sects. It then describes how the different Lebanese communities took part in the establishment of the 'Greater Lebanon' upon the disintegration of the Ottoman Empire, under the French Mandate; and how the Lebanese notables eventually compromised the National Pact, *Mithaq al-Watani*, and institutionalized the country's confessional political order.

This chapter also concentrates on the role of Imam Musa Sadr, his unique personality, and how his perception about the political structure of Lebanon – the context – has revived the Shiʿi community in Lebanon. To this end, the brief activities of the Imam will be discussed to describe how he succeeded in mobilizing the community and transforming it from being a quiet yet ineffective sect to becoming the single most active community in Lebanon during the 1960s to the 33-Days War of

2006. This section begins by introducing Imam Musa Sadr as the leader who seized the opportunities and actively sought to elevate the community's status for the first time in the history of Lebanon. Relatively speaking, by recalling snapshots of his activities in Lebanon and presenting his unique ijtiahd, the chapter goes on to emphasize his legacies for the community.

The chapter tries to shed further light on the rise of Shiʿi political activism prompted by the mysterious disappearance of Imam Sadr and the establishment of the Islamic Republic of Iran. For the first decade after the loss of its charismatic leader, the Shiʿi community experienced an interim phase full of hostilities and inter-sectarian conflicts, until the establishment of Lebanon's second republic in the early 1990s. The final part of the chapter covers the role of Shiʿi political activism in forming the solid resistance movement against the threat of Israel. The termination of the Cold War, the start of a new phase in the Arab–Israeli conflict and the emergence of the so-called Resistance-Axis in the Middle East have formed the post-1990s politics of the community and Lebanon at a broader level. Therefore, the focus here is to elaborate on the merging form of political activism, which the Shiʿi community of Lebanon currently represents, under the leadership of its new charismatic leader, Sayyid Hassan Nasrallah. To this end, the political opportunity structure of post-2000 Lebanon is examined in relation to the Shiʿi community and its overarching influence throughout the country and the region.

Second-class citizens: The Shiʿis of Lebanon

Lebanon has formed a bridge between the West and East since ancient times. Phoenicians, the early inhabitants of the territory which is known today as Lebanon, were among those pioneer civilizations who were influential in creating language and developing regulated trade. This history, along with its fertile land, is an innate part of Lebanon's context. The distinctiveness of the Lebanese entity in relation to other parts of the Ottoman Empire, especially Syria, has its roots in the historical events that happened during the nineteenth century.[1]

The demographic distribution of its three major sects, which has had an important impact on the sociopolitical development of the country up until today, follows the contours of its three distinctive geographical clusters: coastal cities, mountainous areas and peripheries.[2] Afraid of Egypt's Sunni Mamluk Dynasty and, later, of the Ottoman rulers, the Shiʿi community settled in peripheral areas, including the South of Lebanon and Baalbek in the Beqaa Valley, in order to protect themselves from oppression. Following the rise of sectarian conflicts and based on the Ottomans' Tanzimat land reforms, aiming to preserve the Sultanate's territorial integrity, Mount Lebanon Mutessarifate was offered to Christians and they became exempt from military service.[3]

By the late nineteenth century, the sociopolitical structure of Lebanon had been formed with every religious sect attached to certain geographical areas: Sunni became a majority within the coastal cities; the mountains became the Christians' stronghold, while the Shiʿis were marginalized in the peripheries of the South and the Beqaa. The geography, and the unique sectarian characteristics of Lebanon, have led to the development of an elite class, with an extensive role in the politics of the country, and the concept of Za'imism.[4] The Zu'ama were notable Lebanese families and figures whose power perhaps first emerged based on land, as they were among the major landowners in rural areas.[5]

The Za'im was the focal point of the feudal client–patron relationships that formed in the eighteenth century, alongside the sectarianism that developed in the late nineteenth century and shadowed the country's political structure at least until the late twentieth century. Hence, the Lebanese became more attached to their communities that conglomerated around a Za'im than to their religious sects or national identity. For example, a Shiʿi commoner in Beqaa tended to introduce himself firstly as a member of the Haidar Family, then a Shiʿi and, maybe eventually, as Lebanese. Therefore, to understand the politics of Lebanon, one must consider the characteristics of this elite class and the relationship which it has with the laity in each sect's geographical stronghold. This Zai'm–laity relationship has been influenced by the political opportunity structure, at an individual, societal and national level since then.[6]

Nevertheless, with the emergence of modern commercial centres around Lebanese ports, especially Beirut, feudal power was complemented with business professionalism. The agriculture industry lost its influence in the country's economy, while industries like tourism, banking and finance were becoming the main ingredient of economic development as well as the sources of political power.[7] Obviously, to become an influential businessman in the expanding metropolitan cities, one needed to be among those who had previously been major rural landowners.[8] In this regard, the rural Zu'ama, who had built their political apparatus within their relevant communities, became the elite political actors in urban areas like Beirut, and the most influential political players, especially at the dusk of the Ottoman Empire.

In the early years of the twentieth century, the region witnessed the emergence of two major developments: the Arab Awakening throughout the Ottoman Empire, and the direct intervention of European powers in the aftermath of the Great War.[9] There was an active ideology of Arab unity, from Morocco at the western edge of the Atlantic Ocean to Oman neighbouring the Arabian Sea; it was a pervasive ideology during the early twentieth century. Arabism had become an 'oppositional cultural-political identification' against the Ottomans.[10] In Lebanon, Muslims, especially the Sunni community, embraced the ideology to elevate their social status. This, however, promised a series of conflicts in Lebanon as, concurrently, Britain and France were keen to protect the confessional groups of Mount Lebanon after the demise of the Ottoman Empire. The Maronites, and more generally Christians, were under the sponsorship of France, the *Merciful Mother* of Christians of the region. With the victory of the Allies in the Great War, France was offered the mandate over Syria and Lebanon. The inhabitants of the new mandate were divided into two groups: the Muslims, most of whom were seeking to establish the Greater Syria; and the mainly non-Muslim majority in Mount Lebanon, who sought to establish an independent Lebanon through the annexation of the coastal cities of Beirut, Tripoli and Sidon, along with the fertile Beqaa Valley in the north.[11] Eventually, in September 1920, the French High Commissioner, General Gouraud, declared the establishment of Greater

Lebanon with Beirut as its capital. However, predictably, this signalled the outbreak of internal tensions between Christians and Muslims, who felt defeated.

The Shiʿi community played a critical role in easing the conflict. While the French administration acknowledged the Shiʿi as an independent sect, it hoped to attain the support of the community for Lebanese statehood. In January 1926, Shiʿis were granted the right to have their own sectarian court based on the Ja'fari School of Jurisprudence.[12] For them, it was indeed a more promising outlook to become a minority with guaranteed rights in a smaller Lebanon rather than to be a minority in a Greater Syria in which they would have no tangible power.[13] The gamble paid off for the French and Christians in Lebanon, as the divide between Muslims finally led to the establishment of the Democratic Republic of Lebanon under the French Mandate in September 1926. Though the Shiʿis were recognized, not as a minor part of the Muslim community but as an autonomous sect among other Lebanese sects, the new structure was disadvantageous for the community to some extent. In the South, the rural Shiʿi farmers became disconnected from Haifa, as it was then under the British Mandate, and in the North, the Shiʿis of the Beqaa, were cut off from Damascus. This was drastic for Shiʿis. Moreover, in contrast to Christian farmers, who were mainly landowners, the majority of Shiʿi farmers were poor peasants working within a major feudal system. Subsequently, the Shiʿi community was split in two: those who acknowledged pan-Arabism and those who believed that Lebanese identity would provide them with greater prosperity. This schism resulted in the emergence of an amorphous community which, in coming decades, suffered even more as Shiʿis in Lebanon were trapped between the two major communities of Lebanon geographically: Sunni Muslims from central Lebanon and Maronite Christians from the heights.[14]

Independent Lebanon: The outcast Shiʿi community

The tension between the Sunni adherents of Greater Syria and the Maronites became an enduring issue in the politics of the country. It was in such circumstances that a Sunni leader from Tripoli, Muhammad al-Jisr, became the first to indicate Sunni willingness to take a more direct role in the politics of Lebanon under the French Mandate and to settle the sectarian conflict. In 1927, he was appointed Speaker of Lebanon's Chamber of Deputies. After this, more Sunnis became eager to take part in the politics of the new republic.[15]

In order to protect the Christian stronghold in Lebanon, the French administration conducted the first, and the last until the present day, National Census in 1932. The census was structured in a way that provided Lebanese Christians, and especially the Maronites, with a disproportionate share of political authority in relation to the other Lebanese sects.[16] This ramification of the Lebanese 1932 census became the political cornerstone of the country for the coming decades. The confessional apparatus, economic development, political mobility and, perhaps, all the policies of the state from the 1930s to the 1980s were derived from the demographic 'findings' of this census; and as long as its data favoured the Maronite community, it became the sect's touchstone for political supremacy in Lebanon.

In 1934, in the aftermath of the census, the post of president of the Republic went to a Maronite,[17] the single majority sect in the country, while three years later, the Sunni, the second largest sect, received the same guarantee of control over the post of the premiership. Perhaps one of the main factors that provided the Sunni with a significant share of political power in Lebanon was their bargaining power, which was brokered by the Sunni Zu'ama from the coastal cities. Since 1923, the Sunni notables had pursued a systematic policy of cooperating with the Maronites and the French, based on opposition to attaching Beirut, Tripoli and Sidon to a Greater Lebanon. The lack of organization structure among the Shiʿi community in Lebanon, coupled with internal rivalry among Shiʿi Zu'ama, had prevented the community from seizing the political opportunity, in contrast to their co-religionists, the Sunni Muslims. Without these factors, they could have guaranteed for themselves a more viable authority, as they constituted the third biggest sect in Lebanon in those years – they missed the opportunity and any breakthrough as their sectarian interests were postponed to at least a decade later.

However, the conflict between pro-Western Maronites and the Sunnis, who were more inclined towards Arab Nationalism, was far from having reached a clear settlement in Lebanon as a result of the power-sharing formula that the two communities had concluded.[18] The Maronite fear of being overwhelmed by the pan-Arabism of Muslim countries on the one hand, and the Lebanese Sunni community's worry over Western hegemony on the other hand, resulted in a series of intra-sectarian negotiations. The Zu'ama of both communities were hoping to come up with a more pragmatic solution to the future of Lebanon. Having interfered in Lebanese politics, Damascus and Cairo – which had had a successful set of negotiations with the Western powers – sent a green light to Lebanese Sunni leaders with regard to accepting the independence of Lebanon and cooperating with more moderate Maronite political figures.[19] The weak position of France as a result of its involvement in the Second World War provided an opportunity to a Maronite politician, Bechara al-Khoury, and a Sunni Za'im, Riad al-Solh, to lay down a framework for the country's independence and the abolition of the French Mandate in Lebanon in 1943. The unwritten covenant agreed between the two on behalf of their respective sects became known as the National Pact, *Mithaq al-Watani*. According to this Pact, which formed the backbone of the country's political structure for the next five decades, Christians agreed not to seek Western intervention and to accept the Arab character of Lebanon, while Muslims agreed to give up their aspiration to unite with Syria and to stay loyal to the Lebanese borders of 1920.[20] The National Pact was designed, in a way, to guarantee the Lebanese political status quo at the time; Maronite presidency and Sunni premiership became a formal agreement based on the Pact. Later in 1946, the post of Speaker of the National Assembly went to the Shiʿi sect, the third largest community in Lebanon at the time. The Pact guaranteed Maronite leaders the ability to make the most of their demographic power and guaranteed the Zu'ama of other sects the institutionalization of their power to mediate between their own sects and the government over Muslim participation in the political processes of the country. As mentioned earlier, the Pact was enacted as a way of dealing with the confessional diversity of Lebanon. However, it was founded on defective assumptions that the political opportunity structure would remain intact, the demographic proportions of the country would remain unchanged and the regional and international balance of power would never alter. Subsequent events proved these assumptions to be invalid and pushed Lebanon towards the violent conflicts in 1958 and the fifteen years of civil war that commenced in 1975.

The Republic of Lebanon: The Shiʿis plea for new leadership

The major impact of the National Pact on the politics of a sectarian and fragmented Lebanon was to give a monopoly of power to two sects, Maronite Christians and Sunni Muslims, and to disregard the other sects. It initiated a new political structure in Lebanon, which could be characterized as 'Political Maronite';[21] in such a political system, all other Lebanese sects were under the supremacy of Maronite rule. The president and the chief of the National Army were to be Maronite, while the majority of cabinet seats and the National Assembly were reserved for the Christians according to terms of the Pact. For a Shiʿi Za'im to become the Speaker of the National Assembly, he had to have the support of the Maronite leadership. The Speaker of the Assembly had been appointed for a shorter term than both president and prime minister. If he maintained Maronite support, he would hope to remain in office for another year; otherwise, he had to step aside and give up his position to another Shiʿi Za'im who had succeeded in attaining the support of the Maronite president. These factors all meant that the Shiʿi notables and their relevant communities were in a lower position than those of the Maronites and Sunni Zu'ama. Adding to this, as of the discontents in Lebanon's geography, at the midst of the new Republic, while Maronite and Sunni elites were in a position to serve the interests of their respective sects closer to the centre, the Shiʿi Zu'ama of notable families predictably became more disassociated from the community and its demands.[22] Since the majority of Shiʿi laities lived at a distance from the most developed areas of the country (central Mount Lebanon, Beirut and Tripoli), this gap was expanded inadvertently. Less than two decades after independence, Lebanon's commercial hubs, the strongholds of Sunni Muslims and Maronite Christians, were flourishing economically more than ever, due to the development of tourism and finance industries;[23] yet the majority of the Shiʿi community was marginalized in the peripheries of the country, excluded from enjoying the benefits of national economic growth.

Seeking for better lives and hoping to find more opportunities, the downtrodden Shiʿis of the south flooded into and settled in the peripheries of Beirut.[24] In addition to this rural–urban migration that, perhaps, had been started decades earlier, some Shiʿi groups, mainly from the sect's middle class, migrated abroad and dispersed to various countries, ranging from the Persian Gulf to South Africa; this created a substantial Shiʿi Lebanese diaspora mostly employed in high-ranking businesses. They became some of the most reliable financial supporters of their community back in Lebanon, later in the 1970s.[25] These two Shiʿi migration trends, from peripheries to the outskirts of Beirut, as well as to overseas, changed the political opportunity structure in favour of the community over the coming decades. Although, at the time, most Shiʿis still relied on the Zu'ama. In urban areas, to be recruited by a decent employer, they still needed to trust their Zu'ama and their mediating brokerage with the Zu'ama of other sects.[26]

The Arab Nationalism–Western Imperialism encounters influenced the political mise en scène of the Middle East for decades. Egypt, Syria, Jordan and Iraq, along with Arab Palestinians, became involved in the war with the newly established Israel, challenging its very existence in 1948. Although Lebanon declared its reluctance to participate on the Arab front, the first Arab–Israeli war had a tangible impact on the country's internal politics. Divided at home around the Palestinian cause issue, Lebanon's government signed the armistice with Israel to secure the country's border.[27] The war resulted in the defeat of Arab forces, occupation of Arab territories in Palestine, and the mass immigration of Palestinian refugees to the neighbouring Arab countries, including Lebanon. Since then, the Palestinian refugees and their quest to return to their homeland has played a determining role in shaping the realpolitik of the region.

With the outbreak of the Cold War, the activities of Leftist parties, which were extremely appealing to the Arab masses at the time, were strengthened in the Middle East countries, including Lebanon.[28] Leftist groups active in Lebanon, were more successful in recruiting among the middle classes, inhabitants of the bigger cities and, especially, rural emigrants who had been moving from the peripheries of the country to settle around major cities. The Shiʿi youths, willing to play a more prominent social role and to gain access to sources of income, were among the major new members of these parties.[29]

Therefore, the deficiencies of the Lebanese National Pact became clear for the first time in 1958. President Camille Chamoun's refusal to break diplomatic relations with France and Britain, two of the countries that initiated military action against Egypt in the Suez War, put him in direct opposition to Nasser, and to Nasser's supporters within Lebanon, including Lebanon's Prime Minister, Rashid Karami. This ignited a conflict of interests between Chamounists, mostly Maronites, and opposition groups, among them the followers of Sunni and Druze Zu'ama, who were excluded from national politics by the president, and eventually prompted the national turmoil in 1958.

Then, the opposition rebelled and demonstrated in the streets against the government, while supporting Nasser's aspirations and the Arabic face of Lebanon. With the fall of the pro-Western Iraqi monarchy on 14 July 1958, Chamoun asked for US military intervention. The United States responded by sending about 14,000 Marines to Lebanon.[30] The country was on the verge of a civil war, and bloodshed in some cities, like Tripoli, escalated. During the turmoil, the Lebanese Army and its Maronite chief commander, General Fouad Chehab, remained neutral towards both hostile parties, aiming to preserve the country's territorial integrity.[31] Conceivably, this was the single most important factor that made the opposition parties, mainly Muslims, reach a compromise on the presidency and settle the dispute. Over the next six years, Chehab initiated a new phase in the history of Lebanon, later to be known as the Chehabist era. Despite some internal opposition, especially from Christians,[32] Chehab's political policies were continued through the election of a pro-Chehabist president, Charles Hilu, in 1964, thus extending Lebanon's prosperous civil society for six more years.[33]

Chehab's reforms undermined the reign of the Zu'ama and opened a new phase in Lebanon.[34] His administrative reforms were designed to promote national unity by involving all Lebanese sects in state power. Whereas historically Christians, especially Maronites, held the majority of public posts, Chehab started to change the established sectarian set-up in favour of minorities. Until then, Maronites had ensured that public offices were filled by individuals whose views were in accord with those of Maronite leaders and powerful families. Chehab began to dismantle this oligarchy that had controlled Lebanese politics since 1945.[35] This move was especially favourable for Sunni and Druze Muslims, who were among the most educated minorities. However, it also provoked a dramatic rural–urban migration, especially among those populations who were living in poverty in the peripheral areas of the country, and who were willing to seek better jobs in the big cities.[36] Chehab's policies were also targeted at the Shiʿi community, mainly rural dwellers without higher education.[37]

During the Chehabist era in Lebanon, Muslims became more involved in national affairs; hence, the Lebanese identity was institutionalized among them for the first time since independence. Chehab's reforms were sometimes implemented to the dismay of some Christians and members of the Shiʿi and Sunni Zu'ama; yet what encouraged the majority of middle- and lower-class Lebanese to wholeheartedly support his initiatives was rooted in political evolutions that were going on outside Lebanon as well.

To the favour of the Shiʿi community in Lebanon, the rise of Chehabism coincided with the emergence of a novel clerical leadership. To this end, the migration of an Iranian-born cleric, Musa Sadr, to Lebanon in the middle of the 1958 conflict, marked the beginning of a historic era, not only for the Shiʿi community but also for contemporary Lebanon. Franz König, a Cardinal of the Catholic Church, expressed this when he addressed Sadr saying: 'Your Majesty, I heard a lot about you. I believe that the history of Lebanon should be divided into two phases: the era of pre- Musa Sadr, and the Musa Sadr's era.'[38]

The Reformist mujtahid: Musa Sadr's perceptions and postures

In the volatile context of the post-1958 conflict in Lebanon, the migration of Musa Sadr to Lebanon was seen as a golden opportunity for the Shiʿi community as it coincided with the mass rural–urban migration of Shiʿi peoples, and the commencement of the Chehabist reform era in Lebanon. He himself changed Lebanon's opportunity structure, on an individual level, for the Shiʿi community for the coming decades. Born in 1928 to the elite Shiʿi family of Sadr in Qum, Musa's ancestors were among the most prestigious Shiʿi clerical elites of Jabal Amel in Lebanon, with widespread activities and fame in Iraq and Iran at the time. Musa started to study Shiʿi jurisprudence under the teachings of his father, brother and many other Shiʿi elites of the Qum seminary, including Ayatollah Khomeini.[39]

Young Musa was among the most reformist clerics of the Qum seminary. Nonetheless, after a while, he perceived that the structure of Qum and its powerful traditionalist clergy were themselves obstacles in the way of his aspirations. The opportunity structure was not favourable for him and his colleagues to become active independently. At the same time, he was offered two opportunities: to act as Grand Ayatollah Burujirdi's ambassador in the Vatican,[40] and to go to Lebanon upon the receipt of an invitation from his relatives, Allameh Sharaf al-Din's sons. In 1959, he chose the latter offer, seeking an opportunity to follow his aspirations to elevate the Shiʿi position in the modern world. His older brother, Sayyid Reza Sadr, mentions that, if Sayyid Musa had not been offered such an option to go to Lebanon, he would have chosen to take off his religious attire and to start a different life as a civilian lawyer in Iran.[41] Thus, Musa Sadr indeed owed his future status as one of the most prominent Shiʿi clerics of the century, to Lebanon, a debt that he started to pay off to all Lebanese from the first day he set foot in Lebanon.

Sadr had visited Tyre in Lebanon once in 1955, as a guest of Allameh Sharaf al-Din, the Shiʿi leader of the area. Abd al-Husayn Sharaf al-Din was among the renowned students of Akhund Khorasani in Najaf. After he finished his studies in the Najaf seminary, he moved back to live in the city of Chehour and later in Tyre for the rest of his life. Hoping to reduce the enduring Sunni pressures on the Shiʿi community since the rule of the Ottomans, he devoted his activities to Islamic unity.[42] The main facet of Sharaf al-Din's leadership in Lebanon was the foundation of modern schools in the area.[43] Historically, the Lebanese Shiʿi clerical elites relied on the financial support of the Shiʿi Zu'ama; but, in what was perhaps the first time in the modern history of Lebanon, the laity and their endowments solely financed a school for the Shiʿi students of Tyre, established by Sharaf al-Din. He believed that the first step towards activating the community was to diminish their illiteracy so that they could grasp equal opportunities along with other sects in Lebanon. Although Sharaf al-Din succeeded in preserving a degree of independence from the Shiʿi Zu'ama of the south, the scope of his activities barely extended beyond the city of Tyre and its suburbs. However, his school, al-Ja'fariyya, was one of the cornerstones on which Musa Sadr built his legacy in Lebanon over the following decades.

Upon the recommendation of Sharaf al-Din and invitations from his sons, Musa Sadr went to Lebanon to reside there in 1959. With the Shiʿi community having lost its prominent leader, Allameh Sharaf al-Din, the Shiʿi Zu'ama of the south, who felt threatened by the arrival of the young aspirant Sadr, sought to engender hostility among Shiʿi clerics in order to divide and rule.[44] Nonetheless, Jabal Amil had continued to enjoy the status in the Shiʿi world that it had developed as a result of its more than four centuries of religious heritage. During Safavid Persia, there were Shiʿi ulama of this region that contributed to the rule of the Shiʿi monarch for the first time in history. However, the constant pressure of Sunni Ottomans over the community and its religious scholars had, over the course of two centuries, left the Shiʿi of Lebanon in a pitiful state. Furthermore, Shiʿi clerics in Lebanon had been transformed into some of the most inactive and ineffective elements within the community. In general, Shiʿi clerical elites had become the Zu'ama's brokers, and the laity had become used to seeing them in this light.[45] Their activities were limited to reading funeral or wedding sermons in return for the money they would receive from Shiʿi laymen. Musa Sadr changed these circumstances; and while this provided him with the support of the Shiʿi community, it also earned him the resentment of some Shiʿi clerics.[46] Indeed he mentioned once that he had come to Lebanon in order to 'wipe away the dust that has been sitting on the Shiʿi Cleric's habit'.[47]

Sadr's grand ambition was to elevate the status of the Shiʿi community in Lebanon, to reshape its organizational structure, to make it a sect distinct from, rather than inferior to, other Lebanese sects. He believed that, based on its geographical situation, Lebanon was a unique showroom in which the acts of its inhabitants were revealed to the view of Western communities, and that it, thus, was essential for Shiʿi scholars, including himself, to represent their sect to the rest of the world and to improve the status of Lebanese Shiʿis in Lebanon.[48] It was this perception that led him to commence intra-religious talks from his early days in Lebanon. Contrary to the leaders of some other Lebanese sects, he desired that all Lebanese, irrespective of which religion, should live together peacefully, free from sectarian discrimination. This was the goal to which he devoted his life, up until his last days in Lebanon.[49]

As a result of his mould-breaking ideas, in the late summer of 1961, Sadr was approached by a group of Christian Patriarchs, Cardinals and Bishops in Lebanon, as a representative of the new Muslim elite, seeking his support and a mutual relationship.[50] In his dealings with the state, then led by President Fouad Chehab, Sadr had indicated his sincere support for Chehabist reforms by visiting him personally several times. The alignment of Musa Sadr and Fouad Chehab deepened over the coming years based on their mutual interests in pursuing an inclusive approach to Lebanese national sovereignty and integrity, despite its multi-sectarian nature. Consequently, Chehab remained one of the most significant supporters of Musa Sadr among other Christian politicians.

With regard to intra-sectarian cooperation, Musa Sadr had believed that the Lebanese could benefit from their heterogeneous society if they interacted more with each other and developed a mutual understanding. For him, sectarian discrimination was one of the greatest factors threatening Lebanon's integrity at the time. He expressed this view in an address to a gathering in Tyre in 1962:

> We have lived in Lebanon for decades. Yet most of us have not developed a sense of national patriotism . . . have you ever seen Christian clerics stress that Muslims are deprived? Have you ever seen Muslim clerics worry about the underprivileged Armenians in Lebanon? If we lose the sincere nationalistic sense, our home becomes strange to us while we also become strangers in our home. My concern is that if we continue our current sectarian behaviour, soon nothing will remain of Lebanon.[51]

For his part, Sadr intended to influence the political structure in Lebanon and to mitigate the devastating role of sectarianism that had crippled the country for decades. After six years in Lebanon, Musa Sadr visited Iran in 1965, and was received warmly by his companions in Tehran, Qum and several other cities where he visited as a guest speaker. He was willing to attract the alignment of his fellow clergy all around the Shiʿi world, to facilitate a transnational network that may one day help him to mobilize the Shiʿi community in the region. At the time, Musa Sadr had become a famous cleric. This drew SAVAK's—Iran National Organization for Security and Intelligence (1957–1979)—attention to his trips to Iran and its concern to discover more about Sadr's opinions about the Shah's regime and the region. However, the intelligence documents disclosed after the collapse of the Shah's regime confirm that SAVAK had misunderstood Sadr's political affiliation and ideology.[52] He continued his visit in Iran in spite of all SAVAK's controls and, in a speech he delivered in Shiraz, asked Iranians to rise up and become more active in the politics of their country. In his speech he said:

> I do not know why you people are inactive. Why do our women not have religious gatherings? Why do they not study in modern schools? You people should not leave your religious leaders alone. You should believe that a Muslim is always successful either to achieve his goals or not . . . . Fear is misery, we have to rise up and proceed courageously, believing that God is the saviour of Muslims and the patron of their leaders.[53]

His speech clearly indicates how the supposedly quiet Shiʿi clerics had become politically active during six years, and invites the community to assume their place among other politically active nations in the Muslim World.

Back in Lebanon, Musa Sadr's activities began to explicitly advance his aim to establish a Shiʿi Council, an official body able to support the rights of the deprived Shiʿi in Lebanon and represent their demands to the central government. In a meeting with the president, Charles Hilu, Musa Sadr clearly presented what the southerners were seeking, and asked that the state support the development of the underprivileged areas.[54] Such activities brought Sadr incomparable popularity within the community. He was seen as a person who not only wanted to engender a sense of nationalism within all sects, but also backed the rights of the Shiʿi community. Nonetheless, the more popular he became in Lebanon, the more he attracted hostility from other sources of power, especially the Shiʿi Zu'ama.[55] It seemed that Sadr was more successful in seizing the opportunity to attract the support of the community than the traditional Zu'ama. The activities of Sadr and his initiatives were going to change the balance of power, to the dismay of the traditional feudal landowners. This did eventually provoke them to do whatever was in their power to protect their client–patron relationship. However, this new actor who had emerged on the political scene of Lebanon, Musa Sadr, was changing the political opportunity structure so that it was unfavourable to the Zu'ama at least within the Shiʿi community.

Later, Musa Sadr attended a rally in Beqaa and addressed those who were urging the appointment of a Shiʿi leader to represent the community. He stated:

> Half of Shiʿi villages are underprivileged . . . the question is why are we oppressed and deprived? We are oppressed due to the lack of religious integrity among ourselves, and to compensate for this shortage, we require a religious council that can deal with commoners' religious demands . . . . We need to be organised like other Lebanese sects.[56]

These were the initial moves made by Musa Sadr to gain an effective sociopolitical role in Lebanon, and towards founding the Supreme Islamic Shiʿi Council, an assembly representing the Shiʿi community in government, which was eventually acknowledged by the National Assembly in May 1967. Later, in 1969, he was officially elected as the council's first leader, with the title of Imam. Yet he was under serious attack from some of the Shiʿi Zu'ama who were witnessing how their political power over the community was fading due to the Imam's ever-increasing popularity, not only within the community but also throughout Lebanon and perhaps among some regional leaders.

At the same time as the Arab Defeat in the Six-Day War, Imam Musa Sadr issued a statement asking all Arabs to learn from this experience, to retreat and to believe that the war with Israel was not yet finished. He then promised that 'with the support of God the final triumph is ours'.[57] This was the public commencement of the Imam's 'resistance discourse' against what he entitled the 'Absolute Evil', Israel. He declared:

> The illegitimacy of the Israeli regime is evident to everyone, as is the legitimacy of the Palestinian resistance. We all know that from the early history of the Israeli government, they had adopted a racist stance. We are facing an illegitimate regime, which does not even act according to its own religious book . . . . Therefore, I should announce here, that to support the Palestinian cause, to liberate al-Quds, we all have to actively ally ourselves together. We have to put our marginal disparities aside in order to achieve victory over Israel.[58]

However, the Palestinian question was not as straightforward as it appeared initially in Lebanon. The Israeli threats, the inability of Arab leaders to deal with them, and an increasing number of Palestinian refugees in Lebanon became three of the most influential factors in Lebanon's politics and came to overshadow most of the Imam's endeavours to solve the problems of the South. In this, Imam Sadr was still under attack from some Shiʿi Zu'ama, which placed additional restrictions on his activities.[59]

Imam Sadr considered the Palestinian question to be one of the most important humanitarian and religious concerns for all citizens. However, the irresponsible activities of Palestinian Liberation Organization (PLO) fighters in the South brought more misery to the Lebanese inhabitants of the area. Imam Sadr sought to maintain a balance between support for the Palestinians and for the welfare of the southerners, but his actions were limited by the heterogeneous organization of the PLO, and the fear that the Sunnis might regard the Lebanese Shiʿis as traitors.[60]

Among all Palestinian leaders, Yasser Arafat was the one in whom Imam Sadr had the most faith. The cooperation between the Imam and Arafat's *Fatah* organization provided the foundation for a series of cooperative activities in the coming years. However, it soon became evident that Arafat did not have full authority over all PLO factions and their activities in Lebanon. The Imam valued, above all, the alliance with the Palestinians in pursuit of their sacred cause. He constantly referred to this alliance as the unity between the deprived *in* their homeland, the Lebanese Shiʿi, and the deprived *from* their homeland, the Palestinian refugees.[61]

After Hafez al-Assad assumed the presidency in Syria, Imam Musa Sadr went to Damascus to congratulate him in May 1971. From the Imam's point of view, Assad could be seen as a resourceful regional partner for the Shiʿi community. Historically, all Lebanese sects have had international sponsors: France for the Maronites, Russia for the Greek Orthodox, Britain for the Druze, Saudi Arabia and Egypt for the Sunni Muslims.[62] In the absence of the Iranian regime, which had already showed its reluctance to support the community in Lebanon, the Alawite regime in Syria became the best alternative for the Imam and his companions in Lebanon. This led to a strategic alliance between Hafez Assad and Imam Musa Sadr, from which both parties gained greatly for several years.

In addition to seeking a regional ally that could put pressure on Lebanon's government, Imam Sadr started to organize an inter-sectarian institute that could pursue redress for the demands of all of Lebanon's underprivileged citizens. With the election of Suleiman Frangieh to the presidency in Lebanon in 1970, the development of the South had been halted again. The government's disregard left the Imam no choice but to independently pursue plans for the development of the South. In his opinion, Lebanon had two classes: the 'privileged', mainly comprised of Lebanon's renowned and powerful families, and the 'underprivileged' citizens.[63] While the former class was mainly settled in coastal cities and Mount Lebanon, the latter was driven to the peripheries; while the privileged class was receiving plenty of attention from the government, the underprivileged class was suffering from the negligence of officials. Thus, Imam Sadr became determined to reduce the gap between those classes: a passion that not only gave him popularity among Lebanese of all sects, but also attracted powerful enemies, mainly from the powerful privileged class. Despite this, he eventually founded a sociopolitical organization, not exclusive to the Shiʿi community, but belonging to all underprivileged Lebanese. Some leaders of other Lebanese sects, especially Armenians and Geek Orthodox, who were mainly settled in the South, joined him in pursuing this mission. In 1974, the Movement of the Deprived, *Harakat al-Mahrumin*, was born to advance the demands of all underprivileged Lebanese, no matter what sect they belonged to. Accusing the government of not fulfilling its responsibilities for the security of the inhabitants of the South, the Imam threatened that he would have no choice but to ask people to take up arms and to become actively engaged in establishing security for themselves.[64] He believed – and he expressed this belief through his actions – that praying and fasting and executing religious duties were not sufficient, and that God would not accept these religious obligations from those who did not perform their social responsibilities for their homeland and compatriots.[65] This turning point in the development of his political activism became apparent in his historic speech in Baalbeck, supporting the cause of the Movement. On 17 March 1974, coinciding with the Arbaeen of Imam Husayn, he addressed a crowd of 75,000 supporters, almost 10,000 of whom were armed. He stated:

> 1335 years ago, when the captive family of Imam Husayn, the resident of Baalbek welcomed them and made the troops of Yazid flee and commemorated the martyrdom of Imam Husayn for the first time in history. Today we are witnessing that just like in those eras, the void is pervasive and nobody in the government cares about the right. We have gathered here once again to oppose something that our ancestors had opposed rightfully. Upon our legitimate demands to the government officials, they accused me of dreaming the presidency; now I declare loudly, clear to all, that I do not have such an objective. I challenge the officials that, if they fulfill our rightful civil demands, I shall immediately step down forever . . . . Lebanese will remember that whatever Musa Sadr, his companions and followers have done so far was to maintain Lebanon's integrity and its security.

Resembling his movement to that of Imam Husayn's, Imam Sadr wanted to seize the most he could from the available political opportunity to attract the support of his laity followers as well as sending a strong message to the state. He then reproached Lebanese politicians, including the Shiʿi Zu'ama, who were criticizing his involvement in politics and stated,

> Now they advise me to confine myself to religious duties. I am asking them, what is religion? The religion that protects your unjust mandate and that makes people tolerate oppression is indeed not a worthy religion. How can I peacefully go to bed, while the South is under constant attacks of Israel?

At the time, Sadr was willing to broadcast his ijtihad about the sociopolitical role of Shiʿi clergy. The situation in Lebanon had made the Imam a political activist. In the middle of 1974, the turmoil between Lebanese sects, Palestinian guerillas and the warnings from Israel had reached a point that threatened a drastic encounter. It was in this political opportunity structure that Imam Sadr sought an alternative to protect deprived Lebanese and the endeavours that he had been working on for the sake of Lebanon's national integrity over the previous two decades. He had already gained enough popularity to enable him to speak loudly on behalf of deprived Lebanese of all sects. To show his determination to pursue the path he had chosen, he asked the crowd in Baalbeck to make this oath:

> We swear to God, to his Prophet. We swear by human dignity, that we shall go on to vindicate the rightful demands of our community and stand fearlessly beside all oppressed Lebanese. We stand beside what is right, throughout our homeland; we remain enemy to its enemies and hostile to Israel and its supporters.[66]

To this end, the Imam succeeded in mobilizing the community behind his grand ambition. The Baalbek gathering halted all other Lebanese politicians' activities for days. The size of the Imam's armed supporters who attended the gathering persuaded the majority of Lebanese leaders to urge the government to adopt their requested demands. In the coming days, Ghassan Tueni, the Christian editor of *An-Nahar Daily*, described the gathering as a non-sectarian revolution that 'was not a revolution of a specific sect against other sects but it was a revolution of a specific sect representing all other Lebanese sects'.[67] A group of Lebanese religious elites, politicians, and intellectuals showed their support for the Imam's statement by visiting him personally.[68]

Twenty days after the Baalbeck gathering, Maruf Saad, the Nasserist leader of Sidon, invited Imam Sadr to give a talk in the city. For the Imam, to speak in the Sunni-dominated city, was a golden opportunity to present his non-sectarian position and challenge his rivals' accusations. This time, a larger gathering showed up to support him. He addressed the gathering and said:

> If we restrict ourselves to religious praying and ignore the righteous demands of the deprived Lebanese, the oppressors would hang our pictures on walls and would worship us. But the Prophet Muhammad did not behave like this, and as his true

followers we will not stay quiet over the oppressions . . . . God has advised us to take our adornment in every mosque, today the man's adornment is his weapon.[69]

Then Imam Sadr walked and stood at the *Mihrab*[70] of the mosque, saying:

The place I am standing within, is called Mihrab. Have you ever asked yourselves, what is the relationship between war and mosque? It is called so, as this is the place to fight with the Evil; the oppressor and those who stay silent against him are both evils.[71]

These two gatherings clearly show the political manifesto of Imam Sadr and his perception around the political opportunity structure in Lebanon at the time. In April 1974, all of Lebanon saw a Shiʿi cleric who had wisely exploited his opportunities and become one of the most active political figures in the country. His perceptions about the sufferings of the Shiʿi community, along with the state's neglect, had pushed him to abandon quiescence and to become politically active in order to fight for his community's rightful demands. His reformist ijtihad and charisma made him a religious leader who was able to orchestrate social mobilization. Indeed, his supporters did not exclusively belong to the Shiʿi community, but included the majority of Lebanon's underprivileged citizens.[72] Imam Sadr's political activities were also received warmly throughout the region. A unique document in this regard is the letter Ayatollah Khomeini wrote to him while he was in exile in Najaf. In his letter, the Ayatollah addressed him warmly and wrote to him:

I wish you the best and have to send my utmost gratitude for your deeds and struggles to assert Shiʿi rights and to cut the hands off oppressors of the community in Lebanon. I pray to God to save you for all of us; I pray to God to help you in mobilising Shiʿi youths, who are ready to sacrifice themselves in the path of God . . . . I pray to God Almighty to make us, the old clerics, young and active like you . . . and let me ask you to pray for me and my future success before God.[73]

Imam Sadr's civil disobedience coincided with the 1975 turmoil in Lebanon.[74] Though Lebanon would become divided between two fronts – Leftist elements and the PLO forming one side, and their rival Maronite groups forming the other – a common goal for both fronts was to become allied with Imam Sadr and to exploit his pervasive popularity in their own interests.[75] However, the intra-sectarian status that Imam Sadr had already chosen for his political stance did not allow him to incline towards either side. Although the Palestinians were expecting the Imam to make an alliance with them in opposition to the Maronite front, there was a critical issue impeding this. Imam Sadr had always appreciated the liberation of Quds, yet treated Palestinian refugees as guests of the Lebanese and especially southerners, not as a community that sought refuge in Lebanon to settle there forever. Unlimited Palestinian settlement in the south, *Tawṭīn Filasṭīni fi janūb Lubnān*, was indeed one of the main aims of the PLO alliance with the Lebanese National Movement, and the scheme which attracted utmost strong objection from Imam Sadr.[76] In his opinion, the indefinite settlement of

Palestinians in Lebanon would spoil their sacred cause to liberate the land of Palestine, and was indeed what Israel would like to achieve. On the one hand, Imam Sadr could not ally himself with Maronite fundamentalists who were seeking the aid of Israel, the absolute evil in his view, and who were willing to establish a Maronite clone of the Jewish state of Israel in north Lebanon.[77]

Left outside the bipartite conflict in Lebanon, Imam Sadr felt obliged to form a defensive militia wing for the movement, AMAL,[78] which could protect the deprived Lebanese from the extremism of both fronts. Having militia became more vital, when the majority of deprived southerners were trapped between the strongholds of both fronts. Therefore, AMAL was established as defensive militia belonging to all Lebanese who were threatened by hostility from other political parties. The organization's charter clearly indicates two general terms for its members: believing in God and in human dignity.[79] Unlike other sectarian militia in Lebanon at the time, to become a member of AMAL, being a Shiʿi or Muslim was not obligatory. Contrary to what some scholars claim, that Imam Sadr's popularity was diminishing at the time due to his direct engagement in founding the militia,[80] the support he received from hundreds of Lebanese intellectuals from various sects who signed a petition in his support proves his message had an appeal throughout the country by the mid-1970s.[81] Imam Sadr and his supporters were committed to an independent position that not only challenged the historical status of Lebanon's Zu'ama but was also incompatible with the belligerents in the civil war at its commencement in 1975.

During the early stages of the civil war, Imam Sadr, who at the time was trusted by all Lebanese political parties, strived to arbitrate between hostile fronts, and invited them to develop a ceasefire plan and pursue reconciliation negotiations. On 20 April 1975, he invited a group of Muslim, Christian and Palestinian leaders to form a peace committee at the Supreme Islamic Shiʿi Council (SISC) office in Beirut, in order to come up with a comprehensive peace plan. He was also voted sole coordinator for the group, responsible for meeting with all hostile parties and transmitting their demands between them.[82] Praising his unique role in promoting national understanding, Karim Pakradouni, a Christian leader of the Kataeb Party, wrote in an open letter to Imam Sadr that,

> Until yesterday, we were witnessing your moves fearfully, yet today we feel concern about your own security . . . . This is not the first time that you have put yourself forward to solve a problem in our country, but it is the first time that you are the only person who could possibly play out a positive role . . . . Today you are the only politician who can come up with an exit policy for the Palestinian-Lebanese conflict . . . . And what more I can add to Gemayel's opinion, when he called you *the peace Messenger of Lebanon*.[83]

However, in the face of fierce opposition to the Imam's initiatives, mostly from the LNM and their PLO allies, who were witnessing their victory in the conflict,[84] the Imam felt obliged to organize a huge strike in order to transmit his message throughout the country. In May 1975, he took refuge at al-Safa Mosque, located in the heart of the conflict in central Beirut, and commenced a hunger strike, asking all hostile parties to put down their arms and start negotiations. In his letter, he addressed all Lebanese and said:

> Lebanon's conflict has crippled the country today . . . I have done my utmost civil and national responsibility to avoid the drastic war in our beloved homeland, yet let me add that we have never been threatened by anything more dangerous than this conflict throughout our history . . . . Ironically I believe that the conflict does not have anything to do with our sectarian disparities or even the Palestinian refugees in Lebanon at its principles . . . . Therefore, from the very first hours of its commencement, I and a group of my friends from all sects, have done our best to solve the problem, though we have not reached any definite outcome . . . . It seems that negotiations are meaningless, it seems that all ears are deaf. I hereby believe that our country requires a device more powerful than weapons, and more efficient than words, hence I found myself in the house of God to oppose those hostile parties who have polluted the soil of our country. I will continue my hunger strike, until the moment that this conflict will be wiped out from our Lebanon. I sacrifice my life to my homeland's peace, as this is the last thing I have to offer. However, for this to become fruitful, I demand the support of you Lebanese, from every corner of the country. I urge all of you to respect my action's peaceful nature and not to support it by arms. Today, I, as the helpless slave of God, am sheltered in his house, hoping he will save us all and our homeland.[85]

Through this letter and symbolic act, Imam Sadr aimed to explain to people Lebanon's political opportunity structure and how he foresaw the outcome of the conflict. Six days on, with the massive support of Lebanese civilians, the military cabinet resigned, and a new government was formed to reconcile the conflict. The ceasefire, however, was not durable since Lebanon was trapped in a heterogeneous network of internal and regional hostilities. In response to the request of the Imam and his companions from other sects, the Syrian army intervened in the conflict in Lebanon. This coincided with far more dangerous encounters between PLO guerilla fighters and the Arab Deterrent Force under the leadership of Syria.[86]

While different Lebanese parties were involved in the civil war, the blind arrogance of the Palestinian guerilla fighters in the south brought enormous misery to Lebanese inhabitants by provoking the Israeli invasion in March 1978. At the time of the invasion, Imam Sadr was in Paris attending a religious conference. In a statement he issued right after the invasion, he restated his position with respect to Israel. However, this time he indirectly blamed Palestinians and their actions as a cause of the costly consequences for the Lebanese.[87] Although over the years Imam Sadr had called Israel the most formidable threat to the region's and to Lebanon's stability, the constant disregard of Lebanon's integrity by Palestinian guerilla fighters had left him with a sense of resentment. During the 1978 invasion by Israel of Lebanon, for which thousands of inhabitants in the south paid the price, it seemed that Imam Sadr was seeking a more pragmatic solution.[88] It was then that he started to seek the assistance of some regional Arab leaders who were major financial supporters of the Palestinians at the time, to mediate in the conflict and to control the movement of the guerrillas in Lebanon. During these visits, he was constantly in contact with President Sarkis, informing him of his progress.[89] He visited King Hussein of Jordan, and King Khaled of Saudi in April 1978, and finally went to Algeria to meet with President Boumedienne in June, when he was advised to seek the assistance of Ghaddafi who, at the time, was among the most revolutionary leaders of the region.[90] Imam Sadr left Lebanon for Libya on 28 August 1978, to meet with Ghaddafi, a trip from which he never returned, leaving the Lebanese and the Shiʿi community abandoned and without a charismatic leader.

After twenty years of Imam Sadr's activities in Lebanon, his popularity among other Lebanese leaders in 1978 had never been greater.[91] He had become the voice of the Shiʿi community in Lebanon by challenging the traditional Zu'ama's position. A major catalyst for his popularity among the community was the amount of support he had received from Maraji' of Najaf and Qum. From the moment he entered Lebanon, he was in close contact with Grand Ayatollahs Al-Hakim and Khoei in Iraq, and Grand Ayatollahs Shariatmadari, Golpayegani, Milani and Marashi in Iran.[92] Additionally, he had family relations with Grand Ayatollah Khomeini who, at the time, was in exile in Iraq. Having gained massive support for his activities in Lebanon, Imam Sadr became the one and only Shiʿi religious figurehead in the community in Lebanon.

At a broader regional level, Imam Sadr contributed to the Shiʿi community in Iran during their uprising against the Shah's regime. For years, it was clear to the regime's secret service that the Imam had provided the revolutionaries with a safe haven in Lebanon. However, at the funeral of Ali Shariati, he publicly criticized the Iranian regime, calling Shariati a true hero who had connected with the silent people and made them become actively involved and rise up against the oppressor, the Shah.[93] Additionally, Imam Sadr expressed his full-fledged support for Ayatollah Khomeini and his Islamic movement and did all he could to help the Iranian movement under the leadership of the Ayatollah.[94] It is interesting that, in his last surviving written communication, his published article in *Le Monde*, dated 23 August 1978, Imam Sadr foresaw the Islamic Revolution in Iran. In his article, Imam Sadr describes the Iranian uprising as a unique movement that challenges the hegemonies of the West and the East, and that seeks to fulfil the will of the masses. He expressed his support for the movement, saying that,

> This wave that will transform the face of Iran reminds the *Call of Prophets for* revitalizing human dignity and morality . . . hence all free people around the world should support Iranians and their leader; all should condemn the bloodshed of the Shah's regime.[95]

His prediction came true just weeks later though, unfortunately for the Iranians and the Lebanese, Imam Sadr was not present to witness this victory in person. It was, however, evident that the development of Imam Sadr's robust sociopolitical network in the region, and his unique pragmatic experiences, on the one hand, and the massive support of Iranians for Imam Khomeini, on the other hand, held out the prospect of a far more prosperous future for Shiʿi Islam in the modern Middle East.[96]

The Islamic Republic of Iran, and birth of revolutionary Shiʿism in Lebanon

Almost two decades after the Imam entered Lebanon, the majority in the Shiʿi community had become politically mobilized in response to his political stance. His reformist activities addressing the country's political opportunity structure, his unique and unsurpassed charisma and personality, and his novel ijtiahd over the role of clergy in society shaped and mobilized the community's activities from the time he introduced his movement. With Imam Sadr removed from the scene, the question of the community's leadership became the most significant threat to the Shiʿi of Lebanon. The issue became even more complicated when, just 6 months after the Imam's disappearance, the first Shiʿi state of the modern Middle East was established in Iran. Nevertheless, although his mysterious disappearance added to the miseries of what had become a politically ambitious community, it provided his two main inheritors, the leaders of the SISC and AMAL, with an opportunity to prevail in their authority over the community in Lebanon.[97] The crucial dimension of the traditional political structure, namely the Shiʿi Zu'ama, had been crippled by the activities of Imam Sadr and the sociopolitical transformation of the community. Although Kamel Asaad was Speaker of the National Assembly at the time, six years after the last general election, the escalation of civil strife and the transformation of the national and regional political balance, were all a dismayed response to Shiʿi Zu'ama status. The Imam's presence had undermined their authority among the Shiʿi community, but to some extent his absence further alienated the community from the Zu'ama, whose hostility towards Imam Sadr, then the sacred occulted Imam, was evident. Despite all these factors, it seems that the last nail in the Shiʿi Zu'ama's coffin came in the aftermath of the Islamic Revolution in Iran. Prior to the rise of revolutionaries in Iran, the Zu'ama were considered to be the Shah's allies. This, ultimately, led to their being regarded as an enemy of the Islamic Republic and, hence, blocked any chance for Iranians, the new foreign supporter of the community, to back the Zu'ama in Lebanon.

Another possible alternative for the leadership of the community was a group of religious figures and their supporters who, although they had respected Imam Sadr, had been critical of his moderate political stance. With the Imam out of the way and the triumph of the Islamic Revolution in Iran, this group got carried away with the idea of replicating the Iranian Revolution in Lebanon. The group, however, comprised a heterogeneous pool of Shiʿi elite personalities. It ranged from the most accredited cleric, Sayyid Muhammad Husayn Fadlallah, to some lower-ranking clerics who were considered to be the apostles of Sayyid Muhammad Baqir Sadr, the Lebanese branch of the Dawa Party.[98] With the rise of their allies in Iran and the enduring relationship which they had with the revolution's leader, Imam Khomeini, they were given an opportunity to dominate with their political practice throughout the community. However, initially their stronghold was restricted to the suburbs of Beirut, and areas of the Beqaa Valley, especially the city of Baalbeck. While Ayatollah Fadlallah was settling in Naba'a in eastern Beirut from 1966, upon his return from Najaf, Lebanon's Dawa Party members were active in the Beqaa.

The formation of the Interim Government in Iran was an auspicious development for the Lebanese companions of Imam Sadr, especially the leaders of AMAL and SISC. The members of the new government were mostly among those Iranian elite who, over years of struggle to topple the Shah, had built a close relationship with Imam Sadr and had enjoyed his full-fledged support. Mustafa Chamran, the founding member of AMAL, was later appointed defense minister in Iran.[99] Imam Sadr's nephew, Sadeq Tabatabai, was the government's spokesperson. However, they were not the only active Islamic faction in Iran at the time. Indeed, they comprised only a small group within the moderate front in post-revolutionary Iran, and there were groups of Islamists along with them who not only possessed a more hard-line approach but were also waiting for their extremist political stance to prevail over the new revolution.[100]

Notwithstanding, with the rise of the Shiʿi government in Iran, the abandoned Shiʿi community of Lebanon turned their eyes towards Iran and its religious supreme leader, Imam Khomeini; they were first, asking Iranians to use all available political measures to bring Imam Sadr back to Lebanon and, second, demanding both moral and financial support.[101] However, the direct inheritors of Imam Sadr's legacy in Lebanon, who might have assumed leadership of the community in his absence, confronted a set of internal and external obstacles. Perhaps one of the main internal impediments that AMAL and SISC confronted was the lack of a multi-faceted personality similar to Imam Sadr.

During the time Imam Sadr was the president-elect of the SISC, he founded the AMAL as an intra-sectarian defensive militia. While the former was devoted solely to pursuing sociopolitical rights for the Shiʿi community in Lebanon, the latter was established to protect the rights of deprived Lebanese regardless of their sect. The only fact that related the SISC to AMAL during Imam Sadr's time in Lebanon was his unique personality and his perception about the world around. This did not imply that the president of the SISC should govern AMAL. After Imam Sadr disappeared in 1978, conflict between Sheikh Muhammad Mahdi Shams al-Din, the Imam's deputy at the SISC,[102] and Husayn al-Husseini who led AMAL after Imam Sadr, escalated around this issue.[103] While Shams al-Din was reserving the AMAL's leadership for himself as the new head of SISC, Husseini, consistent with AMAL's charter, was keen to preserve the secular face of the movement and so opposed SISC involvement.

Shams al-Din was among a group of Shiʿi clerics who had relatively similar views to those of Imam Musa Sadr, though he lacked the charisma of his predecessor. Like Imam Sadr, Shams al-Din was born in Iraq, but he was Lebanese by descent. While in Najaf as an esteemed student of Grand Ayatollahs Muhsin Al-Hakim and Khoei, he was involved in reformist religious groups and was acquainted with Imam Sadr there. After coming to Lebanon in 1969, he assisted Imam Sadr in the formation of the Shiʿi Islamic Supreme Council and, in 1975, was appointed vice president of the Council. The main difference between Shams al-Din and the Imam was their different personalities: while Imam Sadr was more engaged with laymen, Shams al-Din's activities and avant-garde ideas had more appeal among Shiʿi clerical elites. In other words, Imam Sadr had *walked with* the community, step by step, while Shams al-Din, as a Shiʿi modern-thinking cleric, was *far ahead* of the community; thus, the relationship between the Shiʿi of Lebanon and Shams al-Din was not established as robustly as with the Imam Sadr.[104] He was less of a political personality, though he was a reformist, Shiʿi cleric who was not as successful as

Imam Sadr in building a social base among the masses. However, his thoughts on Islamic government and sectarian coexistence were revolutionary among the Shiʿi clerics of Lebanon, Iran and Iraq.[105] On the other hand, AMAL's leading committee was dominated by a group of nouveau riche, secular Shiʿi political figures who had become known during the Imam's reign in Lebanon and included, most prominently, personalities like Husayn al-Husseini and Nabih Berri.[106] However, the lack of collaboration between the religious faction of the SISC, and the political wing of the AMAL movement, worked to the detriment of both groups with regard to replicating the leadership of Imam Sadr; and it was as a consequence of this that their influence over the Shiʿi community in Lebanon diminished during this period. Imam Musa Sadr's reputation had provided an anchor between SISC and AMAL after he disappeared. Nevertheless, SISC's role was confined to trivial religious activities, while the escalation of the civil war pushed AMAL leaders to engage in the war against other Lebanese citizens, in direct opposition to what Imam Sadr had wished.[107]

Confusion concerning its leadership entrapped the Shiʿi community in Lebanon in a series of national and regional developments. The Southern Lebanon Army was operating in the south on behalf of Israel, and the conflict between PLO fighters was at its peak after Imam Sadr's disappearance. It was at this time that a group of Iranian hardliner Islamists saw an opportunity to 'export the revolution'. Among them was the World Liberation Movement (WLM), headed by Muhammad Ali Montazeri, an Iranian extremist member of the clergy and member of the Islamic Republican Party, who had been based in Syria and Lebanon prior to the revolution in Iran. He was among the Iranian revolutionaries who had had a long-term relationship with Fatah and Colonel Gaddafi of Libya.[108] In the summer of 1979, Montazeri visited Lebanon along with 300 Iranian volunteers with the aim of engaging in Lebanon's civil war, expelling the Israeli army from the south, and supporting the PLO and the Shiʿi community. In a press conference held in a mosque in Beirut, he explained that he and those who had accompanied him from Iran had come to Lebanon 'to fight alongside our Muslim brothers and Palestinians to liberate Lebanon from the filthy hands of the Zionist regime and its Imperialist agents'. When he was asked how he would carry out this aim, he responded by raising his hand and shouting 'with our clenched fists, as we have done in Iran'.[109] However, the course of events that unfolded in the Islamic Republic in the months following the revolution restricted the activities of hardliner groups and prevented them from extending the revolution beyond the borders of the country.

Lebanon, like many other states in the region felt the impact of the Iran-US confrontation and the Iran–Iraq War. Perhaps the foremost consequence of the US approach towards Iran, formed mainly in the aftermath of the Hostage Crisis, was the rise of Israel's regional strategic value to Washington.[110] This provided Israel with more flexibility in pursuing its regional interests. With the Israeli withdrawal from Sinai on April 1982 and prospects of a long-lasting peace with Egypt, the security of the northern borders with Lebanon became the first priority for Israel. At the same time, the course of the Iran–Iraq War had shifted dramatically: the Iranian army liberated Khorramshahr on 24 May 1982 after two years of Iraqi occupation and gained leverage over the Iraqi army for the first time since the commencement of the War.[111]

Saddam was not only defeated on the battleground, but also his plan to represent the war with Iran as an Arab–Persian encounter was cast into doubt when the Syrian

Arab Republic signed a strategic treaty with the Islamic Republic and shut its borders to Iraqi oil exports in early 1982.[112] For Saddam Hussein, Lebanon provided an opportunity to kill two birds with one stone: the Syrian army was present there at the time, and Iran exercised a large influence on its Shiʿi community. In Israel, on the other hand, the right-wing government of Prime Minister Menachem Begin, along with the defense minister, Ariel Sharon, was preparing a plan to expel PLO guerilla fighters from Lebanon and to restore security on its borders. However, the new PLO attitude, in disengaging from provocative activities against Israel from within Lebanese territory, had stopped Israel from advancing its master plan, at least until a major excuse could be found. The excuse was provided by Iraq, when the Iraqi Intelligence Service along with its client Palestinian terrorist group, Abu-Nidal, attempted to assassinate the Israeli ambassador in London on 3 June 1982.[113] Although, Abu-Nidal had left the PLO nine years earlier for Israel, as long as the plot provided an internationally recognized provocation, this was enough reason to invade Lebanon, and Israel targeted PLO guerrilla fighters just three days after the incident.[114]

At the same time as the invasion of Lebanon by Israel, two divisions of the Iranian army and the Revolutionary Guards were transferred to the Beqaa via Damascus. While the Israeli army was heading towards the capital, the Iranian soldiers were forming positions alongside Syrian forces to engage in a war with Israel. However, the sudden ceasefire between Syria and Israel, and the call of Imam Khomeini asking forces to return to the battleground with Iraq, prevented any further engagement by Iranian troops. The majority of them headed back to Iran, while a few dozen remained in the Beqaa to train Lebanese.[115] In his message to the Iranian forces, Imam Khomeini acknowledged the whole plot as a hostile conspiracy against Iran and reminded his supporters that the 'path to liberate al-Quds runs across Karbala'. He declared:

> The Islamic Republic's enemies have manipulated us for a while; they were aware of our sensitivity to Lebanon; therefore, they came up with a plot to distract our attention from the war with Iraq. They knew that we are sensitive to Lebanon; thus, they came up with this plot.[116]

The Imam confessed that he had misperceived the transnational political opportunity structure at the midst of Iran–Iraq War, and had, thus, hastened to undo his moves by asking the Iranian forces to return. Although the Israeli invasion ultimately led to the PLO's expulsion from Lebanon, it also provoked a paradigm shift among the Shiʿi of Lebanon. In the aftermath of the invasion, groups of Lebanese Shiʿi raised the banner of resistance against Israel with the close collaboration of forces from the Islamic Republic. As Israeli Prime Minister Rabin later recalled, the invasion had 'let the genie out of the bottle'.[117]

Lebanese mujtahids in the political arena: The establishment of Hezbollah

Two weeks after the Israeli invasion, west Beirut came under siege. Prior to closing the siege around Beirut, the Israeli army, with the assistance of Lebanese militia forces, confronted AMAL resistance in Khaldeh for some days, though eventually all militia members, along with thousands of Palestinian fighters, were confined in west Beirut.[118] It was at this point that President Sarkis called for a National Salvation Committee to decide upon the fate of the PLO presence in Lebanon and the Israeli ultimatum. The group comprised six members from predominant Lebanese sects.[119] Nabih Berri, then the leader of AMAL, was invited to represent the Shiʿi community on the committee. For the AMAL members and clerical elite of the SISC that was a once-in-a-lifetime opportunity to consolidate their leadership over the community in Lebanon, since it was the first time that they had been called upon at this national decision-making level to represent the Shiʿi of Lebanon. While, ostensibly, Nabih Berri was reluctant to take part in the committee, the majority of AMAL and SISC leading clerics, including Shams al-Din, voted on his participation.[120] The deliberation of the committee on the issue of Palestinian expulsion from Lebanon was restricted to the decision of the Sunni Prime Minister and Saeb Salam, who acted as the mediator between Arafat and the US envoy Habib. West Beirut was a Sunni stronghold and, traditionally, was under the rule of the Salam and Solh families. Out of the committee's six members, the Christians were in favour of PLO expulsion while, in reality, the eventual decision of the Muslim bloc was in hands of Wazzan and those he was representing, the Sunni Zu'ama of west Beirut.[121]

Nevertheless, with the incompetency of the SISC, Berri's participation in the committee caused a schism within the community in the summer of 1982. While the secular wing of AMAL was still under siege in Beirut, Husayn Musawi, the chief of the AMAL office in Baalbeck, announced his break from the movement and the formation of the Islamic AMAL, an organization more inclined towards the Islamic Republican cause. This marked the rise of a strong rivalry within the Shiʿi community between the joint leadership of AMAL and the SISC. Unfortunately for the Shiʿi of Lebanon, the legacy of Imam Sadr, based on the unity of the community, human dignity and non-sectarian coexistence, was falling apart in the absence of a united and all-embracing leadership. The Council did not have effective authority, the AMAL leadership was entangled with the hostile attacks from Israel in the south and in Beirut, and the Shiʿi of the Beqaa were about to sectarianize the Imam's movement by labelling it as 'Islamic'. Therefore, the schism that Musawi initiated, contrary to what he claimed later, was not consistent with Imam Sadr's political stance but, more probably, was influenced by Fatah affiliates and their allies among Iranian politicians who were based, at the time, inside the Iranian embassy in Damascus.[122] At the time, when the south and Beirut were under Israeli occupation, the Iranian ambassador in Syria, Ali Akbar Mohtashamipour, made contact with Muslim figures in the Beqaa and in Tripoli, areas outside the sphere of the Israeli occupation, to form a Lebanese resistance group against Israel and its allies. The common denominator within all of these groups and among these figures was opposition to the Zionist regime within the framework of the Islamic Republic, namely the theory of the Guardianship of the Jurist. Islamic AMAL, Lebanon's al-Dawa Party and a group of young clerics who had settled in the newborn seminary of Baalbeck were the main groups who responded to Mohtashamipour's call.[123]

In the autumn of 1982, while Israel and its allies were preoccupied with the conflict in Beirut and the South of Lebanon, the Lebanese Shiʿi of Beqaa formed a clandestine resistance group, later called Hezbollah, with the direct support of the

Islamic Republic.[124] Dozens of Iranian Revolutionary Guard members who had been stationed in the Baalbeck seminary began training the Lebanese to ready them for an engagement with Israeli forces in the South. Later on, the 'leftover' Shiʿi members of the PLO, who were rejected by AMAL, joined Hezbollah and made the group even more formidable.[125] The emergence of Hezbollah in Lebanon not only promised a dramatic change for the Shiʿi community, but also introduced a new force into the balance of power in Lebanon and the region in the mid-1980s. However, the leaders of this new group had a long way to go in order to consolidate their authority throughout the community and to mobilize the Shiʿi masses through their extremist political stance. As a result, the Shiʿi community of Lebanon was polarized between those in the south and in the suburbs of Beirut, on the one hand, and a faction in the Beqaa bordering Syria under the rule of the new Islamic Resistance Party, on the other. When on 11 November 1982, a bomb detonated inside the Israeli base in Tyre, all the countries and parties involved in Lebanon were baffled by this new extremist trend.[126] Nonetheless, evidence confirms that in this action and all other major activities against Israel until 1985, AMAL was cooperating with the Islamic Resistance group in the Beqaa.[127]

In its efforts to gain leadership of the community and to make the most out of the available opportunities, Hezbollah had pursued a multi-faceted policy from the outset: opposing the multinational forces presence in Lebanon, as a proxy for the Islamic Republic; legitimizing Islamic Resistance against the Israeli occupation of the south; and consolidating its position as the only legitimate voice of the community.[128] To act on behalf of the Islamic Republic, and perhaps the extreme faction in its leadership, the Shiʿi resistance carried out a series of attacks against the western fronts inside Lebanon (e.g. the US embassy bombings in 1983, and the taking of Western citizens as hostages). Hezbollah can be acknowledged to have attempted to import the Islamic Revolution from Iran and, as a matter of fact, the Islamic Republic had taken every opportunity to exploit the activities of its loyal Shiʿi party in Lebanon.[129] The Islamic Republic's authority over Hezbollah, however, lessened in the late 1980s.

In order to engage with the resistance against the Israeli occupation of the south, Hezbollah needed to expand its operations beyond the Beqaa. This aim was advanced by the activities of two important Shiʿi clerics, Sheikh Raqib Harb in Jebsheet, a village in the south, and Muhammad Husayn Fadlallah in the suburban areas of Beirut. Both were fully devoted to Imam Khomeini and his discourse. Muhammad Husayn Fadlallah had been born in Najaf to a Lebanese parent, and returned to Lebanon in 1966 to be settled in Naba'a, in the east of Beirut. His return to Lebanon coincided with the rise of Imam Sadr as an active Shiʿi leader in Lebanon. Although they respected each other, Fadlallah's perception of the political opportunity structure was very different from that of Imam Sadr at the time;[130] though he hoped to spread his more extreme stance within the Shiʿi community, Fadlallah lacked Sadr's charisma.[131] During the Imam Sadr's reign in Lebanon, Fadlallah was perhaps his most significant critic within the Lebanese Shiʿi clergy.[132] The disappearance of Imam Sadr encouraged Shiʿi clerics with similar political stances to that of Fadallah to attempt to raise their religio-political stature within the community. His political activism had further escalated by the eve of the Israeli invasion and with the establishment of Hezbollah by a group of his young companions.[133] Similarly to all the other major Shiʿi clerics in Lebanon, Fadlallah opposed the Israeli occupation of the south and supported the cause of Islamic resistance; yet what singled out his political stance at the time from other Shiʿi clerics was, consistent with Hezbollah's policy, his prioritizing of the establishment of the Islamic government in Lebanon above the liberation of the occupied territories.[134] At the time, his writings and sermons about the culture of Martyrdom and Jihad inspired his followers in Lebanon, especially Hezbollah's leading cadre. Moreover, he was seen as a religious figure loyal to the Palestinian cause, and when Israel was initially portrayed as a beautiful white stallion at the break of dawn that liberated the Shiʿi of the south from the hostility of Palestinians, it was he who was the first to call this viewpoint an 'illusion'. From his point of the view, the only choice for Shiʿis was to resist Western hegemony and Israel in the name of loyalty towards Jihad, and by using all means.[135]

With the ever-expanding activities of Hezbollah within the community, and partial withdrawal of Israeli forces from the south in early 1985, the party publicly announced its existence through an open letter on 16 February 1985.[136] This marked a turning point in the history of Hezbollah and indeed the Shiʿi community in Lebanon. As of that date, this new trend in Lebanon emerged publicly and announced its full compliance with the Islamic Republic and its unique interpretation of Islamic governance. The timing of the open letter coincided with the rise of AMAL in Beirut and the south. It seemed that, by announcing its existence publicly, Hezbollah wanted to prevent AMAL, then its internal rival, from claiming all credit for the resistance.

The clash of Shiʿi political activism: AMAL and Hezbollah

In late 1982, when multinational forces entered Beirut, Israelis were pulled back and stationed in restricted areas within the so-called security zone. On 17 May 1983, a biased agreement was signed between Lebanon's president and Israel through the mediation of the United States. The terms of the treaty were not only seen by Muslims as evidence of the president's servility towards the Israeli government, but also undermined the authority of President Gemayel over the Maronite community, as well.[137] The first active protests against the 17 May agreement were held on that day by a group of Shiʿi clerics in Beirut, including Shams al-Din and Fadlallah, who took refuge in the Imam Reza Mosque.[138] With the intervention of the Lebanese armed Forces, under the command of the president, the government was shown, evidently for the first time, to have formed a front against the Shiʿi community. The president appeared to still believe in the traditional political structure in Lebanon, the strategic alliance between Sunni Muslims and Maronite Christians, and was underestimating the Shiʿi community. Nonetheless, as a result of Lebanon's sociopolitical transformation and consistent with transnational events, the Shiʿi community's status in Lebanon was not something that could be easily ignored in 1984. Perhaps Gemayel's misperception of the new structure was among one of the last examples of such practice.

Relatively ineffectual since the summer of 1982, Nabih Berri's AMAL found an opportunity to strengthen its grip over the leadership of the Shiʿi community in Beirut and in the south in February 1984.[139] Berri urged the Muslim members of the cabinet to step down in opposition to the president and, in response to this call, the cabinet submitted its resignation to Gemayel pushing him to a political impasse; later Nabih Berri and his allies took control of the west of Beirut.[140]

For the first time in the history of Lebanon, Shiʿis held authority over most of the country, an area that consisted of almost two-thirds of the territory of Lebanon.[141] The following day, President Reagan ordered US Marines to evacuate Lebanon, and the ratification of the 17 May agreement was thrown into doubt. The credit for enabling the Shiʿi community to deploy its power throughout the country should be split between AMAL and Hezbollah, whose attacks on the barracks of the MNF had resulted in severe casualties months earlier.

Later in 1984, for the first time in the history of Lebanon, at the national level, Kamel Asaad, a Shiʿi Zai'm, stepped down, and Husayn al-Husseini, the former AMAL leader, was appointed as Speaker of the Assembly. When he used his gavel for the first time in Parliament, thousands of Shiʿis in Lebanon were chanting in the streets and celebrating the dawn of a new era in the history of their community in Lebanon. This involved the achievement of a status that had developed through the early endeavours of their Imam and which was now advancing rapidly through the efforts of his companions.[142] However, subsequent events demonstrated that perhaps the festivities were premature, for the oppression of the Shiʿis was not yet over in Lebanon.

The retreat of Israeli forces to the security zone in 1985, and the empowerment of AMAL and the Progressive Socialist Party (PSP) militia in the west of Beirut followed the withdrawal of the MNF from Lebanon. Concurrently, groups of Palestinian guerilla fighters who had been expelled from Lebanon wished to go back to refugee camps and to restore their pre-1982 authority. It was at this time that, with the green light from Syria, the AMAL and PSP militia encountered Palestinians in the Sabra, Shatila and Bourj al-Barajneh camps who were allied to some Sunni militia including Al-Mourabitoun. Eventually the 'War of Camps' broke out in April 1985 in west Beirut, and the Shiʿi and Druze militias, backed by Syrian forces, succeeded in dissolving the power of the Al-Mourabitoun and in controlling Palestinian activities inside their camps to some extent. In reality, however, the war was between Assad's Syria and Arafat, a hostility that had caused Lebanon, and its Shiʿi community particularly, nothing but despair. Moreover, evidence confirmed that the War of the Camps was partly initiated by President Gemayel and his Maronite allies, in the aftermath of the Tripartite Agreement,[143] to mitigate the military power of AMAL and PSP forces in west Beirut.[144] Three years on from the outbreak of the tension, AMAL had achieved no definite results but a drastic decrease in its military power. At this time, Berri, who had, perhaps, understood how he was being used by his rivals, declared the end of the camps' confinement as 'a gift for the Palestinian Intifada' in the West Bank, and officially removed his forces in the summer of 1988.[145]

AMAL's confrontation with the Palestinians not only caused huge distress within the Shiʿi community in Lebanon, but also worsened its already unsteady relationship with Iran. For a faction of the community which was sympathetic to Hezbollah, Nabih Berri appeared to be emerging as a new Shiʿi Zai'm, a secular political broker who himself was active as a client to a more dominant source of power, in this case Syria.[146] A group of Iranian MPs accused AMAL of exploiting the Zionist will in order to perpetrate sectarian conflict and to violate the sacred Palestinian cause.[147] During a ceremony in 1987 marking the ninth anniversary of Imam Sadr's disappearance, Nabih Berri addressed a gathering in Sidon to clarify AMAL's position and to criticize the extremist actions of his Shiʿi rivals. For the first time since the disappearance of Imam Sadr, one of his descendants harshly criticized its fellow Shiʿis and said: 'with due respect, not everyone who wears a turban becomes a scholar'. His statement was directed at the Hezbollah figures who had recently criticized AMAL's political position by calling them 'insects who should be crushed by the hands of true Shiʿi'.[148] Recalling Israel as the absolute evil and the enemy of Muslims and Christians in Lebanon, Berri continued,

> We adhere to the UN resolutions and continue to support the UNIFIL, who watch over our rights and the enduring presence of our people on their land. Any attacks against the UNIFIL means an attack against the resistance. The slogan is resistance, not terrorism. A very thin thread separates terrorism from the struggle. We are not against the peoples, but the rulers of the peoples are against us.[149]

He had announced his and AMAL's doctrine vis-à-vis Lebanon's political structure at the time. He clearly accused an extreme faction within the Iranian leadership, who in opposition to the will of Imam Khomeini, the supreme leader, had tried to obliterate the name of Imam Sadr and his companions in Lebanon and to propagate its fundamentalist doctrine within the Shiʿi community.[150]

In response to Berri's actions, Hezbollah organized a rally in Baalbeck on 3 September, four days after the Sidon gathering. There, Subhi Tufayli associated the party's actions fully with Imam Khomeini's doctrine and added that 'the UN soldiers witnessed Lebanon's loss with indifference, just as they witnessed the Palestinians' loss'.[151] The point of divergence between AMAL and Hezbollah at the time was around a number of critical issues, mostly rooted in each party's essential identity. Opposing Lebanon's political sectarian structure and Maronite supremacy, AMAL nonetheless, was believed to participate in the government and to dedicate itself to reform from within. Therefore, the party claimed that it fully complied with the UN resolutions, with UNIFIL and protecting the sovereignty of the country against Israel until its forces withdrew completely from Lebanese territories.[152] In pursuing this cause, although the movement's leaders constantly declared their devotion to the cause of Imam Khomeni as 'the religious political leader of all Shiʿis in the world', they critically needed a strategic alliance with the Syrian regime.[153] Therefore, AMAL's clash with Palestinians during the War of the Camps should be analysed within the framework of the Assad–Arafat conflict. A bitter conflict that eventually mitigated both PLO's and AMAL's military powers, thus, provided their national rivals with more political leverage.[154] On the other hand, Hezbollah fully embraced the idea of establishing a replica of the Islamic Republic of Iran in Lebanon and the actions of their hardliner influential leaders at that time, like Tufayli, challenged every aspect of AMAL's political position.[155] The party was representing the will of its *Wali e Faqih*, Imam Khomeini, and thus opposed the very existence of the Zionist regime of Israel, while it was devoted to the Palestinian cause unconditionally. Therefore, any compromise with Israel or its allies, and any dispute with Palestinians, by any party, whether AMAL or Assad's regime would consequently provoke the hostility of Hezbollah against those parties.[156]

The war-of-words phase terminated when, in early 1988, military clashes broke out between supporters of both groups in the south. With Israel continuing to strengthen its client, the SLA, and inflaming hostilities, the balance of power within the Shiʿi community shifted more towards Hezbollah. Consequently, when on 7 February, the US Colonel and UNIFIL officer William Higgins was taken hostage near Tyre, internal conflicts inside AMAL escalated, and days later, the movement commenced pre-emptive attacks against Hezbollah's bases in the south and in Beirut. The AMAL–Hezbollah fights erupted in the suburbs of Beirut on 6 May 1988. This eventually resulted in confining AMAL's authority to the territories in the south, where the movement still had strong public support.[157] But while the more extremist Hezbollah was consolidating its authority over the majority of the community in Lebanon, the party's fundamentalist caretakers in Iran were gradually losing their political bases inside the Islamic Republic leadership. Eventually, in late 1988, Iran officially announced that it was revising its foreign policy in Lebanon.[158] The Iranian call coincided with the joint meeting of the Tufayli, Fadlallah and Shams al-Din with the Islamic Republic leadership in Tehran, and the successful mediations of Iranian envoys between the hostile Shiʿi parties in Lebanon.[159]

The change in the Islamic Republic's policy towards the Shiʿi community in Lebanon, notwithstanding, was rooted in some internal and regional factors as well. Just months after the Islamic Revolution, Iran had instigated the US embassy hostage crisis and, in 1980, entered into a full-fledged war with Iraq. The moderate political elite inside the country's leadership, without any meaningful pragmatic experience in politics, found itself at the centre of multi-faceted national, regional and international pressures. At the same time that the government was confronting internal pressures from groups, ranging from secular nationalists to Islamic Leftists, demanding a share in ruling post-revolution Iran, the newly formed Islamic state was thrust into a war by Saddam's regime, supported by almost all of Iran's Arab neighbours, all of which were allied to Europe and the United States. In 1982, after a partial settlement with internal opposition groups and initial victories in the war with Iraq had been achieved, the regime's foreign policy in Lebanon came to be directed by a more fundamentalist faction that had strategic alliances with the PLO and its leader Yasser Arafat. It was not until halfway through the war with Iraq, that the doctrine of a group of moderate pragmatic political players, led by Hashemi Rafsanjani, gradually became embodied in the internal and foreign policy of the Islamic Republic. In mid-1985, the relationship between Yasser Arafat and the Islamic Republic had been strained because of the PLO's covert support for Saddam Hussein. However, Palestinians still had strong connections with the office of Ayatollah Montazeri, then the deputy supreme leader of the Islamic Republic.[160] The last nail in the coffin for the fundamentalist faction inside the Islamic Republic leadership and for Arafat's network in Iran in the post-revolution era was the execution of Sayyid Mehdi Hashemi, Ayatollah's Montazeri's relative and the mastermind behind the 'World Liberation Movement', in late 1987.[161] After that, the Iranian leadership inclined more towards realpolitik in their dealings with neighbouring states, reconsidered its ideological aspirations, and reformed its foreign policy. The change in Tehran's attitude towards the Shiʿi community in Lebanon was concurrent with the transformation of the leadership inside Iran.

As a result of Iran's new policy and its strategic understanding with Syria, the leaders of AMAL and Hezbollah were summoned to Syria and, on 30 January 1989, signed a peace treaty. According to the terms of the agreement, Hezbollah committed itself to respect AMAL's authority in the south, not to violate the AMAL–UNIFIL alliance, and not to facilitate the re-migration of PLO fighters to their pre-1982 bases in the south. On the other hand, AMAL agreed to respect Hezbollah's right to coordinate its resistance operations against Israel from the southern territories.[162] Ten months later, while tensions were easing between the two parties, the Ta'if agreement was concluded. This agreement called for the disarming of all Lebanese militia. As a result, while the hostility between AMAL and Hezbollah had been abating, it now erupted once again in the summer of 1990 in the Iqlim al-Tuffah area in the south. The rigidity of Sheikh Subhi Tufaily, who was at that time the secretary general of Hezbollah, was responsible for re-igniting hostilities.[163] After a hundred days of exchanging fire, shuttle diplomacy between Tehran and Damascus succeeded in producing a treaty based on mutual understanding once again. Later, after the death of Ayatollah Khomeini, new post-war leadership in Iran, and regional and national political shifts, Hezbollah's fundamentalist stance became gradually more moderate. AMAL and Hezbollah were both recognized as the legitimate representatives of Lebanon's Shiʿi community and joined the newly formed Resistance-Axis, headed by Iran and Syria in the post-1990 Middle East.[164] While AMAL was more inclined towards involvement in political activities, Hezbollah maintained armed resistance to the Israeli occupation of the South.

The power of mujtahids' solidarity in Lebanon: The politics of resistance

The death of Ayatollah Khomeini in Iran and with the introduction of the new and pragmatic foreign policy in the aftermath of the war with Iraq marked a turning point in the Iran–Lebanon relationship in the late 1980s. Recognizing both the position of AMAL as the representative of Imam Musa Sadr, and the popularity of Hezbollah within the community in Lebanon, the Islamic Republic tended to support both parties as equally essential players in the country and in the region.[165] The Iranian leaders' perceptions about the political opportunity structure in Lebanon had become more accurate after a decade of trial and error. During the previous eight years, though Shiʿi elites in Lebanon, like Shams al-Din and Fadlallah, had engaged in trivial disputes and disagreements, they constantly supported the resistance against Israel and promoted the rights of the Shiʿi community. Shams al-Din had moved away from AMAL in 1983 and was keen, after that, to represent the Shiʿi clergy as the head of SISC. On the other hand, although the West regarded Fadlallah as the leader of Hezbollah, in 1990 he had become a Shiʿi cleric who was more interested in Shiʿi scholastic life. Both were serving the Shiʿi community in Lebanon as representatives of Najaf's and Qum's Maraji' until 1990. After Imam Khomeini passed away and Saddam's regime lost control over the Najaf seminary following the 1991 Shiʿi uprising in Iraq, Fadlallah presented himself as a new Lebanese Shiʿi Marjaʿ, and gradually removed himself from the political scene.[166] Shams al-Din had already attained a prestigious position within the Shiʿi world for his reformist thoughts on Political Islam with respect to coexistence with non-Muslim communities. Soon both of these distinguished Shiʿi clerics stepped aside from the activities of AMAL and Hezbollah and became known as supporters of the Shiʿi resistance, with the aim of achieving rights for the community within the country's new political structure.[167]

Nevertheless, in order to assume joint leadership of the Shiʿi community in Lebanon with AMAL, Hezbollah needed to reform itself towards greater moderation. Therefore, with a green light from Iran, Sheikh Subhi Tufaily[168] was replaced by Sayyid Abbas Musawi in 1991, after the Hezbollah–AMAL alliance had been strengthened.[169] It seemed that, although the rights of the Shiʿi community had been effectively ignored following the conclusion of the Ta'if agreement, the disunity among the various Shiʿi political actors held out the possibility of triumph.

The rise of Sayyid Abbas Musawi in Hezbollah pushed the community one step further towards political compromise. In 1968, as a young student, he had met Imam Sadr and had enrolled in Tyre's Institute of Islamic Studies. Later he was recommended to Muhammad Baqir Sadr in Najaf, and soon Sayyid Abbas entered Sadr's circle of students in Najaf. Loyal to Imam Sadr, he was forced to leave Iraq in 1978, when he moved to Baalbeck, where he, with help from some other Shiʿi clerics, including Hassan Nasrallah, established a small seminary with the permissions of Shams al-Din and Fadlallah. After the rise of Imam Khomeini in Iran and in the aftermath of the Israeli invasion in 1982, he became one of the founders of Hezbollah. Trained by the Revolutionary Guards in Baalbeck, he had been appointed as Hezbollah's commander in the South.[170] His unique personal characteristics, with touches of moderation, and his devotion to resistance against Israel, once again reminded the community of Imam Sadr in some respects.[171] When, in 1991, he was appointed as Hezbollah's leader, the future of the community seemed to promise unity and mutual understanding. However, he did not last long in the post, as he was assassinated in an Israeli air raid along with his family on 16 February 1992.

Musawi had played a crucial role in transforming Hezbollah's identity from a military resistance group aiming to 'establish an Islamic state', to a sociopolitical party willing to participate in the new political structure in Lebanon. Consequently, his martyrdom contributed to the community's internal unity, as an all-embracing front – including Lebanese Shiʿi clerics, AMAL, Lebanese Parliament members and the government – condemning his assassination and demanding full-fledged support for resistance efforts in the South.[172] Hours later, Hezbollah's leadership council appointed Hassan Nasrallah, closest advocate of Musawi in the party, as the new secretary general.[173]

The combatant mujtahid: The political posture of Hassan Nasrallah

The first post-war general election in Lebanon was considered a triumph for AMAL and Hezbollah's coalition lists in the South. Nabih Berri was elected the new Speaker of the

Parliament, leading the political front in Beirut to advance the community's rights, while Hezbollah led an Islamic Resistance front in the south. The new prime minister, Rafik Hariri, along with the majority of politicians, supported the resistance in the South in order to force Israel to terminate its occupation and to comply with UN resolutions. This new internal Lebanese balance of political power and the resistance cause were tested for the first time on 13 September 1993 with the conclusion of the Oslo Accord. Still facing continual Israeli aggressions, the Shiʿis of the south along with Palestinian refugees demonstrated in Beirut showing their resentment over the agreement between Arafat and Yitzhak Rabin. Minutes after the start of the demonstration, and in violation of a pre-set agreement with the government regarding the demonstration, the Lebanese armed forces opened fire on the public and killed nine demonstrators.[174] It was only Hezbollah's self-restraint that prevented civil strife from sweeping across Lebanon once again. This clearly showed that Lebanese people were fed up with the miseries of the civil war and had matured over the course of the preceding decade. Ten years earlier, an incident much less important than this, which occurred in September 1993, was considered a dangerous national dilemma.[175] There had been a dramatic change in perception of the political structure among the Lebanese political actors.

The war between the Islamic Resistance and Israel continued throughout the 1990s while the rest of Lebanon was moving rapidly forward to restore its economic and political order. However, in spring 1996, Israel commenced a military operation, 'Grapes of Wrath', against the Resistance and expanded its war – this time beyond the security-zone areas. By attacking the newly built civil infrastructure in Lebanon, the Israeli administration tried to put pressure on the Resistance and the flow of arms from within. Yet the nature of Israel's attack, especially the shelling of the UN compound in Qana, attracted international condemnation. Two weeks after the operation, for the first time in the history of the Resistance, a written agreement, known as the April Accord, was finalized with Israel through the arbitration of Iran, Syria, France and the United States. According to its terms, the belligerents would refrain from involving civilians in their military encounters and the monitoring committee, including the arbitrators, would ensure the accord's ratification; in this respect, the accord was a success, though marginal, for the Resistance-Axis comprised Syria and Iran, along with the Shiʿi Lebanese combatants in the south.[176] The resistance of the Shiʿi community to the Israeli-supported SLA, and the support of Lebanon's government under Nabih Berri in Beirut, eventually succeeded in forcing Israel to comply with UNSCR 425 in May 2000; its withdrawal from the south resulted in an unexpected collapse of SLA missionaries, and south Lebanon, except for the disputed Shebaa territories in the Golan Heights, was liberated. For the first time in the history of the Arab–Israeli conflict, Israel withdrew from an occupied land unconditionally. The incident gave the community and their leadership unsurpassed popularity throughout the Arab world. In the aftermath of the victory, Hassan Nasrallah appeared in front of his supporters in Bint Jbeil, praising Imam Khomeini and Imam Musa Sadr, as founders of the resistance in Lebanon, and acknowledging President Lahoud and Prime Minister Selim al-Hoss for their role in the victory over Israel. He declared that this is 'not a victory for one sect and a defeat for another; this is Lebanon's victory', and he promised that this victory would 'not be used by anyone to the detriment of this nation, or any part of his dear nation's population'.[177]

Furthermore, he called Ehud Barak's peace recommendations deceitful, and confirmed that the Islamic Resistance, with the backing of Lebanon's government and population would continue to confront Israel until the release of all Lebanese detainees and the liberation of the remaining occupied territories. The Israeli withdrawal from Lebanon consequently marked a turning point in Arab–Israeli relationships; it became evident that military force could be defeated by the culture of resistance and martyrdom, masterfully exploited through the activities of the Shiʿi community in Lebanon. The resistance struggles coincided with the rise of a new elite governing party in Israel, whose foreign policy was concerned with the country's internal security and the start of a new political paradigm that would limit Israel's historic expansionist strategy.

At the outset of the new Millennium, and a month after the Israeli withdrawal from Lebanon, Hafez Assad, leader of Syria for almost three decades, passed away in June 2000. His legacy, however, continued through the Syrian Baʿath Party which supported Assad's son, Bashar, as the new president of the Republic. In July, Ehud Barak and Arafat met at Camp David to negotiate over mutual issues and perhaps to establish a more enduring peace agreement. The failure to reach a comprehensive agreement resulted in the commencement of the Second Intifada within the Palestinian territories in autumn 2000. Nevertheless, at the same time, the international community and the region were confronting an even more complicated situation, involving a new paradigm initiated following the terrorist attacks on 11 September 2001. This new paradigm cast a shadow over the future of the Middle East and questioned hopes of an imminent settlement of regional conflicts.

In the aftermath of the 9/11 incidents, President Bush introduced his new 'war on terror' doctrine with invasions of Afghanistan and Iraq, propagating the establishment of a new Middle East order. After the overthrow of Saddam's regime, the Resistance-Axis became the first target of the government in Washington.[178] Over the initiatives of France and the US governments, the UN Security Council passed Resolution 1559 on 2 September 2004 urging Syria to withdraw its forces from Lebanon and calling for the disarming of Hezbollah.[179] From the pro-Syrian bloc point of view, the Resolution was planned to influence the Lebanese Parliament session on 3 September, when members were going to decide on the extension of the pro-resistance Emile Lahoud presidency.[180] Article 5 of the UNSC Resolution opposed the action and demanded a new presidential election in Lebanon without any 'foreign interference or influence'.[181] The majority of the Parliament, however, voted for the constitutional amendment, and postponed the presidential election for three years.[182] Nevertheless, the proponents of UNSCR 1559 had already ignited a catastrophe for 'Lebanon's internal stability'.[183]

A handful of cabinet members resigned after the constitutional amendment, later on Prime Minister Hariri also submitted his resignation to Lahoud, and was replaced by Omar Karami.[184] Soon the country became divided between supporters and opponents of the Syrian regime. One of the earliest attempts on behalf of the latter group was the Bristol Hotel Gathering in late 2004, when the Christian–Druze alliance issued a statement asking the new government to resign because the new prime minister's pro-Syrian policies were aimed at 'further deepening differences between the Lebanese' during a period which they also labelled as a 'very dangerous phase' for Lebanon.[185]

Although Hariri did not attend the gathering, he was soon singled out as the leader of the Syrian opposition. In early 2005, the UN Security Council issued another resolution, confirming that Israel had fully exploited the terms of UNSCR 425,[186] and asking the Syrian regime to comply with the UN resolutions and to withdraw its forces from Lebanon.[187] The Lebanese political structure became increasingly volatile, and violence erupted when, on 14 February 2005, a bomb was detonated in central Beirut, which killed Rafik Hariri and dozens of his companions.

The Syrian regime was among the first to be suspected. A week later, thousands of Lebanese demonstrated in the streets of Lebanon demanding the withdrawal of Syrian forces, and so commenced what was later known as the Cedar Revolution.[188] This marked a new phase in the recent history of the country.

For years, Syria had formed the strategic backbone that held together the ideological bounds between Iran and the Shiʿi in Lebanon within the Resistance-Axis. The strategic understanding between Hezbollah in Lebanon and the Syrian regime was made even more enduring because of joint resistance to Israel and the goal of liberating the Golan and Shebaa. However, when in 2005, the anti-Syria consensus inside Lebanon strengthened, Hezbollah, as one of the greatest representatives of the Shiʿi community, complied with the will of the majority in response to the perceivably close political opportunity structure. Nasrallah, though, called upon his supporters to demonstrate in Beirut on 8 March 2005, as a farewell to the Syrians and a gesture of gratitude. On 14 March, anti-Syrian elements staged another demonstration claiming they were continuing the late Hariri's policy. These two demonstrations, later on, led to the establishment of two main political camps inside Lebanon. By the end of April 2005, all Syrian forces had left Lebanon and the country celebrated its independence from foreign forces after decades of Palestinian, Syrian and Israeli occupations.

In the aftermath of the Cedar Revolution and with the resignation of Karami, the Lebanese tycoon, Najib Mikati was appointed to form a new cabinet in April 2005. For the first time, to protect its resistance status, Hezbollah nominated a member for the Lebanese cabinet. The tactic was to undermine international opposition against the party and the Resistance-Axis.[189] Furthermore, Hezbollah, AMAL, Walid Jumblatt's PSP and Saad Hariri's Future Movement signed a formal Quartet Alliance for the upcoming election in May 2005, the first post-Ta'if election without the interference of Syria. This was a strategic initiative by the Shiʿi elites to show their intention to become actively involved in national politics. The election outcome was victorious for all four of these parties.[190] Nevertheless, months after the election, Walid Jumblatt, known for his flip-flop politics,[191] unilaterally called off the Quartet Alliance. In response to this move, seen as a betrayal of the Shiʿi community and the resistance cause, Hezbollah and AMAL ministers boycotted Prime Minister Fouad Siniora's government for 7 weeks when Nasrallah publicly announced the dissolution of the Quartet Alliance.[192] Hezbollah's announcement was followed by the declaration of a new memorandum of understanding between Nasrallah and Michel Aoun, leader of the Free Patriotic Front, two days later. The last article of the memorandum under the title of 'The Protection of Lebanon' clearly asserts that carrying arms is an honourable means for any party whose land is occupied to achieve sacred and political resistance.[193] The new mutual understanding between the Shiʿi community and one of the most significant Maronite leaders in Lebanon not only granted both communities favourable political opportunity in Lebanon but also showed the political weight and popularity of Hezbollah, which had easily formed a new alignment to promote its causes.

Hezbollah, representing the Shiʿi community, had seized a great deal of political opportunity. Aligned with Nasrallah, Nabi Berri called for a National Dialogue meeting in March 2006. Fourteen Lebanese elites from a wide range of political parties and sects, including Nasrallah, Saad Hariri and Amine Gemayel, were gathered mainly to discuss five topics: the case of Hariri's assassination, Palestinian arms and the situation in the refugee camps, the future of the Lebanese–Syrian relationship, Lebanon's claims over the Shebaa Farms, the presidency of Emile Lahoud, and the arming of the Islamic Resistance.[194] Through a series of talks, a consensus was reached over the first three issues. However, no settlement was reached over the termination of Lahoud's presidency.[195] Supporting the arm of the Islamic Resistance, Hezbollah's secretary asked for a comprehensive Strategic National Defence scheme that could satisfy Lebanon's national security concerns and align the armed resistance with the Lebanese armed forces. The decision on disarming Hezbollah was referred to as a 'working-group' while the participants agreed to resume talks over the issue of the presidency two months later; the issue remained unresolved at that time.[196]

The 33-Days War: A case of networked Shiʿi politics

To the disappointment of the international and regional opponents of the Resistance-Axis, one year after the Syrian withdrawal from Lebanon, Hezbollah and AMAL were playing a joint and pivotal role in Lebanese politics, something which became apparent during the National Dialogue sessions. Added to this, the situation was deteriorating for Israel, as Hamas, another party loyal to the Resistance-Axis at the time won the majority of votes in the Legislative Election of January 2006.[197] In retaliation against Hamas's abduction of Gilad Shalit,[198] Israeli forces invaded Gaza targeting Hamas. The Israeli operation in Gaza was still at its heights when Hezbollah ambushed an Israeli patrol on 12 July in Shebaa Farms, and captured two Israeli soldiers with the aim of restarting the prisoner-exchange scheme that had been halted unilaterally by Israel two years before. Hours later, Israel commenced a full-fledged military campaign against Lebanon, with airstrikes targeting civilian infrastructure in Beirut, followed by a ground invasion that began a week later. Although at the outset Israeli foreign minister Olmert claimed the Israeli response would be 'restrained but very painful',[199] on 17 July Olmert stated: 'our nation is under attack from the southern and northern borders. We will then continue to operate with full force [against Lebanon] until the return of our two soldiers and the expulsion of Hezbollah from the area, and the fulfilment of UNSCR 1559.'[200]

Taking everything into account and based on the historical relations between Hezbollah and Israel, especially in aftermath of the 2000 withdrawal, the Israeli reaction was far beyond what was expected by observers, and perhaps even beyond the perceptions of Hezbollah's leaders. The April Agreement of 1996 had committed both parties to a relationship that came to be known as 'rules of the game'.[201] According to this mutual non-written understanding, while Hezbollah and Israel respected the UN blue line, the Shebaa Farms area would be considered a fire-free zone for Hezbollah, and the Lebanese resistance would comply on the basis of 'an eye for an eye' principle, based on which it could respond to Israeli aggression with the same level of aggression.[202] Taking this structure into account, the harsh and comprehensive Israeli reaction had a seemingly far stronger motive than the return of its two soldiers from the Shebaa Farms area.

Although Hezbollah had not expected an Israeli response of such a kind, its swift engagement on the battleground proved that during the preceding years it had been strengthening its warfare capabilities. Concurrent with its military defence, Hezbollah commenced an all-embracing psychological war strategy. The first radio speech of Nasrallah on 14 July is one of the most influential examples of this. Addressing Israeli civilians, he said that, although Lebanon was under severe attack from Israeli forces, the ultimate victory belonged to the Resistance's combatants, as they are 'children of Muhammad, Ali, Hassan and Hussein' and they possess a 'faith that the earth has never seen'. To the surprise of every listener, he then continued by stating: 'At this very moment, off the coast of Beirut, there is an Israeli battleship that struck our homes and the lives of our civilians during last two days; you can see it burning and sinking along with dozens of its Israeli crew. This is only the beginning, and there will be a lot more said before the battle ends.'[203]

Seconds after his speech, the Israeli battleship that was harboured in Beirut was hit by Resistance rockets and sank, while everyone watched the scene through the televised commentaries of Hezbollah propagating that the leadership of Hezbollah and its supporters had proven their devotion to the Shiʿi culture of Martyrdom and Jihad, and had boldly challenged the Israeli military for the first time in sixty years. For their part, Hezbollah's leaders would like to change the political structure in their own favour.

Thirty-three days after the outbreak of the tension, the UN Security Council passed Resolution 1701 calling for an immediate ceasefire between Hezbollah and the Israel Forces extending the mandate of UNIFIL over the south of Lebanon, and asking the hostile parties to restore their prisoner-exchange plans.[204] During the course of the warfare, almost a thousand Lebanese were killed as a result of the widespread attacks by Israel. However, since Olmert's two preconditions to the ceasefire were not fulfilled, Hezbollah claimed a 'divine victory' over the operation which is known in Lebanon as 'the Truthful Pledge'.[205] In addressing his Lebanese supporters, Nasrallah stated:

> Once again, I repeat my statement in Bint Jbeil in 2000 that this victory belongs to Lebanon and its people and all noble people of the world. Therefore, do not confine this great success within the bounds of sectarianism. Arab armies and their peoples now believe that they can easily, if they are determined enough, liberate all of Palestine from the Sea [Mediterranean] to the River [Jordan].[206]

Nasrallah's speech aimed to present Hezbollah's resistance as Lebanese or more broadly Arabic. Consequently, in the eyes of Hezbollah's leaders, the party had become influential in changing the political opportunity structure in favour of resistance against the aggressors – to become an inspiration to the masses in the Middle East.[207]

Nevertheless, the consequence of this incident, which raised the status of the Shiʿi community, goes beyond the issue of who was the winner or loser on the battleground. In Lebanon, during the war, the majority of Lebanese, ranging from Christians to Sunni Muslims, supported the resistance cause.[208] Throughout the Arab world, the community enjoyed the full support of the laity and Islamic movements, and Nasrallah was emerging as the new leader of the Arabs.[209] Among the regional leaders, although they criticized Hezbollah's adventurous activities at the outbreak of the conflict, later on they preferred not to explicitly condemn the war in the light of the increasing popular support for Nasrallah.[210]

In the face of such popular support throughout the region, perhaps the notable achievement for the Shiʿi community in Lebanon was the effectiveness that the alignment between Shiʿi elites, the leadership of Nasrallah-Berri, had presented during the conflict. While Nasrallah was leading the war on the battleground in the south, Berri was exploiting his capabilities in Beirut. When Hezbollah had the support of Iran and the Qum seminary, along with all its settled Marajiʿ, on 30 July 2006, in the midst of the war and when the chance of a ceasefire was waning mainly due to the US veto, Berri came up with the idea of asking for a more forceful reaction from the leader of the Najaf seminary, Grand Ayatollah Sistani.[211] In response, the Grand Ayatollah sent a message to President Bush through an Iraqi courier, reminding him about the regional consequences of postponing the ceasefire.[212] The communication paid off, as a result of Ayatollah Sistani's status and the engagement of American forces in Iraq at the time. This was a successful seizure of political opportunity on a broader transnational scale. It was in the aftermath of the 33-Days War that it became evident that the Shiʿi community in Lebanon, which used to be among the most isolated and deprived communities in the region, had found a balance in its political activism under this new leadership. This undeniable political status deserves more thorough consideration, especially given that it contributes to an understanding of Shiʿi transnational networks prevailing through Iraq and Iran.

* * *

Although Shiʿi clerical elites did not enjoy a favourable political opportunity structure at bureaucratic level, at least until recently, they have played a pivotal role in mobilizing the community during the last fifty years (see Figure 6.1 for the illustrative trajectory of activism by Shiʿi clerical elites in modern Lebanon). In 1958, when Imam Musa Sadr, then a young Shiʿi cleric in his thirties, set foot in Lebanon, he had envisioned a thorough awakening for the Shiʿi community in Lebanon. He had come from a new generation of Shiʿi clerical elites. His perception of the modern world made him draw the deprived Shiʿi community of Lebanon along a route towards sociopolitical development. He believed that Lebanon's unique geopolitical structure provided a window through which international audiences could view the message of Shiʿi Islam. His understanding of Shiʿism, as it appears in his writings and activities, was concentrated on the struggle over the rights of oppressed people, no matter what their belief or ideology. For Imam Sadr, the most important characteristic of humans that distinguishes them from other species is their dignity. Thus, he believes that in

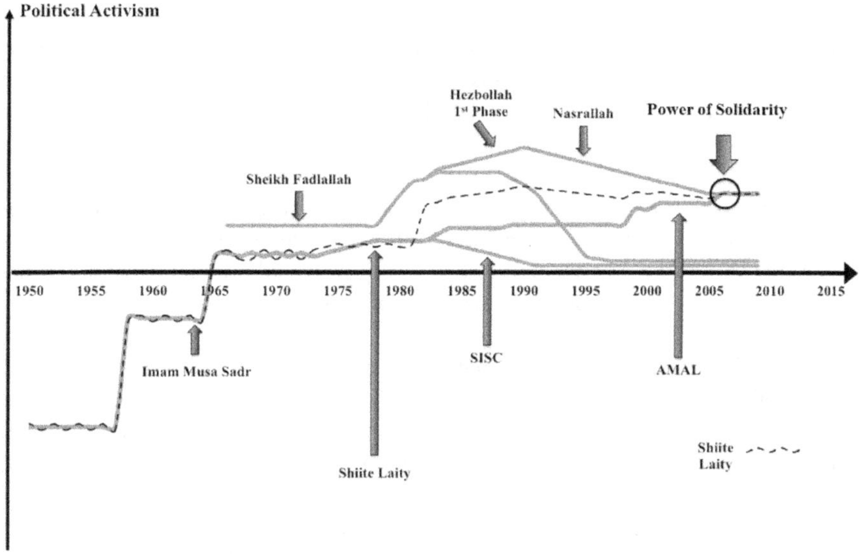

Figure 6.1 Political activism of mujtahids in modern Lebanon.

order to restore their dignity, the Shiʿi community must become actively involved in Lebanese society. What enabled this end, which indeed facilitated his activities, was the economic and sociopolitical structure, which Lebanon was going through at the time that Imam Sadr migrated there in late 1950. In other words, the favourable opportunity structure of Lebanon at the time accelerated the Imam's involvement in political activism. The factor that made his political posture resonate within the Shiʿi community in Lebanon was his unsurpassed personality and charismatic leadership. He truly believed in bottom-up change. Thus, thanks to his personal characteristics, the Shiʿi community that had become ready to mobilize at the time of the country's socioeconomic transformations was more open to his initiatives.

Hence, Imam Musa Sadr became the architect of Lebanon's new Shiʿi activism. In 1969, with the official establishment of the Supreme Islamic Shiʿi Council, which enjoyed the support of the community, he became known as one of the most active political figures in Lebanon. However, the path that he had taken did not reach its ideal destination. While Lebanon and the Shiʿi community were still in need of his leadership, he had been wiped off the political scene in the country. The Imam's disappearance in 1978 left the community with a leadership vacuum. This critical dilemma has been a constant one throughout the history of Shiʿi Islam. The community, without a charismatic leader, therefore, was directionless in its attempts to attain stability and its final goal of revitalizing its sociopolitical status in Lebanon. The alternative leader, who was nominally the Imam's successor, Sheikh Muhammad Mehdi Shams al-Din, although adhering to the political stance of his predecessor, was unable to mobilize the masses in the way that Imam Sadr could, perhaps as a result of changes in the political opportunity structure. He was forced to become politically quiet and left the political sphere to the secular AMAL leaders to fill the leadership role of Imam Sadr, although only partially. While AMAL leaders hoped to provide the community with leadership in the absence of Imam Sadr, they were weak successors in this position, as they lacked a religious facet. Therefore, it was Sayyid Muhammad Husayn Fadlallah who became the prime candidate for this leadership role. At the time, and based on his perception about the political opportunity structure, Fadlallah was holding the active posture. However, it was due to his encounters with Imam Sadr that an alliance between him and AMAL was impossible. For Fadlallah and his political posture to fill the community's leadership vacuum, and for him to become a popular leader, he had to hope for the emergence of a political wing among his followers that could succeed AMAL. The emergence of Hezbollah was a step towards fulfilling that idea. However, the Shiʿi community, at least in the south, which was loyal to Imam Sadr and his doctrine, did not fully embrace this new trend in leadership. This became concurrent with Fadlallah's personal decision in the aftermath of Imam Khomeini's and Ayatollah Khoei deaths, when he desired to devote his life more to scholastic jurisprudence and to become a Marjaʿ, hoping to strengthen the clerical elite organizational structure in Lebanon.

Consequently, the leadership of the community was in the hands of two groups: AMAL, a secular politically moderate movement, and Hezbollah, a religious fundamentalist party under the leadership of Sheikh Subhi Tufaily. Considering the political opportunity structure at the time, neither of those parties was capable of mobilizing the masses behind their objectives. The secular AMAL, which was seen to be hostile to the favourable Islamic Republic government, and the extremist Hezbollah that could not comply with the realities of Lebanon, did not provide a fulfilment of the Shiʿi community's desires at the time. While in the early 1990s, both groups were active and somehow engaged in the community's leadership, albeit from different angles, the discharge of Tuafily from Hezbollah and the party's new strategy changed the calculus entirely.

The ascent of Sayyid Abbas Musawi as the new secretary general of Hezbollah, promised the emergence of a new Shiʿi leader who could possibly fill the vacuum that had been caused by the disappearance of Imam Sadr. In post-war Lebanon, he had the opportunity to lead the Shiʿi community towards the new political agenda of Hezbollah while building a bridge with AMAL. Nevertheless, his reign did not last long, and his assassination was perceived as another miserable incident for the abandoned community in Lebanon. It was at this point that a new charismatic leader emerged onto the political scene in Lebanon in 1992. Sayyid Hassan Nasrallah was, perhaps, the most capable figure within the Hezbollah cadre, and he had become ready to assume the leadership of the Shiʿi community during the previous decade. Fortunately for the Shiʿi community, his accurate perception of the political opportunity structure empowered the community on the verge of the Taʾif agreement. Later, it became evident that the association between AMAL and Hezbollah, under the leadership of Nasrallah, perhaps, provides a leadership capable of mobilizing the community behind its political doctrine. In the current international, regional and national context this auspicious association has displayed all the characteristics of the leadership that the Shiʿi of Lebanon have been seeking for decades.

7

The power of Shiʿi clergy's solidarity and the future of the Middle East

Shiʿi clerical activism in the Middle East is entwined with the political context. The case studies set out through this book tried to explore this activism within a context defined by a particular structure of objective political opportunity coupled with the mujtahids' interpretations of that structure. As discussed in Chapter 2, Shiʿi political doctrine maintains that during the Occultation era, in the absence of an infallible source of leadership, it is the responsibility of competent Shiʿi clerics to lead the community. As the general deputies of the Occulated Imam, the main duty of Shiʿi mujtahids is to protect the citadel of Islam, and to safeguard the community until the reemergence of the infallible Imam. Based on this doctrinal belief, whenever the clergy perceives an open political opportunity structure, it becomes actively engaged in politics. Nonetheless, the extent of political activism may differ from one figure to another, as every mujtahid has its own unique ijtihad and perception over a given circumstance. Therefore, so-called activism and quietism should be understood as different tactics and political postures that clerics assume, rather than as representing the existence of a strategic disparity among them.

This book has sought to understand the ends for which the Shiʿi clergy become engaged in politics and the specific context within which they pursue an explicitly active role in politics. The so-called end for each mujtahid is to receive a sociopolitical status and authority through which he can fulfil the divinely assigned responsibilities (i.e. *Ifta* and *Qadha*). Shiʿi mujtahids believe that to protect the community, they need to hold the legislature and judicial authorities during the Occultation era. It challenges the view that a serious divide exists among Shiʿi clerics over the issue of their participation in the political affairs. It employs an analytical framework confirming that so-called Shiʿi 'quietism' and 'activism' are tactical postures assumed by different clerics in response to different contexts. The context, as defined in this book, consists of the intersection between a given political opportunity structure and the perception that Shiʿi clerical elites have of it. This book argues that when the context is permissive – that is, when there exists a favourable political opportunity structure and Shiʿi clerical elites perceive it accurately – it is more likely that they will adopt an activist posture in pursuing the fulfilment of their roles and responsibilities. But when there is a favourable objective political opportunity structure and Shiʿi clerical elites *fail* to perceive it accurately, then the context will be restrictive for activism, and the clergy will assume a relatively quiet posture.

Since its formation, Shiʿi Islam has adhered to a concrete political doctrine. Diverging from most Sunni counterparts, Shiʿi doctrine implies that the twelve infallible Imams are those most suited to rule and lead the community. They have sought to observe this belief in highly restrictive contexts since the early emergence of the sect. Shiʿi belief entails that it took almost twenty-five years for Ali, the first Imam, to seize an opportunity to take his rightful role as successor (caliph) to the Prophet. Subsequent to Ali's rule, his son Hassan concluded a treaty (in 661 CE) in which he agreed to temporarily cede the caliphate to Muawiyah, a provincial governor of Syria who, reneging on the treaty, went on to establish the Umayyad dynasty. Since then, Shiʿi Imams were never again provided with an opportunity to form a government; pushed out of politics, they focused, instead, on leading their followers. Until 941 CE, the commencement of the Major Occultation of the twelfth Imam, the main responsibility of Shiʿi Imams was to focus on spiritual leadership and developing the 'true' message of the Prophet. By teaching hundreds of students, and forming a network of deputies, infallible Imams tried to protect the foundational principles of Shiʿism.

The occultation of the twelfth Imam marked the emergence of a group of Shiʿi scholars, who are known as his general deputies and are responsible to carry out his duty. For the next centuries, as the era has been extended, this group of Shiʿi elites formed a 'fully-fledged corps of religious professionals' to lead a community threatened by the absence of an infallible source of leadership.[1] And as discussed, the backbone of this transitory 'fallible' leadership is 'ijtihad', the deducting of laws from the faith's principles.

For the majority of Shiʿi clerics, the Usulis, ijtihad is considered the essential practice in continuing the leadership of infallible Imams. It is incumbent upon them to use their ijtihad to render judgements within the varying contexts faced by the community until the 'promised day', the reemergence of the twelfth Imam.

Concurrent with the occultation of the last Imam, the rise of the Shiʿi Buyids in Persia (934–1062 CE) provided the scholars with a permissive context within which they further developed and formulated the faith's doctrines. Early Shiʿi works, including those of Muhammad Ibn Yaqub al-Kulayni (d. 941), Sheikh al-Saduq (d. 991) and Sheikh al-Tusi (d. 1067), were all compiled during this era. Above all, it was under the same favourable context that al-Tusi later succeeded in establishing the Najaf seminary in early eleventh century.

After centuries of Shiʿi scholarly stagnation under the Abbasids, a turning point for Shiʿi clerical elites occurred when Baghdad, the seat of Sunni rulers, fell to the Mongols.[2] Relatively free from the state repressions, Shiʿi elite figures, among them Nasir al-Din Tusi (d. 1274) and Allameh Hilli (d. 1325), were provided with a context in which they could further develop Shiʿi doctrines. The context for the Shiʿi community became so permissive under the rule of the Mongol Ilkhanid dynasty, that in 1309 the ruler, Uljeitu, declared Shiʿi Islam the official religion of his reign. This, coupled with the rising Persian's piety for Shiʿi Imams, eventually led to the establishment of the Safavid dynasty in the early sixteenth century.

It was now six centuries after the occultation of the twelfth Imam and, with the establishment of the Shiʿi dynasty in Persia, the community and its clerical leadership found themselves in an open and favourable circumstance. The search for suitable political practices to fit these new contexts inaugurated the political activism of the Shiʿi clergy in modern time. The institutionalization of the Safavid dynasty provided an opportunity for Shiʿi clerics to develop their ijtihad along with novel lines. Hundreds of Shiʿi scholars were invited to the Safavid's courts and were requested, while sitting by the side of the monarch, to paint the newly established Shiʿi rule with religious legitimacy.

The rise of the Safavids provided a favourable political opportunity structure to Shiʿi clerical elite activism. For a good part of Shiʿi Safavid's reign in Persia, Shiʿi mujtahids had paramount political power.[3] However, this changed with the rise of anti-ijtihad scholars, the Akhbāris, in the early seventeenth century. Rejecting the role of mujtahids, the proponents of the Akhbāri School did not believe in the deputyships of the infallible Imam.[4] The emergence of Akhbārism, therefore, was a factor that closed the opportunity structure for Shiʿi clerical activism for decades.

With the demise of the Safavid dynasty in 1722 and the establishment of the Afsharid a decade later, the context became even more restrictive for clerical activism. The Shiʿi clergy were forced to abandon politics, their ties with the state were loosened, and the majority of them migrated to Iraq, which was then under the rule of the Sunni Ottomans. For the following century, Shiʿi clerical elites focused on teaching at seminaries and remained quiet politically due to the absence of a favourable political opportunity structure. Yet, with the crackdown of the Akhbāris and the establishment of the Qajar dynasty in Persia (1794–1935 CE), the political opportunity structure was once again transformed for many of the Shiʿi clerical elite.

At the international level, the world was engaged with the hegemonic rivalries among the colonial powers of the time. Sovereign states were forming in the region and the introduction of new transport and communication technologies fostered the development of a sort of transnationalism among the Shiʿi community. This factor is considerable when taking into account the fact that, in the post-Safavid era, the clergy–state relationship had been replaced by the clergy–laity relationship to some extent: in contrast to their Sunni counterparts, Shiʿi clerical elites had been successful in reducing their dependency on rulers and, instead, becoming more dependent on the public especially for their religious endowments and financial supports. This, and the growing transnational links among clerical elites contributed, regionally, nationally and societally, to producing a relatively open political opportunity structure for clerical activism. As it is mentioned in Chapter 3, it was because of this uniquely open structure of opportunities, and clerical elite appreciation of it, that Shiʿi clerical elites played an active role in the Russo-Persian Wars (1826–8 CE), the Tobacco Protest (1890–2 CE) and the Persian Constitutional Revolution (1905–11 CE).

However, a review of Shiʿi history from the commencement of the occultation to the start of the modern era confirms that the clergy failed to accomplish its goals through its political activism on various occasions. According to the argument of this book, this outcome results from a mismatch between the political opportunity structure and clerical elite perceptions of it – and, specifically, a situation in which there exists a closed opportunity structure which clerics misperceive as being open. A case in point is Shiʿi clerical activism during the Persian Constitutional Revolution of 1906. In this case, some clerics, having misperceived the nature of the political opportunity structure at that time, became actively involved in the political arena, with the consequence that their activism produced an outcome that delivered a drastic blow to clerical authority (see Chapter 3). Three case studies were developed to further elaborate the role of context in determining the Shiʿi clerical elite activism in the Middle East. During the Islamic Revolution in Iran, in post-Saddam Iraq and with the rise of Hezbollah in Lebanon, clerical political activism materialized when the clerical leadership was confronted with a relatively open political opportunity structure and, having accurately perceived it to be open, became politically active.

The contemporary Middle East, political opportunity structures and Shiʿi activism

For almost four decades, the concept of 'political opportunity structure' has been at the core of the study of social movements and contentious politics. Proponents of this widely used concept in the fields of Political Science and Sociology tended to define 'political opportunities' more-or-less along lines consistent with Sidney Tarrow's definition: '*consistent but not necessarily formal, permanent, or national signals to social or political actors which either encourage or discourage them to use their internal resources to form social movements*'.[5] But in 1990s, most researchers, in an evident departure from this viewpoint, began to recognize the significance of actors' perceptions of the 'objective conditions'. Recent researchers argue that the perception, accurate or not, is important in the formation of contentious politics.[6] However, little has been done to explore the implications of this idea.[7]

This book has endeavoured to understand the means through which actors and, specifically, the Shiʿi clerical elite perceive objective structures. It argues that the majority of Shiʿi clergy, in their role as general deputies of the infallible Imam during the Occultation era, believe that in order to lead their laity followers, it is incumbent upon them to render judgements that will protect the community from threats. The means by which a Shiʿi clerical elite interprets and, therefore, perceives the nature of the existing opportunity structure at any given time is through engaging in ijtihad. A qualified mujtahid perceives his surrounding world through the lens of ijtihad. His ijtihad is influenced both by his understanding of the objective conditions as well as, to some extent, his own personal characteristics. Therefore, when facing a similar objective political opportunity structure, it is possible that two mujtahids may arrive at two different interpretations. As long as they are endeavouring to apply Islamic principles to the current circumstances, each is abiding by his divinely assigned responsibility.

Encountering the political opportunity structure at a given time and place, the Shiʿi clerical elite would become politically active only when he perceives the opportunity structure to be open. If his perception is accurate, his activism will be successful; if it is inaccurate he will not achieve his goals. On the other hand, when the objective political opportunity structure is closed, a cleric who accurately perceives that structure will remain quiet; if he perceives the structure inaccurately, he will become active, but his activism will likely be unsuccessful.

The argument, therefore, is that the differences of Shiʿi clerical elites' political postures – in modern Iran, Iraq and Lebanon – are just attributable to distinctions in the objective political opportunity structures, that they have faced, and not, for example, to the existence of fundamentally different versions of Shiʿism. 'Activism' and 'quietism', therefore, should be understood as representing not a strategic or doctrinal divide in Shiʿism, but only tactical political postures that vary according to a given context.

To develop a comprehensive and systematic assessment of the objective political opportunity structures that Shiʿi clerical elites faced in the three case studies presented in previous chapters, these structures are conceived of as consisting of different levels of analysis – different levels of social organization or generality, ranging from the international system to individuals. The objective political opportunity structures relevant to the case studies of Iran, Iraq and Lebanon presented in the last three chapters exhibited both recurrent and unique factors.

At the international level, the political opportunity structure was somehow overlapping for the Shiʿi communities in the Middle East. Especially, Shiʿi elites faced threats arising from the Cold War until the early 1990s. The US–Soviet rivalries represented the potential threat of a non-Muslim conquest of the Islamic abode. While Iran was inclined towards the western camp for the most of its pre-revolution era, the Republic of Iraq tended towards the east, and Lebanon was vacillating between the two camps during the course of the Cold War. The Shiʿi clergy strived to protect its followers from both the detrimental influences of anti-religious communism and the religious laxity and secularism introduced by western liberalism. Based on factors which contributed to the opportunity structure at other levels, some clerics succeeded, and others failed, to mitigate these perceived threats to their communities.

At the regional level, the abolition of the Ottoman Caliphate in the aftermath of the First World War and the rise of Kamal Ataturk changed political structures in Iraq and Lebanon and influence those of Iran (See the overview of clerical concerns about the event in Chapter 4). The rise of Iraq republic in 1958, the civil war in Lebanon and most significantly the establishment of the Islamic Republic of Iran had impacts at regional level, on political opportunity structures of the neighbouring countries. One impact of these regional upheavals was the development of a sense of religious transnationalism among Shiʿi communities in the Middle East. For instance, the popular uprising in 1963 in Iran attracted a response from the leadership of the Najaf seminary in Iraq (see Chapter 5), as did the devastating civil war in Lebanon from 1975 to 1990 (see Chapter 6). Religious leaders in Iran opposed the atrocities of the Baʿth regime against the Shiʿi community in Iraq (1968–2003) and condemned the Israeli invasion of Lebanon in the 1980s (see Chapters 5 and 6).

An important element of political opportunity structure at the national level is represented by the attitude of the state towards the Shiʿi religious community. Throughout the modern era, the Shiʿi community and its clerical leadership have been subject to relentless repression by Iranian and Iraqi states. The rise of Reza Shah Pahlavi in Iran became concurrent with his pressure on clerical establishments in Iran. Although during the early stages of Muhammad Reza Pahlavi's reign, some restrictions against the clergy were lifted, and during the second half of his rule, clerics were the target of sanctions by the regime (see Chapter 4). Due to the weakness of the central state, the Shiʿis in Lebanon were faced with a more open political opportunity structure; but the situation was worse for the Shiʿis in Iraq. The rise of the Baʿth regime in Iraq in 1968 heralded the start of the most severely repressive era for the Shiʿi community and for clerics settled in the holy cities. The state did not tolerate even the least amount of activism among the clergy and responded to them with the utmost harshness.[8] Over the course of the two decades that ended with Operation Iraqi Freedom in 2003, the Shiʿi clerical elite in Iraq faced a closed political opportunity structure as a result, mainly, of state repression.

At the societal level, the political opportunity structures that existed in Iran, Iraq and Lebanon at the time of the events detailed in the case studies had few similarities. The vast majority of the population of Iran is Shiʿi; Iranian nationalism and Shiʿism construct the identity of most of the population of the country in the modern era. In as much as each Iranian national shows patriotism towards his country, he cherishes Shiʿi Islam, though not necessarily the activities of the Shiʿi clerics. This is a factor that is unique to the objective political opportunity structure faced by political actors in Iran, including the Shiʿi clergy. Thus, during the eight-year war with Iraq, Iran's Shiʿi leaders took advantage of this to promote an Iranian–Shiʿi discourse as a means of mobilizing the masses in Iran. The opportunity structures in Iraq and Lebanon are, to some extent, different. While both are hugely influenced by sectarianism, Iraqi society is still relatively dependent on tribal values as well.

The Shiʿis of Iraq came to constitute the majority of the population of the country during the process of conversion by Sunni tribesmen to Shiʿi Islam in the early twentieth century.[9] Therefore, the traces of strong Arab and nomadic ties should not be underestimated in studying the Shiʿis of Iraq. Some Iraqi tribes still have both Sunni and Shiʿi members, both of whom show relatively strong patronage to their tribal values and sheikhs. Shiʿi clerics in Iraq have always faced the dilemma of how to respond to this tribalism when considering how to undertake their sociopolitical responsibilities (see Chapter 5). The Shiʿi clerical elite is less likely to engage in politics, or to expect a successful outcome if he becomes active, unless he has the support of tribal chiefs. This is also reflected in Lebanon, but through the lens of sectarianism. Lebanese identity is constructed along sectarian lines. Therefore, the main concern of the Shiʿi clerical leadership in Lebanon is to evaluate the consequences of their actions vis-à-vis the almost sixteen other religious sects that are found throughout the country. Nevertheless, the sectarianism of Lebanon's society has enabled Shiʿi clerics to form a strong relationship with the Shiʿi laity.

At a bureaucratic level, clerical elite organization structures vary in the three cases. The Najaf seminary in Iraq, established ten centuries ago, has been the most important centre for Shiʿi studies throughout Islamic history. In contrast, the Qum seminary in Iran is only about a hundred years old. In Lebanon, and despite the enormous influence of Shiʿi Amili scholars (see Chapter 3) on contemporary jurisprudence, the country does not currently have any important seminary. It was only during Ayatollah Burujirdi's leadership of the seminary in Qum (1947–61) that the centre became known globally and that its status, to some extent, superseded that enjoyed by the Najaf seminary. At the same time, Najaf seminary was entangled with post-British Mandate discontents. It is noteworthy that the majority of Najaf seminary leaders, excluding Ayatollah Muhsin Al-Hakim, are Iranian by descent. This ultimately, especially at the individual level, further closed the opportunity structure for the activism of the Shiʿi clergy in Iraq. The seminary in Qum has not had this problem. The centre was able to survive the threats of Reza Shah's rule under the providential leadership of Ayatollah Hairi, and further strengthened its foundations under the leadership of Burujirdi. By the late 1950s, the Qum seminary was known as the most important Shiʿi centre in the world. It was through this capacity that it succeeded in developing a robust network of clerics extending to the most remote cities in Iran. The exploitation of this network on the eve of the Islamic Revolution played a most crucial role in orchestrating mass demonstrations against the rule of Muhammad Reza Pahlavi. In Lebanon, the absence of bureaucratic institutions for the Shiʿi clergy-led Imam Musa Sadr to seek to establish the Supreme Islamic Shia Council in the late 1960s. Although its establishment succeeded in promoting the clerical leaderships' mission throughout the Shiʿi community in Lebanon, later, with Sadr out of the picture, the Council's effectiveness decreased and was largely replaced by AMAL and, later, by the Hezbollah Juristic Council.

The political opportunity structure for Shiʿi activism on an individual level has been relatively dependent on a handful of charismatic leaders, high-ranking mujtahids, who have been active in Iran, Iraq and Lebanon during the modern era. As leaders of their relevant communities, each of these figures has sought to seize the opportunity, when it has been available, to pursue their sociopolitical roles and responsibilities. Facing different objective political opportunities on broader levels, these figures have, through their ijtihads and other activities, contributed to the structure on an individual level. The novel ijtihad of Khomeini in the 1970s outlining the role of the clergy as participants in sociopolitical affairs was not only crystalized as a response to the structure he perceived at the time, but it also changed the objective political opportunity structure for his colleagues and followers and further developed contention against the regime of the Shah in Iran. This was similar to the role that Imam Musa Sadr played in revitalizing the Shiʿi community in Lebanon. In contrast, the ijtihad of Ayatollah Khoei, influenced by his interpretation of what was a relatively closed political opportunity structure in Iraq during 1980s, pushed him towards assuming a quietist posture and, hence, further closed the political opportunity structure.

Evaluating the objective political opportunity structures at different levels further explains the rationale behind the political postures of different Shiʿi clerical elites in contemporary Iran, Iraq and Lebanon. The course of events that led to the current Shiʿi revival in the Middle East is mainly influenced by the contextual changes which have occurred in recent years and which, consequently, provided a relatively more open political opportunity structure for clerical activism. For their part, the Shiʿi clergy were able to accurately perceive opportunities where they existed and seize them in order to benefit their followers. This constitutes a remote connection among the clerical elites and their followers in different communities across the region. The transnational Shiʿi network that has formed in the region is based on clerical authority, their responsibility to protect the Shiʿi community and clergy–laity religious relationships.

The transnational mujtahids

The charismatic Marja'iyya network in modern times constitutes the backbone of Shi'i transnationalism. Nevertheless, the development of this network has been started since the eighteenth century. The fall of the Safavid capital, Isfahan, in 1722 marked a turning point in the Shi'i clergy's relationship with the state and with its laity followers. During the two centuries of Safavid rule in Persia, Shi'i elites had been engaged in a give-and-take relationship with monarchs and, to some extent, shared power with the state. During the same period, thousands of mosques and hundreds of seminaries were built throughout the country and the clergy, who had strong support from the state at the time, also succeeded in constructing a robust relationship with the laity. Clerics became the point of reference for religious matters and, in every corner of Persia, people abided by their verdicts in mediating conflicts, marriages, divorces and deaths. There was an obvious vertical expansion of the clergy through Persian Shi'i society. However, as a result of the Afghan invasions (1722 CE), and later the restrictive policy of Nader Shah (1736–47), the majority of clerical elites preferred to leave Persia and settle in the holy cities in Iraq. However, contrary to what everyone expected, the clergy–laity relationship was not diminished and, in fact, became relatively stronger over the course of subsequent decades (see Chapter 3).

Though pious followers still sought the advice of clerics in religious affairs, the absence of a supportive Shi'i state made clerical elites in Iraq dependent on financial support from the wealthy classes and on religious taxes coming from their laity followers in Persia. Every year, hundreds of trustworthy couriers were responsible for mediating between the Persian laity and the Maraji' who were residing in seminaries in Iraq. These couriers were responsible for collecting both religious taxes and religious inquiries from Persia, and bringing back the signed responses of the clerical elites. Later on, the introduction of new communication technologies (e.g. telegram) further facilitated this process. In the mid-nineteenth century, concurrent with the leadership of Sheikh Murtada Ansari (d. 1864), the sense of a transnational clergy–laity relationship was formed in Najaf seminary. The Qajar dynasty in Persia was more open to the activities of the clerical elite, Usuli mujtahids had ousted the dogmatic Akhbāri School, and the Persia–Iraq telegram line facilitated communications. It was in such circumstances that the leader of Najaf seminary was known as the sole Marja' of all Shi'is throughout the Islamic world. Since then the eyes of the Shi'is in Persia and other countries in the region focused on Najaf, the centre of this ever-expanding religious transnational network. The undeniable role of Mirza Shirazi, who resided in Samarra and was the highest-ranking Shi'i Marja' of the time, in the Tobacco Protest in Persia can be understood in relation to this structure (see Chapter 3).

A hundred years later, the rise of an Islamic state in Iran, run by the Shi'i clergy, raised the fresh question of the possibilities of religious and political Shi'i transnationalism. A new stream of literature within Middle East studies and Political Science has tried to address this question. Louër sheds some light on the nature of this transnationalism. Observing Shi'i political movements within some Persian Gulf countries, she states that, although the Islamic Revolution in Iran energized Shi'i activism throughout the region, it failed to create a robust transnational network (see Chapter 5). She believes that the ambition to 'export the revolution', initiated by the clerical leadership of the Islamic Republic of Iran, failed; and maintains that what emerged, instead, to the dismay of the religious leaders of Iran, was a bipolarization of the Shiʿi Muslim community.[10]

The argument of this book confirms Louër's claim about the importance of 'domestic space' in the formation of Shiʿi politics,[11] in that the political postures assumed by the clergy are influenced by national and societal level factors that contribute to the political opportunity structure and, hence, by the domestic affairs of countries. But, can one declare the end of transnationalism in Shiʿi politics? Again, the analysis presented here implies the existence of a Shiʿi transnational network. This is based on scrutinizing the role of Shiʿi Marja'iyya in the routine affairs of their laities (which Louër and other scholars acknowledge). The religious responsibility of Shiʿi Marja' is not confined to a nation, tribe or a specific ethnic group; principally, its authority encompasses all the Shiʿis. A Shiʿi Marja', the most righteous mujtahid at a given time, is responsible towards the community and should act respectively. However, when he perceives a restrictive context, he may prefer to remain quiet politically. Imam Khomeini's views, based on his ijtihad, applied to the Shiʿi communities throughout the world. He constantly addressed 'all Muslims', the 'Islamic Ummah', the 'oppressed Shiʿis' of Iraq, Lebanon, Saudi Arabia, Kuwait and other countries hosting Shiʿi Muslims, and conveyed personal judgements about ongoing developments in those countries. This was not the case only when he became the supreme leader of the Islamic Republic; this position had characterized his sense of his religious responsibility decades before. As a Shiʿi Marja', he was responsible for leading all Shiʿis, whether Iranian, Arab, Kurd or other. In Iraq, the same can be said of Ayatollah Muhsin Al-Hakim (d. 1970), Ayatollah Abu al-Qasim Khoei (d. 1992) and Ayatollah Ali Sistani, who, on different occasions, have expressed, and continue to express, positions on the affairs of non-Iraqi Shiʿi communities. Similarly, in Lebanon, Imam Musa Sadr, Muhammad Husayn Fadlallah (d. 2010) and, currently, Sayyid Hassan Nasrallah have all been outspoken about the affairs of Shiʿi communities in other countries.

Therefore, the activities of Marja'iyya go beyond the borders of the country in which they reside. This extends far further than family ties (e.g. Sadrs, Khoeis, Shirazis and Hakims) among members of the Shiʿi clerical elite. It is even far broader than the network of the Prophet's Descendants, *Sayyids*, throughout the Islamic world, as detailed in some studies.[12] It includes a strong, to some extent personal, relationship between the Marja' and his followers, which has been formed for centuries and is still valid despite all the discontents of the modern era. It is the case for the religious Iranian laity who follow the verdicts of Ayatollah Sistani in Najaf, as for Lebanese laymen who follow Ayatollah Khamenei, in Iran. This relationship forms the very foundation of Shiʿi transnationalism in the contemporary Shiʿi world.

Throughout this book, and its case studies of Shiʿi politics in the historical and contemporary Shiʿi world, examples of this network have been suggested. Apart from the relationship between Marja' and laity followers, the clergy as a whole supports the strengthening of Shiʿi transnationalism. An Iraqi Marja' who endorses a colleague residing in Iran is reinforcing Shiʿi clerical authority (which is a Shiʿi principle in the eyes of the clerical elite) and benefiting a clergy that forms a networked social stratum throughout the Shiʿi world. This dynamic also challenges the categorization of Shiʿi clergy as principally quietist or activist.

The myth of 'quietism' versus 'activism': How does the Shiʿi clergy read its history?

It has been argued that there does not exist any strategic disparity among Shiʿi clerical elites in their political engagements. Those known as active Shiʿi clerics as well as those famous for their quietism all believe they have the same roles and responsibilities vis-à-vis the Shiʿi community as a whole. During the Occultation era, the Usuli mujtahids, who represent the majority of Shiʿi clerical elites, reserve for themselves the exclusive right to issue *Ifta* and *Qadha*. Shiʿi clerical elites universally believe that it is incumbent upon them to issue legal opinions and interpretations of Islamic law in given circumstances. The majority of the clergy also reserve the right of issuing judgements to their followers among the laity, *Qadha*. These were among the responsibilities of the Prophet and the infallible Imams, and have been inherited by their general deputies and clerical elites during the Occultation era.

Faced with the contingencies of the contemporary era and the structural changes that had occurred in the late 1970s, a group of clerics in Iran seized an opportunity and established an Islamic Republic. Imam Khomeini, the most famous cleric of the time, believed that institutionalizing the Shiʿi clerical *Qadha* requires the acquisition of executive power; to this end, the context was favourable for the Shiʿi clergy in post-Revolution Iran.

At the first step, Shiʿi clerics succeeded in forming a judicial system in Iran based mainly on Islamic Sharia. A theme in documents found in historical archives, supported by excerpts of interviews conducted for this book with a handful of those closely affiliated to Khomeini, confirmed that, in post-revolutionary Iran, where the judicial system remained unchallenged, and the role of the clergy and its judgements were respected, clerics did not engage in political activism. However, the perception of potential threats by internal and external forces, have led the clerical elite to seek to further strengthen their authority in Iran by assuming a more activist political posture. So, for instance, the supreme leader, who had not agreed to allow Sayyid Muhammad Beheshti to be fielded as a candidate in the January 1980 presidential election, on the grounds that he was a cleric, in 1981 encouraged Sayyid Ali Khamenei to participate in elections in response to what he perceived as a threat to the very foundations of the Islamic Republic.

On the other hand, internal schisms among the revolutionaries were highest during the first decade after the revolution. International sanctions, and a devastating war with Iraq, ignited a sense of irrational inconsistency among active clerics at the forefront of politics. Nonetheless, the spiritual and charismatic leadership of Imam Khomeini helped to mitigate these threats. This turn of events favoured the moderate, yet active clergy in Iran in the last months of Khomeini's life. By the late 1980s, a group of active clerics had succeeded in consolidating their political position in Iran, and these sought to promote Iran as a crucial regional power and to abide with the norms of the international community.

With the end of Cold War, the consolidation of the regional role of the Islamic Republic, the expulsion of the internal opposition that had represented an existentialist threat to the Islamic state in the eyes of many clerics, and the expansion of clerical authority throughout the country, Iranian leaders confronted a new political opportunity structure, and so were obliged to redefine their political postures. Ever since, despite some critical upheavals (e.g. the nuclear crisis), they have pursued a relatively rational set of policies based on realpolitik and diplomacy.[13] This can be understood as the development by activist clerical elites of a new ijtihad that enables them to both fulfil their responsibilities and to act as members of the international community.

The objective political opportunity structure in Iraq is, to some extent, different to that in Iran. Although the Shiʿi community constitutes the majority of the population, it has experienced Sunni supremacy since the emergence of the independent state in the 1920s. Nevertheless, with the fall of the Baʿth regime, the clerical leadership offered an opportunity to consolidate the rights of the community. As a first step, Ayatollah Sistani insisted on a one-man-one-vote standard and asked the Iraqi Shiʿis to participate in the 2005 election. He pragmatically sought a way for the Shiʿi community to make the most out of its numerical majority in today's Iraq.[14]

Perceiving the political opportunity structure to be relatively favourable, the Ayatollah became active in politics – though, for example being of Iranian descent, with some reservations. He sought to strengthen and protect the community at that critical moment. In an interview I held with Sayyid Muhammad Reza Sistani, he implied that the endeavours of his father were mainly focused on lobbying with elected members of the Provisional Assembly to prevent the ratification of 'anti-Sharia laws' in the new Iraqi constitution.[15] The objective political opportunity structure for Shiʿi activism in Iraq in 2005 was fundamentally different from that of Iran in 1980. The clerical leadership in Iraq had been a witness to the experiences of its colleagues in Iran over the previous three decades. This was mainly responsible for the seeming divergence of the views of Khomeini's and Sistani, two of the most distinguished Shiʿi leaders of their times. Eventually, the pragmatism pursued by Sistani rewarded the Shiʿi community and its religious leadership in Iraq with the maximum degree of authority they have received since the birth of the modern country.

Since 2005, the clerical leadership in Iraq, though not directly active in routine executive political matters, has been the source of legitimacy for the state to which most people refer to. In a handful of cases, and whenever they are requested, Ayatollah Sistani and his entourage in Iraq have issued fatwas or mediated conflicts among different parties in order to stabilize the country's internal and foreign affairs. However, perhaps the most significant move in post-2003 Iraq was made on the eve of the fall of Mosul to the fanatics of the Islamic State of Iraq and the Levant in June 2014. In the most exceptional act of almost a century of Shiʿi history, Sistani issued the Fatwa of Jihad calling on all Iraqis, Shiʿis and non-Shiʿis, 'to defend the country, its people, the honor of its citizens, and its sacred places'.[16] The Fatwa represents the greatest degree of political activism that has ever been exhibited by a Shiʿi cleric residing in Iraq.

The irony is, however, that it came from the figure who was believed by a majority of analysts to be the most famous advocate of political quietism among the Shiʿi clergy.[17] The political postures taken by Sistani over the course of the last twelve years clearly indicates that he becomes engaged in politics when, in the context of an open political opportunity structure, he perceives both threat to the Shiʿi community, especially when it comes from outsiders. His millions of followers, Iraqi politicians and other regional players regard him as the most influential religious leader in Iraq.[18]

Shiʿi activism in Lebanon also has unique characteristics compared with those of Iran and Iraq. Interestingly, the Shiʿis in Lebanon had succeeded in establishing a legal court dedicated to their sect before the Shiʿis in Iran and Iraq. Indeed, the establishment of Ja'fari court in 1926 was a vehicle for Shiʿi sectarian identity in Lebanon.[19] Due to the relatively closed objective structural opportunity structure in the country and, particularly, the mainly confessional nature of Lebanese politics, the Shiʿi clergy in Lebanon engaged in politics simply to protect the very existence of the sect. It took Imam Musa Sadr, the founder of clerical activism in contemporary Lebanon, more than fifteen years to form AMAL, the military wing of the Deprived Movement, in 1974. The manifesto of the movement indicates that it had formed as a means of protecting the deprived Lebanese communities (Shiʿis), which at the time was entangled geographically between the hostilities of Palestinian refugees in the south and the Maronites of Beirut and northern Lebanon.

Later on, with the commencement of the civil war in 1975 and constant threats from Israel, Shiʿi clerical elites moved further towards assuming an activist posture. Imam Musa Sadr's inheritors did the same. Most notably, the formation of Hezbollah around a handful of clerical figures was a response to the threats of Israeli occupation in post-1982 Lebanon. Although during its early years, the clerical leadership of Hezbollah asked for the establishment of an Islamic state, they later and with the emergence of a new charismatic leadership, moderated their posture consistent with the realities of the country's political structure. Today, Hezbollah of Lebanon forms a strong faction within the state and has a remarkable popular constituency. Moreover, as long as there is a threat of an Israeli invasion in the south, the historical stronghold of the Shiʿis, it is unrealistic to think that the party and its clerical leadership would voluntarily give up their armed resistance.

Reviewing the trajectory of the Shiʿi clergy political activism in the Middle East since the early twentieth century, one could conclude that, when it comes to the protection of the community from outsiders' threats, clerics form powerful associations, either by engaging in activism or supporting their active colleagues. In a post-9/11 World, and with the rise of transnational terrorist groups that impose constant threats to the regional order, it has become clear that what is perhaps the greater threat to stability in the region is the set of doctrines that are embraced by a small group of fanatical Sunni Salafists in the region. Today the active Shiʿi leadership in Iran, Iraq and Lebanon present a coherent pragmatic policy that complies with the norms of the international community. This, and the fact that Shiʿis are numerically a majority of the population of the Gulf, which is at the heart of the Middle East, suggest that this leadership would constitute a significant regional power broker.

Categorizing members of high-ranking Shiʿi clerics as either apolitical quietists or extremist activists obscures the realpolitik that is common to all of them, and the varying political contexts which arise in the Middle East. Shiʿi clerics are always potentially active. The very foundations of the faith have been constructed on politics. Above all, in times of threat, the clerical leadership is capable of orchestrating political contention whenever they perceive a relatively open political opportunity structure. To this end, especially in modern times, they may go beyond the exclusive domain of spiritual activities and engage in more pragmatic politics. To fulfil their responsibilities, as the heirs to the Prophet and infallible Imams, they form alliances with specific social class against common threats and might even join with autocratic state rulers. The end for them is, indeed, to protect the community during the ever-threatening era in which Shiʿis are deprived of the infallible source of leadership; acknowledging this is a crucial step towards understanding Shiʿi politics in the region today, and how these politics might shape the future.

Glossary

'Alim (plural. **Ulama**): the educated class of Muslim scholars.

Allameh: An honorary title carried by the clerical scholars of Islamic science, jurisprudence and philosophy.

Arbaeen: (lit. 'The Fortieth [day]'): The Shiite religious observation that takes place forty days after the Day of Ashura to commemorate the martyrdom of the third infallible Imam, Hussein Ibn Ali. The day falls on the 20th of Safar, the second month of the Islamic Lunar Calendar.

Ashura: The Shiite observance marking the anniversary of the third Imam's martyrdom in 680. It falls on the 10th of Muharram, the first month of the Islamic Lunar Calendar.

Ayatollah: (lit. 'The Sign of Allah'): A high-ranking title carried by a Shiite clerical elite. In the contemporary era, the clerical elite titles start with *Theqat al-Islam* (The Trustee of Islam), followed by *Hujjat al-Islam* (The Proof of Islam), *Hujjat al-Islam wa al-Muslemin* (The Proof of Islam and to Muslims), *Ayatollah* and *Ayatollah Uzma* (The Grand Ayatollah).

Fatwa: A legal pronouncement issued by a qualified Muslim jurist regarding a specific issue at a given time.

Hadith: Tradition concerning the Prophet Muhammad and the Infallible Imams' lives and utterances.

Hawza: A traditional Shiite seminary where clerics are trained.

Ifta: The act, by a qualified Muslim jurist, of issuing a legal pronouncement (fatwa).

Ijtihad: (lit. 'Striving and exerting'): Making deductions in matters of Islamic law, in cases in which no explicit text is applicable.

Infallible Imams: The twelve saints, from the abode of the Prophet Muhammad, who are his legitimate successors. The first of them is Ali Ibn Abu Talib, the prophet's son-in-law, following by Hassan, the elder son of Ali, Hussein, the younger son of Ali, and the nine descendants of Hussein.

Kalam: (lit. 'Science of Discourse'): A scientific practice in Islamic philosophy that seeks to confirm theological principles through dialectics, debates and argument.

Khums: (lit. 'The One-fifth'): A religious tax, obligatory for Shiite laities, representing a contribution of one-fifth of their annual income to the infallible Imam or his deputies.

Majlis: (lit. 'A place of Sitting'): Technically it refers to the House of Parliament.

Marja' Taqlid (plural **Maraji'**): The highest-ranking clergy who is followed by groups of Shiite laity as the general deputy of the infallible Imam during the Occultation era. Marja'iyya refers to the position held by the Marja'.

Mujtahid: A cleric competent enough to engage in ijtihad.

Mulla: One of the titles generally used, especially in pre-contemporary era, for a man trained in Islamic jurisprudence and law.

Nass: A known and clear legal injunction of the Quran, the Prophet and the Infallible Imams' traditions.

Occultation era: Refers, in Shiite principles, to a period during which the twelfth infallible Imam has disappeared and is unseen. The era is divided into two consecutive periods. The former Minor Occultation era, from 874–941, when the Imam was in contact with his followers through his four special deputies; and the Major Occultation era, since 941, when the Imam appointed no special deputy.

Omour Hesbiah: (lit. 'Non-litigious Affairs'**):** In Shiite jurisprudence it refers to general affairs to which social order is linked.

Ra'y: (lit. 'Verdict'): In Islamic jurisprudence it means a personal opinion in adapting the law.

Sayyid: An honorific title denoting to the descendants of the Prophet Muhammad.

Sharia: The Islamic Law. In Shiite Islam it refers to the body of canonical laws deducted from the Quran, and from the Prophet's and infallible Imam's traditions, which lays down certain responsibilities for Muslims.

Sheikh: (lit. 'The Elder'): A title in Arabic that carries the meaning of 'chief' of the community, tribe, family or village.

Taqiyya: In Shiite jurisprudence, it refers to a form of dissimulation of the faith in order to diminish the risk of enemies' persecution.

Waqf (plural Awqaf): An Islamic endowment of a building, plot of land and sometimes cash that is used for charitable and religious purposes.

Zann: (lit. 'Dubious Supposition'): Valid conjecture or speculation of a jurist about the soundness of an Islamic tradition, which does not entail more than a probability.

Notes

Chapter 1

1 Abdolreza Kefayi, interview with the author, Qum, August 2011.
2 Twelver Shiʿism, *Ithnā 'Asharīyya*, or Imam Shiʿism, is the largest branch of Shiʿi Islam. Its adherents believe in a succession of twelve divinely guided Imams that served as leaders of the community following the death of the Prophet Muhammad. Throughout this book, the term 'Shiʿi' is used to refer to this main branch, unless otherwise stated.
3 Writing just twenty years prior to the 1979 Revolution, observers maintained that Shiʿi sects could be divided into two general groups: 'moderate and extreme', with Twelvers classified as the 'most moderate sect'. See Bullard, *The Middle East*, p.44.
4 Ajami, 'Iran: The Impossible Revolution', p. 135.
5 A case in point is studies of the Islamic party, *Fadaian e Islam*, in Western academia (see, e.g. Behdad, 'Islamic Utopia in pre-revolutionary Iran'). The group was politically active in Iran during the 1940s and 1950s under the leadership of a young cleric, Mojtaba Navvab Safavi. It is noteworthy that except for a number of short reports that appeared in *Time Magazine* in February and December 1952, which addressed what was characterized as a 'Fanatical Islamic Group', there was not much research on the party prior to the 1979 revolution in Iran. More information on this party and its ideology will be presented in Chapter 4.
6 Nasr, 'Regional Implications', p. 9.
7 It is believed that the Shiʿi uprising in Saudi Arabia in late 1979 and Shiʿi revolts in Bahrain during the 1980s were inspired by the Islamic Revolution in Iran. See Kechichian, 'The gulf cooperation council'.
8 Norton, 'Changing Actors and Leadership'.
9 Nasr, 'When the Shiʿis Rise', p. 59.
10 Wright and Baker, 'Iraq, Jordan See Threat'.
11 For insights on the Shiʿi Crescent, see Cole, 'A 'Shiʿi Crescent'?'; Haji-Yousefi, 'Whose Agenda is Served'; and Barzegar, 'Iran and the Shiʿi Crescent'.
12 Visser, 'Sistani, the United States and Politics in Iraq'.
13 Cook, 'Activism and Quietism in Islam', p. 21.
14 Gleave, 'Quietism and Political Legitimacy', p. 102.
15 Nakash, 'The Shi'ites and the Future of Iraq'.
16 See Keddie, *Religion and Politics in Iran.*
17 See Marcinkowski, *Twelver Shi'ite Islam.*
18 Cole, 'The United States and Shi'ite Religious Factions'.
19 Hamoudi, 'Between Realism and Resistance'.
20 Braam, 'All Roads Lead to Najaf'.
21 Ibid., p. 14.
22 Hamoudi, 'Between Realism and Resistance', p. 111.
23 Ibid., p. 118.

24 Puelings, 'Fearing a Shi'i Octopus'.
25 Schmidt, 'The Role of Religion in Politics'.
26 Visser, 'Sistani, the United States and Politics in Iraq'.
27 Rahimi, 'Ayatollah Ali al-Sistani'.
28 However, the exponents of the quietist posture have often been, in practice, supporters of authoritarian politics and have offered unquestioning and immediate obedience to almost any Muslim authority that publicly adhered to the Sharia. See Sachedina, 'Prudential Concealment in Shi'ite Islam', p. 237.
29 Sachedina, 'Activist Shi'ism in Iran, Iraq, and Lebanon'; Enayat, *Modern Islamic Political Thought*, pp. 175–83.
30 Rahimi, 'The Discourse of Democracy in Shi'i'.
31 Hamoudi, 'Between Realism and Resistance', pp. 107–20.
32 For the viewpoints of Shi'i ulama about *the Guardianship of the Jurist* from eleventh century to date, see Al-Mufid, *Al-Muqni'a*, p. 810; Al-Tusi, *al-Nihāyah*, p. 704; Al-Muhaqqiq al-Hilli, *Sharā'i' al-Islām*, Vol I, p. 266; Al-Karaki, *Rasā'il al-Muḥaqqiq al-Karakī*, Vol I, p. 142; Al-Shahid al-Thāni, *Masālik Al-Afhām*, Vol. III, p. 9; Al-Ardabili, *Majma' Al-fā'idah wa-Al-Burhān*, Vol. XII, p. 11; Naraqi, *'Awā'id al-ayyām*, p. 529; Al-Najafi, *Jawāhir Al-Kalām*, Vol. XXI, p. 397; Al-Ansari, *Kitāb Al-Makāsib*, Vol. III, p. 557; Akhund Khurasani, *Ḥāshiyah kitāb al-makāsib*, p. 96; Yazdi, *Al-'Urwah al-wuthqá*, Vol. IV, p. 111; Araki, *al-Makāssib al-muḥarramah*, pp. 93–5; Na'ini, *Tanbīh Al-ummah*, p. 72; Burujirdi, *Istiftā'āt*, Vol. II, pp. 471–82; Al-Hakim, *Nahj Al-faqāhah*, Vol I, pp. 299–300; Sadr, *Al-Fatāwá Al-wāḍiḥah*, Vol. I, p. 115; Khawnsari, *Jāmi' Al-madārik*, Vol. III, p. 100; Shariatmadari, *Taḥqīq wa-taqrīrāt fī bāb al-bay'*, Vol. IV, p. 37; Khomeini, *Kitāb Al-Bay'*, Vol. II, p. 467; Khoei, *Ṣirāṭ al-najāh fī ajwibat al-istiftā'āt*, p. 10; Makarem Shirazi, *Anwār al-Faqāhah*, Vol. I, pp. 506–8; Muntaziri, *Dirāsāt fī wilāyat al-faqīh*, Vol. II, pp. 168–9; Sobhani, *Mabānī-i Ḥukūmat-i Islāmī*, p. 197; Jawadi Amoli, *Wilāyat-i faqīh*, p. 242; Khamenei, *Ajwibat Al-Istiftā'āt*, Vol. I, p. 11.
33 Visser, 'Sistani, the United States and Politics in Iraq'.
34 This book focuses on those clerical elites who adhere to the traditionalist Usuli Schools. Unless stated otherwise, the terms 'clerical elite', 'the clergy', 'Ulama' and 'Mujtahid' refer to this category of clergy, which represents the majority of Shi'i clerical elites in modern time.
35 The necessity of forming a group of scholars, or a Muslim clerical elite, was explicitly mentioned in the Quran. The relevant verse reads: 'it is not for the believers to go forth all at once; for there should be separate from every division of them a group to obtain understanding in the religion and warn their people when they return to them' (IX: 122).
36 The term 'protecting the citadel of Islam (and/or the faith)', *hefz beyzat al-Islam*, literally protecting Islam's testicles, is a common concept in the lexicon of political jurisprudence. It refers to those Islamic and Shi'i principles that the faith's very existence is dependent upon. For more details see Kalantari, 'Protecting the Citadel of Islam in the Modern Era'.
37 According to the fundamental principles of Shi'i Islam, the Shi'i clerical elite is 'the proof' of the Infallible Imam to all members of the community. Consequently, according to Shi'i thought, Shi'i clerical elites, by definition, cannot form a social class, as this would imply the existence of a schism in their relations with other elements within society. Some scholars maintain that it is more relevant to describe membership in the Shi'i clerical elite, the *Shi'i Ulama*, as a social status (Litvak, *Shi'i*

Scholars of nineteenth-century Iraq, p. 2); or as a social category (Moaddel, 'The Shi'i Ulama and the State in Iran', p. 520).

38 Muhammad Javad Alavi Burujirdi, interview with the author, Qum, January 2012.
39 Amanat, 'In Between the Madrasa and the Marketplace'.
40 According the Shiʿi traditions, during the time in which the twelfth Imam was serving his Minor Occultation (873–941), a Shiʿi follower wrote a letter to him asking for his guidance concerning a series of issues that had arisen for his followers. In response, a deputy of the Imam provided a signed script, *tawqi*, stating that: '[a]s for the events which may occur in future, refer to the transmitter (*ruwat*) of our traditions (*hadith*); who are my proof (*Hujjat*) to you, and I am the proof of Allah to you all' (al-Saduq, *Kamāl al-dīn wa-tamām al-niʿmah*, Vol. II, p. 483).
41 Ibid.
42 Meyer and Minkoff. 'Conceptualizing Political Opportunity'.
43 Tarrow, 'States and Opportunities', p. 54.
44 Della Porta, 'Political Opportunity/Political Opportunity Structure'.
45 Gamson and Meyer, 'Framing Political Opportunity', p. 277.
46 Goodwin and Jasper, *Rethinking Social Movements*, pp. 3–30.
47 Suh, 'How do Political Opportunities Matter'.
48 Banaszak, *Why Movements Succeed or Fail*, p. 31.
49 Hallaq, 'Was the Gate of ijtihad Closed?'.
50 Thus while, at some points in this book, these terms (as well as 'quietist/activist', and 'quietistic/activist') are used, they are used as descriptive – not analytical – concepts, and only in order to distinguish between different political postures assumed by Shiʿi clerics in relation to specific contexts.
51 Kurzman, 'Structural Opportunity and Perceived Opportunity', p. 154.
52 For more information see Kalantari, 'The Shiʿi Clergy and Dilemma of the Separation of Powers'.
53 See Kalantari, 'The Shi'i Clergy and Perceived Opportunity Structures'.
54 Full-text available at http://english.khamenei.ir/news/7284/Ayatollah-Sistani-s-message-to-Imam-Khamenei-on-the-martyrdom (accessed 27 January 2020).
55 Just months before the revolution, the Shah of Iran was believed to be one of the strongest regional leaders. In his famous visit to Iran in early 1978, President Carter offered a New Year's toast saying: 'Iran, because of the great leadership of the Shah, is an island of stability in one of the more troubled areas of the world. This is a great tribute to you, Your Majesty, and to your leadership and to the respect and the admiration and love which your people give to you.' Quoted in Ibid.
56 Jones, *Negotiating Change*, p. 257.
57 Fawaz Gerges, 'Hezbollah and the Future of Lebanon', *Dissent Magazine*, 1 June 2008. http://www.dissentmagazine.org/online_articles/hezbollah-and-the-future-of-lebanon (accessed 28 February 2018).
58 Press Conference with Hasan Nasrallah, Al-Manar TV, 12 July 2006.
59 Helena Cobban, 'The 33-Day War', *Boston Review*, 2 November 2006. http://www.bostonreview.net/cobban-33-day-war (accessed 28 February 2012).
60 The statistics are based on data from various scholarly reports, local governments and Western NGOs. For detailed statistics on Shiʿi population, see 'Mapping the Global Muslim Population', *Pew Research Center's Forum on Religion & Public Life*, 7 October 2009. http://www.pewforum.org/2009/10/07/mapping-the-global-muslim-population/ (accessed 30 June 2015).
61 Cottam, *Nationalism in Iran*, p. 134.

62 Nakash, 'The Conversion of Iraq's Tribes to Shiism'.
63 Pahlavi, 'The 33 Day War'.

Chapter 2

1 Quran, V: 67.
2 While the Shiʿis were bereaved to have lost direct access to the divine and infallible leadership, they believe that the Imam is present and does live on the Earth and is the source of divine blessing for the humanity. According to Shiʿi beliefs, the last Imam lives among people, but he is not recognized by them and does not hold earthly authority until the promised day of his return.
3 'Although the majority of Sunni Muslims account Shiʿi Muslims as *rawāfid*, defectors from Islam, Shiʿi Muslims believe that true Islam, the one, which God and his prophet, Muhammad, desired, is the one that is now expressed in Shiʿi Islam' (Muhammad Javad Alavi Burujirdi, interview with the author, January 2012).
4 The Quran clearly asserts that the Prophet has neither gone astray nor has erred, nor does he speak of his own desire and what it says is all revealed and is the message of God to humans (Quran, LIII: 2–4).
5 [Shiʿi] Muslims believe that the ultimate authority over humans belongs to God and that he asserts this authority through his last Prophet. He asks the believers to obey the Prophet unconditionally in Quran where he states: 'Obey Allah and obey the Messenger [Muhammad] and those of you who are in authority' (Quran, IV: 53).
6 Shiʿi scholars believed that such role has clearly been identified for the Prophet in Quran when it states: '[Muhammad] judge between them by what God has revealed to you' (Quran, V: 48).
7 In support of this belief, Shiʿis point to a series of occasions when the Prophet clearly nominated Ali. Among the most significant of these incidents, was the grand Muslim gathering in *Ghadīr Khumm* on 19 March 632, during the Farewell Pilgrimage of the Prophet Muhammad.
8 Madelung, 'Hiṣẖām b. al-Ḥakam', p. 497.
9 Tabatabai, *Shi'ite Islam*, p. 70. Shiʿis believe that Allah has revealed the divine message to Muhammad through the holy Angel, and the Prophet taught the message to his only legitimate successor, Ali, directly. Thus, the divine knowledge has been inherited from every Imam to his next successor and finally to the twelfth Imam. Therefore, the twelve Shiʿi Imams are the divine experts of Islam and the sole infallible religious reference for Muslims. In general, Shiʿis believe that the Quran and the people of the House, the twelve Infallible Imams, are two weighty and complementary sources inherited by Muslims from the Prophet to achieve the God's will.
10 Tabatabai, *Shi'ite Islam*, p. 15.
11 *Nahj al-Balāgha*, Sermon III.
12 Jafri, *Origins and Early Development of Shi'a Islam*, p. 253. The early consolidation of the Shiʿi jurisprudence is owed to the teachings of the fifth Imam. As his son, the sixth Shiʿi Imam states: 'Before him [Muhammad Ibn Ali], the Shiʿi Muslims did not know what should be considered as lawful or unlawful, except that which they had heard from the ordinary people [which were not necessarily based on the Shiʿi doctrine]. It was just after my father's endeavors that his students, the Shiʿi elites, began to publish what they have learned from him directly throughout the Islamic world.'
13 Tabatabai, *Shi'ite Islam*, p. 44.

14 The Sixth Shiʿi Imam, Ja'far Ibn Muhammad al-Sadeq, is known as the *Sheikh al-A'immah*, the eldest of the Imams. In commemoration of his role in spreading Shiʿi Islam, the Twelvers have ever since also been known by his name as *the Ja'faris*.
15 Qummi, *Muntahá al-Āmāl*, Vol. II, p. 871. Some of these elite figures, among them Zurareh ibn A'yan al-Sheybani, even have specific verbal endorsements of the Imams. A case in point is when the Ja'far al-Sadeq states: 'If this man [Zurarah], did not exist my traditions would have been lost.'
16 See, for example, Sachedina, *Islamic messianism*.
17 Shiʿi tradition holds that four deputies acted in succession to one another: Uthman Ibn Sa'id al-Asadi, Abu Jafar Muhammad Ibn Uthman, Abul Qasim Husayn Ibn Ruh al-Nawbakhti, and Abul Hasan Ali Ibn Muhammad al-Samarri.
18 These two roles are known in Shiʿi lexicon as *Iftā*, giving legal opinions, and *Qadhā*, arbitration based on the faith's regulation.
19 For full details of the letter, see Majlesi, *Biḥ2r al-Anwār*, Vol. LI, p. 361.
20 Al-Saduq, *Kamāl al-dīn wa-tamām al-niʿmah*, Vol. II, p. 483.
21 Al-Kulayni, *Uṣūl al-Kāfī*, Vol. I, p. 334. Shiʿi mainstream belief entails that the twelfth Imam is living among people on earth. To this end, they refer to a tradition narrated from Prophet Muhammad in numerous Shiʿi sources, when he states, 'if the earth would remain without a Hujja [the infallible Imam] for a momenet, the earth will be injested along with its dwellers'.
22 Ibid., p. 34. In a trustworthy tradition, the Prophet refers to clerical elite, 'the Ulama', as the heirs of the prophets.
23 Sheikh Al-Ḥurr Al-Āmili, who is among the most renowned Shiʿi scholars, narrates from the sixth Imam, who, in addressing one of his students, Hisham Ibn al-Salem, states: 'We lay down the principles for you, and it is your duty to develop the subsidiary practices, *tafri'*, from those you were taught.' See Al-Ḥurr Al-Āmili, *Wasā'il al-Shīʿa*, Vol. XVIII, p. 51.
24 For the full text of *Hadith*, see Majlesi, *Biḥ2r al-Anwār*, Vol. II, p. 6.
25 In a tradition from Hassan Ibn Ali, the eleventh Shiʿi Imam, the Imam clarifies that believers should follow those of the Shiʿi elite who are 'pious, keepers of the faith, pursue reason independent of their own desire, and are obedient to Allah'. See Al-Tabarsi, *Al-iḥtijāj ʿalā ahl al-lijāj*, Vol. II, p. 263.
26 One of the most renowned elite at the time was Sheikh al-Tusi (996–1067) – known as *Sheikh al-Tai'feh* (the master of the faith) – who initiated the first phase of the evolution of the Shiʿi Jurisprudence. While the Abbasids in Baghdad were under the tutelage of the Buyids, he made the most out of the political opportunity, and developed a robust network of students. Yet, with the empowerment of the Sunni Seljuqis in Baghdad, he migrated to Najaf, and founded the first Shiʿi seminary there in 1038. For the details of his role and that of the other Shiʿi elites in Evolution of the Jurisprudence, see Kadivar, *Taḥavvul-i guftimān-i siyāsī-i Shīʿah*.
27 Watt, *The Formative Period of Islamic Thought*, p. 294.
28 Al-Sharif al-Murtada, *Al-shāfī fī al-imāmah*, p. 31.
29 See 'Following a Mujtahid'. http://sistani.org/index.php?p=251364&id=48&pid=2116 (accessed 12 January, 2018).
30 For the first time in the modern history, circumstances became permissive enough for Sheikh Muhammad Hassan al-Najafi, the leading Marja' of the time, to write one of the most comprehensive books on Shiʿi jurisprudence, *Jawāhir al-kalām*, which ran over more than 20,000 pages. This extensive volume (compared to Sheikh al-Tusi's, for example), is another example of how Shiʿi jurisprudence was developed over nine centuries, as the situation, and perhaps laymen's inquiries, changed dramatically.

31 Amanat, 'In Between the Madrasa'.
32 Momen, *An Introduction to Shia Islam*, p. 140.
33 See 'Following a Mujtahid'. http://sistani.org/index.php?p=251364&id=48&pid=2116 (accessed 12 January 2018).
34 Quran, IX: 122.
35 See Kazemi Mousavi, 'The Establishment of the Position of Marja'iyyt-i Taqlid'; Amanat, 'In Between the Madrasa and the Marketplace'; and Gleave, 'Conceptions of Authority'.
36 This mundane misinterpretation has been reproduced in speech of an Iranian Professor Hashim Aghajari, dated November 2002. He went further and criticized the Marja'iyya system by declaring that 'the people are not monkeys who merely imitate. The pupil understands and then acts, and then tries to expand his own understanding, so someday he will not need the teacher.' For a review on Aghajari's speech, see Thomas Friedman, 'A Story Worth Watching: An Islamic Reformation', *The New York Times*, 4 December 2002.
37 Motahhari, *Imāmat wa rahbarī.*
38 Makarem Shirazi, *Dā'irat al-ma'ārif-i fiqh-i muqārin.*
39 Kazemi Mousavi, *Religious Authority in Shi'ite Islam*, p. 225.
40 As in Safavid era, Shi'i clerical elite was extensively dependent to the monarchs' endowments financially. The dissolution of Safavid dynasty and rise of the Afsharid in Iran made them to migrate from Iran to Iraq and to seek other sources of financial means. For more information, see Kazemi Mousavi, *Religious Authority in Shi'ite Islam*, Chapter 7.
41 Lambton, 'A Reconsideration of the Position of the Marja' al-Taqlid'. In principle, lay Shi'i's should pay one-fifth, Khums, of the remaining of their annual profit to their Marja' Taqlid. Half of these religious taxes is the share belonging to the infallible Imam and should be spent on the furtherance of Shi'i Islam. The other half should be distributed among the destitute descendants of the Prophet, known as Sayyids.
42 Khomeini, *Ṣaḥīfeh-ye Imām*, Vol. XIII, p. 248.

Chapter 3

1 *Nahj al-Balāgha*, Sermon 73.
2 Amin al-Amili, *A'yān al-Shī'ah*, Vol. VIII, p. 371.
3 Ansari, *Kitāb al-Makāsib*, p. 56.
4 'God does not charge a soul except [with that within] its capacity. It will have [the consequence of] what [good] it has gained, and it will bear [the consequence of] what [evil] it has earned', Quran, II: 286.
5 Kohlberg, *A Medieval Muslim Scholar*, p. 11.
6 Momen, *An Introduction to Shia Islam*, p. 75.
7 Madelung, 'A treatise of the Sharif al-Murtada'.
8 The development of Shi'i Islam in Iraq, and especially in Baghdad, had begun centuries before the Buyids, at the time of Salman's government of Madian during the caliphate of Umar Ibn al-Khattab. Consequently, from the early days of the city's establishment, its western suburb, known as Karkh, had always been a Shi'i stronghold. Although Persians, all authors of the Shi'i Four Books had lived in Baghdad for decades: Al-Kulayni spent the last years of his life in Baghdad and was

buried there in 941. Al-Saduq was in Baghdad during 966, and Sheikh al-Tusi was the leader of Baghdad seminary until the fall of city at the hands of the Seljuqids in 1055. The power of the Shiʿi of Baghdad reached such a level that in 897 that the Abbasid caliph, al-Mu'tadhid, ordered that a curse be pronounced on Muawyyah in mosques willing to appeal to their community. See Ibn al-Jawzi, *Al-Muntazam fī tārīkh*, Vol. XII, p. 371.

9 Ibn Tiqtaqa, *Al-Fakhrī fī al-adab*, p. 315.

10 Jafarian, *Tārīkh-i Tashayyuʿ dar Iran*, pp. 646–65. Some sources, mainly written by Sunni historians, accuse Nasir al-Din Tusi and Ibn Alqami of treason and encouraging Hulagu to go to war with the Abbasids. Reviewing the corruption of the Caliphate at the time, and the roots of these narrations back to the works of IbnTaymiyyah, Jafarian argues that the destructive role of Shiʿi statesmen in the incident is more a false allegation than a historical reality.

11 Mar'ashi, *Tārīkh-i Ṭabaristān va Rūyān*, p. 85.

12 Tusi, *Akhlāq-e Nāṣerī*, p. 252.

13 Ibn Tawus, *Kashf al-maḥajjat*, pp. 168–70.

14 The term 'Muslim' when it appeared in the phrase 'an unjust Muslim ruler' implied the 'Sunni' at the time as, during the period, the appointment of a Shiʿi ruler seemed beyond the imagination of anyone. Therefore, Ibn Tawus's response should be regarded in its relevant context. For full details, see Kohlberg, *A Medieval Muslim Scholar*, p. 10.

15 Reportedly, another reason that motivated Shiʿis to collaborate with the Mongols against the Abbasids was that they were expecting such an incident based on their traditional beliefs. They believed that Imam Ali had predicted the overthrow of the sons of Abbas by an army of *Turks with round faces and folded eyes*. Allameh Hilli narrates the tradition when he introduces his father, Sadid al-Din Hilli, who represented the city at the court of the Hulagu asking for safe-conduct prior to the outbreak of the war with the caliph. He says that Sadid al-Din promised the Mongol ruler a momentarily triumph over the Abbasids, reading to him the prophecy of Imam Ali. See Al-Allama Hilli, *Nahj al-ḥaqq wa-kashf al-ṣidq*, p. 6.

16 Bausani, 'Religion under the Mongols', p. 542.

17 Vassaf Shirazi, *Tārīkh-i Vaṣāf*, p. 302.

18 For the full text of the treatise see Rahimlou, 'Risāla favāyid-i Ūljāytū'.

19 The Sufi and Shiʿi rapprochement took place concurrently with the start of the Mongol invasion of the Islamic world in the early thirteenth century. This newborn approach received popular support, especially after the fall of Baghdad. For the transformation of Sufi and Sunni movements to the Shiʿi Islam, see Jafarian, *Tārīkh-i Tashayyuʿ dar Iran*, pp. 677–89.

20 Momen, *An Introduction to Shia Islam*, p. 93.

21 Al-Shahid al-Thāni, *Al-Rawda al-Bahiyah*, Vol. I, p. 143.

22 Established by Timur, they ruled throughout a vast part of Iran and central Asia from 1370 to 1507. Their authority over Iran declined with the rise of the Safavids. For a history of Timurid Iran, see Manz, *Power, Politics and Religion*, pp. 146–77.

23 One significant example of those movements was the rise of militancy among Sheikh Safi's household. The Sufi Safavid order became militant in the mid-fifteenth century, under the leadership of Sheikh Junayd (d. 1460), the grandfather of Ismail. See Jafarian, *Tārīkh-i Tashayyuʿ dar Iran*.

24 Savory, *Iran under the Safavids*, p. 18. A group of Shiʿi Ghulat warriors strongly committed to the Safavid supreme spiritual leader. Since the era of Sheikh Haydar,

Ismail's father, they became fully at the service of the Safavids against their enemies and played a crucial rule in the establishment of the dynasty by Ismail.

25 Khwandamir, *Ḥabīb al-siyar*, Vol. IV, pp. 467–8. The operation of Shiʿi Islam as the state religion was generally limited by Ismail to six elements: (1) reading prayer sermons in the name of the changing Twelve Imams, (2) the following of Shiʿi rituals by Prayer leaders, (3) changing the Adhan to the Shiʿi style, (4) inscription of the name of the Imams on coin, (5) cursing the first three Caliph in public, and (6) killing whoever opposed these orders. Therefore, the conversion to Shiʿi Islam, at least during the early stages of Safavid rule, encompassed nothing more than a few insubstantial changes. In sum, the rise of Ismail and declaration of Shiʿi Islam as the religion of his reign did not abolish Shiʿi social institutions and order in Persia.

26 Numerous studies have focused on the role of the Jabal Amil Shiʿi scholars and their migration to Persia and involvement in the Safavid's court. Beyond the numbers of Jabal Amili Shiʿi scholars who migrated to Persia after the founding of the Safavid dynasty, the role that their jurisprudential school has played is undeniable. As we have seen over this chapter, three main issues should be noted in this regard: (1) the majority of Shiʿi ulama supported the Safavids; and though some may have been critical of some of its activities, at least during the rule of the Sunni Ottomans, nobody was opposed to its very existence; (2) while Persian Shiʿi scholars were inclined towards philosophical and theosophical schools of thought, Arab Shiʿi scholars were devoted to the jurisprudential school, and (3) the impact of Jabal Amili Shiʿi scholars was not limited to those who migrated to Persia; there were some scholars, like Al-Shahid al-Thāni, who had never been in Persia but greatly influenced the development of Shiʿi political thoughts through their teachings and students, during and after the Safavids. For detailed background, see Abisaab, *Converting Persia*; and Newman 'The Myth of the Clerical Migration to Safawid Iran'; and Newman, *Safavid Iran*.

27 Lambton, 'Concepts of Authority in Persia'.

28 Minorsky, *Tadhkirat al-Mulūk*, p. 13.

29 Shaybi, *Tashayyuʿ va Taṣavvuf*, p. 391. The Shiʿi Imams were popular among Persians throughout post-Islamic history. Consequently, one major factor for the development of the Safavid apparatus in Iran was the claim that they belonged to the Sadat progeny. However, the reliability of this claim is believed to be quite controversial.

30 Amir Sadr al-Din Ibrahim Amini Hiravi (d. 1535), the writer of *Futūḥāt -i Shāhī*, narrates that in the aftermath of Uzbek's overthrow from Khorasan, 'Shah Ismail entered Herat on 31 December 1510 and was regularly visited by the elite and notables from Iraq, Khorasan, Sabzevar, and Azerbaijan. While some Shiʿi scholars settled in Khorasan close to the Eighth Imam's shrine, others headed back to where they came from.' See Amini Hiravi, *Futūḥāt -i Shāhī*, pp. 357–8.

31 Shaybi, *Tashayyuʿ va Taṣavvuf*, p. 411. One of the major characteristics of Shahid Awwal's jurisprudential thought was the unique role he reserved for Shiʿi scholars and their guardianship over the community. While he was leading the seminary of Jabal Amil, he used to send his deputies to the neighbouring cities in order to propagate the faith and perhaps to collect money for developing the religious schools.

32 Khawnsari, *Rawḍāt al-jannāt*, Vol. IV, p. 363. After conquest of Baghdad, Shah Ismail cherished Shiʿi clerics by endowing them great deals of properties. Along with land grants, the Shah gave orders for seventy thousand dinars to be given to al-Karaki to spend among the religious students.

33 One of the earliest works of al-Karaki is his treatise on Khar āj, written months before his travel to Iran. He implies in the introduction of the treatise, which does not mention anything about Safavid rule contrary to his later works, that he wrote the treatise to address the criticism of his fellow Shiʿi jurists. In this sense, his acceptance of the royal endowments resembled Sayyid Radhi's behaviour when encountering the unjust ruler of his era. Eight years later, Ibrahim Ibn Sulaiman Qatifi (d. 1538), known as the most famous critics of al-Karaki, wrote a response to this treatise. See al-Karaki, *Al-Kharājīyāt*.

34 Stanfield-Johnson, 'The tabarra'iyan', p. 59.

35 Al-Karaki, *Nafaḥāt al-lāhūt*, p. 35.

36 The congregational prayer on Friday, *Jumu'ah*, has always been a sign of the religio-political bond between the Muslim ruler and the community. While among the majority of Sunni Muslims, anyone who is appointed by the ruler could lead the Friday Prayer; the leadership of this prayer was generally exclusive to the infallible Imams and their specific deputies in Shiʿi Islam. The rise of the Shiʿi Safavid dynasty, along with the accusations of the Sunni Ottomans in regard to recitation of the prayer, led Shiʿi scholars to consider the conditions of conducting the Friday Prayer during the Occultation era. Although al-Karaki's treatise paved the way for some Shiʿi jurists to lead the Friday Prayer, the discussion was so sensitive that it took decades for Shiʿis to conduct the congregational Friday Prayer routinely. For a detailed history of the Friday Prayer in Shiʿi Islam and during Safavids era, see Jafarian, *Ṣafavīyah dar 'arṣah-'i dīn*, pp. 15–102.

37 Al-Karaki, *Rasā'il al-Muḥaqqiq al-Karakī*, Vol. I, p. 168. Al-Karaki believed that the mujtahid of the Age should encompass thirteen different characteristics, including faith, justice and a strong memory.

38 Al-Karaki had not been given the opportunity during the Shah Ismail's era due to the two major reasons: first the Shah who projected a great charisma did not require an alternative source of legitimacy for his rule, and secondly, the Safavid court at disagreement with the clergy, perhaps fearing the danger of losing their positions to an Arab Shiʿi jurist. One of the Persian Shiʿi Scholars who opposed al-Karaki was Mir Jamal al-Din Astarabadi, who was the Safavid's Sadr between 1514 and 1525 under Shah Ismail and Shah Tahmasb. While he was responsible for the Awqaf and Royal endowments to the Shiʿi clerics, between 1514 and 1518, al-Karaki had been excluded from grants previously offered to him. For more information on disputes between al-Karaki and some Safavids' court members, see Abisaab, *Converting Persia*, pp. 17–19.

39 Khawnsari, *Rawḍāt al-jannāt*, Vol. V, p. 170.

40 Ibid., p. 162.

41 However, because of some internal hostilities, perhaps from his historic enemies, al-Karaki headed back to Najaf after three years. Later, Shah Tahmasb issued another decree and tried to induce him to travel to Persia once again. In his letter, Shah Tahmasb states that the development and propagation of Shiʿi Islam, as a means to bring about the emergence of the Imam, is the utmost goal of the Safavids; and that, to achieve this goal, everyone should follow the Ulama, among whom al-Karaki possessed the greatest prestige (Afandi, *Riyāḍ al-ʿulamā'*, Vol. III, p. 460). Preparing to travel to Persia, however, al-Karaki passed away in 1533. The coincident prompted a theory that he had been poisoned. Consequently, some contemporary Shiʿi scholars of al-Karaki, acknowledged him as the *Al-Shahid al-Thāni*, the Second Martyr (Ibid., p. 442).

42 Jafarian, *Ṣafavīyah dar 'arṣah-'i dīn*, p. 146.
43 Khawnsari, *Rawḍāt al-jannāt*, Vol. I, p. 203.
44 Quran, XI: 113.
45 Al-Ardabili, *Majma' al-fā'idah wa-al-burhān*, Vol. XIII, p. 68.
46 Golsorkhi, 'Ismail II and Mirza Makhdum Sharifi'. Shi'i clerics in alliance with some Qizilbash commanders, forced Shah Ismail II to rescind his anti-Shi'i Islam orders, which were made under the influence of the king's master and pro-Sunni Sadr, Mirza Makhdum Sharifi.
47 Falsafi, *Zindagānī-i Shāh 'Abbās-i Avval*, pp. 185–93. Shah Abbas killed Murshid Quli Khan Ostaglu, the kingmaker army leader, along with some other Army leaders, on a grand scale to show his independence in Royal affairs. After that, the autocratic rule of Shah Abbas was established, and no religious or political figures were able to disobey his orders throughout his reign.
48 Turkaman, *Tārīkh-i 'ālam'ārā-yi 'Abbāsī*, Vol. II, p. 532.
49 Della Valle, *Safarnāmah*, p. 309. Pietro Della Valle, the Italian traveller who was a contemporary of Shah Abbas, states that the king criticized the clerical elite who were demanding him to stop the war with the Muslim Ottomans, and said 'they have become irritating, and if I hear from them once again, I will order them all to be massacred'.
50 Falsafi, *Zindagānī-i Shāh 'Abbās-i Avval*, pp. 877–81. After his decisive victory over the Ottomans, Shah Abbas offered to allocate a huge portion of his possessions to Awqaf in the name of the Prophet and Infallible Imams.
51 Gleave, *Scripturalist Islam*.
52 Astarabadi, *Al-Fawā'id al-Madanīyah*, pp. 172–3.
53 For a detailed list of differences between the Akhbāri and Ususli schools of thought, see Gleave, *Scripturalist Islam*, pp. 311–14.
54 Khawnsari states that Astarabadi's activities 'degraded the grand Ulama of the faith and ruined the principal foundations of the religion' (*Rawḍāt al-jannāt*, Vol. I, p. 136).
55 Ibid., Vol. VII, p. 96. Muhammad Baqir Majlesi, along with Muhammad Ibn Hassan, known as Al-Ḥurr Al-Āmili (d. 1693), the writer of *Wasā'il al-Shī'a*, and Mulla Muhsin Muhammad Fayḍ Kashani (d. 1679), the writer of *al-Wāfi*, known as 'the three later Muhammads, the collectors of the faith's traditions', were all adherents of the Akhbāri School.
56 For a list of causes of the Safavid decline, see Minorsky, *Tadhkirat al-Mulūk*, p. 23.
57 Lockhart, *The Fall of the Safavi Dynasty*, p. 298.
58 Amoretti, 'Religion in the Timurid and Safavid Periods'.
59 Astarabadi, *Tārīkh-i Jahāngushā-yi Nādirī*, p. 349.
60 Roemer, 'The Safavid Period'.
61 Marwi, *Nāme-ji 'Ālamārā-ji Nādirī*, p. 416.
62 Roemer, 'The Safavid Period'. When the central Safavid state was toppled in 1722, their popularity by no means came to an end, at least among Shi'i Persians who honoured their progeny. Nader was promoted among Persians as the ally of the Safavid princes, Tahmasb II, and Abbas III and was accounted as their regents until the establishment of the Afsharid dynasty. After Nader, Karim Khan and his allies became regent to another Safavid prince, Ismail III, who died in 1773.
63 Some years earlier, after a century of decline, the Usuli Shi'i Islam had been strengthened when Wahid Behbahani (d.1791) overthrew Akhbāris' domination over the Shi'i seminaries of Iraq and Persia. Born in Isfahan, Behbahani fled to Behbahan,

then Najaf, and when he ceased to find its seminary useful, he finally resided in Karbala, in the late 1740s. At that time, its strong Akhbāri School was under the leadership of the moderate, Sheikh Yusuf Bahrani (1695–772). It was then that, at a point, he started to challenge his Akhbāri counterparts and engaged in a series of religious discussions with Bahrani. The last nail in the coffin of Akhbāri domination came in 1772, when the then prestigious Usuli leader of Karbala seminary read the funeral prayer of Bahrani and consolidated his power throughout the Shiʿi clerical network. Beyond Wahid's endeavours against the Akhbāri School, his role in fostering a handful of students, who shaped the future of Usuli Shiʿi clerical network, is substantial and promised a more active political role for them. See Cole, 'Shi'i Clerics in Iraq and Iran'.

64 Quoted in Lehovich, 'The Testament of Peter the Great'.

65 Mahmood, *Tarīkh-i ravābit-i siyāsī Irān va Inglīs*, Vol. I, pp. 33–181. In 1801, Sir John Malcolm, the British representative, entered Persia and signed a treaty that enlisted the support of the Qajar of India against the ruler of Afghanistan, and to prevent the rising power of French nationals in Persia. It is significant that later in 1806, the Shah, trapped in a war with the Russians and disappointed by the lack of British support, accepted Napoleon's proposal to sign a peace treaty with France, which was concluded a year later (the Treaty of Finckenstein). Upon the conclusion of this Treaty, Persia declared war against Britain and received military training from France. No French military aid was given to Persia, however, as just less than 2 months later Napoleon signed an agreement with Tsar Alexander of Russia, the Tilsit Treaty. Persia failed once again to attract the support of European powers in the course of the war with Russia; it is said that Persians were threatened by Russians, scoffed by French, and never had been treated fairly by Britain's forces.

66 Nategh, *Az mā'st kih bar mā'st*, p. 18.

67 Mirza Abul Qasim Jilani, known as Mirza Qummi, from Qum, Mulla Ahmad Naraqi, from Kashan, and Mir Muhammad Hussein Khātoonābādi, from Isfahan, were among a group of famous Shiʿi personalities who wrote treatises supporting the sovereignty of Islamic Persia against Russian invaders. See Sepehr, *Nāsikh al-tavārīkh*, Vol. I, p. 181.

68 Kashif al-Ghita, *Kitāb Kashf al-ghiṭā'*, Vol. IV, p. 334.

69 Sepehr, *Nāsikh al-tavārīkh*, Vol. I, p. 363. Years earlier, Abbas Mirza's agents had informed the Shiʿi clerics about the resentments of Muslim inhabitants of North Persia who had been under the authority of Russia since the treaty of Gulistan. It was in this context that the religious elite decided to support the Jihad against Russia and mobilized their followers to participate in the second war.

70 Ibid., p. 365. Historians named 500 Shiʿi scholars from Iraq and Persia who joined the military campaign directly.

71 Kashmiri, *Nujūm al-samā'*, p. 388. Born as Sayyid Muhammad Tabatabai in 1767 in Karbala, he was the son of Sayyid Ali Tabatabai, the writer of *Riyad al-masa'il*, who had supported the Jihad against Russia during the first war. It is written that when he joined the campaign, he was so popular among the Shiʿi community that, in Qazvin, people consecrated the water left from his ablutions and accompanied him up to the frontline of the war with Russia.

72 Ibid., p. 389. Some believed that after the first triumphant phase of the war, Abbas Mirza was told by some of his corrupt advisers that if 'the warfare ends with rapid victory, then Sayyid Muhammad will become a great threat to the throne, as he enjoys the utmost popularity amongst Persians and plays a vital role in mobilising the

masses and in the defeat of the Russians'. Consequently, the crown prince decided to accept the Russian envoy's offer of a ceasefire in September 1826. This was a factor in turning the tide against the Persian army.

73 Keddie and Amanat, 'Iran under the later Qajars'.

74 Nategh, *Az mā'st kih bar mā'st*, pp. 9–42. The latter disclosed documents, including reports of Sir Henry Willock, the British envoy to Persia (1815–26) and a manuscript of Mirza Saleh Shirazi, the Persian attaché to Russia, which accused Abbas Mirza of manipulating the clerics to support the second war against Russia, though Persian forces had no chance of resisting their opponents.

75 Algar, 'Religious Forces in Twentieth-Century Iran'. Although clerical popularity declined with these accusations, the religious elite still exercised great influence over the Shiʿi community. On a smaller scale, Mirza Masih Mujtahid, the famous clergy of Tehran, led a protest against the Russian envoy, Gribayedoff, in 1829, and some minor Shiʿi clerics supported Muhammad Shah's campaign against the British in Heart. However, their support never provided them with the consensus that had been forged with respect to the second Russo-Persian war.

76 Tehrani, *Tabaqāt a'lām al-Shī'ah*, Vol. IV, p. 323. The migration of Shiʿi ulama from Iraq to Persia reached such a level that, at some point, Muhammad Shah Qajar sarcastically asked Sheikh Muhammad Hassan al-Najafi (d.1849), then the leader of Najaf Seminary, 'if you have opened a factory to produce Mujthaids'.

77 Ramezani, *Nāṣir al-Dīn Shāh Qājār*, p. 28. Amir Kabir (d.1852), Naser al-Din Shah mentor and his first chancellor, and the Kingmaker, mentioned the inconsistencies of the Monarch once in a letter, where he criticized the Shah and his evasive orders about the court reform process and says: 'you cannot rule if you escape from reform. Let's say one day I become sick or deceased, do you want to rule or not? If your answer is positive, then why do you refuse to reform?'

78 Prior to the Shah's first visit to Europe in 1872, Paul Julius Freiherr von Reuter, a British subject, obtained from the Persian government a seventy-year concession that would grant him substantial authority over the economy of the country. As Curzon states, the concession was 'found to contain the most complete and extraordinary surrender of the entire industrial resources of a kingdom into foreign hands that has probably ever been dreamed of, much less accomplished, in history' (Curzon, *Persia and the Persian question*, p. 480). Although almost a year later the concession was withdrawn in the face of popular protest, Mulla Ali Kani, the esteemed mujtahid of Tehran, and Reuter the opponent of Russia, received the major share of the Persian Imperial Bank. See Abrahamian, *Iran Between Two Revolutions*, p. 56.

79 Adamiyat, *Shūrish bar imtīyāzńāmah-'i Rizhī*, p. 10. One of the first signs of opposition came from an editorial in the Akhtar Newspaper, which named the concession as a 'traitorous act of the monarchy against the innate rights of the nation' and criticized Major Talbot in an interview that was conducted in Istanbul, comparing the terms of the agreement with the one that the British Régie Company had signed with the Ottomans.

80 Teymouri, *Taḥrīm-i tanbākū*, p. 42.

81 Quoted in Ibid., p. 69.

82 For the full text of the telegram see Karbalayi, *Tārīkh-i dukhānīyah*, p. 88. Sheikh Hassan Isfahani Karblayi was stationed in Samara at the time and was among Mirza Shirazi's students. His book, *Tārīkh-i dukhānīyah*, which was written during the revolution, describes the events of the Tobacco Protest from the religious elite's point of view.

83 After the demonstration in Shiraz and its follow-ups in Tabriz, Naser al-Din Shah reviewed the terms of the concession that had been granted. To calm the Azerbaijani protesters, in September 1891 he sent a telegram to Tabriz indicating that 'he had started to contact the company hoping to withdraw the concession' yet asked for some time to sort things out. For details of this telegram, see Adamiyat, *Shūrish bar imtīyāzňāmah-'i Rizhī*, p. 41.
84 Keddie, *Religion and Rebellion in Iran*, p. 94.
85 Adamiyat, *Shūrish bar imtīyāzňāmah-'i Rizhī*, p. 59.
86 Karbalayi, *Tārīkh-i dukhānīyah*, p. 96.
87 Quoted in Ibid., p. 118.
88 Ibid., p. 167.
89 For a detailed account of the event see Feuvrier, *Trois Ans à la Cour de Perse*, p. 330.
90 Teymouri, *Taḥrīm-i tanbākū*, pp. 205–23. The Persian government was forced to accept 500,000 Sterling as compensation for the British company. The amount, which was lent from the Imperial Bank of Persia, owned mainly by Britain, and laid a huge debt on the Persians' shoulders.
91 Some studies have emphasized the role of Russia as one of the main reasons for the Revolt's success (see e.g. Keddie, *Religion and Rebellion in Iran*). Although Russia was among the main opponents to the concession from the outset, its role in managing and shaping the popular protests was minimal. See Moaddel, 'Shi'i political discourse'.
92 Abbasi Fardoyi, *Taḥrīm-i tanbākū wa mashrūṭiyat*, p. 103. Later Hassan Modarres, one of Mirza Shirazi's students wrote that with the victory of the Tobacco Protest based on the central role of the Shiʿi clerical elite, the sole Marja' of the time was surprisingly unhappy about the whole circumstances. In replying to Modarres, Mirza states: 'Now, the superpowers realized that what the real source of the people's authority is, and what the driving force behind the Shiʿi masses is. Thus, from today they will work hard to destroy this source [the Shiʿi clerical popularity]. I am concerned about the future of the Islamic nation.'
93 Japan's victory over Russia in the 1904–5 War, and the Russian Revolution of 1905 which resulted to the establishment of a limited constitutional monarchy, were among the most important regional incidents that influenced the Persians, especially the intelligentsia. Furthermore, the Persians interpreted the Japanese victory over Russians in the war as the victory of the only Asian constitutional power over the only major non-constitutional country of the time.
94 Adamiyat, *Īdi'ūlūžī-i nahḍat-i mašrūṭīyat*, p. 30.
95 Rezwani, *Lawāyiḥ-i Āqā Shaykh Faẕl Allāh*, p. 67. During their protests, people chanted against the despotic rule of the Shah and his chancellor, Ein al-Dowleh, and asked for the dismissal of Mr Naus, the customs minister of Persia who was accused of humiliating Islam and the religious elite by attending a masque ball wearing a turban and clergy attire.
96 This incident, from 13 December 1905 to 1 January 1906, is known as the 'minor migration' in the lexicon of the Persian Constitutional Revolution. The 'Major Migration' occurred when the Shiʿi clerical elite left Tehran for the city of Qum in July 1906 and resulted in the Shah's agreement to sign the constitutional monarchy.
97 Kermani, *Tārikh-i bidari-yi Irānīān*, Vol. I, p. 358. It is believed that the idea of establishing the house of justice, which at the outset was solely a judicial demand rather than a political one, was not among the clerical elite's list initially. After consultations with the Turkish ambassador and some secular figures, like Yahya

Dowlat Abadi, who had been among the refugees, this article was later added to the list.

98 Quoted in Ibid., p. 366.

99 Dowlat Abadi, *Ḥayāt-i Yaḥyā*, Vol. II, p. 35.

100 Mohit Mafi, *Muqaddamāt-i Mashrūṭīyat*, p. 92. Sheikh Fazlollah, who had not accompanied the earlier sanctuary in Rey, promised not to abandon his fellows who were opposing the government in the future. He answered the Two Sayyids that whenever they would like to organize another anti-government movement, they could count on him.

101 Malakzadeh, *Tārīkh-i inqilāb-i mashrūṭīyat*, Vol. I, p. 366.

102 Kasravi, *Tārīkh-i mashrūṭah-'i Īrān*, p. 113.

103 Kermani, *Tārikh-i bidari-yi Irānīān*, Vol. I, p. 552.

104 Quoted in Ibid., p. 558.

105 Dowlat Abadi, *Ḥayāt-i Yaḥyā*, Vol. II, p. 82. The religious elite stationed in Qum was presented with the second decree, the one that mentions the establishment of the Islamic Assembly, and they had responded to that. Through the will of the secular constitutionalists who had succeeded in gaining a royal promise concerning the establishment of a National Assembly, they pretended that religious elites were aware of the contents of the third handwriting. This marked the first setback for the religious constitutionalists vis-à-vis their former strategic allies, the secular constitutionalists. Later, the religious elite did not find an opportunity to declare that secular figures had manipulated them.

106 More specifically, Sheikh Fazlollah and his followers opposed Article No. 8 which implied that 'the Persians [from any sect or with any religion] are to enjoy equal rights', Article No. XX that endorses the free press. For a detailed list of the Articles, see Browne, *The Persian Revolution*, pp. 372–84.

107 Kasravi reports that after the opening of the first Majlis and during the writing of the Supplementary Law, the Two Sayyids and Sheikh Fazlollah were still supporting the Assembly. Since they 'considered themselves the ones who had brought about the Constitution, they did not cease looking after it'. They were participating in the Majlis' deliberations, although they had different aspirations; Sheikh Fazlollah in this sense was looking for 'promulgation of the Sharia' through the Assembly (*Tārīkh-i mashrūṭah-'i Īrān*, p. 285).

108 Ibid., p. 323. Outside the Assembly also, the responsibility for putting pressure on the religious elite was divided between the secular newspapers, like Habl al-Matin and Sur Israfil, and the people of Tabriz, who under the influence of the secular constitutionalists were chanting against the Sheikh saying: 'We want a constitutional law, not the [law of] sharia.'

109 For the full English translation, see Browne, *The Persian Revolution*, p. 372.

110 Kasravi, *Tārīkh-i mashrūṭah-'i Īrān*, p. 372.

111 Zargarinejad, *Rasā 'il-i mashrūtiyat*, Vol. I, pp. 36–41. On 19 June 1907, some constitutionalist hardliners attacked the gathering of Islamic Constitutionalists in the Bazaar's mosque and, when they succeeded in dispersing the gathering, agreed to attack the houses of the Islamic Constitutionalist leaders and to expel them from the city. Although the upheavals calmed down as a result of the initiatives of Sayyid Muhammad Tabatabai, the lives of Sheikh Fazlollah and his followers were placed in serious danger by the actions of fanatical constitutionalists.

112 For the full account of the public letter, see Rezwani, *Lawāyiḥ-i Āqā Shaykh Faẓl Allāh*, p. 44.

113 Zargarinejad, *Rasā'il-i mashrūtiyat*, Vol. I, pp. 75–9. His later support for the Shah in opposition to National Assembly members gives clear evidence of his perceptions and *ijtihad* concerning the existing opportunity structure.
114 Kasravi, *Tārīkh-i mashrūṭah-'i Īrān*, p. 287. He also wrote once that the constitutionalist religious elite of Najaf and Tehran 'did not understand the proper meaning of the Constitution and the implications of the spread of European laws. They were not properly aware of the obvious great incompatibility between the Constitution and the Shi'i sect. On the one hand, these zealous people saw the chaos in Iran and the weakness of the government and saw no other solution for this than a constitution and Majlis and supported them very resolutely. On the other hand, they were in the grip of their faith and could not ignore it. They remained stuck in the middle.'
115 Browne, *The Persian Revolution*, p. 172. Russia and Britain also came up with an agreement in regard to their foreign policies in the region, including Persia. Eventually, an Anglo-Russian agreement was concluded on 31 August 1907, in order to decrease rivalries between the two powers. Persia was divided into three spheres: North of the country was to come under the influence of Russia, the Southeast would go to Britain, and the centre was to remain under the authority of the central government.
116 Turkaman, *Majmū'ah'ī az rasā'il, i'lāmīyah'hā*, Vol. I, pp. 363–6.
117 Quoted in Kermani, *Tārikh-i bidari-yi Irānīān*, Vol. II, pp. 187–8.
118 For the full account of the telegraph from the constitutionalist clerics of Najaf, Khorasani, Mazandarani, and Tehrani, see Kasravi, *Tārīkh-i mashrūṭah-'i Īrān*, p. 730.
119 See Turkaman, *Majmū'ah'ī az rasā'il, i'lāmīyah'hā*, Vol. I, p. 106.
120 Na'ini, *Tanbīh al-ummah*, pp. 46–8.
121 Quoted in Abu al-hasani, *Ākhirīn āvāz-i qū*, p. 151.
122 Khomeini, *Ṣaḥīfeh-ye Imām*, Vol. 18, pp. 135–7.

Chapter 4

1 Charles Kurzman discussed this context briefly in his oft-cited article, 'Structural Opportunity and Perceived Opportunity in Social-Movement Theory: The Iranian Revolution of 1979'. Through a more detailed historical analysis focused on the specific role of Shi'i clerical elites, this chapter tries to illuminate an additional facet of the Islamic Revolution in Iran.
2 The theory of Guardianship of the Jurist, as was explained in Chapter 1, has always been embedded in Shi'i jurisprudence. It was the influence of new contextual factors that enabled Khomeini to build up new readings based on the theory and to institutionalize this sociopolitical role for the Shi'i clerical elite in Iran in the aftermath of the revolution. For more information on the development of the theory, see Khomeini, *Islamic government*.
3 Abdolreza Kefayi, interview with the author, Qum, August 2011.
4 Internal politics became polarized over this Agreements: the government campaigned for its ratification by the National Assembly, while opposition to it was formed of forces ranging from religious politicians like Sayyid Hassan Modarres, to Mustawfi, a Qajari notable politician (Katouzian, *State and Society in Iran*, p. 125). Ahmad Shah, however, flip-flopped between these two camps. Eventually, while

visiting Britain just weeks after signing the Agreement, he hesitantly expressed his support for it and left its fate to be decided by the National Assembly. Historians have two distinctive views about Ahmad Shah's political life. Some believe he sacrificed Qajar dynastic rule because of his approach towards the ratification of the 1919 Agreement, others believe that he was a selfish ruler who lost his throne because of his personal laxity. See Sheikholeslami, *Simaye Ahmad Shah Qajar.*

5 Sadr al-Din Sadr (d. 1954), Muhammad Hujjat Kuh Kamarei (d. 1953) and Muhammad Taqi Khawnsari (d. 1952) who, from 1936, led the seminary for eight years, are known as the *Three Maraji'*.

6 Khomeini, *Ṣaḥīfeh-ye Imām*, Vol. I, p. 145.

7 Ghani, *Iran and the Rise of Reza Shah*, p. 21.

8 Ansari, *The Politics of Nationalism*, p. 66.

9 Akhavi, *Religion and Politics in Contemporary Iran*, p. 29.

10 Hairi, *Shi'ism and Constitutionalism in Iran*, p. 136. Prior to this, between 1900 and 1906, Hairi had settled in the city of Arak, just a few miles from Qum. However, with the rise of Constitutionalism in Tehran, he preferred to leave Persia and to settle, first, in Najaf and, then, in Karbala. In 1913, he left Karbala and went once again to Arak, from where he moved to Qum to re-establish the seminary.

11 Ibid.

12 Abrahamian, *Iran Between Two Revolutions*, pp. 123–5. The campaign reached its zenith in early 1924 when articles appeared in newspapers demanding a secular state and warning Iranians of the threat posed by the corrupt Qajar dynasty, foreigners and the clerics.

13 Bahar, *Tārīkh-i mukhtaṣar-i aḥzāb*, Vol. II, p. 42.

14 For a more detailed description of the expulsion of the Najaf clerical elite from Iraq to Qum, see Chapter 5.

15 For the full text of the letter signed by Na'ini, Isfahani and Hairi, see Mustawfi, *Sharḥ-i zindigānī-i man*, Vol. III, p. 601.

16 Akhavi, *Religion and Politics in Contemporary Iran*, p. 29.

17 Herz al-Din, *Ma'ārif al-rijāl*, Vol. I, p. 49. Reza Khan later visited Na'ini and Isfahani in Najaf to seek their support for his future political plans, and he promised to employ Article II of the Supplementary Fundamental Law, which provided for the monitoring by five Shi'i mujtahids of the activities of the National Assembly in order to prevent the ratification of laws that might be in non-compliance with Islam. Sheikh Muhammad Herz al-Din, a contemporaneous biographer of the ulama, claims that Reza Khan, then the minister of War to Ahmad Shah, met with the clerics of Najaf, including Isfahani and Na'ini, in the holy Shrine of Imam Ali in Najaf, and promised that upon ascending the throne, he would obey the clerics and deploy Article II of the Supplementary Fundamental Law. He goes on to state, 'however, after he returned and ascended to throne, he did not fulfil what had been promised'.

18 Algar, 'Religious Forces in Twentieth-Century Iran'.

19 Quoted in Makki, *Tārīkh-i bīst sālah*, Vol. IV, p. 379.

20 Najafi, *Andīshah-'i siyāsī va tārīkh-i nahẓat-i Ḥājj Āqā Nūr Allāh*. Born in 1859, Muhammad Mahdi Najafi Isfahani was one of the prominent religious leaders of Iran who, along with his brother, Aqa Muhammad Taqi (d. 1914), was actively involved in the Tobacco Revolt and the Constitutional Revolution.

21 Makki, *Tārīkh-i bīst sālah*, Vol. IV, p. 417.

22 Quoted in Mahdavi, *Bayān subl al-hidāyah*, Vol. II, p. 149.

23 Makki, *Tārīkh-i bīst sālah*, Vol. IV, p. 282.

24 Ibid., Vol. I, p. 210.
25 Abd al-Hussein Hairi, interview with *Hawzah Journal*, No. 125, December 2004.
26 For a detailed review of Reza Shah's modernization initiatives, see Banani, *The Modernization of Iran*, chapters 5–7. For a review of how these initiatives restrained Shi'i clerical authority in Iran, see Faghfoory, 'The Impact of Modernization'.
27 Throughout this study, the term 'Persia' has been used to refer to the country of Iran prior to 1935. It was in 1935 that Reza Shah Pahlavi requested that the international community refer to the country as 'Iran' instead of 'Persia'.
28 Faghfoory, 'The Impact of Modernization'.
29 Based on the Dress Unification Law, for a cleric to become exempt from the law he has to have a license from two prominent mujtahids or be a full-time member of a seminary and have passed an official examination. *Ettelaat Daily*, 25 December 1928, Tehran, Iran.
30 There are a handful of stories and memoirs of students who, in order to retain their religious attire, were forced to leave town during daylight hours and take sanctuary from police forces in the suburbs. Imam Khomeini, a student at the time, states that 'fearing the reinforcement police of Reza Shah, the religious students in Qum either imprisoned themselves in their rooms or would leave town and spend the day in the suburbs'. For a detailed story of the life of clerical students at the time, see Khomeini, *Ṣaḥīfeh-ye Imām*, Vol. XI, p. 396.
31 Abd al-Hussein Hairi, *interview with Hawzah Journal*, No. 125, December 2004.
32 National Archives of Iran, Document No. 116001-17, Pack-198.
33 It is said that, following the telegram, Reza Shah made a personal visit to Hairi's house in Qum and, referring to developments in Turkey, were a similar law was due to be ratified, warned him not to interfere. Reportedly, Reza Shah addressed Hairi saying: 'As if I am Yazid and you are Imam Hussein. What do you want from me? You should change your behaviour otherwise I will crush the seminary to debris' (Muhammad Hussein Fazel Isfahani, eyewitness of the meeting; quoted in *Yaad Quartely*, Qum1989, Vol. 14, p. 106).
34 Quoted in Vahed, *Qīyām-i Gawharshād*, p. 77.
35 For the first and contemporaneous account of Qumi's activities in regard to the incident, see Adib-Heravi, *Al-ḥadīqah al-riḍawīyah*, p. 282.
36 Abrahamian, *A History of Modern Iran*, p. 94.
37 Khomeini, *Ṣaḥīfeh-ye Imām*, Vol. II, p. 207.
38 The grandson of Hairi, Abd al-Hussein Hairi, states that his major concern was to protect the new seminary from threats emanating from the Pahlavi regime. As he once stated to one of his fellows, Sheikh Muhammad Khalesizadeh: 'the seminary is the most significant one at this time. To preserve its very foundation is the foremost priority at this time and I do not involve myself in any activity that may threated its security'. See *Hawzah Journal*, No. 125, December 2004.
39 Abrahamian, *A History of Modern Iran*, p. 111.
40 After the death of Hairi, a group of reformist clerics in Qum initiated a campaign to ask Burujirdi to go to Qum and assume the leadership of the seminary. The most active member of this group was a, then, middle-aged teacher of the Seminary, Ruhollah Khomeini, a former student of Hairi. Khomeini had been in contact with Burujirdi, sending him letters and envoys to persuade him to move to Qum. The campaign achieved its goal in 1946, and for years to come, Khomeini was one of the closest companions of Burujirdi (Muhammad Javad Alavi Burujirdi, interview with the author, January 2012).

41 Ibid. In December 1944, Burujirdi was admitted to a hospital in Tehran for medical treatment. During the month he was in Tehran, groups of people, including Muhammadreza Shah, members of the merchant class, and Shiʿi clerical elites, visited him in Qum. The main demand of the latter group was that he should go to Qum and assuming leadership of the seminary after his discharge from the hospital. Burujirdi agreed to visit Qum, but with some reservations. The main concern of the Grand Ayatollah at the time was the situation of those three Shiʿi clerics who had already been leading the seminary. All three were ranked lower than Burujirdi, based on their age and teachers; and it was believed that, over the Burujirdi's migration to Qum, their status would be damaged among the community and their followers. Eventually, Burujirdi entered the holy city of Qum on 10 February 1945, to reside there for the rest of his life. The political opportunity structure had already made it possible for Shiʿi clerics to fulfil their sociopolitical vision and now, together with the unique characteristics of Burujirdi, the situation for the Shiʿi clerical elite in Iran could not have been more promising.

42 Ali Davani, a contemporary historian of Qum seminary, relates that Burujirdi once told him: 'I had attended the sittings of Akhond Khorasani during the Constitutional Revolution in Najaf . . . . I witnessed how he made a mistake in the execution of Sheikh Fazlollah Noori and how he had blamed himself over the incident . . . since then whenever it comes to politics, I worry that I might also make a mistake' (*Yaad Quarterly*, Vol. 6 [Spring 1987]: 25).

43 Muhammad Javad Alavi Burujirdi, interview with the author, Qum, January 2012.

44 Martin, 'Religion and State'. During the early 1940s, relieved of the secular policy of Reza Shah, clerical authority was about to rise again in Iran. Fretful of its re-empowerment, a group of Iranian scholars, the most famous of which were Ahmad Kasravi, Reza Qoli Shariat-Sangelaji, and Ali Akbar Hakamizadeh, wrote books and initiated campaigns attacking the principles of Shiʿi Islam. In response, members of the Shiʿi clergy counter-attacked by writing treatises and preaching in mosques to refute the accusations. One of those refutations is contained in the book, *Kashf al-Asrār* (The Unveiling of Secrets), which Khomeini had written in 1944 in response to Hakamizadeh's book, *Asrār-i Hezār Sale* (*The Secrets of a Thousand Years*). Some clerics, like Navvab Safavi chose a more combatant approach in dealing with the insults of this group of scholars.

45 Quoted in Khoshniyat, *Sayyid Mujtaba' Navvāb Ṣafavī*, p. 21.

46 Davani, *Nahḍat-i rūḥānīyūn-i Īrān*, Vol. II, pp. 195–6. At a religious gathering in Tehran, and in response to the concern of Sheikh Muhammad Tehrani who was shouting from the pulpit that 'Kasravi openly insults Imam Jafar Sadeq and Imam of the Age and there is nobody who could suffocate him', a young cleric, Mojtaba Mirlowhi, stood up and said loudly that 'the sons of Imam Ali are alive and will respond to him'. He said that, later, when Navvab Safavi went back to Najaf after the death of Kasravi, everyone in Najaf recognized him.

47 Sharif Razi, *Ganjīnah-'i dānishmandān*, Vol. I, pp. 267–71. During the Great War, he had fought against British forces in Iraq along with groups of other Shiʿi clerics. During the anti-British revolt in Iraq that led to the 1920 rebellion, Kashani, who was young at the time, was in the forefront of the fight along with his famous father, Sayyid Mustafa Kashani. It was through this experience that a close relationship had been built between Kashani and Muhammad Taqi Khawnsari, who had also been active in the fighting.

48 Qanatabadi, *Khāṭirāt*, pp. 262–4. In the summer of 1944, Kashani, who was harshly critical of British policies in Iran, was arrested for his pro-German activities and spent almost a year in the Allied Forces' detention camps. When, at the end of the Second World War, he was freed and went back to Tehran to support his followers, he was more hostile to foreign forces and their supporters in the country. Thus, he again started to accuse the government of Qavam and his Democratic Party of being British Agents. This led to a second arrest in July 1946.

49 Davani, *Nahḍat-i rūḥānīyūn-i Īrān*, Vol. II, p. 197. At the time of the appointment of Burujirdi as the leader of Qum seminary, Navvab Safavi had clearly shown his support for Kashani. In a gathering to mark the death of Isfahani, the late leader of Najaf Seminary, Navvab took the podium and asked the crowd to demand that the Iranian government set Kashani free. The demand was fulfilled just a few months later.

50 Rahnema, *Nīrū'hā-yi maẕhabī*, pp. 67–8. Asking support from the sole leader of the seminary, a group of Fadaian affiliates took sanctuary at the house of Burujirdi in Qum. However, following days of the Grand Ayatollah's cold reception, which had been prompted by the group's rough actions, they left the city and returned to their own cities. Nevertheless, it is believed that it was in response to Burujirdi's lobbying that the government agreed to banish Kashani to Lebanon instead of convicting him in court.

51 Abrahamian, *Iran between Two Revolutions*, p. 250. The Shah also ordered the creation of Iran's second Constituent Assembly, which offered him a set of powers beyond what he had already been granted under the existing constitution. The Assembly was formed under the Martial Law. Its members finally voted for the establishment of the senate, with half of its members to be appointed by the Shah. The Shah was also given the right to dissolve Parliament and to nominate the prime minister, which the Parliament could either confirm or reject.

52 *Ettelaat Daily*, 14 February 1949, Tehran, Iran.

53 Ibid., 21 February 1949.

54 On 17 July 1949, a controversial agreement was signed between Golshayian (Iran's minister of Finance) and Neville Gass (the representative of the Anglo-Persian Oil Company), as a supplement to the 1933 Oil Agreement. Although the Shah agreed to the new terms, in order for it to be ratified, the agreement needed a favourable vote from Parliament. Activities of some Nationalist members of the fifteenth Parliament, like Hussein Makki, delayed the decision over the fate of the agreement, and the matter ultimately passed to the next session of Parliament. It was in this context that the government, along with British affiliates in Iran, were keen to structure the parliamentary election in a way that would guarantee the passage of the agreement. See Makki, *Kitāb-i siyāh*, Vol. III, pp. 9–33.

55 Iraqi, *Na Gofteha*, p. 39.

56 Abrahamian, *A History of Modern Iran*, pp. 115–16. In the campaign against the supremacy of the British and their affiliates in Iran, Muhammad Mosaddeq founded a National Front in 1949 comprised of several political groups. The Front, which had as its main objective to nationalize the oil industry, was closely associated with Kashani and his religio-political network.

57 For their part, Fadaian-e-Islam assassinated Hazhir, the minister of the court in May 1949. Within days, the assassin, Hussein Imami, was executed and a day later, the election in Tehran was cancelled, giving another opportunity for a religio-nationalist coalition. The irony was that to prove their willingness to take part in a free

democratic election, this coalition had no option but to make use of terror (Kinzer, *All the Shah's Men*, p. 66). Eventually, the result of the new election was declared in April 1950, in which Muhammad Mosaddeq and Kashani, who was still in exile in Lebanon, were elected to represent the people of Tehran in the new Parliament. Two months later, Kashani came back from exile, and met with the members of the National Front and Mosaddeq. Just days after he arrived in Tehran, Kashani went to Qum to meet with the Shiʿi clerics. It was there that Burujirdi met him at the house of Grand Ayatollah Khawnsari and the two exchanged views. It is said that Kashani, who had a different posture from that of Burujirdi at the time, addressed him and said: 'I do not want you to confirm whatever policy I follow, but just not to falsify it'; to which the leader of Qum seminary responded: 'I will say to all that I recognise you as the qualified mujtahid.' The rapprochement of these two religious and political leaders of the time clearly shows that, despite there being previously a degree of mutual resentment, they shared a common strategy, though with different approaches. For the full account of the meeting, see Rahnema, *Nīrū'hā-yi maẕhabī*, p. 142.

58 Makki, *Vaqāyiʿ-i sī'um-i tīr 1331*, p. 82. He was considered to be a traitor in the eyes of both nationalists and religious elite factions of the National Movement. On the day he went to the Parliament asking for a vote of confidence in his cabinet, Mosaddeq addressed him and said: 'God is our witness, that even if they would kill us and tear us to shreds, we will not tolerate the injustice of these people . . . we will beat them and will die . . . if you are from the army I am more armed than you, I will kill, I will kill you right here.'

59 Turkaman, *Asrar-e Ghatl-e Razmara*, p. 413. It is said that in planning the plot, Navvab Safavi met with members of the National Front, including Makki, Baqai and Fatemi, and some affiliates of Kashani, and that he assured them of Razmara's annihilation. Days after the assassination of the prime minister, a bill to nationalize the oil industry was passed in Parliament and approved by the senate. Following this, demonstrators filled the streets of Teheran chanting anti-British slogans and a comprehensive strike commenced in the oil fields of the southern provinces.

60 The anti-state positioning of Fadian-e-Islam reached the point at the time that they directly attacked the Shah and directly threatened for the first time to 'deploy the Islamic Law without any reservation', and that he, along with other members of the government apparatus, should expect a harsh retribution. For the full text of the declaration, see Khosroshahi, *Fadaian e Islam*, p. 128, and pp. 177–8.

61 Following the expulsion of the British affiliates from Iran and the nationalization of the oil industry, Britain threatened to launch a military response. Burujirdi sent a delegate to the Shah and informed him that, if Britain continued its threats against Iran and the popular government of Mosaddeq, the Shiʿi leadership would issue the Fatwa of Jihad against British forces and retaliate accordingly (Muhammad Javad Alavi Burujirdi, interview with the author, Qum, January 2012).

62 Iraqi, *Nāguftah'hā*. Soon after the premiership of Mosaddeq, Fadaian requested his government to submit to Islamic Law, and more specifically to (1) make public praying obligatory in state organizations, (2) make Hijab obligatory in Iran, (3) ban the selling of alcohol, (4) and dismiss all female employees from public organizations.

63 Makki, *Vaqāyiʿ-i sī'um-i tīr 1331*, p. 304. Rejecting the demands of Fadaian and referring to those untimely questions, Kashani stated that 'some would like to disrupt our battle [against Britain] by making these requests at this time . . . these are either servants of Britain, its mercenaries, or stupid'.

64 For details, see Nejati, *Junbish-i mili,* pp. 223–4.
65 Ibid., p. 226. Fretful because of popular support for Kashani, Qavam sent his envoys to change Kashani's attitude towards the government. However, the Ayatollah did not agree to support the new cabinet and asked for that Mosaddeq be returned to office.
66 Rahnema, *Nīrū'hā-yi maẕhabī,* p. 118.
67 Gasiorowski, 'The 1953 Coup D'etat in Iran'.
68 In the aftermath of the 1953 Coup, Mosaddeq was put on trial and then kept under house arrest for the rest of his life. In 1956, Kashani, who had at that time lost his social base, was questioned about the case of the Razmara Assassination and was about to be imprisoned. However, Kashani was released and acquitted of all charges following an ultimatum from Burujirdi in which he threatened the Shah that he would 'come personally to Tehran' if Kashani was not released immediately. See Sadeqkar, *Rūḥānī-i mubāriz,* Vol. II, pp. 744–51.
69 Ahmadi, *Chashm va charāgh-i marja 'īyat,* p. 118. Sayyid Hussein Budala, a close affiliate and student of Burujirdi, describes his teacher's concerns about the schism among all three sides of 'the triangle of the oil nationalisation movement', namely Mosaddeq, Kashani and Fadaian-e-Islam. He quotes Burujirdi as saying that 'if these three sides fall apart, not only will every side be hurt but it will also damage the clerical authority and the status of Islam as well'.
70 For a first-hand account of this bilateral relationship, see interviews with Grand Ayatollah Burujirdi's students compiled in Ibid., p. 53, p. 118, p. 163, and pp. 183–4.
71 *Ettelaat Daily,* 25 August 1953, Tehran, Iran. Muhammadreza Pahlavi had travelled to Rome, Italy, during the coup.
72 Muhammad Javad Alavi Burujirdi, interview with the author, Qum, January 2012.
73 For some cases of Burujirdi–Shah relationships, see interviews with Sayyid Hussein Budala and Sheikh Ali Safi Golpayegani in Ahmadi, *Chashm va charāgh-i marja 'īyat,* pp. 105–42.
74 Akhavi, *Religion and Politics in Contemporary Iran,* p. 72.
75 Following Burujirdi's death, a group of clerical elites and religious modern thinkers published a series of papers re-examining the role of Shi'i institutions compatibility with the contingencies of the time. The book, entitled *Baḥs̱ī Darbārah-'i marja 'īyat wa rawḥānīyat* (A Discussion about Marja'iyya and Clerics), was published in 1962. For a brief English review of the book see Lambton, 'A Reconsideration of the Position of the Marja' al-Taqlid'. An excerpt of the book's introduction reads as: 'Marja'iyya not only oversees individual religious practices, but also performs social and political functions in our country. It encompasses a huge weight in this world and hereafter' (Tababtabai et al., *Baḥs̱ī Darbārah-'i,* p. 5).
76 In some cases, for instance land reform initiatives, Burujirdi had discreetly warned the government against pursuing its planned policies. The Shah himself acknowledged the role of Burujirdi in postponing the Reform Initiatives in a later commemoration of the White Revolution. A detailed overview of Burujirdi's actions concerning the land reform initiatives is available at: http://Burujirdi.org/content/view/1066/68/ (accessed 10 May 2014).
77 Nevertheless, the Qum seminary in 1961 was strong enough to lead the Shi'i community. As a result of Hairi and Burujirdi activities in revitalizing the seminary, days after the death of Burujirdi, in Qum, the most renowned Shi'i elite gathered and nominated Muhammadreza Golpayegani (1898–1993), Kazem Shariatmadari (1905–1986), and Shahab al-Din Marashi Najafi (1897–1990) as those responsible for the financial affairs and leadership of the seminary. Within the meeting, Khomeini

declared that he 'prefer to go on with his academic responsibilities' as the seminary teacher and does not want to involve with financial issues'. Although, Khomeini was among the famous teachers of the seminary, quite distinctive among clerical elite of the city, and close in age and ability with the other three Ayatollahs, the evidence shows that in 1961, he did not have the intention of holding the conventional Marja'iyya position. Until the date, he had not been published his jurisprudential manual, neither been distributing religious taxes among his students, two main prerequisites of the position-holder in Shiʿi Islam. It was the upcoming events along with the demands of his close disciples and followers that pushed him to nominate himself as a Shiʿi Marja'. (Akbar Hashemi Rafsanjani, interview with the author, Tehran, November 2013).

78 Arjomand, *The Turban for the Crown*, p. 72.
79 Davani, *Nahḍat-i rūḥānīyūn-i Īrān*, Vol. III, p. 29.
80 For the text of the telegrams, see Ibid., pp. 31–8.
81 See Ibid., p. 36. In his telegram to the elite of Qum, the Shah addressed the leaders of Qum seminary as 'Hujjat al-Islam', a title lower in rank to 'Ayatollah' in Shiʿi hierocracy, in order to humiliate them.
82 Khomeini, *Ṣaḥīfeh-ye Imām*, Vol. I, p. 80.
83 A collection of telegrams against the six-points bill are compiled in the second volume of *Asnad-i Inqilab-i Islami* published in 1995 by Markaz-i Asnad-i Inqilab-i Islami in Tehran.
84 A first-hand account of the clerical elite's threats of mass mobilization against the government initiatives has been given in in memoires of the leading preacher of that time, Muhammad Taqi Falsafi. See Falsafi, *Khāṭirāt*, pp. 238–41.
85 Rajabi, *Zindigīnāmah-i siyāsī-i Imām Khumaynī*, p. 181.
86 Khomeini, *Ṣaḥīfeh-ye Imām*, Vol. I, p. 133.
87 The high-ranking clerics who signed the declaration were Morteza Langaroodi, Ahmad Zanjani, Muhammad Hussein Tabatabai, Muhammad Mohaghegh Damad, Muhammad Golpayegani, Kazem Shariatmadari, Rouhallah Khomeini, Hashem Amoli and Morteza Hairi. For the full text of the declaration, see Husseinian, *Sih sāl satīz marjaʿīyat-i Shīʿah*, pp. 204–6.
88 Quoted in Moin, *Khomeini*, p. 89.
89 Algar, 'Religious Forces in Twentieth-Century Iran'.
90 The clergy in Iraq supported their colleagues in Iran in this. Seemingly quiet, the leader of Najaf Seminary, Muhsin Al-Hakim, sent a telegram of condolence to his fellow Iranian clerics in early April 1963 and invited them to make an exodus to Iraq in order to issue a unanimous decree against the Shah. Although the elite of Qum did not agree to go to Najaf, the telegram from Al-Hakim shows the possibility that existed of a 'Jihad decree' against the Iranian government and, as the Shah had recognized him as the Shiʿi leader of the time, it was very costly for the Iranian regime. The harsher reaction, however, came from Khoei, a renowned teacher of Najaf seminary at the time. Through a set of questions and answers, which later was distributed in a pamphlet called 'Serious Warning of Ayatollah Khoei about the Jewish involvement in Iranian politics', he issued a harsh decree against the Shah and threatened him and his regime with utmost opposition and no concession. In this regard, the rise of Najafi clerics in support of the Iranian people and clerics is reminiscent of the Persian Constitutional Revolution era. http://www.alkhoei.net/arabic/pages/book.php?bcc=17&itg=61&bi=132&s=ct (accessed 8 May 2014).
91 Khomeini, *Ṣaḥīfeh-ye Imām*, Vol. I, p. 243.

92 Algar, 'Religious Forces in Twentieth-Century Iran'.
93 Martin, *Creating an Islamic State*, p. 58.
94 Among all of Khomeini's teachers, Mirza Muhammad Ali Shahabadi (1874–1950), the ascetic scholar of Philosophy and Gnosticism, had the most influence in his life, as the Grand Ayatollah himself later recalled. For the role of Philosophy and Gnosticism on the formation of the political doctrine of Shiʿi clerical elites in contemporary Iran, see Fadayi Mehrabani, *Ḥikmat, maʿrifat va siyāsat*.
95 Moin, *Khomeini*, pp. 39–52.
96 More than fifty high-ranking Shiʿi figures were travelled from their cities to take part in this protest and to support Khomeini; among them were Shariatmadari, Marashi Najafi, Morteza Hairi from Qum and Milani the leader of Mashahd seminary. For a full list of who were present in this civil protest and their activities while they were in Tehran see Davani, see *Nahḍat-i rūḥānīyūn-i Īrān*, Vol. VI, p. 131.
97 One of the most famous declarations that was issued over the incident and in support of Khomeini's movements at the time, was the one which came from the Freedom Movement of Iran, an Islamic faction of the National movement, entitled 'the dictator sheds blood'. In this declaration they emphasized that, with the blessings of the religious elites and upon their decrees, 'anyone who give up the opposition [against the regime] at this time, is a traitor to Islam, Quran, and Freedom'. This declaration caused the leaders of the movement, namely Mehdi Bazargan, Yadollah Sahabi and Mahmoud Taleqani, who were in prison already due to their opposition to the White Revolution, severe consequences and each were sentenced to a long imprisonment. For a full text of the FMI, see Ibid., Vol. IV, p. 142.
98 Husseinian, *Sih sāl satīz marjaʿīyat-i Shīʿah*, p. 452.
99 *Ettelaat Daily*, 5 April 1964, Tehran, Iran.
100 Following his return to Qum, Khomeini, then at the centre of attention, denounced the rumours of his compromise with the regime and advised his fellow clerics to not lose their thunder against the unjust rule of Shah. In one of his public sermons after his release, he clarified the duty of Shiʿi clerics and stated: 'today it is not the time to sit in our house and to pray, it is the day of fighting. Today is the day that the government attacks the religion, thus we should stand against it, and I will stand until the last drop of my blood . . . . You [clerics] should also loudly declare that and warn the people on the pulpits that a danger is threatening the religion . . . the government does not want to see a powerful clerical authority in Iran.' See Khomeini, *Ṣaḥīfeh-ye Imām*, Vol. I, p. 305.
101 Ibid., p. 415.
102 A simple comparison of Shariatmadari's speech with that of Khomeini's shows that, in the context of a similar political structure, and with similar opinions concerning the role the Shiʿi elite should play in political affairs and in protecting their community, it is the personal perceptions of Khomeini that pushed him towards making a more active and blatant response (Ali Akbar Mehdipour, interview with the author, Qum, May 2013).
103 Martin, *Creating an Islamic State*, p. 201.
104 When Khomeini entered Najaf, the high-ranking clerics of the seminary separately visited him. On the second night following his arrival that Al-Hakim visited him and advised him to start teaching in Najaf. Later, in a routine visit, Khomeini met Grand Ayatollah Al-Hakim to thank him for his hospitality. It was at this meeting, on 19 October 1965, that the two engaged in an exceptional discussion about the Shiʿi community in Iran and the role that the Shiʿi elite should take in its protection

at that time. When Khomeini asked Al-Hakim to 'visit Iran and see what is going on against the Shi'i community personally' and to take a more active position against the Iranian regime, Al-Hakim responded in this way: suppose that after 'I find out what is going on in Iran precisely', if I take an action that does not have sufficient influence, it will 'be doomed'. Still attempting to persuade Al-Hakim to rise up and lead the opposition Khomeini reminds him that 'with the amount of people who follow you, you have the greatest power'. Al-Hakim then responded, 'I could not see that many people would listen to me thoroughly and obey my orders.' Years later, after the establishment of the Islamic Republic of Iran, Imam Khomeini confessed that the perception of Grand Ayatollah Al-Hakim that, at the time, Shi'i clerical activism would not have popular support, was accurate. For detailed accounts of the Al-Hakim-Khomeini meeting in Najaf, see Tabarayian, *Iḥyāgar-i ḥawzah-i Najaf*, Vol. II, pp. 177–90. For Khomeini's recollections of the posture of Al-Hakim at the time, see Khomeini, *Ṣaḥīfeh-ye Imām*, Vol. XIV, p. 175.

105 Moin, *Khomeini*, p. 152.

106 Jafarian, *Jeryanhā va sāzmanhāye-ye mahzabi*, p. 291.

107 Khomeini, *Islamic Government*, p. 7.

108 Ibid., p. 23. He clearly states soothe reasons for arguing the necessity of establishing an Islamic Government led by the clerical elite: (1) the existence of a non-Islamic political order necessarily results in the non-implementation of the Islamic political order; (2) all non-Islamic systems of government are systems of *kufr,* since the ruler in each case is an idolater, and it is our duty to remove from the life of Muslim society all traces of *kufr* and destroy them; (3) it is also our duty to create a favourable social environment for the education of believing and virtuous individuals, an environment that is in total contradiction with that produced by the rule of idolatry and illegitimate power; (4) in order to assure the unity of the Islamic community, in order to liberate the Islamic homeland from occupation and penetration by the imperialists and their puppet governments, it is imperative that we establish a government; and (5) it is our duty to be a helper to the oppressed, and an enemy to the oppressor; thus, clerics have a duty to struggle against all attempts by oppressors to establish a monopoly over sources of wealth or make illicit use of them.

109 Khomeini, *Islamic Government*, p. 35.

110 While the Qum seminary was the cradle and shaped the core of Shi'i political activism in Iran, the seminary of Tehran, which was 200 years old at the time, had an influence in mobilizing the people of the capital and the merchants of the Bazaar in support of the objectives of the religious revolutionaries. Grand Ayatollah Sayyid Ahmad Khawnsari (1891–1985) was the centre's leader at the time of the Islamic Revolution. Although he never engaged in blatant political activism during his life, perhaps due to his personal asceticism, he supported Khomeini all through the movement. Following his death, Imam Khomeini praised his personality by stating that he was among the most pious clerics in Shi'i history and one resembling the infallibility of the Shi'i Imams (Mostafa Mohaghegh Damad, interview with the author, Tehran, November 2013).

111 For more documents about Marashi's role, see Marashi Najafi, *Ḥaẓrat-i Āyat Allāh al-'uẓmá Ssayyid Shihāb al-dīn Mar'ashī Najafī.*

112 Following Khomeini's arrest in 1963, Marashi was the first Shi'i Marja' who issued a declaration demanding that the government release him. When Khomeini was expelled from Iran, Marashi sent his son to meet with the Ayatollah to see if there was anything the leadership of Qum seminary could do to support the anti-

government uprising. And after the revolution, he repeatedly expressed his support for Khomeini's leadership saying: 'I am not capable as you to lead the country even for an hour.' For a detailed role of Marashi in the revolution, and his postures, see Sayyid Mahmood Marashi Najafi, interview with Khamenei's website, dated January 2012. http://farsi.khamenei.ir/others-dialog?id=10848 (accessed 15 May 2014).

113 Like most of the clergy who were active during the Shah's rule, Golpayegani was by no means a supporter of the regime. For a list of his declarations against the state's actions prior to the revolution, see Emami, *Zindagīnāmah-i Āyat Allāh al-'uẓmá Gulpāyagānī*.

114 For the text of his declaration, see *Asnad-i Inqilab-i Islami*, Vol. I, pp. 136–7.

115 Ali Akbar Mehdipour, interview with the author, Qum, May 2013.

116 At its birth, the establishment of *Dar al-Tabligh* in Qum was regarded as an act that might cause an internal schism among the clergy who were engaged in anti-state activities and it, thus, prompted a series of objections, mostly from political active clerics, including Khomeini. However, through the mediations of some renowned religious elites, the dispute between Shariatmadari and Khomeini was settled later. For an account of the arguments of both sides and the resolution of the dispute, see Jafarian, *Jeryanhā va sāzmanhāye-ye mahzabi*, pp. 327–41.

117 Ibid., p. 327.

118 The publication of *Maktab-e Islam* magazine, at the time was considered among the most avant-garde activities of the religious elite. The spiritual and financial sponsor of the magazine was Grand Ayatollah Shariatmadari and the initial editorial board was compromised of some modern Shiʿi thinkers like Musa Sadr. The role of its articles in awakening the Shiʿi community in Iran and bridging the elite-laity gap is undeniable. For a first-hand account of how the magazine was formed, see Davani, *Naqd-i 'umr*.

119 In Najaf, Grand Ayatollah Khoei read the prayer over the body of Sayyid Mostafa, who was to be buried in the holy shrine of Imam Ali. In Qum, just in one case, 6000 people gathered in the A'zam Mosque accompanying Golpayegani, Marashi Najafi and Shariatmadari to mourn the death of Khomeini's son. SAVAK officers reported that great numbers of anti-government declarations signed by 'the Combatant Clerics of Qum' and 'the Iranian Student Confederation' were distributed among the attendees. (Archives of Markaz-i Asnad-i Inqilab-i Islami, Revived No. 393: 4).

120 *Ettelaat Daily*, 6 January 1978, Tehran, Iran.

121 Husseinian, *Yik sāl mubārazah*, p. 165.

122 Kurzman, 'The Qum Protests.'

123 Algar, 'Religious Forces in Twentieth-Century Iran.'

124 Quoted in Tabatabai, *Khāṭirāt-i siyāsī*, Vol. III, p. 59.

125 Martin, *Creating an Islamic State*, p. 156.

126 Khomeini, *Ṣaḥīfeh-ye Imām*, Vol. VI, p. 54.

127 In April 1980, Imam Khomeini had a heart attack and was rushed to Tehran. When he was discharged from the hospital, upon the advice of his doctors, he resided in the northern suburbs of Tehran in the village of Jamaran where the climate was better for his health. He lived in Jamaran for the rest of his life. The migration of the Imam to Tehran was auspicious for the interim government and for Prime Minister Bazargan who had struggled to control the post-revolution situation with respect to the activities of the Revolutionary Council. With the Imam in Tehran, the meetings and perhaps arbitrations between various members of the government and the council, it became much easier (Sadeq Tabatabi, interview with the author, Tehran, November 2012).

Chapter 5

1 Batatu, *The Old Social Classes*, p. 40. The demographic trend has been much the same for the last sixty years. The 1947 Iraqi census recorded that about 51.4 per cent of the population in Iraq was made up of Shiʿi Arabs, while Sunni Arabs comprised 19.7 per cent, and Sunni Kurds comprised 18.4 per cent of the population.
2 Nakash, 'The Conversion of Iraq's Tribes to Shiism'. The late eighteenth century saw the beginning of a series of massive conversions of Iraq's Sunni tribes to Shiʿi Islam, which continued until as late as 1917.
3 Ottoman-Safavid hostile rivalries during the sixteenth and seventeenth centuries affected Iraq. Shah Ismail Safavi conquered Iraq in 1509, but in 1535, the Ottomans, under Suleiman, succeeded in reacquiring Iraq. Again in 1623, Persia, under Shah Abbas, was able to annex Iraq, only to lose the area to Ottomans in 1638 forever.
4 Vakili Qummi, 'Tashkīlāt-i maḏhab-i Shī'ah'.According to this research conducted fifty years ago by the Institute for Social Studies and Research in Tehran, thirty-four of over fifty-eight Shiʿi Marja' who had led the seminary since its foundation were originally Persian, while only sixteen were Iraqi nationals, among them the late Muhsin Al-Hakim. The nationality of the Shiʿi leadership in Iraq played a pivotal role in constraining the political activism of the centre, especially during the modern history of Iraq when pan-Arab ideology prevailed throughout the Middle East.
5 See Nasr, *The Shia Revival*; and Nakash, *Reaching for Power.*
6 Makiya, *Republic of Fear.*
7 For a detailed primary source about the negative effects of the Persian Constitutional Revolution on dividing the seminaries of Najaf and Karbala, see Najafi Ghoochani 2007.
8 For the text of Yazdi's fatwa against the British, see Davani, *Nahḍat-i rūḥānīyūn-i Īrān*, Vol. I, p. 212.
9 With the 1917 Bolshevik Revolution in Russia, the Ottoman Empire invaded Russia's northern border, thus decreasing their armed presence in the south where they had been engaged with British troops. The Arab Revolt of the Sharif of Hejaz also fuelled tension between Turks and the Arab ethnic groups of the Empire during this critical time. Moreover, harsh policies by the Ottoman government against the people of some Iraqi cities, especially Hilla, as well as increases in taxes, alienated other Iraqis from the Ottomans. For a series of other factors that fuelled the Arab-Turkish Ottoman schism during the Great War, see Sluglett, *Britain in Iraq*, pp. 8–41.
10 The full text is available at http://wwi.lib.byu.edu/index.php/The_Proclamation_of_Baghdad (accessed 7 July 2017).
11 See Toby Dodge, 'Failing in Baghdad – The British Did It First', *The Washington Post*, 25 February 2007.
12 Ansari, *Tārīkh-i 'Irāq*, Vol. II, p. 330.
13 Nakash, *Reaching for Power*, p. 75.
14 Al-Asadi, *Ṯawraẗ al-Najaf*, p. 169.
15 Sluglett, *Britain in Iraq*, p. 221.
16 Al-Hassani, *Al- 'Irāq fī dawray al-iḥtilāl*, Vol. I, p. 38.
17 During the Iraqi revolt, British hegemony throughout the Middle East was undergoing dramatic changes. Neighbouring Iran, where the majority of Shiʿi Muslims resided, was falling apart, and Britain was forced to propose an Anglo-Persian treaty as a means of protecting its interests. In Egypt and Sudan, there were

anti-imperialist rebellions that resulted in restricting British troops to the Suez Canal zone; and turmoil in Palestine appeared increasingly unpromising for British interests. For details of anti-British developments in the Middle East at that time, see Fromkin, *A Peace to End All Peace*, pp. 415–64.

18 Nakash, *The Shi'is of Iraq*, 63.
19 Nakash, *Reaching for Power*, 78.
20 Āl Fir'awn, *Al-Ḥaqā'iq al-nāṣi'ah*, p. 9. The committee consisted of five Shiʿi clerical figures: Sheikh Mahdi Khalesi, Sayyid Abu al-Qasim Kashani, Sayyid Hebat al-Din Shahrestani, Mirza Ahmad Khorasani and Sheikh Muhammadreza Shirazi.
21 Al-Wardi, *Lamaḥāt ijtimā'īyah*, Vol. V, p. 128.
22 Quoted in Ibid., Vol. IV, p. 183.
23 Quoted in Āl Fir'awn, *Al-Ḥaqā'iq al-nāṣi'ah*, p. 195.
24 Nakash, *The Shi'is of Iraq*, p. 77.
25 Tripp, *A History of Iraq*, p. 43.
26 Nakash, *The Shi'is of Iraq*, p. 72.
27 Tripp, *A History of Iraq*, p. 44.
28 Al-Badri, *Al-Islām bayna al-'ulamā' wa-al-ḥukkām*, p. 244.
29 The full text of the letter is available at http://www.gerty.ncl.ac.uk/letter_details.php?letter_id=425 (accessed 29 June 2017).
30 Sluglett, *Britain in Iraq*, p. 31.
31 For a full account of the conference's outcome, see Ibid., pp. 39–41.
32 Nakash, *The Shi'is of Iraq*, pp. 76–7. The Shiʿi clerical elites' support of Faisal was conditional; he had apparently assured Khalesi that, upon receipt of the throne, he would protect the monarchy from the British. In any case, the Shiʿi clerical leadership had very little room for manoeuvre in the nomination of Faisal given the sociopolitical context of the country at the time.
33 The full text of the treaty is available at http://www.galeuk.com/iraq/pdfs/Treaty%20of%20alliance%20btw%20GB%20&%20Iraq%2010%20Oct%201922%20CO%20730%20167%201.pdf (accessed 1 July 2017).
34 Nakash, *The Shi'is of Iraq*, p. 78.
35 Ibid., p. 79.
36 For the text of the government's proclamation, see Al-Hassani, *Tārīkh al-wizārāt al-'Irāqīya*, Vol. I, p. 130.
37 Nakash, *The Shi'is of Iraq*, p. 82.
38 Marr, *The Modern History of Iraq*, p. 28.
39 Hadi Ansari, interview with the author, Tehran, August 2013.
40 Al-Wardi, *Lamaḥāt ijtimā'īyah*, Vol. VI, p. 261.
41 Wiley, *The Islamic Movement of Iraqi Shi'as*, p. 22.
42 Kubba, 'Iraqi Shi'i Politics', p. 143.
43 Dekmejian, *Islam in Revolution*, p. 120. The Shiʿi clerical leadership in Iraq saw the emergence of a Nasserist orientation as a threat, as they would lose their popular status if Iraq were to become a Sunni-dominated, secular pan-Arab state headed by Nasser.
44 The founders of the Association were among the most renowned members of the clerical elite in Najaf, just a level lower than the seminary's leadership circle. Among them were Sheikh Murtada A'l-Yasin (the maternal-uncle of Muhammad Baqir Sadr), Sayyid Muhamamd Taqi Bahr al-Ulum, Sheikh Muhammadreza Mozaffar and Sayyid Ismail Sadr. For a thorough review of founding members and their political missions, see Al-Siraj, *Al-Imām Muḥsin al-Ḥakīm*, p. 116.

45 Tabarayian, *Iḥyāgar-i ḥawzah-i Najaf*, Vol. I, p. 46.
46 Ibid., p. 194. Other famous members of the Shi'i clergy in Najaf at that time were the Grand Ayatollahs Sayyid Abdul Hadi Shirazi, Hassan Bojnourdi, Sayyid Mahmoud Shahroodi, Sayyid Abu al-Qasim Khoei and Sheikh Hussein Hilli.
47 The estimated number of students in the Najaf seminary had increased sixfold after Muhsin Al-Hakim took its leadership. Interview with Sayyid Muhammad Baqir Al-Hakim quoted in Ibid., p. 311.
48 Wimmer, 'Democracy and Ethno-Religious Conflict in Iraq'.
49 Sluglett and Sluglett, *Iraq Since 1958*, p. 57.
50 Nakash, *The Shi'is of Iraq*, p. 135.
51 Al-Alawi, *Shī'ah va ḥukūmat*, p. 243.
52 Wiley, *The Islamic Movement of Iraqi Shi'as*, p. 37.
53 Aziz, 'The Role of Muhammad Baqir al-Sadr'.
54 Al-Alawi, *Shī'ah va ḥukūmat*, p. 244. During this period, a series of essays by Muhammad Baqir Sadr was published in *Al-Hurriya*, the journal run by Iraqi Nationalists and Ba'thists. This is indicative of the existence of an unwritten alliance between Shi'i religious forces and Arab Nationalist activists against the rule of Qasim in Iraq.
55 Mallat, *The Renewal of Islamic Law*, 15.
56 Al-Alawi, *Shī'ah va ḥukūmat*, p. 255. On 18 November 1963, Arif broke his alliance with the Ba'thists and formed a new government, supported mostly by Nasserist army officers. On the same day, he issued a proclamation and called the Shi'is of Iraq *Shuyuis* – communists – who should step down from any key positions they held in Iraq.
57 Quoted in Tabarayian, *Iḥyāgar-i ḥawzah-i Najaf*, Vol. I, p. 490.
58 Wiley, *The Islamic Movement of Iraqi Shi'as*, p. 40.
59 Tabarayian, *Iḥyāgar-i ḥawzah-i Najaf*, Vol. I, p. 513.
60 Sluglett and Sluglett, *Iraq since 1958*, p. 220.
61 With the rise of the Ba'th in 1968, the office of the Presidency was abolished, and the Revolutionary Command Council became the ultimate decision-maker in Iraq. Ahmad Hassan al-Bakr, an Iraqi army officer from the city of Tikrit, became the first chairman of the Council. Through exclusivist rule of the Ba'thists in Iraq, the inhabitants of Tikrit and its neighbouring towns and cities, irrespective of their religious identities and propensities, were awarded the highest political and army positions. For the exclusivist policies of the Ba'th in recruiting from among specific regions in Iraq, see Al-Alawi, *Shī'ah va ḥukūmat*, pp. 275–89.
62 Michel Aflaq planned a conspiracy against Muhsin Al-Hakim and instructed Ba'thist rulers to impose a series of restrictions on Shi'i seminaries in Iraq. For full details of his confession, see confessions of Hardan al-Tikriti, the ex-Ba'thist vice president of Iraq quoted in in Tabarayian, *Iḥyāgar-i ḥawzah-i Najaf*, Vol. II, pp. 62–4.
63 His proposed amendment to the Constitution of the Islamic Republic of Iran has been published along with four other articles in a book entitled, *Al-Islām yaqūdu l-ḥayāt*.
64 Muhammad Baqir Sadr is the first cousin and brother-in-law of Imam Musa Sadr, the religious leader associated with Lebanon's Shi'i revivalism.
65 Husseini Hairi, *Zindagī va afkār-i shahīd-i buzurgvār*, pp. 82–3. The first five editorials of *al-Dawa*, the journal of the Ulama Association published since June 1960, were written by Sadr and signed as 'the Ulama Association of Najaf'. Under pressure from hostile elements in the city, who accused Sadr of imposing his political

posture on other Shiʿi elites in the seminary, he stopped publishing editorials in the journal.

66 *Jamaat al-Ulama fi Najaf al-Ashraf*, 'Resalatuna', *al-Adwa* I (9 June 1960): 1.
67 Mallat, 'Religious Militancy in Contemporary Iraq'.
68 Quoted in Sluglett and Sluglett, *Iraq Since 1958*, 196.
69 Some believe that the Dawa Party was founded years earlier than the Ulama Association in 1957 by a group of young Shiʿi students of the Najaf seminary. The Party's main founders were Muhammad Baqir Sadr, Sayyid Mahdi Al-Hakim and Sayyid Muhammad Hussein Fadlallah. For a review of the Party's role in the politics of Iraq, see Dai, 'Transformation of the Islamic Da'wa Party'.
70 Aziz, 'The Role of Muhammad Baqir al-Sadr'.
71 Wiley, *The Islamic Movement of Iraqi Shi'as*, p. 32.
72 Ibid., p. 39. Apart from the government of Qasim and his early communist tendencies, which had basically been the target of al-Dawa's social activities, Arab Nationalists were also targets of the party's opposition activities.
73 Years later, during the rule of the Baʿth in Iraq, Sadr issued a fatwa forbidding students and affiliates of the Najaf seminary to join political parties. His close disciples would argue that this action was a case of *taqqiya*, meant to protect the seminary from pressures from the regime and that, to the last day of his life, he supported the activities of religious political parties. For a first account narrative, see Husseini Hairi, *Al-Shahīd al-Ṣadr*, p. 142.
74 The activities of some reformist Shiʿi clerical elites of Qum in introducing a new definition of the Marja'iyya position after the death of Burujirdi has been discussed in Chapter 4.
75 Aziz, 'The Role of Muhammad Baqir al-Sadr'.
76 In terms of this, there is evidence that proves Khoei's personal support. In general, Sadr was among the most notable of his students, and there always remained a great teacher–student relationship between the two. In an interview with Khoei's son, Abd al-Saheb Khoei, he mentioned that the Grand Ayatollah had stated, 'had Sadr been alive; he would have been the best alternative for leadership of the seminary after my death' (interview with the author, Tehran, July 2012).
77 Tripp, *A History of Iraq*, 208.
78 Nu'mani, *Al-Shahīd al-Ṣadr*, p. 212. Muhammad Baqir Al-Hakim (d. 2003), the student close to Sadr and founder of the Supreme Council for Islamic Revolution in Iraq, was arrested after the February Incident and sentenced to life in prison; yet he later escaped and went to Iran. Sadr himself stated that, while he was in custody in Baghdad, Izzat al-Douri, then the minister of State, threatened him with revenge for the role he had played in the uprising.
79 Quoted in Aziz, 'The Role of Muhammad Baqir al-Sadr'.
80 In an open letter to Iranian revolutionaries in December 1978, months before their victory, Sadr had advised them to support Imam Khomeini and to obey his orders and promised them that their 'triumph is nigh'. This letter was accompanied by numbers of others that were issued by him confirming the incidents in Iran after the establishment of the Islamic government. For a text of the letter, see Al-Ameli, *Muḥammad Bāqir al-Ṣadr*, Vol. IV, pp. 8–10.
81 While Sadr was under house arrest in Najaf (in July 1979), he issued an open letter, addressed to Iraqis, stating: 'It is incumbent on every Muslim in Iraq and every Iraqi outside Iraq to do whatever he can, even if it cost him his life, to keep the jihad and struggle to remove this nightmare from the land of beloved Iraq, to liberate

themselves from this inhuman gang, and to establish a righteous, unique, and honourable rule based on Islam.' For the detail of his open letter to Iraqis, see Ibid., Vol. IV, p. 201.

82 Sadr also contributed in drafting the Islamic Republic's constitution by sending copies of his jurisprudential verdicts on the role of Shiʿi clerical elites in modern politics to Iran after the victory of the revolution. For a full text of his treatise, see Sadr, *al-Islam Yaqud al-Hayat*, Chapter I.

83 For the full text of his note, see Ibid., pp. 14–19.

84 Mallat, *The Renewal of Islamic Law*, p. 51.

85 Nu'mani, *Al-Shahīd al-Ṣadr*, p. 327.

86 In his message on the death of Sadr, Imam Khomeini showed that he had cherished Sadr's activities: 'it is not a matter of wonder that the late Ayatollah is martyred. The wonder is here that the Islamic nations, particularly the noble nation of Iraq and more particularly the tribes of Tigris and Euphrates and the Iraqi youth and university students, have remained indifferent at this agony and havoc that has hit Islam . . . . It is, indeed, strange that they give the cursed Baʿth party of Iraq the opportunity to kill the pivots of our pride one after the other . . . I hope [the Iraqi nation] will eradicate this element of shame from Iraq. I pray God to wipe out this tyranny from Iraq.' See Khomeini, *Ṣaḥīfeh-ye Imām*, Vol. XII, pp. 253–4.

87 A historical irony is that Baʿth ideology had been brought from its cradle, Syria, to Iraq in 1951 by a group of Shiʿi activists, headed by Fuad Rikabi. However, by the time the Baʿthists had consolidated their power and seized the government in 1968, its key members had been dramatically transformed. For a historical review of Shiʿis and Baʿthism in Iraq, see Sluglett and Sluglett, 'The Historiography of Modern Iraq'.

88 Tabarayian, *Intifā̤zah Sha'bānīyah*.

89 Nakash, *Reaching for Power*, p. 72.

90 Muhammad Sadeq Rouhani, interview with the author, Qum, Autumn 2013.

91 Otterman, 'Iraq: Grand Ayatollah Ali al-Sistani'; and Patel, 'Ayatollahs on the Pareto Frontier'.

92 For Khoei's position at the time, see Chapter 4, FN. 90.

93 For the full text of the letter, see *Asnad-i Inqilab-i Islami*, Vol. III, p. 143.

94 Eslami, *Ghurūb-i khvurshīd-i faqāhat*. Khoei was one of the first members of the Shiʿi clergy in Najaf to meet with Khomeini; he greeted him in 1964. In the winter of 1977, it was Khoei who prayed over the body of Sayyid Mostafa, the deceased son of Khomeini in Najaf. He also issued a proclamation and supported the constitution of the Islamic Revolution and asked people to vote for it.

95 Contrary to some of his fellow Maraji', such as Khomeini, Khoei believed that 'the qualified Shiʿi jurist has the right to issue a fatwa for aggressive Jihad during the Occultation era'. Thus, the circle of clerical authorities that adhered to Khoei's ijtihad could go far beyond that of Khomeini's, who limits the Guardianship of the Jurist to only the 'defensive Jihad'. For the characteristics of his ijtihad, see the interview with Ahmad Madadi, *Mehrnameh Monthly*, Tehran, Iran, No. 12, May 2011.

96 For a detailed analysis of this conflict, its background, course of events and outcomes, see Chubin and Tripp, *Iran and Iraq at War*; Rajaee, *Iranian Perspectives on the Iran-Iraq War*; and Karsh, *The Iran-Iraq War*.

97 Potter and Sick, *Iran, Iraq, and the Legacies of War*, p. 8.

98 Nakash, 'The Shi'ites and the Future of Iraq'.

99 Bakhash, 'The Troubled Relationship', p. 22.

100 Quoted in Ahmadi, *Islands and International Politics*, p. 124.

101 Al-Khafaji, 'War as a Vehicle'.

102 For a review of Ba'th propaganda through the course of the war with Iraq and the emergence of Saddam's 'Aggressive Arabism' and 'New Iraqism', see Ibid.

103 Karsh, 'Geopolitical Determinism'.

104 For the full account of his speech see Khomeini, *Ṣaḥīfeh-ye Imām*, Vol. XIII, pp. 253–4.

105 Although not a single written verdict from the Grand Ayatollah has been found in support of the Iranian army during the war, perhaps for security reasons, it is said that the Khoei had allowed his representatives, *wukala*, to spend his followers' religious taxes on Iranians. See Eslami, *Ghurūb-i khvurshīd-i faqāhat.*

106 For the list of SCII actions, mainly conducted by the entourage of Muhammad Baqir Sadr and the Al-Hakim family, see International Crisis Group Report 2007, *Shi'i Politics in Iraq: The Role of the Supreme Council.* https://www.crisisgroup.org/middle-east-north-africa/gulf-and-arabian-peninsula/iraq/shiite-politics-iraq-role-supreme-council (accessed 5 June 2017).

107 The main reason for Saddam's invasion of Kuwait was the dispute over the repayment of loans Iraq had received from Persian Gulf countries during the war with Iran. For an analysis of the Gulf War, see Mearsheimer and Walt, 'An Unnecessary War'.

108 For the Iraq–US relationship during the war with Iran and at the beginning of the Iraq–Kuwait conflict, see Pollack, 'How Saddam Misread the United States'.

109 Addressing the Iraqi army and people, President Bush stated: 'Iraqi military and the Iraqi people to take matters into their own hands and force Saddam Hussein, the dictator, to step aside, and then comply with the United Nations resolutions and rejoin the family of peace-loving nations. We have no argument with the people of Iraq. Our differences are with that brutal dictator in Baghdad.' The full account of President Bush's statement is available at http://www.gpo.gov/fdsys/pkg/PPP-1991-book1/html/PPP-1991-book1-doc-pg148.htm (accessed 1 August 2017).

110 Tabarayian, *Intifā.zah Sha'bānīyah*, p. 230. During the 1991 uprising, the government maintained its authority in just four provinces, those of Baghdad, Saladin, Anbar and Nineveh.

111 The Committee had nine members, among them Sayyid Muhammad Taqi Khoei, son of the Grand Ayatollah, and Sayyid Muhammad Sabzevari, the son of Grand Ayatollah Sayyid Abd al-'Ala Sabzevari, another politically active Marja' of Iraq during the uprising. For a comprehensive list of the Executive Committee members and brief biographies of them, see Ibid., pp. 279–83.

112 Ibid., p. 281.

113 For a detailed insider account of the Shi'i Marja'iyya's role over the uprising, see the interview of Abdul Majid Khoei with *al-Sharq al-Awsat Daily*, 6 March 2000.

114 Marr, *The Modern History of Iraq*, 232.

115 One of the main factors that alarmed the US-led coalition into not supporting the popular uprising was the bold role the Iranian-backed Badr brigade forces throughout the turmoil in Iraq. For a series of other factors that led to the collapse of the 1991 Shi'i uprising, see Abdul-Jabar, 'Why the Uprising Failed?'.

116 Cole, 'The United States and Shi'ite'.

117 In the recent history of Iraqi Shi'is, *Muhammad Baqir Sadr* is known as the first Sadr, his cousin *Muhammad Muhammad Sadeq Sadr* is titled the second Sadr, while *Muqtada Sadr*, the founder of the Mahdi Army in Iraq, has been named the third Sadr.

118 Allawi, *The Occupation of Iraq*, p. 54.

119 Haugh, 'The Sadr II Movement'.
120 Allawi, *The Occupation of Iraq*, p. 58. Ayatollah Muhammad Sadr introduced 'jurisprudence for the tribes'. As his perception over the political opportunity structure at societal level matters, the Ayatollah had accurately perceived that, to become actively engaged in the politics of Iraq, it was necessary for him to come up with a coherent resolution for Shiʿi tribes. Yet as the upcoming events unfolded, this was not the whole picture in Iraq during the 1990s.
121 Allawi, *The Occupation of Iraq*, p. 58.
122 Cole, 'The United States and Shi'ite'.
123 Allawi, *The Occupation of Iraq*, p. 60.
124 Ibrahim Bahr al-Ulloum, interview with the author, Najaf, December 2013.
125 Marr, *The Modern History of Iraq*, p. 170.
126 Nakash, 'The Shi'ites and the Future of Iraq'.
127 Elhadj, *The Islamic Shield*, p. 178.
128 See 'What Role for the Iraqi National Congress in Iraq', *Council on Foreign Relations*, 1 February 2002. http://www.cfr.org/iraq/role-iraqi-national-congress-iraq/p4330 (accessed 10 June 2017).
129 Ehrenberg, *The Iraq Papers*, p. 29.
130 Marr, *The Modern History of Iraq*, p. 258.
131 Ibrahim Bahr al-Ulloum, interview with the author, Najaf, December 2013.
132 Al-Khaffaf, *Al-Nuṣūṣ al-ṣādirah*, p. 30.
133 Quoted in Arato, 'Sistani v. Bush'.
134 Rahimi, 'Ayatollah Ali al-Sistani'.
135 Marr, *The Modern History of Iraq*, p. 278. The National Iraqi Alliance consisted of Shiʿi parties (e.g. Dawa, SCIRI, Islamic Action Organisation, and Iraqi National Congress) won the majority of 140 out of 275 seats on the Council of Representative of Iraq in the January 2005 parliamentary election. Later that year, in December, when Sunni parties ran for election, again, Shiʿi parties won the majority of seats.
136 Nasr, 'When the Shiites Rise'.
137 Abd al-Jabbar, *The Shīʿite Movement in Iraq*, pp. 264–73.

Chapter 6

1 Hourani, 'Political Society in Lebanon'. At the time, the Ottoman territories comprising Mount Lebanon, Tripoli, Beirut, Sidon, the Beqaa Valley and Jebel Amil, were home to more than fifteen different sects. Sunni Muslims were settled in the big port cities of Tripoli, Sidon and Beirut; Mount Lebanon was the stronghold of Christians and Druze, while Shiʿis were found mainly in the South as well as in the Beqaa Valley.
2 Harris, *Faces of Lebanon*, p. 23.
3 For the first time in the history of Lebanon, the Mutasarrifate scheme institutionalized different sects' identities see Farah, *Politics of Interventionism*, 256. In association with the Ottomans' central government, the Christian governor of Mount Lebanon was obliged to seek assistance from an administrative council consisting of twelve members from six different religious sects, namely Maronite, Druze, Sunni, Shiʿi, Greek Orthodox and Greek Catholic Makdisi, *The Culture of Sectarianism*, p. 84.

4 Hottinger, 'Zu'ama' in Historical Perspective'. Zu'ama, plural for Zai'm, refers to elites among all Lebanese sects who serve as patrons to the laymen and peasant clients.
5 Dekmejian, *Patterns of Political Leadership*, p. 11.
6 A noteworthy case of Zu'ama authority is, indeed, the rise of Shiʿi Zu'ama in the South during the early years of the last century. During the first Balkan War, while the Sunni community was under the full-fledged support of the Ottoman Sultan and Christians, as *dhimmis,* were exempt from participating in the War, the pressure intensified on the Shiʿi laity to go to the warfront. Taking the circumstances into account, the chances of return for the Ottoman soldiers were at their lowest. As a result, the Shiʿi community rose up against the discrimination. Eventually, the central government agreed that each Shiʿi soldier could be exempt from mandatory military participation with a payment of 75 Liras. This resembled blood money to most of the Shiʿi young men. As a result, groups of Shiʿi peasants who had land, or any other kinds of property sold them to large Shiʿi landowners in order to acquire the exemption money; others who did not have property were forced either to participate in the war or to acquire the money from elites and remain in debt to them for several years. Thus, the Shiʿi Zu'ama became even more powerful and expanded their influence over the community. For a full account of the incidents see Chamran, *Lubnān*, p. 38.
7 Dekmejian, *Patterns of Political Leadership*, p. 22.
8 Great landowner families in different parts of Lebanese territories were among the most influential political leaders in later Lebanon. Maronite figures like Frangieh and Khazen, Sunnis like Karami and Solh, Druzes like Jumblatt and Shiʿi like Asaad and Osseiran were all among the major rural landowners in Lebanon in the late nineteenth century. For a comprehensive list, see Ibid., p. 17.
9 See for example Kayali, *Arabs and Young Turks;* and Dawn, 'From Ottomanism to Arabism'.
10 Dawn, 'From Ottomanism to Arabism'.
11 Hourani, *Syria and Lebanon: A Political Essay*.
12 Halawi, *A Lebanon Defied*, p. 157.
13 Shanahan, *The Shia of Lebanon*, p. 52.
14 Hanf, *Coexistence in Wartime Lebanon,* p. 27.
15 Solh, 'The Attitude of the Arab Nationalists'.
16 Maktabi, 'The Lebanese Census of 1932'. A biased policy in conducting the census was to take Lebanese immigrants into account. The result of the census depicts that out of 254,987 Lebanese immigrants, constituting over 22 per cent of the country's total population, 215,844 were Christians.
17 A Greek Orthodox, Charles Debbas (d. 1935), was the first president of Lebanon and served for eight years between 1926 and 1934. Upon the disclosure of the census results, Habib Pasha al-Saad, a prominent Maronite political figure, became the first Maronite president of the Republic of Lebanon under the French Mandate in January 1934.
18 Regional incidents had fuelled tensions between the two communities, as well. In the 1930s, following the gradual rise of Arab Nationalism against the French and British presence in the region, the colonial powers were seeking a more indirect role in the politics of Arab countries. This trend started with the Anglo-Iraqi treaty of 1930, in which the Kingdom of Iraq received nominal independence from the British Mandate and became an independent member of the League of Nations. In September 1936, an anti-French strike led by a Syrian nationalist bloc resulted in a

treaty of independence for Syria (see Thomas, *The French Empire between the Wars*, p. 312). In the same year, the Anglo-Egyptian treaty was signed which required Britain to withdraw its troops from Egypt, except for the Suez Canal, and granted the country a great deal of independence from the British. These developments, along with the Arab revolt against the Jewish community in Palestine from 1936 to 1939, made the political scene in Lebanon more volatile than ever. It was in this situation that Sunni and Maronite elites had come up with a kind of compromise in order to protect Lebanon's national unity.

19 Khazen, 'The Communal Pact of National Identities', p. 18.

20 Al-Jisr, *Ri'āsah wa-siyāsah wa-Lubnān al-jadīd*, p. 145.

21 While based on the constitution, the president had the utmost executive authority; he was not accountable to the National Assembly. Parliament could ask for interpellation of the cabinet but not the Maronite president.

22 Hani Fahs, interview with the author, Beirut, Lebanon, August 2012.

23 Kasaba et al., 'Eastern Mediterranean Port Cities'. The Eastern Mediterranean Ports have had an importance in World trade for centuries. During the last decades of the Ottoman Empire, in the late nineteenth century, they regained their significant economic position once again thanks to the new trends in World Trade and transportation evolutions. This unique characteristic influenced the formation of a bourgeois class dwelling in those areas at the beginning of the twentieth century.

24 Khuri, 'A Comparative Study of Migration'.

25 Muhammad D. Nasrallah, interview with the author, Beirut, Lebanon, August 2012.

26 Hamzeh, 'Clientalism, Lebanon'.

27 'Lebanese-Israeli General Armistice Agreement 23 March 1949'. Full text available at http://unispal.un.org/UNISPAL.NSF/0/71260B776D62FA6E852564420059C4FE (accessed 27 December 2016).

28 Halperin, 'The Post-Cold War Political Topography', pp. 1139–42. Leftist groups were introduced to the region just years after the Bolshevik Revolution in 1917. During the following decades, the ideology became more pervasive among the countries of the region and became one of the main concerns of the Western superpowers at the verge of the Cold War.

29 Ibid. In general, the Middle East had become an arena for US and Soviet Russian confrontation in general, in the sense that each superpower was seeking to ally with different regional states, and social classes. While oil rich monarchies of the Persian Gulf were more inclined towards the West, the rest were looking for an alliance with the East; whereas, generally, the notable merchant class in each state was more interested in Western Capitalism, Eastern Socialism seemed more appealing to the middle and lower classes. Communism and leftist ideology in the Middle East had taken root in the aftermath of the Great War.

30 See Dragnich, 'The Lebanon Operation of 1958'.

31 Salibi, 'Lebanon under Fuad Chehab'.

32 One of the major opposition movements against Chehab and his seemingly pro-Muslim politics resulted in a failed coup in 1961 by middle ranking Christian army officers. See Beshara, *Lebanon: The Politics of Frustration*, Chapter 6.

33 Fouad Chehab was from a notable family from Mount Hermon in South Lebanon bordering western Syria. He became the first commander of the Lebanese armed Forces after independence in 1945, an official entity which had gathered groups of underprivileged Lebanese soldiers, mainly from Shi'i, Druze and Greek Orthodox sects, who sought a source of income by joining the army. This had given the

General a unique understanding of the country's social situation and, evidently, had influenced his political initiatives from the day he became president. Most notable among these were reforms in public administration jobs, and rural development policy. While in office, Chehab embarked on public reforms that, contrary to the decisions of his predecessors, Khuri and Chamoun addressed the needs of all Lebanese, especially deprived civilians who lived in peripheral areas. See Barak, *The Lebanese Army*, p. 54.

34 Winslow, *Lebanon: War and Politics*, p. 128.

35 Salibi, 'Lebanon since the Crisis of 1958'.

36 Kobeissi, 'Rural Urban Migration'.

37 Traboulsi, *A History of Modern Lebanon*, p. 141. As an example, one of the plans was to build a dam on the Litani River in order to develop the irrigation of vast agricultural lands in the western Beqaa Valley and in Southern Lebanon.

38 Sadeq Tabatabai, interview with the author, Tehran, Iran, November 2012.

39 During his studies in Qum seminary, Musa Sadr was a member of a larger group of pioneering young Shiʿi clerics along with others like Morteza Motahhari (d. 1971), one of the main ideologues of the Islamic Revolution of Iran, Muhammad Beheshti (d. 1981), who later became leader of the Iran Islamic Republican Party, and Abdul-Karim Mousavi Ardebili (b. 1926), who was the Chief of the Islamic Republic of Iran Judiciary between 1981 and 1989.

40 Muhsin Kamalian, interview with the author, Tehran, Iran, October 2012.

41 Ibid.

42 His influential book, *Al-Murājaʿāt*, is one of the first attempts to develop a Shiʿi-Sunni intra-faith dialogue; the book comprises more than a hundred correspondences between Allameh Sharafuddin and Sheikh Salim al-Bashiri, then head of Al-Azhar University.

43 Halawi, *A Lebanon Defied*, p. 108.

44 Ajami, *The Vanished Imam*, p. 45.

45 Hani Fahs, interview with the author, Beirut, August 2012.

46 Muhammad D. Nasrallah, interview with the author, Beirut, August 2012.

47 Hawra Sadr, interview with the author, Tehran, October 2012.

48 Imam Musa Sadr, recorded speech in Iran, date unknown.

49 The impact of the then unconventional *ijtihad* of Musa Sadr extended beyond Lebanon's borders and influenced Shiʿi religious students in the Najaf and Qum seminaries in the 1960s and 1970s. One of the first examples of his unconventionality was his daring opinion concerning what Shiʿi jurisprudence refers to as *Nijāsat al-Ahl al-Kitāb*: the 'impurity of the people of the book'. At the time, a majority of Shiʿi jurists believed that non-Muslims, including Christians and Jews are defiled and that Muslims should thus be cautious in their dealings with them. The Lebanese Shiʿi community had been counselled about this well-established Fatwa and, perhaps, most of Lebanon's Shiʿi clerics were its exponents. This simply made it impossible to achieve a peaceful relationship between a Lebanese Shiʿi Muslim and his Christian or Jewish neighbours. It was in such a circumstance that Musa Sadr stood against this belief through a very simple action in Lebanon, which surprisingly made the Shiʿi elites of Najaf and Qum reconsider their verdicts (Muhsin Kamalian, interview with the author, Tehran, October 2012).

50 *Lisan al-hal Daily*, Beirut, Lebanon, 25 August 1961.

51 *Al-Asr Daily*, Sidon, Lebanon, 5 December 1962.

52 SAVAK document No. 241/574 dated 26 June 1965 claimed that Sayyid Musa Sadr was an Egyptian agent in Lebanon and had recently been given a car by the Egyptian Embassy in Beirut. In some other documents, SAVAK officers claim that he might be a CIA or MOSSAD agent. See SAVAK 2000.
53 SAVAK document No. H/7/8771 dated 5 October 1965.
54 *Al-Hayat Daily*, Beirut, Lebanon, 19 February 1966.
55 Khalil Hamdan, interview with the author, Nabatieh, August 2012.
56 *Al-Hayat Daily*, Beirut, Lebanon, 20 August 1966.
57 Ibid., 26 July 1967.
58 Ibid., 17 September 1968.
59 One of the Imam's critics was Kamil Asaad, one of the main feudal Shiʿis of the South, who employed his maximum capability to prevent the Imam's leadership of the SISC. When he lost on this front, he then focused on a variety of means by which to push the Imam to give up politics, and to limit him and the SISC to solely pursue religious issues. His wish was never fulfilled (Samih Haydous, interview with the author, Beirut, August 2012).
60 Hujjati Kermani, *Lubnan be Revayate Imam Musa Sadr*, p. 89. In correspondence with one of his students, Imam Musa Sadr once refers to a statement by the Egyptian philosopher, Ahmad Amin: 'It is absolutely fair to say that Shiʿi Muslims have always provided a safe haven for those who have betrayed Islam.' He bitterly discloses that some religious Sunni intellectuals had labelled Shiʿis in Lebanon as the enemy's fifth column.
61 Ibid., p. 65.
62 Sadeq Tabatabai, interview with the author, Tehran, Iran, November 2012.
63 Muhammad Ali Muhtadi, interview with the author, Tehran, October 2012.
64 *An-Nahar Daily*, Beirut, Lebanon, 12 January 1974.
65 Mehdi Firoozan, interview with the author, Tehran, January 2013.
66 *An-Nahar Daily*, Beirut, Lebanon, 18 March 1974.
67 Ibid.
68 Pierre Gemayel, the leader of Phalanges Party, Sheikh Khaled, the Sunni Mufti, and Sheikh Abu-Shaqra, the Druze leader, were among those who visited Imam Sadr in the aftermath of the gathering, declaring their support for his righteous demands. See *Al-Hayat Daily*, Beirut, Lebanon, 24 March 1974.
69 *An-Nahar Daily*, Beirut, Lebanon, 5 April 1974.
70 An architectural dent in every Mosque showing the direction of Mecca; Mihrab with the Arabic root of H-R-B literally means place of war.
71 *An-Nahar Daily*, Beirut, Lebanon, 5 April 1974.
72 Muhammad D. Nasrallah, interview with the author, Beirut, August 2012.
73 Letter dated 22 December 1974. See AMAL 2010: 395–6.
74 From 1975 to 1990, Lebanon was entangled in a devastating civil war. For detailed information and various narratives of the Lebanese civil war see Hanf, *Coexistence in Wartime Lebanon*; Winslow, *Lebanon: War and Politics*; Fisk, *Pity the Nation*; and Khazen, 'Ending Conflict in Wartime Lebanon'.
75 Khalil Hamdan, interview held in Nabatieh, August 2012.
76 Hawra Sadr, interview with the author, Tehran, Iran, January 2013.
77 Muhammad Ali Muhtadi, interview with the author, Tehran, Iran, October 2012.
78 *Afwaj al-Muqawamah al-Lubnaniyyah*, or Lebanese Resistance Regiments. As its name portrays, AMAL was formed as a Lebanese militia in 1974, non-aligned to either hostile fronts or a specific sect in Lebanon.

79 Samih Haydous, interview with the author, Beirut, Lebanon, August 2012.
80 For the English text of the AMAL charter, see Norton, *Amal and the Shia*, Appendix 1.
81 More than 190 Lebanese intellectuals and politicians signed a petition in support of the movement. They were moderate leaders and scholars of all Lebanese sects, from Maronite, Orthodox, Armenian, Sunni, and Shiʿi. See *Al-Hayat Daily*, Beirut, Lebanon, 20 November 1974. Later when the public found out about AMAL's militia activities in July 1975, the Lebanese intellectuals announced their support for AMAL and its cause once again. See *Al-Anwar Daily*, Beirut, Lebanon, 12 July 1975.
82 Adel, *Ma ʿa al-i ʿtidhār*, p. 125.
83 *Al-A'mal Daily*, Beirut, Lebanon, 30 April 1975.
84 In general, they were against the role of the Shiʿi Council acting as the key player in the crisis. Palestinians opposed the Imam at the time, as they were concerned over the disclosure of the terms of the Cairo Accord, something that might impact negatively on their settlement in Lebanon. See *Ousbou Al-Arabi* Weekly, Beirut, Lebanon, 5 May 1975.
85 *Al-Anwar Daily*, Beirut, Lebanon, 28 June 1975.
86 Dahir, *Masīrat al-Imām al-Sayyid Musá*, pp. 104–6. In September and November 1976, Imam Sadr visited Anwar Sadat in Cairo, Hafez al-Assad in Damascus, King Khaled in Riyadh, and Sheikh Sabah in Kuwait, inviting them to hold an extraordinary Arab League Summit dealing with the Lebanon's conflict. On 16 October these four along with Yasser Arafat, PLO leader, and Elias Sarkis, then the president of Lebanon, gathered in Riyadh appointing Syria as their representative in Lebanon and urging Palestinian groups to respect the Lebanese sovereignty.
87 *An-Nahar Daily*, Beirut, Lebanon, 17 March 1978.
88 Sadeq Tabatabai, interview with the author, Tehran, November 2012.
89 *An-Nahar Daily*, Beirut, Lebanon, 28 May 1978.
90 Muhsin Kamalian, interview with the author, Tehran, Iran, November 2012.
91 Salah Zawawi, interview with the author, Tehran, Iran, January 2013.
92 The hundreds of telegrams he had received from Maraje' in Iraq and Iran, in support of him, show Imam Sadr's esteemed position among the Shiʿi communities of Iran and Iraq. See SAVAK 2000.
93 Sadr, *Dīn dar khidmat-i Insān*, p. 115.
94 In April 1978, Musa Sadr facilitated between Khomeini and Lucien George, a correspondent for *Le Monde* in Beirut for an interview. For the first time, the world became familiar with the opinions of the Ayatollah regarding the situation in the region and Iran. (Muhsin Kamalian, interview with the author, Tehran, November 2012).
95 *Le Monde*, Paris, France, 23 August 1978.
96 Sadr al-Din Sadr, interview with the author, Beirut, August 2012.
97 Ajami, *The Vanished Imam*, p. 24. To some extent, his fate resembled, for the Shiʿi, the Occultation Discourse, as his disappearance embodied Shiʿi twelfth Imam's status in modern times. This presented Imam Sadr's religio-political apostles with an initial advantage in assuming leadership of the community. Nonetheless, to consolidate their authority, they had to encounter two main rivals: the Shiʿi Zu'ama and a group of Shiʿi activist figures that had been active even during the Imam Sadr's era.
98 Davoodabadi, *Sayyid 'Azīz*, p. 26. In early 1980, with the mass expulsion of Lebanese Shiʿi students from Najaf, they mostly joined this trend of political activism upon their return to Lebanon.

99 Three days before the victory of the Revolution in Iran, Chamran along with 500 militia members of AMAL tried to parachute to the centre of Tehran and to engage with the Shah's army. However, while their plane was in the air heading towards Iran, they were informed that the Iranian Chief Commanders of the army declared its neutrality towards the revolutionaries, and the regime toppled (Adel Aoun, interview with the author, Tehran, January 2013).

100 Ironically, the majority of these hardliners were among those revolutionaries who were trained in Lebanon and Syria during the Shah's regime and were subsequently among the critics of Imam Sadr's activities in Lebanon. Muhammad Ali Montazeri, son of the Grand Ayatollah Montazeri, Jalaleddin Farsi, a member of the Islamic Republican Party, Muhammad Gharazi, and Abbas Agha Zamani, co-founders of the Revolutionary Guards, were among the active revolutionary combatants in Lebanon who were among the Shah's opponents. They generally had strong ties with the PLO and Fatah, and opposed Imam Sadr's moderate political views at the time in Lebanon. All were recipients of key positions in the first decade of post-revolutionary Iran (Sadeq Tabatabai, interview with the author, Tehran, Iran, November 2012).

101 Just months earlier, in December 1978, Imam Khomeini had encouraged the Lebanese Shiʿis in his interview with an AMAL journal correspondent to 'assist their Iranian co-religionists in toppling the regime of Shah, as the revolutionaries are opposing Israel alongside them and will compensate them when they achieve victory'. See Khomeini, *Ṣaḥīfeh-ye Imām*, Vol. 5, 7 December 1978.

102 As a honorary gesture to Imam Sadr, the position of the SISC president was not awarded to anybody else after his disappearance. After 1978, and until 1997, when Imam Sadr would have been sixty-nine-year-old and, thus, would have been barred from serving as the president of the Council, other presidents of the SISC were given the title of vice president.

103 Muhammad Ali Muhtadi, interview with the author, Tehran, October 2012.

104 Samih Haydous, interview with the author, Beirut, August 2012.

105 Kadivar, *Naẓarīyah'hā-yi dawlat dar fiqh-i Shīʿah*, pp. 159–74. While in Iraq, Shams al-Din wrote *The Governance and Management System in Islam* (1954), one of the earliest books written by a Shiʿi cleric concerning modern Islamic government. Years later, in the early 1990s, he introduced his theory of 'the Guardianship of the Nation', that assumed a place alongside that of Imam Khomeini's and Ayatollah Muhammad Baqir Sadr's thoughts concerning Shiʿi governance during the Occultation era.

106 Norton, 'Changing Actors and Leadership'.

107 Hani Fahs, interview with the author, Beirut, August 2012.

108 After the Iranian Revolution, the proponents of this political doctrine had a close relationship with the PLO and Libyan Ambassadors in Iran, Hani Hassan and Saad Mujber. In addition to their extreme Islamic propensities, they were advocates of the left-inclined Islamic Internationalism, and hence became loyal to rejectionist Arab leaders like Gaddafi and Arafat in order to advance their views throughout Islamic countries. Therefore, in Lebanon, while they were against the Israeli occupation, they did not believe in sectarian coexistence between Muslims and Christians and were thus against Imam Sadr and his more moderate political posture (Muhsin Kamalian, interview with the author, Tehran, November 2012).

109 Muhammad Ali Muhtadi, interview with the author, Tehran, October 2012.

110 Ramazani, *Revolutionary Iran*, p. 180.

111 Karsh, *The Iran-Iraq War*, pp. 22–3. The first major engagement between the Iraqi army and Iranian forces occurred in Khorramshahr, the main non-oil port of Iran in

the province of Khuzestan. Iraq succeeded in occupying the city within thirty-four days of its invasion of Iran and imposed its mandate over the city for almost two years.

112 Agha and Khalidi, *Syria and Iran*, p. 12.
113 Later reports released by Scotland Yard confirmed that the three assassins were in contact with the Military Attaché's office at the Iraqi Embassy in London. See *Haaretz Daily*, Tel Aviv, Israel dated 6 December 1982.
114 Goodarzi, *Syria and Iran*, p. 61.
115 Muhsin Rafiqdoost, interview with the author, Tehran, January 2013.
116 . Khomeini, *Ṣaḥīfeh-ye Imām*, Vol. XVI, pp. 351–2.
117 Norton, *Hezbollah*, p. 33.
118 Muhammad Ali Muhtadi, interview with the author, Tehran, October 2012.
119 The Sunni Prime Minister Shafik Wazzan, the Druze Walid Jumblatt, the Maronite Bachir Gemayel, the Orthodox Fouad Petros Sarkis, the Catholic Nasri Maalouf, along with the Shiʿi Nabih Berri, were members of the committee (Muhammad Ali Muhtadi, interview with the author, Tehran, October 2012).
120 Haytham, *Nabīh Birrī*, p. 150.
121 Muhammad Ali Muhtadi, interview with the author, Tehran, October 2012.
122 Anonymous, interview with the author, Beirut, August 2012.
123 The Sunni Islamic Unification Movement, which was a splinter group of the Lebanese branch of the Muslim Brotherhood, under the leadership of Sheikh Said Shaaban in 1982, and was based in Tripoli, was among the attendees. See Mohtashamipour interview with *Shahed-e-Yaran Quarterly*, Tehran, Iran, Vol. 40 Autumn 2006.
124 Crooke, *Resistance*, p. 175.
125 Imad Fayez Mughniyah, then the head of Hezbollah's security division, was among those Shiʿi youth who were abandoned by the AMAL militia upon the expulsion of the PLO from Lebanon and were well received by the newly formed Hezbollah in the Beqaa Valley (Muhammad Ali Muhtadi, interview with the author, Tehran, October 2012).
126 At the time of the operation, no party claimed responsibility. Later in 1985, when Deir Qanoun al-Nahr, Qasir's hometown was liberated from Israeli occupation, Hezbollah revealed his name and claimed responsibility. Israeli officials, however, attributed the casualties to a gas leak, which resulted in 144 of them getting killed and injured. For the detailed chronology, see http://www.mfa.gov.il/MFA/Foreign%20Relations/Israels%20Foreign%20Relations%20since%201947/1982-1984/HIGHLIGHTS%20OF%20MAIN%20EVENTS-%201982-1984 (accessed 10 March 2016).
127 Adel Aoun, interview with the author, Tehran, January 2013.
128 Khashan, 'The Religious and Political Impact'.
129 During the Reagan presidency, a group of extreme revolutionaries inside the Islamic Republic leadership had used Hezbollah several times. An example of those activities can be recalled in the case of the US Christian Missionary in Lebanon, Benjamin Weir, who was taken hostage in May 1984. He was freed after sixteen months, just hours after the covert arms deal between the United States and Iran. For a full account of the story, see Parsi, *Treacherous Alliance*, pp. 119–20.
130 Muhammad D. Nasrallah, interview with the author, Beirut, August 2012.
131 Khashan, 'The Religious and Political Impact'.
132 Later in 1999, Fadlallah repented of his deeds against Imam Sadr. After approving all of the Imam's actions and political viewpoint, he confessed that Imam Sadr's

approach at the time was more suitable in response to the situation. See the interview with *al-Diyar Daily*, Beirut, Lebanon, 1 September 1999.

133 Davoodabadi, *Sayyid 'Azīz*, p. 58. Sayyid Hassan Nasrallah claims that Allameh was barred from joining Hezbollah officially as the party leader in 1982. However, he remained one of the ardent voices of Islamic Resistance among the Shiʿi clerics in Lebanon.

134 Mallat, 'Aspects of Shi'i Thought from the South'.

135 Kramer, 'The Oracle of Hizbullah'.

136 For the full text of the open letter, see Norton, *Amal and the Shia*, pp. 167–87.

137 Eisenberg & Caplan, *Negotiating Arab-Israeli Peace*, p. 67.

138 Qassem, *Hizbullah: The Story from Within*, p. 133.

139 Norton, *Amal and the Shia*, p. 99.

140 Haytham, *Nabīh Birrī*, pp. 208–9.

141 *Al-Watan al-Arabi Magazine*, Beirut, Lebanon 2 March 1998.

142 Muhammad Ali Muhtadi, interview with the author, Tehran, Iran, November 2012.

143 Deeb, Syria's Terrorist War on Lebanon and the Peace Process, pp. 118–20. The Agreement was signed among the Druze Walid Jumblatt, the Shiʿi Nabih Berri, and the commander of Lebanese Forces, Elie Hobeika on December 1985. It was seen as aiding Syria in its will to achieve further domination of Lebanon. However, President Gemayel and some other Christian militia commanders, like Samir Geagea who later replaced Hobeika in LF, rejected the agreement and asked for the further involvement of their relevant parties in political structure of Lebanon.

144 From 1985 to 1987, fearing the rising power of the Shiʿi community as a result of the activities of AMAL, some Phalangist leaders supported Arafat and his Palestinian supporters by selling them Lebanese passports to facilitate their return to Lebanon. See Thomas Friedman, 'New Lebanon Allies: Christians and the PLO', *The New York Times*, 8 January 1987.

145 Haytham, *Nabīh Birrī*, p. 270.

146 Ali Fahs, interview with the author, Beirut, Lebanon, August 2012.

147 'Proceedings of the Parliament of the Islamic Republic of Iran', 5 June 1985. Full text available at http://www.ical.ir/index.php?option=com_content&view=article&id=2378&Itemid=13 (accessed 5 March 2016).

148 Anonymous, interview with the author, Beirut, Lebanon, Summer 2012.

149 *Al-Nahar Daily*, Beirut, Lebanon 31 August 1987.

150 His speech provoked a mixed response from the community. The Iranian representative walked out of the ceremony, and Shiʿi groups marched in the streets following the speech chanting against Iran and saying, 'We clearly announce today that we do not want to see Iranians in our neighbourhood ever again.' As a result, Iranian nationals were banned from commuting to south Lebanon, and the AMAL militia tightly controlled their movements in the area until late 1988 (Muhammad Ali Muhtadi, interview with the author, Tehran, November 2012).

151 Radio Free Lebanon Reportage on 4 September 1987, as published in *Daily Report, Near East & South Asia*, FBIS-NES-87-172.

152 Muhammad D Nasrallah, interview with the author, Beirut, August 2012.

153 Nabih Berri, interview with *Al-Sharq al-Awsat*, London, UK, 22 January 1989.

154 Hani Fahs, interview with the author, Beirut, August 2012.

155 Alagha, *Hizbullah's Identity Construction*, p. 51.

156 Ali Fahs, interview with the author, Beirut, August 2012.

157 Qassem, *Hizbullah: The Story from Within*, p. 145.

158 *Tehran Times Daily*, Tehran, 18 December 1988.
159 Ali M. Besharati, interview with the author, Tehran, November 2012.
160 Yasser Arafat interview with *al-Qabas Daily*, Kuwait, 6 June 1985.
161 For an example of encounters between moderate-extremist factions inside the Islamic Republic leadership, see Parsi, *Treacherous Alliance*, pp. 100–38.
162 Syrian Arab News Agency, Damascus, 30 January 1989, as published in *Daily Report. Near East & South Asia*, FBIS-NES-89-019.
163 Muhammad Yazbeck, interview with *Rah Magazine*, Tehran, Iran, October 2011.
164 Muhammad Ali Muhtadi, interview with the author, Tehran, November 2012.
165 Akbar Hashemi Rafsanajani, a written correspondence with the author, January 2013.
166 Abisaab, 'Lebanese Shiites and The Marjaiyya'.
167 It was believed that Muhammad Hussein Fadlallah was going to bring back long lost prestige to the Shi'i Marja'yiat office in Lebanon after four centuries. However, after he declared controversial opinions challenging the reliability of some incidents of early Islamic history, he became somehow obsolete within the Shi'i scholastic mainstream for the rest of his life. See Rasoul Jafarian, 'The Lebanon's Seminary and Iran', *Bulletin of History of Iran and Islam Library*, 26 May 2008.
168 Davoodabadi, *Sayyid 'Azīz*, pp. 53–4. Sheikh Subhi Tufaily was among the most extremist leaders in Hezbollah and maintained a strong relationship with Palestinians, especially the PFLP. As the secretary general of Hezbollah, he constantly condemned Shams al-Din's moderate position. Although he served in Hezbollah until the end of the party's fifth enclaves, he later split from Hezbollah and opposed the party and the Islamic Republic in the post-1992 Lebanese general election.
169 Ali M Besharati, interview with the author, Tehran, Iran, November 2012.
170 *Shahed-e-Yaran Quarterly*, Tehran, Iran, Winter 2008.
171 Qassem, *Hizbullah: The Story from Within*, p. 161.
172 *An-Nahar Daily*, Beirut, Lebanon, 17 February 1992.
173 Ibid.
174 Qassem, *Hizbullah: The Story from Within*, p. 161.
175 The conflict between Hezbollah and the central government over the incident was resolved 20 months later when, in May 1995, the government issued a decree that characterized the nine casualties as 'National Martyrs'. *Al-Ahd* Weekly, Lebanon, Vol. 19, May 1995.
176 Ibid., p. 168.
177 Noe, *Voice of Hezbollah*, p. 240.
178 Parsi, *Treacherous Alliance*, pp. 223–37. Washington's approach against Iran in the aftermath of the Allied operation in Iraq came as a surprise to the then reformist government of the Islamic Republic which had been closely complying with the United States and its allies since the commencement of the 'War on Terror' doctrine. The Iranian government had been providing crucial intelligence support to the Coalition Forces in Afghanistan against the Taliban regime, hoping for a more benign approach from the US government.
179 France was the main sponsor of the Resolution. Given Rafik Hariri's close relationship with French President Chirac, in Lebanon it was speculated that the prime minister was the promoter of the Resolution. See 'Trial by Fire: The Politics of the Special Tribunal for Lebanon', *International Crisis Group*, 2 December 2010, p. 6.
180 Emile Lahoud was elected as president in 1998, after being the Republic's Army commander-in-chief for almost eight years.

181 The full text of UNSCR 1559 is available at http://www.unhcr.org/refworld/docid/41516a7e4.html (accessed 12 March 2013).
182 Hariri's bloc voted in favour of the amendment. See *Al-Diyar Daily*, Beirut, Lebanon, 4 September 2004.
183 Blanford, *Killing Mr. Lebanon*, p. 103.
184 Lahoud and Hariri had a history of conflict since 1998, when the then new President Lahoud launched an anti-corruption case against Hariri and his companions. See Robert Fisk, 'Lebanon's Vast Web of Corruption Unravels', *The Independent*, 6 December 1998.
185 Blanford, *Killing Mr. Lebanon*, p. 116.
186 Hezbollah's official claim that the UNSC endorsement over the compliance of Israel with its resolutions was in violation of the Lebanese claim over the occupied territories of Shebaa and Kfar Shuba in the south. Qassem, *Ḥizb Allāh-i Lubnān*, p. xvii.
187 Available at http://www.unhcr.org/refworld/docid/42c3a5a2d.html (accessed 13 March 2013).
188 The name 'Cedar Revolution' appeared for the first time on 27 February in a press conference in Washington held by Paula Dobriansky, the US under secretary of state for Democracy and Global Affairs. It seems that it was an effort to compare the Lebanese situation to that which occurred in Ukraine and Georgia years earlier rather than using the Arabic word 'Intifada' which might link Lebanon's situation with that of the Palestinian uprisings in Israel. See Jefferson Morley, 'The Branding of Lebanon's Revolution', *The Washington Post*, 3 March 2005.
189 Qassem, *Ḥizb Allāh-i Lubnān*, p. xvii.
190 AMAL and Hezbollah together received eight more seats in the new Parliament bringing their total number of seats to twenty-eight. However, the ultimate winner of the election was Jumblatt and his PSP which received sixteen seats in comparison to a mere six seats that it had won in the 2000 general election. See Inter-Parliamentary Union Website for the details of Lebanon's general election results, available at http://www.ipu.org/parline/reports/2179_A.htm (accessed 1 March 2013).
191 For a brief account of his political personality, see 'Walid Jumblatt: Mountain Leader and Redeemer of Political Imbalances', *The Majalla*. http://www.majalla.com/eng/2009/05/article554201 (accessed 28 March 2013).
192 Qassem, *Ḥizb Allāh-i Lubnān*, p. xviii.
193 The full text of the memorandum is available at http://yalibnan.com/site/archives/2006/02/full_english_te.php (accessed 27 February 2013).
194 *Al Safir Daily*, Beirut, Lebanon, 15 March 2006.
195 Qassem, *Ḥizb Allāh-i Lubnān*, p. xxi. AMAL, Hezbollah, Free Patriotic Movement, ex-Prime Minister Omar Karami and Talal Arsalan, a Druze, were among the supporters of Lahoud.
196 *Al Mustaqbal Daily*, Beirut, Lebanon, 17 May 2006.
197 *The Guardian*, London, UK, 26 January 2006.
198 An Israeli soldier who was captured by HAMAS commandos in a cross-border raid on 25 June 2006. After five years of captivity, he was returned to Israel in 2011 in a prisoner-exchange agreement with HAMAS. See Ronen Bergman, 'Gilad Shalit and the Rising Price of an Israeli Life', *The New York Times*, 9 November 2011.
199 *Haaretz*, Tel Aviv, Israel, 12 July 2006.
200 Ibid., 18 July 2006.
201 Norton, 'The Shiite "Threat" Revisited'.

202 Sobelman, 'New Rules of the Game'.
203 Available at http://english.moqawama.org/essaydetails.php?eid=11707&cid=286 (accessed 25 February 2013).
204 The full text of UNSCR 1701 is available at http://www.un.org/News/Press/docs/2006/sc8808.doc.htm (accessed 14 March 2018).
205 Qassem, *Ḥizb Allāh-i Lubnān*, p. xxiv.
206 Hassan Nasrallah speech on 22 September 2006. For the full text see Noe, *Voice of Hezbollah*.
207 Amal Saad-Ghorayeb, 'Hezbollah's Apocalypse Now', *The Washington Post*, 23 July 2006.
208 El-Husseini, 'Hezbollah and the Axis of Refusal'. Polls confirmed that during the conflict, 87 per cent of Lebanese supported Hezbollah's military response to the Israeli attacks; that included 89 per cent of Sunni Muslims and 80 per cent of Christians.
209 Hamzawy and Bishara, 'Islamist Movements in the Arab World'.
210 Andy Mosher, 'From Arab Leaders, Sympathy for Civilians but Not Hezbollah', *The Washington Post*, 18 July 2006.
211 Hamed al-Khaffaf, interview with the author, Beirut, Lebanon, November 2012.
212 For the full story, see *Al-Safir Daily*, Beirut, Lebanon, 1 October 2011.

Chapter 7

1 Louër, *Transnational Shia Politics*, p. 69.
2 Abbasid Caliphate was considered as the major Muslim rulers from 750 to 1258. Even during the reign of Shiʿi Buyids dynasty, they did not abolish the Abbasid Caliphate. Rather, over some political reservations, they preferred the caliph's bestowment. For more details, see Nagel Tilman. 'Buyids', *Encyclopaedia Iranica*, 1990. http://www.iranicaonline.org/articles/buyids (accessed 28 March 2018).
3 Arjomand, 'The Mujtahid of the Age and the Mulla-bashi', p. 81.
4 Allameh Majlesi (d. 1698), one of the most famous Akhbāri clerics, narrates a tradition from the twelfth Imam: 'If someone claims himself to be the deputy of the Imam during the occultation, he is a liar, ousted from Allah's religion, calumniating Allah; he himself has gone astray and is leading others into error too.' See *Biḥār al-Anwār*, Vol. XIII, p. 884.
5 Tarrow, 'States and Opportunities', p. 54.
6 Kurzman, 'The Qum Protests'.
7 Giugni, 'Political Opportunities: From Tilly to Tilly'; Suh, 'How do Political Opportunities Matter'.
8 Kadhim, *The Hawza Under Siege*.
9 Nakash, 'The Conversion of Iraq's Tribes to Shiism'.
10 Louër, *Transnational Shia Politics*, p. 218.
11 Ibid., p. 299.
12 See for example Mauriello, *Descendants of the Family of the Prophet*.
13 During the Iranian nuclear crisis, Meir Dagan, director of the Mossad since 2011, declared in an interview that 'the regime in Iran is very rational . . . they are considering all the implications of their actions'. Such a statement expressed by an Israeli high-ranking official reflects the nature of the Iranian leadership's policymaking

during the last three decades. For the full excerpt of the interview, see Lesley Stahl, 'Ex-Israeli spy chief: Bombing Iran a Stupid Idea', *CBS News*, 8 March 2012. http://www.cbsnews.com/news/ex-israeli-spy-chief-bombing-iran-a-stupid-idea/ (accessed 11 June 2018).

14 Nasr, *The Shia Revival*, p. 175.

15 Interview with the author, Najaf, August 2013.

16 For a detailed review of the Fatwa, see Abbas Kadhim and Luay Al-Khatteeb, 'What Do You Know about Sistani's Fatwa?' *Huffington Post*, 10 July 2014. http://www.huffingtonpost.com/luay-al-khatteeb/what-do-you-know-about-si_b_5576244.html (accessed 11 June 2018).

17 For thorough background on Sistani's activities prior and after Iraq War 2003, see Khalaji, *The Last Marja;* Arato, 'Sistani v. Bush'.

18 Larry Kaplow, 'Iraq's Most Influential Man Gets Pulled Back into Politics', *National Public Radio*, 24 June 2014. http://www.npr.org/sections/parallels/2014/06/24/325169087/iraqs-most-influential-man-gets-pulled-back-into-politics (accessed 11 June 2018).

19 Weiss, 'Institutionalizing Sectarianism'.

Bibliography

Non-English Sources

Abbasi Fardoyi, G. A. (2007). *Taḥrīm-i tanbākū wa mashrūṭiyat*. Qum: Zā'ir.

Abu al-Hasani, A. (2012). *Ākhirīn āvāz-i qū: bāzkāvī-i shakhṣīyat va 'amalkard-i Shaykh Faẓl Allāh Nūrī*. Tehran: Mu'assasah-i Muṭāla'āt-i Tārīkh-i Mu'āṣir-i Īrān.

Adamiyat, F. (1976). *Īdi'ūlūžī-i nahḍat-i mašrūṭīyat-i Īrān*. Tehran: Payam.

Adamiyat, F. (1981). *Shūrish bar imtīyāzńāmah-'i Rizhī*. Tehran: Payam.

Adel, R. (1981). *Ma'a al-i'tidhār--lil-imām al-Ṣadr*. Cairo: Maktabat Madbūlī.

Adib-Heravi, M. H. (1948). *Al-ḥadīqah al-Riḍawīyah*. Mashhad: Bina.

Afandi, A. (1980). *Riyāḍ al-'ulamā' wa ḥiyāḍ al-fuḍalā'*. Tehran: Khayyam.

Ahmadi, M. (2009). *Chashm va charāgh-i marja'īyat: muṣāḥabah'hā-yi vīzhah-i Majallah-i Ḥawzah, bā shāgirdān-i Āyat Allāh Burūjirdī*. Qom: Būstān-i Kitāb.

Al-Alawi, H. (2011). *Shī'ah va ḥukūmat dar 'Irāq: 1914–1990* (M. N. Ibrahimi, Trans., 2nd ed.). Tehran: Intishārāt-i Sūrah-i Mihr.

Al-Allama al-Hilli. (1993). *Nahj al-ḥaqq wa-kashf al-ṣidq*. Qum: Dār al-Hiğra.

Al-Ameli, A. (2006). *Muḥammad Bāqir al-Ṣadr: al-Sīrah wa al-Masīrah fi Haqai'q wa Wata'iq*. Beirut: Al-'Ārif lil-Maṭbū'āt.

Al-Ansari. (2003). *Kitāb al-Makāsib*. Qum: Majma' al-Fikr al-Islmai.

Al-Ardabili. (1986). *Majma' al-fā'idah wa-al-burhān fī sharḥ Irshād al-adhhān*. Qum: Al-Nashri Islāmī.

Al-Asadi, H. (1975). *Ṯawraẗ al-Najaf 'alá l-Inkilīz: aw, al-Šarāraẗ al-ulá li-ṯawraẗ al-'Išrīn*. Baghdad: Wizāraẗ al-I'lām.

Al-Badri, A. (1966). *al-Islām bayna al-'ulamā' wa-al-ḥukkām*. Medina: al-Maktabah al-'Ilmīyah.

Al-Basir, M. M. (1924). *Tārīkh al-qaḍīyah al-'Irāqīyah*. Baghdad: Maṭba'aṭ al-Falāḥ.

al-Ghita, Kashif. (2001). *Kitāb Kashf al-ghiṭā' 'an mubhamāt al-sharī'ah al-gharrā'*. Qum: Daftar-i Tablīghāt-i Islāmī-i.

Al-Hakim, M. (1951). *Nahj al-faqāhah (Ta'liq ala' Bay' al-Makasib)*. Najaf: Matbaat al-'ilmiyya.

Al-Hassani, A. a.-R. (1935). *Al-'Irāq fī dawray al-iḥtilāl wa-al-intidāb*. Sayda: Maṭba'at al-'Irfān.

Al-Hassani, A. a.-R. (1988). *Tārīkh al-wizārāt al-'Irāqīyah*. Baghdad: Dār al-Shu'ūn al-Thaqāfīyah al-'Āmmah.

al-Hilli, Al-Muhaqqiq. (1988). *Sharā'i' al-Islām fi masā'il al-ḥalāl wa-al-ḥarām*. Tehran: Istiqlāl.

Al-Ḥurr Al-Āmili. (1993). *Wasā'il al-Shī'a*. Tehran: Kitābfurūshī-i 'Ilmīyah-i Islāmīyah.

Al-Jisr, B. (1964). *Ri'āsah wa-siyāsah wa-Lubnān al-jadīd*. Beirut: Dār Maktabat al-Ḥayāh.

Al-Karaki. (1989). *Rasā'il al-Muḥaqqiq al-Karakī*. Qum: Maktabat Āyat Allāh al-'Uẓmá al-Mar'ashī al-Najafī.

Al-Karaki. (1991). *Al-Kharājīyāt*. Qum: Mu'assasat al-Nashr al-Islāmī.

Al-Karaki. (2003). *Nafaḥāt al-lāhūt fī la'n al-jubbat wa-al-ṭāghūt*. Qum: Manshūrāt al-Iḥtijāj.

Al-Khaffaf, H. (2010). *al-Nuṣūṣ al-ṣādirah 'an samāḥat al-Sayyid al-Sīstānī fī al-mas'alah al-'Irāqīyah* (2nd ed.). Beirut: Dār al-Mu'arrikh al-'Arabī.
Al-Khaffaf, H. (2012). *Al-Riḥlah al-'ilājīyah li-samāḥat al-Sayyid al-Sīstānī wa-azmat al-Najaf 'ām 1425 H. / 2004 M* (2nd ed.). Beirut: Dār al-Mu'arrikh al-'Arabī.
Al-Kulayni. (1990). *Uṣūl al-Kāfī*. Tehran: al-Maktabah al-Islāmīyah.
Al-Mufid. (1989). *Al-Muqni'a* (2nd ed.). Qum: Mu'assasah-i Nashr-i Islāmī.
al-Murtada, Al-Sharif. (1996). *Al-shāfī fī al-imāmah*. Tehran: Mu'assasat al-Imām al-Ṣādiq.
Al-Najafi, M. H. (1983). *Jawāhir al-kalām fī sharḥ Sharā'i' al-Islām*. Beirut: Dār Iḥyā' al-Turāth al-'Arabī.
Al-Saduq. (1975). *Kamāl al-dīn wa-tamām al-ni'mah* (2nd ed.). Tehran: Dār al-Kutub al-Islāmīyah.
Al-Siraj, A. I. (1993). *Al-Imām Muḥsin al-Ḥakīm 1889-1970*. Beirut: Dar al-Zahrā.
Al-Tabarsi. (1982). *Al-iḥtijāj 'alā ahl al-lijāj*. Mashhad: Nashr Al-Murtada.
al-Thāni, Al-Shahid. (1966). *Al-Rawda al-Bahiyah fi Sharh al-Lum'ah al-Dimashqiya*. Najaf: Jami'a al-Najaf al-Diniyya.
al-Thāni, Al-Shahid. (1992). *Masālik al-afhām fi sharḥ sharāyi' al-islām*. Qum: Mu'assasah al-Ma'ārif al-Islāmīyah.
Al-Tusi. (1978). *Al-Nihāyah fī mujarrad al-fiqh wa-al-fatāwā*. Qum: Quds Muhammadi.
Al-Wardi, A. (1974). *Lamaḥāt ijtimā'īyah min tārīkh al-'Irāq al-ḥadīth*. Baghdad: Maṭba'at al-Irshād.
Āl Fir'awn, F. q. a.–M. (1952). *Al-Ḥaqā'iq al-Nāṣi'ah: fī al-Thawrah al-'Irāqīyah Sannat 1920 wa-Natā'ijihi*. Baghdad: Maṭba'at al-Najāḥ.
AMAL. (2010). *Sīrah va sarguẕasht-i Imām Mūsá Ṣadr*. Tehran: Mu'assasah-i Farhangī-i Taḥqīqātī-i Imām Mūsá Ṣadr.
Amin al-Ameli, M. (1998). *A'yān al-Shī'ah*. Beirut: Dar al-Ta'aruf.
Amini Hiravi, S. a.-D. (2005). *Futūḥāt -i Shāhī*. Tehran: Āṯār wa Mafāḫir-i Farhangī.
Ansari, H. (2010). *Tārīkh-i 'Irāq*. Tehran: Chāp va Nashr-i Bayn al-Milal.
Ansarian Khansari, M. T. (2017). *Sham'-i hamīshah furūzān: Āyat allāh al-'Uẓmá Khū'ī*. Qum: Intishārāt-i Anṣāriyān.
Ansarian Khansari, M. T. (2018a). *Marja'-i muttaqīn āyat allāh al-'uẓmá ḥāj Sayyid Aḥmad Khvānsārī*. Qum: Intishārāt-i Anīn āyat.
Ansarian Khansari, M. T. (2018b). *Sitārah-i dirakhshān: āyat allāh al-'uẓmá Sayyid Muḥsin Sayyid Muḥsinkhs*. Qum: Intishārāt-i Anhshān.
Ansarian Khansari, M. T. (2019). *Ḥ. 9.ian Khansari/example.com?id=journal"áSayyid Aḥmad Khvānsārītā' Za'īm va marja' Ḥājj Aqā Ḥusayn Burūjirdī*. Qum: Intishārāt-i Anri/exam.
Araki, M. A. (1992). *Al-Makāsib al-Mu//exampl*. Qum: Mu'assasat Fī Ṭarīq al-Ḥaqq.
Astarabadi, M. (2004). *Tārīkh-i Jahāngushā-yi Nādirī*. Tehran: Hāmi.
Astarabadi, M. A. (2005). *Al-Fawā'id al-Madanīyah*. Qum: Nashr-i Ma'ārif.
Bahar, M. T. (1992). *Tārīkh-i mukhtaṣar-i aḥzāb-i siyāsī dar Īrān* (Second ed.). Tehran: Intishārāt-i Amīr-i Kabīr.
Burujirdi, H. (2014). *Istiftā'āt*. Qum: Āyat Allāh al-'Uẓmá Burujirdi.
Chamran, M. (2009). *Lubnān: guzīdah'ī az majmū'ah-i sukhanrānī'hā va dast'nivishtah'hā-yi sardār-i pur'iftikhār-i Islām Shahīd Duktur Muṣṭafá Chamrān dar bārah-i Lubnān* (6th ed.). Tehran: Bunyād-i Shahīd Chamrān.
Dahir, Y. (2000). *Masīrat al-imām al-sayyid Musá al-Ṣadr: yawmīyāt wa-wathā'iq*. Beirut: Ḥarakat Amal, Hay'at al-Ri'āsah.
Davani, A. (1979). *Nahḍat-i rūḥānīyūn-i Īrān*. Tehran: Bunyād-i Farhangī-yi Imām Riḍā.

Davani, A. (2003). *Naqd-i 'umr : zindagānī va khāṭirāt*. Tehran: Intishārāt-i Rahnamūn.
Davoodabadi, H. (2012). *Sayyid -e 'Azīz*. Tehran: Yā Zahrā.
Della Valle, P. (2005). *Safarnāmah-'i Piyitrū dilā Vālah* (S. Shafa, Trans.). Tehran: Shirkat-i Intishārāt-i 'Ilmī va Farhangī.
Dowlat Abadi, Y. (1992). *Ḥayāt-i Yaḥyā*. Tehran: Zavvar.
Emami, M. M. (2003). *Zindagīnāmah-i Āyat Allāh al-'Uẓmá Gulpāyagānī*. Tehran: Markaz-i Asnād-i Inqilāb-i Islāmī.
Eslami, G. (1994). *Ghurūb-i khvurshīd-i faqāhat*. Tehran: Dār al-Kutub al-Islāmīyah.
Eyn al-Saltanah, Q. M. (1995). *Rūznāmah-'i khāṭirāt-i 'Ayn al-Salṭanah*. Tehran: Asāṭīr.
Fadayi Mehrabani, M. (2014). *Ḥikmat, ma'rifat va siyāsat dar Īrān : andīshah-'i siyāsī 'irfānī dar Īrān, az maktab-i Iṣfahān tā ḥukamā-yi ilāhī-i mu'āṣir*. Tehran: Nashr-i Nay.
Fadlallah, M. H. (1988). *Ḥarb al-irādāt : ṣirā' al-muqāwamah wa-al-iḥtilāl al-Isrā'īlī fī Lubnān*. Beirut: Dār al-Hādī.
Falsafi, M. T. (1997). *Khāṭirāt*. Tehran: Markaz-i Asnād-i Inqilāb-i Islāmī.
Falsafi, N. (1990). *Zindagānī-i Shāh 'Abbās-i Avval*. Tehran: Intishārāt-i 'Ilmī.
Farati, A. (2017). *Gūnah'shināsī-i fikrī - siyāsī-i Ḥawzah-i 'Ilmīyah-i Qum*. Tehran: Sāzmān-i Intishārāt-i Pizhūhishgāh-i Farhang va Andīshah-i Islāmī.
Haytham, N. (2004). *Nabīh Birrī: askunu hādhā al-kitāb*. Beirut: Mukhtārāt.
Herz al-Din, M. (1985). *Ma'ārif al-rijāl: fī tarājim al-'ulamā' wa-al-udabā'*. Qum: Maktabat Āyat Allāh al-'Uẓmá al-Mar'ashī al-Najafī.
Hujjati Kermani, A. (2010). *Lubnān ba-riwāyat-i imām Mūsā Ṣadr wa duktur Čamrān: nigāhī ba-tārīḫ-i ğanghā-i dāḫilī-i Lubnān*. Tehran: Mu'assasah-i Farhangī Taḥqīqātī-i Imām Mūsá Ṣadr.
Husseini Hairi, K. (1996). *Zindagī va afkār-i shahīd-i buzurgvār Āyat Allāh al-'Uẓmá Sayyid Muḥammad Bāqir Ṣadr*. Tehran: Intishārāt-i Vizārat-i Farhang va Irshād-i Islāmī.
Husseini Hairi, K. (2008). *Al-Shahīd al-Ṣadr sumūw al-dhāt wa-sumūw al-mawqif* (2nd ed.). Qum: Dar al-Bashir.
Husseinian, R. (2008a). *Sih sāl satīz marja'īyat-i Shī'ah dar*. Tehran: Markaz-i Asnād-i Inqilāb-i Islāmī.
Husseinian, R. (2008b). *Yik sāl mubārazah barā-yi sarnagūnī-i rižīm-i Šāh*. Tehran: Markaz-i Asnād-i Inqilāb-i Islāmī.
Ibn al-Jawzi, A. (1992). *Al-Muntazam fī tārīkh al-mulūk wa-aluman*. Beirut: Dar al-Kutub al-'Ilmiyah.
Ibn Tawus, A. (1991). *Kashf al-maḥajjat li-s̱amarat al-muhjah*. Qum: Markaz al-Nashr al-Aa'lam al-Islami.
Ibn Tiqtaqa, M. (1966). *Al-Fakhrī fī al-adab al-sulṭānīyah wa-al-duwal al-Islāmīyah*. Beirut: Dār Ṣādir.
Iraqi, M. (1991). *Nāguftah'hā*. Tehran: Rasā.
Jafarian, R. (2000). *Ṣafavīyah dar 'arṣah-'i dīn, farhang va siyāsat*. Qum: Pizhūhishgāh-i Ḥawzah va Dānishgāh.
Jafarian, R. (2008). *Jeryanhā va sāzmanhāye-ye mahzabi - siāsi-ye Irān* (Ninth ed.). Tehran: Khaneh Ketab.
Jafarian, R. (2011). *Tārīkh-i Tashayyu' dar Iran* (4th ed.). Tehran: Nashr-i 'Ilm.
Jamaluddin, N. (2002). *Al-Shī'ah 'alá al-muftaraq, aw, Mūsá al-Ṣadr*. Beirut: Dār al-Balāghah.
Jawadi Amoli, A. (2012). *Wilāyat-i faqīh, Wilāyat-i fuqaha wa Edālat* (12th ed.). Qum: Esra.
Kadivar, J. (1997). *Taḥavvul-i guftimān-i siyāsī-i Shī'ah dar Īrān*. Tehran: Ṭarḥ-i Naw.

Kadivar, M. (1997). *Naẓarīyah'hā-yi dawlat dar fiqh-i Shī'ah* (7th ed.). Tehran: Nashr-i Nay.
Karbalayi, H. (1994). *Tārīkh-i dukhānīyah* (R. l. Ja'fariyān Ed.). Tehran: Markaz-i Asnād-i Inqilāb-i Islāmī.
Kashani, A. A. (2005). *Tārīkh-i Uljā'itū* (2nd ed.). Tehran: Shirkat Intishārāt-i 'Ilmī va Farhangī.
Kashmiri, M. A. (2005). *Nujūm al-samā' fī tarājum al-'ulamā'*. Tehran: Sāzm ān-i Tablīghāt-i Islāmī.
Kasravi, A. (1984). *Tārīkh-i mashrūṭah-'i Īrān*. Tehran: Intishārāt-i Amīr-i Kabīr.
Kermani, N. (1997). *Tārikh-i bidari-yi Irānīān*. Tehran: Tolu-i Āzādi.
Khamenei, A. (1999). *Ajwibat al-Istiftā'āt*. Beirut: Dar al-Islamiyya.
Khamenei, A. (2014). *Insān-i 250 sāle*. Tehran: Mu'assasah-'i Īmān-i Jahādī.
Khawnsari, A. (1984). *Jāmi' al-madārik fī sharḥ al-Mukhtaṣar al-nāfi'*. Qum: Mu'assasat Ismā'īlīyān.
Khawnsari, M. B. (1991). *Rawḍāt al-jannāt: fī aḥwāl al-'ulamā' wa-al-sādāt*. Beirut: Dār al-Kutub al-Islāmīyah.
Khoei, A. (1995). *Ṣirāṭ al-najāh fī ajwibat al-istiftā'āt (Ta'liqah Jawad Tabrizi)*. Beirut: Dār al-Muḥajjah al-Bayḍā'.
Khomeini, R. (1984). *Kitāb al-Bay'*. Qum: Mu'assasat Ismā'īlīyān.
Khomeini, R. (2008). *Ṣaḥīfeh-ye Imām* (M. Limba, Trans.). Tehran: The Institute for Compilation and Publication of Imām Khomeinī's Works.
Khosroshahi, H. (1996). *Fidā'iyān-i Islām*. Tehran: Iṭṭilā'āt.
Khurasani, A. (1986). *Ḥāshiyah Kitāb al-Makāsib* (S. M. Shamsuddin, Ed.). Tehran: Īntishārāti Viyzārāti Farhang va Īrshādi Īslām.
Khwandamir, M. (1983). *Ḥabīb al-siyar fī aḫbār afrād al-bašar*. Tehran: Kitābfurūšī-i Ḫaiyām.
Laroudi, N. (2009). *Nādir, pisar-i shamshīr* (Second ed.). Tehran: Shirkat-i Muṭāla'āt-i Nashr-i Kitāb-i Pārsah.
Ma'adikhah, A. a.-M. (2006). *Jām-i shikastah: khāṭirāt-i Ḥujjat al-Islām 'Abd al-Majīd Ma'ādīkhvāh*. Tehran: Markaz-i Asnād-i Inqilāb-i Islāmī.
Madadi, A. (2014). *Nigāhī bih daryā*. Qum: Mu'assasah-i Kitābshināsī-i Shī'ah.
Mahdavi, M. a.-D. (1988). *Bayān subl al-hidāyah fī ẕikr a'qāb ṣāḥib al-hidāyah, yā, Tārīkh-i 'ilmī va ijtimā'ī-i Iṣfahān dar dū qarn-i akhīr*. Qum: Nashr al-Hidāyah.
Mahmood, M. (1974). *Tarīkh-i ravābit-i siyāsī Irān va Inglīs*. Tehran: Chapkhānah Iqbāl.
Majlesi, M. B. (1982). *Biḥār al-anwār*. Beirut: Dar Ihya'al-Turath al-Arabi.
Makarem Shirazi, N. (1992). *Anwār al-faqāhah*. Qum: Madrasat al-Imām 'Alī ibn Abī Ṭālib.
Makarem Shirazi, N. (2009). *Dā'irat al-ma'ārif-i fiqh-i muqārin*. Qum: Intishārāt-i Imām 'Alī Bin Abī Ṭālib.
Makki, H. (1979). *Tārīkh-i bīst sālah-'i Īrān*. Tehran: Intishārāt-i Amīr-i Kabīr.
Makki, H. (1981a). *Kitāb-i siyāh*. Tehran: Bongah e Nashr e Ketab.
Makki, H. (1981b). *Vaqāyi'-i sī'um-i Tīr 1331*. Tehran: Bongah-e-Nashr wa Trajomeh-e Ketab.
Malakzadeh, M. (1984). *Tārīkh-i inqilāb-i mashrūṭīyat-i Īrān*. Tehran: 'Ilmī.
Mar'ashi, Z. (1984). *Tārīkh-i Ṭabaristān va Rūyān va Māzandarān*. Tehran: Sharq.
Mar'ashi Najafi, S. (2009). *Ḥaẓrat-i Āyat Allāh al-'Uẓmá Sayyid Shihāb al-Dīn Mar'ashī Najafī bih rivāyat-i asnād-i Sāvāk*. Tehran: Markaz-i Bar'rasī-i Asnād-i Tārīkhī-i Vizārat-i Iṭṭilā'āt.
Marwi, M. K. (1960). *Nāme-ji 'Ālamārā-ji Nādirī*. Moscow: Vostočnoj Literatury.

Mohit Mafi, H. (1984). *Muqaddamāt-i Mashrūṭīyat*. Tehran: Intishārāt-i ʻIlmī.
Motahhari, M. (1985). *Imāmat wa rahbarī* (2nd ed.). Tehran: Intišārāt-i Ṣadrā.
Motahhari, M. (2003). *Dah Goftar* (5th ed.). Tehran: Sadra.
Muntaziri, H. A. (1990). *Dirāsāt fī wilāyat al-faqīh wa-fiqh al-dawlah al-Islāmīyah* (M. Salawati Ed.). Qum: Tafakkur.
Muntaziri, H. A. (2001). *Matn-i kāmil-i khāṭirāt-i Āyat Allāh Ḥusayn ʻAlī Muntaẓirī: bih hamrāh-i payvast'hā*. Essen: Nima.
Mustawfi, A. (1998). *Sharḥ-i zindigānī-i man: yā tārīkh-i ijtimāʻī va idārī-i dawrah-ʼi Qājāriyah*. Tehran: Zavvār.
Na'ini, M. H. (2003). *Tanbīh al-ummah wa-tanzīh al-millah* (J. Varaʻī, Ed.). Qum: Mu'assasah-i Būstān-i Kitāb.
Najafi, M. (2005). *Andīshah-ʼi siyāsī va tārīkh-i nahẕat-i Ḥājj Āqā Nūr Allāh Iṣfahānī*. Tehran: Mu'assasah-i Muṭālaʻāt-i Tārīkh-i Muʻāṣir-i Īrān.
Najafi, S. M. H. (1984). *Jawāhir al-kalām fī sharḥ Sharāʼiʻ al-Islām*. Tehran: Dar al-Kutub al-Islamyya.
Najafi Ghoochani, M. H. (2007). *Sīyāḥat-i Sharq* (3rd ed.). Tehran: Ghadyani.
Naraqi, A. (1987). *ʻAwāʼid al-ayyām*. Qum: Maktabah-i Baṣīratī.
Nategh, H. (1975). *Az mā'st kih bar mā'st*. Tehran: Āgāh.
Nejati, G. (1987). *Junbish-i mili shudan-i sanʻāt-i naft*. Tehran: Inteshar.
Nu'mani, M. R. (1996). *Al-Shahīd al-Ṣadr sanawāt al-miḥnah wa-ayyām al-ḥiṣār*. Beirut: Dār al-Hādī.
Qanatabadi, S. (1998). *Khāṭirāt-i Shams Qanāt'ābādī: sayrī dar nahẕat-i millī'shudan-i ṣanʻat-i naft*. Tehran: Markaz-i Bar'rasī-i Asnād-i Tārīkhī-i Vizārat-i Iṭṭilāʻāt.
Qassem, N. (2007). *Ḥizb Allāh-i Lubnān: khaṭṭ-i mashī, guẕashtah va āyandah-i ān* (M. M. Shariatmadar, Trans.). Tehran: Iṭṭilāʻāt.
Qummi, A. (1999). *Muntahá al-āmāl: dar zindagānī va sharḥ-i aḥvāl-i chahārdah maʻṣūm salām Allāh ʻalayhā*. Tehran: Intishārāt-i Payk.
Rahimlou, Y. (1973). Risāla favāyid-i Ūljāytū. *Nashriyeh Daneshkadeh Adabiyat wa Ulum Ensani Tabriz, 106*, 135–56.
Rahnema, A. (2009). *Nīrū'hā-yi maẕhabī bar bistar-i ḥarakat-i nahẕat-i millī* (2nd ed.). Tehran: Gām-i Naw.
Rajabi, M. H. (1999). *Zindigīnāmah-i siyāsī-i Imām Khumaynī*. Tehran: Markaz=-i Asnād-i Inqilāb-i Islāmī.
Ramezani, A. (2004). *Nāṣir al-Dīn Shāh Qājār*. Tehran: Tarfand.
Rau'f, A. (2000). *Al–ʻAmal al-islāmī fī l-ʻIrāq baina l-marǧiʻīya wa-l-ḥizbīya: qirāʼa naqdīya li-masīrat niṣf qarn (1950-2000)*. Damascus: Markaz al-ʻIrāqī li-l-Iʻlām wa-d-Dirāsāt.
Rezwani, H. (1983). *Lawāyiḥ-i Āqā Shaykh Faẕl Allāh*. Tehran: Nashr-i Tārīkẖ-i Iran.
Rumlu, H. B. (2006). *Aḥsan al-tavārīkh*. Tehran: Asāṭīr.
Sadeqkar, M. (2000). *Rūḥānī-i mubāriz, Āyat Allāh Kāshānī bih rivāyat-i asnād*. Tehran: Markaz-i Bar'rasī-i Asnād-i Tārīkhī-i Vizārat-i Iṭṭilaʻāt.
Sadr, M. (2005). *Dīn dar khidmat-i insān*. Tehran: Mu'assasah-ʼi Farhangī-Taḥqīqātī-i Imām Mūsá Ṣadr.
Sadr, M. B. (1980). *Al-Islām yaqūdu l-ḥayāt*. Beirut: Dar al-Ta'aruf li'l-Matbu'at.
Sadr, M. B. (1982). *Al-Fatāwá al-wāḍiḥah wifqan li-maḏab ahl al-bait*. Beirut: Dar al-Taruf lil-Maṭbūʻāt.
Sadr, M. B. (1987). *Buḥūṯ fī al-uṣūl*. Qum: Markaz al-Abḥāṯ wa-'d-Dirāsāt at-Taẖaṣṣuṣīya li-Shahīd aṣ-Ṣadr.
Samiʻi, M. (2018). *Nabard-i qudrat dar Īrān: chirā va chigūnah rūḥāniyat barandah shud?* Tehran: Nashr-i Nay.

SAVAK. (2000). *Imām Mūsá Ṣadr bih rivāyat-i asnād-i Sāvāk*. Tehran: Markaz-i Bar'rasī-i Asnād-i Tārīkhī-i Vizārat-i Iṭṭilā'āt.
Sepehr, M. T. (1958). *Nāsikh al-tavārīkh*. Tehran: Intishārāt-i Amīr-i Kabīr.
Shariatmadari, K. (2009). *Taḥqīq wa-taqrīrāt fī bāb al-bay' wa-al-khiyārāt* (H. Haqani Ed.). Qum: Tawalla.
Sharif Razi, M. (1973). *Ganjīnah-'i dānishmandān*. Tehran: Kitābfurūshī-i Islāmīyah.
Shaybi, K. M. (1991). *Tashayyu' va Taṣavvuf tā āghāz-i sadah-i davāzdahum-i Hijrī* (A. Zekavati Gharagozlou, Trans.). Tehran: Intishārāt-i Amīr-i Kabīr.
Sheikholeslami, J. (1989). *Sīmā-yi Aḥmad Shāh Qājār*. Tehran: Nashr-i Guftār.
Shubayri Zanjani, M. (2014). *Jur'ah-'i az daryā*. Qum: Mu'assasah-i Kitābshināsī-i Shī'ah.
Sobhani, J. (1991). *Mabānī-i ḥukūmat-i Islāmī* (D. Elhami, Trans.). Qum: Tawhid.
Tabarayian, S. (2010). *Iḥyāgar-i ḥawzah-i Najaf: zindagī va zamānah-i Āyat allāh al-'uẓmá Ḥakīm*. Tehran: Markaz-i Asnād-i Inqilāb-i Islāmī.
Tabarayian, S. (2012). *Intifā ẓah Sha'bānīyah*. Tehran: Markaz-i Asnad-i Inqilab-i Islami.
Tabatabai, M. H., Mujtahed Zanjani, A., Motahhari, M., Bazargan, M., Beheshti, M., Taleqani, M., & Jazaeri, M. (1962). *Baḥs̱ī Darbārah-'i marja'īyat wa rawḥānīyat*. Tehran: Shirkat-i Sihāmī-i Intishār.
Tabatabai, S. (2010). *Khāṭirāt-i siyāsī - ijtimā'ī-i duktur Ṣādiq Ṭabāṭabāyī*. Tehran: Mu'assasah-i Tanẓīm va Nashr-i Ās̱ār-i Ḥaẓrat Imām Khumaynī.
Tabatabayifar, M. (2015). *Jarayān'hā-yi fikrī dar ḥawzah-i mu'āṣir-i Qum*. Tehran: Nashr-i Nay.
Tavakkolian, J. (2014). *Nukhbagān-i Īrānī dar dawrān-i guẕār*. Tehran: Nigāh-i Mu'āṣir.
Tehrani, A. B. (1991). *Tabaqāt a'lām al-Shī'ah*. Qum: Mu'assasat Ismā'īlīyān.
Teymouri, I. (1979). *Taḥrīm-i tanbākū: qarār-dād-i 1890 rižī ; awwalīn muqāwamat-i manfī dar Īrān*. Tehran: Kitābhā-i Jībī.
Turkaman, I. (1992). *Tārīkh-i 'ālam'ārā-yi 'Abbāsī*. Tehran: Intishārāt-i Amīr-i Kabīr.
Turkaman, M. (1984). *Majmū'ah'ī az rasā'il, i'lāmīyah'hā, maktūbāt-- va rūznāmah-'i Shaykh Shahīd Faẕl Allāh Nūrī*. Tehran: Rasā.
Turkaman, M. (1991). *Asrār-i qatl-i Razm'ārā*. Tehran: Rasā.
Tusi, N. (1994). *Akhlāq-e Nāṣerī*. Tehran: Chāpkhāne-ye Dāneshgāh.
Vahed, S. (1987). *Qīyām-i Gawharshād*. Tehran: Vizārat-i Farhang va Irshād-i Islamī.
Vakili Qummi, A. (1966). *Tashkīlāt-i maḏhab-i Shī'ah*. Retrieved from Tehran.
Vassaf Shirazi, A. (1967). *Tārīkh-i Vaṣāf*. Tehran: Vizārat-i Farhang va Irshād-i Islami.
Wahid Khorasani, H. (2007). *Āshnā'ī bā uṣūl-i dīn*. Qum: Bāqir al-'Ulūm.
Yazdi, M. K. (1999). *Al-'urwah al-wuthqá: ma'a ta'līqāt 'idat min al-fuqaha*. Qum: Mu'assasat al-Nashr al-Islāmī.
Zargarinejad, G. H. (2011). *Rasā'il-i mashrūtiyat*. Tehran: Nashr Kavir.

English Sources

Abdul-Jabar, F. (2002). *Ayatollahs, Sufis and Ideologues: State, religion and social movements in Iraq*. London: Saqi Books.
Abdul-Jabar, F. (2003a). *The Shī'ite movement in Iraq*. London: Saqi.
Abdul-Jabar, F. (2003b). Why the uprising failed? In M. L. Sifry & C. Cerf (Eds.), *The Iraq war reader: History, documents, opinions* New York: Touchstone.
Abisaab, R. J. (2004). *Converting Persia: Religion and power in the Safavid Empire*. London: I.B.Tauris.

Abisaab, R. J. (2009). Lebanese Shiites and The Marjaiyya: Polemic in the late twentieth century. *British Journal of Middle Eastern Studies, 36*(2), 215–39.

Abrahamian, E. (1982a). 'Ali Shariati: Ideologue of the Islamic revolution. *Merip Report, 102*(Islam and Politics), 24–8.

Abrahamian, E. (1982b). *Iran between two revolutions*. Princeton: Princeton University Press.

Abrahamian, E. (2008). *A history of modern Iran*. New York: Cambridge University Press

Abu-Sharif, B. (2009). *Arafat and the dream of Palestine*. New York: Palgrave Macmillan.

Agha, H., & Khalidi, A. (1995). *Syria and Iran: Rivalry and cooperation*. London: Pinter Publishers.

Ahmadi, K. (2008). *Islands and international politics in the Persian Gulf: The Abu Musa and Tunbs in strategic context*. New York: Routledge.

Ajami, F. (1986). *The Vanished Imam*. London: I. B. Tauris.

Ajami, F. (1988). Iran: The impossible revolution. *Foreign Affairs, 67*(2), 135–55.

Akhavi, S. (1980). *Religion and politics in contemporary Iran: Clergy state relations in the Pahlavi period*. New York: State University Press.

Al-Khafaji, I. (2000). War as a vehicle for the rise and Demise of a State-Controlled Society: The Case of Ba'thist Iraq. In S. Heydemann (Ed.), *War, Institutions, and Social Change in the Middle East*. Berkeley: University of California Press.

Al-Qarawee, H. H. (2017). Sistani, Iran, and the Future of Shii Clerical Authority in Iraq. *Middle East Brief*(105).

Al-Qarawee, H. H. (2018). The 'formal' Marjaʿ: Shiʿi clerical authority and the state in post-2003 Iraq. *British Journal of Middle Eastern Studies, 46*(3), 481–97.

Al-Sarhan, S. (2020). *Political quietism in Islam: Sunni and Shīʿī practice and thought*. London: I.B. Tauris.

Alagha, J. E. (2011). *Hizbullah's identity construction*. Amsterdam: Amsterdam University Press.

Alavi, A. (2019). *Iran and palestine: Past, present, future*. London: Routledge.

Algar, H. (1980). *Religion and state in Iran, 1785–1906: the role of the ulama in the Qajar period*. Berkeley: University of California Press.

Algar, H. (1991). Religious forces in twentieth-century Iran. In P. Avery, G. Hambly, & C. Melville (Eds.), *The Cambridge history of Iran* (Vol. 7, pp. 732–64). Cambridge: Cambridge University Press.

Allawi, A. A. (2007). *The occupation of Iraq: Winning the war, losing the peace*. New Haven: Yale University Press.

Amanat, A. (1988). In between the madrasa and the marketplace: The designation of clerical leadership in modern Shi'ism. In S. Amir Arjomand (Ed.), *Authority and political culture in Shi'ism* (pp. 98–132). New York: State University of New York Press.

Amanat, A. (2009). *Apocalyptic Islam and Iranian Shi'ism*. London: I.B.Tauris

Amanat, A. (2017). *Iran: A modern history*. New Haven: Yale University Press.

Amir Arjomand, S. (1985). The causes and significance of the Iranian revolution. *State, Culture, and Society, 1*(3), 41–66.

Amir Arjomand, S. (1988). The Mujtahid of the age and the Mulla-bashi: An intermediate stage in the institutionalization of religious authority in Shi'ite Iran. In S. A. Arjomand (Ed.), *Authority and Political Culture in Shi'ism*. New York: SUNY Press.

Amir Arjomand, S. (1989). *The turban for the crown: The Islamic revolution in Iran*. New York: Oxford University Press.

Amir Arjomand, S. (2009). *After Khomeini: Iran under his successors*. New York: Oxford University Press.

Amoretti, B. S. (1968). Religion in the Timurid and Safavid periods. In P. Jackson & L. Lockhart (Eds.), *The Cambridge history of Iran* (pp. 610–55). Cambridge: Cambridge University Press.

Ansari, A. (2003). *Modern Iran since 1921: The Pahlavis and after*. New York: Pearson Education.

Arato, A. (2004). Sistani v. Bush: Constitutional politics in Iraq. *Constellations*, *11*(2), 174–92.

Axworthy, M. (2013). *Revolutionary Iran: A history of the Islamic Republic*. New York: Oxford University Press.

Aziz, T. M. (1993). The role of Muhammad Baqir al-Sadr in Shii political activism in Iraq from 1958 to 1980. *International Journal of Middle East Studies*, *25*(2), 207–22.

Bakhash, S. (1985). *The reign of the Ayatollahs: Iran and the Islamic revolution*. London: I.B.Tauris.

Bakhash, S. (2004). The troubled relationship: Iran and Iraq, 1930–80. In L. G. Potter & G. G. Sick (Eds.), *Iran, Iraq, and the legacies of war*. New York: Palgrave Macmillan.

Banani, A. (1961). *The modernization of Iran, 1921–1941*. Stanford: Stanford University Press.

Banaszak, L. A. (1996). *Why movements succeed or fail: Opportunity, culture, and the struggle for woman suffrage*. Princeton: Princeton University Press.

Barak, O. (2009). *The Lebanese army: A national institution in a divided society*. Albany: SUNY Press.

Barzegar, K. (2008). Iran and The Shiite Crescent: Myths and realities. *The Brown Journal of World Affairs*, *15*(1), 87–99.

Batatu, H. (2004). *The old social classes and the revolutionary movements of Iraq*. London: Saqi.

Bausani, A. (1968). Religion under the Mongols. In J. A. Boyle (Ed.), *The Cambridge history of Iran* (pp. 538–49). Cambridge: Cambridge University Press.

Bayless, L. (2012). Who is Muqtada al-Sadr? *Studies in Conflict & Terrorism*, *35*, 135–55.

Behdad, S. (1997). Islamic Utopia in pre-revolutionary Iran: Navvab Safavi and the Fada'ian e Eslam. *Middle Eastern Studies*, *33*(1), 40–65.

Berry, J. M. (2002). Validity and reliability issues in elite interviewing. *Political Science & Politics*, *35*(04), 679–82.

Beshara, A. (2004). *Lebanon: The politics of frustration – The Failed Coup of 1961*. London: Routledge.

Blanford, N. (2006). *Killing Mr. Lebanon: The assassination of Rafiq Hariri and its impact on the Middle East*. London: I. B. Tauris.

Blaydes, L. (2018). *State of repression: Iraq under Saddam Hussein*. Princeton: Princeton University Press.

Bowker, R. (2003). *Palestinian refugees: Mythology, identity, and the search for peace*. Boulder: Lynne Rienner Publishers.

Braam, E. H. (2011). All roads lead to Najaf: Grand Ayatollah Al-Sistani's quiet impact on Iraq's 2010 Ballot and its aftermath. *Journal of International and Global Studies*, *2*(1), 1–21.

Browne, E. G. (1910). *The Persian revolution of 1905–1909*. Cambridge: Cambridge University Press.

Brunner, R. (2020). 'Dropping a Thick Curtain of Forgetting and Disregard': Modern Shi'i Quietism beyond politics. In S. Al-Sarhan (Ed.), *Political quietism in Islam: Sunni and Shī'ī practice and thought* (pp. 185–208). London: I.B. Tauris.

Bullard, R. (1958). *The Middle East: A political and economic survey* (Third ed.). London: Oxford University Press.
Chubin, S., & Tripp, C. (1988). *Iran and Iraq at war*. London: I.B. Tauris.
Churchill, W. (1985). *The Second World War: The Grand Alliance* (Vol. 3). Boston: Houghton Mifflin.
Clarke, L. (2001). The Shi ʿi Construction of Taqlid. *Journal of Islamic Studies, 12*(1), 40–64.
Cobban, H. (1984). *The Palestinian Liberation Organisation: People, power and politics*. Cambridge: Cambridge University Press.
Cobban, H. (1985). *The making of modern Lebanon*. London: Hutchinson
Cole, J. (1985). Shi'i Clerics in Iraq and Iran, 1722–1780: The Akhbari-Usuli Conflict Reconsidered. *Iranian Studies, 18*(1), 3–34.
Cole, J. (2003). The United States and Shi'ite religious factions in Post-Ba'thist Iraq. *Middle East Journal, 57*(4), 543–66.
Cole, J. (2006). A 'Shiite Crescent'? The regional impact of the Iraq war. *Current History, 105*(687), 20–6.
Cole, J. (2009). Meet the Ayatollahs. *New Statesman, 138*(4961), 28–30.
Contractor, C. A. (2011). The Dearborn effect: A comparison of the political dispositions of Shia and Sunni Muslims in the United States. *Politics and Religion, 4*(1), 154–67.
Cook, D. (2011). Waiting for the Twelfth Imam: Contemporary Apocalyptic Shiite literature and speculation in Lebanon and Iran. In U. Martensson, J. Bailey, P. Ringrose, & A. Dyrendal (Eds.), *Fundamentalism in the Modern World*. London: I.B.Tauris.
Cook, M. (1981). Activism and Quietism in Islam: The case of the early Murji'a. In A. S. Cudsi & A. E. H. Dessouki (Eds.), *Islam and Power*. London: Croom Helm.
Corboz, E. (2014). *Guardians of Shi'ism: Sacred authority and transnational family networks*. Edinburgh: Edinburgh University Press.
Corboz, E. (2017). The Najafi Marjaʿiyya in the Age of Iran's Vali-ye Faqih (Guardian Jurist): Can it Resist? In M. Lynch (Ed.), *New analysis of Shia politics*. George Washington University: Project on Middle East Political Science.
Cottam, R. W. (1979). *Nationalism in Iran: Updated through 1978*. Pittsburgh: University of Pittsburgh Press.
Cronin, S. (1999). Conscription and popular resistance in Iran, 1925-1941. In E. Zürcher (Ed.), *Arming the State: Military conscription in the Middle East and Asia, 1775–1925* (pp. 145–68). London: I. B. Tauris.
Crooke, A. (2009). *Resistance: The essence of the Islamist revolution*. London: Pluto Press.
Curzon, G. (1892). *Persia and the Persian question*. London: Longmans Green & Co.
Dabashi, H. (2006). *Theology of discontent: The ideological foundation of the Islamic revolution in Iran*. New Brunswick: Transaction Publishers.
Dabashi, H. (2011). *Shi'ism: A religion of protest*. Cambridge, MA: Harvard University Press.
Dai, Y. (2008). Transformation of the Islamic Daʿwa party in Iraq: From the revolutionary period to the Diaspora Era. *Asian and African Area Studies, 7*(2), 238–67.
Dasgupta, P. (1988). *Cheated by the world: Palestinian experience*. New Delhi: Orient Longman Limited.
Dawn, C. E. (1961). From Ottomanism to Arabism: The origin of an ideology. *The Review of Politics, 23*(3), 378–400.
Dawn, C. E. (1973). *From Ottomanism to Arabism: Essays on the origins of Arab nationalism*. Urbana: University of Illinois Press

Deeb, M. (2003). *Syria's terrorist war on Lebanon and the peace process*. New York: Palgrave Macmillan.

Dekmejian, R. H. (1975). *Patterns of political leadership: Egypt, Israel, Lebanon*. Albany: SUNY Press.

Dekmejian, R. H. (1995). *Islam in revolution: Fundamentalism in the Arab World* (2nd ed.). New York: Syracuse University Press.

Della Porta, D. (2013). Political opportunity/political opportunity structure. In D. A. Snow, D. Della Porta, B. Klandermans, & D. McAdam (Eds.), *The Wiley-Blackwell encyclopedia of social and political movements*. New Jerey: Wiley-Blackwell.

Dragnich, G. S. (1970). The Lebanon Operation of 1958: A Study of the Crisis Role of the Sixth Fleet. (Research Contribution 153).

Ehrenberg, J. (2010). *The Iraq Papers*. New York: Oxford University Press.

Ehteshami, A., & Varasteh, M. (1991). *Iran and the international community*. London: Routledge.

Eisenberg, L. Z., & Caplan, N. (2010). *Negotiating Arab-Israeli Peace, Second Edition: Patterns, problems, possibilities*. Bloomington: Indiana University Press.

Eisinger, P. (1973). The condition of protest behavior in American cities. *American Political Science Review*, *67*, 11–28.

El-Husseini, R. (2010). Hezbollah and the Axis of Refusal: Hamas, Iran and Syria. *Third World Quarterly*, *31*(5), 803–15.

Elhadj, E. (2006). *The Islamic Shield: Arab resistance to democratic and religious reforms*. Baton Rouge: Brown Walker Press.

Enayat, H. (2005). *Modern Islamic political thought: The response of the Shi'a and Sunni Muslims to the twentieth century*. London: I.B.Tauris.

Faghfoory, M. (1993). The impact of modernization on the Ulama in Iran, 1925–1941. *Iranian Studies*, *26*(3/4), 277–312.

Farah, C. E. (2000). *Politics of interventionism in Ottoman Lebanon, 1830–1861*. London: I.B.Tauris.

Feuvrier, J. (2012). *Trois ans à la cour de Perse*. Charleston: Nabu Press.

Fisk, R. (2001). *Pity the nation: Lebanon at war* (3rd ed.). Oxford and New York: Oxford University Press.

Fromkin, D. (1989). *A peace to end all peace: Creating the Modern Middle East, 1914–1922*. New York: H. Holt.

Fuller, G. E., & Francke, R. R. (2000). Is Shi'ism radical? *The Middle East Quarterly*, *VII*(1), 11–20. Retrieved from http://www.meforum.org/35/is-shiism-radical

Fuller, G. E., & Francke, R. R. (2001). *The Arab Shi'a: The forgotten Muslims*. New York: Palgrave MacMillan.

Gaddis, J. L. (2005). *Strategies of containment: A critical appraisal of American National Security Policy during the Cold War*. New York: Oxford University Press.

Gamson, W. A., & Meyer, D. S. (1996). Framing political opportunity. In D. McAdam, J. D. McCarthy, & M. N. Zald (Eds.), *Comparative perspectives on social movements: Political opportunities, mobilizing structures, and cultural framings*. New York: Cambridge University Press.

Ganji, B. (2006). *Politics of confrontation: The foreign policy of the USA and revolutionary Iran*. London: I.B. Tauris.

Gasiorowski, M. J. (1987). The 1953 Coup D'etat in Iran. *International Journal of Middle East Studies*, *19*(3), 261–86.

Gerges, F. (1995). The Kennedy Administration and the Egyptian-Saudi Conflict in Yemen: Co-Opting Arab Nationalism. *Middle East Journal*, *49*(2), 292–311.

Gerges, F. (2002). Israel's retreat from South Lebanon: Internal and external implications. *Middle East Policy*, *8*(1), 106–16.
Gharbieh, H. M. (1996). *Political awareness of the Shi'ites in Lebanon: The role of Sayyid Abd al-Husain Sharaf al-Din and Sayyid Musa al-Sadr*. (Doctoral Thesis). Durham University.
Gholsorkhi, S. (1994). Ismail II and Mirza Makhdum Sharifi: An interlude in Safavid history. *International Journal of Middle East Studies*, *26*(3), 477–88.
Giugni, M. (2009). Political opportunities: From Tilly to Tilly. *Swiss Political Science Review*, *15*(2), 361–7.
Gleave, R. (2007a). Conceptions of authority in Iraqi Shi'ism: Baqir al-Hakim, Hai'ri and Sistani on Ijtihad, Taqlid, and Marja'iyya. *Theory, Culture & Society*, *24*(2), 59–78.
Gleave, R. (2007b). *Scripturalist Islam: The History and Doctrines of the Akhbari Shi'i School*. Leiden: Brill.
Gleave, R. (2020). Quietism and political legitimacy in Imami Shi'i Jurisprudence: Al-Sharif al-Murtada's treatise on the legality of working for the government reconsidered. In S. Al-Sarhan (Ed.), *Political quietism in Islam: Sunni and Shī'ī practice and thought* (pp. 99–128). London: I.B. Tauris.
Goodarzi, J. M. (2006). *Syria and Iran: Diplomatic alliance and power politics in the Middle East*. London: I. B. Tauris.
Goode, J. (1991). Reforming Iran during the Kennedy Years. *Diplomatic History*, *15*(1), 13–29.
Goodwin, J., & Jasper, J. M. (2004). *Rethinking social movements: Structure, meaning, and emotion*. New York: Rowman & Littlefield Publishers, Inc.
Gordon, D. C. (1980). *Lebanon: The fragmented nation*. Stanford: Hoover Institution Press.
Hage Ali, M. (2018). *Nationalism, transnationalism, and political Islam: Hizbullah's institutional identity*. Cham: Palgrave Macmillan.
Hairi, A. H. (1977). *Shi'ism and constitutionalism in Iran: A study of the role played by the Persian Residents of Iraq in Iranian politics*. Leiden: Brill.
Haji-Yousefi, A. M. (2009). Whose agenda is served by the idea of a Shia Crescent? *Turkish Journal of International Relations*, *8*(01), 114–35.
Halawi, M. (1992). *A Lebanon defied: Musa al-Sadr and the Shi'a community*. Colorado: Westview Press.
Hallaq, W. B. (1984). Was the gate of ijtihad closed? *International Journal of Middle East Studies*, *16*(1), 3–41.
Halperin, S. (2005). The post-cold war political topography of the Middle East: Prospects for democracy. *Third World Quarterly*, *26*(7), 1135–56.
Hamoudi, H. A. (2009). Between realism and resistance: Shi'i Islam and the contemporary Liberal state. *Journal of Islamic Law and Culture*, *11*(2), 107–20.
Hamzawy, A., & Bishara, D. (2006). *Islamist movements in the Arab World and the 2006 Lebanon War*. Retrieved from Washington:
Hamzeh, A. N. (2001). Clientalism, Lebanon: Roots and trends. *Middle Eastern Studies*, *37*(3), 167–78.
Hanf, T. (1993). *Coexistence in wartime Lebanon: Decline of a state and rise of a nation*. London: I.B.Tauris.
Harris, W. W. (1997). *Faces of Lebanon: Sects, wars, and global extensions*. Princeton: Markus Wiener Publishers
Hartung, J.-P. (2020). Making sense of 'Political Quietism'-An analytical intervention. In S. Al-Sarhan (Ed.), *Political quietism in Islam: Sunni and Shī'ī practice and thought* (pp. 15–32). London: I.B. Tauris.

Hashemi, N., & Postel, D. (2017). *Sectarianization: Mapping the new politics of the Middle East*. New York: Oxford University Press.

Haugh, T. (2005). *The Sadr II movement: An organizational fight for legitimacy within the Iraqi Shi'a community*. Retrieved from https://apps.dtic.mil/dtic/tr/fulltext/u2/a521548.pdf.

Hiro, D. (2003). The post-saddam problem. In M. L. Sifry & C. Cerf (Eds.), *The Iraq war reader: History, documents, opinions*. New York: Touchstone.

Hitti, P. K. (1967). *Lebanon in history: From the earliest times to the present* (Third ed.). New York: Macmillan.

Hottinger, A. (1961). Zu'ama and parties in the Lebanese Crisis of 1958. *Middle East Journal, 15*(2), 127–40.

Hottinger, A. (1966). Zu'ama' in historical perspective. In L. Binder (Ed.), *Politics in Lebanon* (pp. 85–105). New York: Wiley.

Hourani, A. (1946). *Syria and Lebanon: A political essay*. Oxford: Oxford University Press.

Hourani, A. (1986). *Political society in Lebanon: A historical introduction*. Paper presented at the Seminar, E.B.M.E.

Hudson, M. C. (1997). Trying again: Power-sharing in Post-Civil War Lebanon. *International Negotiation, 2*, 103–22.

Isfahanian, D., & Karimi, A. (2006). Utopia: A reason behind Khawjeh Nasir al-Din Tusi Collaboration with Ilkhanids. *Journal of Historical Researches, 1*(1), 27–38.

Jafri, H. (2007). *Origins and early development of Shi'a Islam*. London: Stacey International.

Jervis, R. (1976). *Perception and misperception in international politics*. Princeton: Princeton University Press.

Jones, J. (2007). *Negotiating change: The new politics of the Middle East*. London: I.B. Tauris.

Kadhim, A. (2013a). *The Hawza under Siege: A study in the Ba'th Party Archive*. Retrieved from Boston University.

Kadhim, A. (2013b). *Reclaiming Iraq: The 1920 revolution and the founding of the modern state*. Austin: University of Texas Press.

Kalantari, M. R. (2019a). The Shi'i clergy and perceived opportunity structures: Political activism in Iran, Iraq, and Lebanon. *British Journal of Middle Eastern Studies*. doi:10.1080/13530194.2019.1605879.

Kalantari, M. R. (2019b). The Shiʿi clergy and dilemma of the separation of powers. In W. M. Amin & M. R. Tajri (Eds.), *Ijtihad & Taqlid: Past, present, and future*. Birmingham: Al-Mahdi Institute Press.

Kalantari, M. R. (2020a). The media contest during the Iran–Iraq war: The failure of mediatized Shiʿism. *Media, War, and Conflict*. doi:https://doi.org/10.1177/1750635220902192.

Kalantari, M. R. (2020b). Protecting the Citadel of Islam in the Modern Era: A case of Shiʿi Mujtahids and the Najaf Seminary in early twentieth-century Iraq. *The Muslim World, 110*(2), 217–31.

Kamrava, M. (2018). Leading the faithful: Religious authority in the Contemporary Middle East. *Sociology of Islam, 6*(2), 97–115.

Karsh, E. (1990). Geopolitical determinism: The origins of the Iran-Iraq War. *Middle East Journal, 44*(2), 256–68.

Karsh, E. (2002). *The Iran-Iraq War, 1980–1988*. Oxford: Osprey Publishing.

Kasaba, R., Keyder, Ç., & Tabak, F. (1986). Eastern Mediterranean port cities and their bourgeoisies: Merchants, political projects, and nation-states. *Review (Fernand Braudel Center), 10*(1), 121–35.

Katouzian, H. (2006). *State and society in Iran: The eclipse of the Qajars and the emergence of the Pahlavis*. London: IB Tauris.
Kayali, H. (1997). *Arabs and Young Turks: Ottomanism, Arabism, and Islamism in the Ottoman Empire, 1908–1918*. Berkeley: University of California Press.
Kazemi Mousavi, A. (1985). The establishment of the position of Marja'iyyt-i Taqlid in the Twelver-Shi'i community. *Iranian Studies*, *18*(1), 35–51.
Kazemi Mousavi, A. (1996). *Religious Authority in Shi'ite Islam: from the Office of Mufti to the Institution of Marja'*. Kuala Lumpur: International Institute of Islamic Thought and Civilization.
Kechichian, J. A. (1985). The gulf cooperation council: Search for security. *Third World Quarterly*, *7*(4), 853–81.
Keddie, N. (1966). *Religion and Rebellion in Iran: The Iranian Tobacco Protest of 1891–1982*. London: Routledge.
Keddie, N. (1983). *Religion and politics in Iran: Shi'ism from Quietism to revolution*. New Haven: Yale University Press.
Keddie, N., & Amanat, M. (1991). Iran under the Later Qājārs, 1848–1922. In P. Avery, G. Hambly, & C. Melville (Eds.), *The Cambridge history of Iran* (pp. 174–212). Cambridge: Cambridge University Press.
Khalaji, M. (2006). The last Marja: Sistani and the end of traditional religious authority in Shiism. *The Washington Institute for Near East Policy*.
Khalaji, M. (2017). The future of leadership in the Shiite community. *The Washington Institute for Near East Policy*.
Khalidi, W. (1971). *From haven to conquest: Readings in Zionism and the Palestine problem until 1948*. Institute for Palestine studies.
Khashan, H. (2010). The religious and political impact of Sayyid M. H. Fadlallah on Arab Shi'ism. *Journal of Shi'a Islamic Studies*, *3*(4), 427–41.
Khazen, F. (1991). *The communal pact of national identities: The making and politics of the 1943 national pact*. Retrieved from Oxford.
Khazen, F. (1998). *Lebanon's First Postwar Parliamentary Election, 1992: An imposed choice*. Retrieved from Oxford.
Khazen, F. (2004). Ending conflict in wartime Lebanon: Reform, sovereignty and power, 1976–88. *Middle Eastern Studies*, *40*(1), 65–84.
Khomeini, R. (1980). *Islamic government* (G. Carpozi, Trans.). New York: Manor Books.
Khuri, F. I. (1967). A comparative study of migration patterns in two Lebanese villages. *Human Organization*, *26*(4), 206–13.
Kinzer, S. (2003). *All the Shah's men: An American coup and the roots of Middle East Terror*. Hoboken: John Wiley & Sons.
Kobeissi, O. I. (2009). *Rural Urban Migration of the Shi'a of South Lebanon to Beirut Southern Suburbs*. (Master of Art). American University of Beirut, Beirut.
Kober, A. (2006). Great-power involvement and Israeli battlefield success in the Arab-Israeli wars, 1948–1982. *Journal of Cold War Studies*, *8*(1), 20–48.
Kohlberg, E. (1992). *A Medieval Muslim Scholar at work: Ibn Ṭāwūs and his library*. Leiden: Brill.
Kramer, M. (1997). The Oracle of Hizbullah: Sayyid Muhammad Husayn Fadlallah. In S. Appleby (Ed.), *Fundamentalist Leaders in the Middle East*. Chicago: University of Chicago Press.
Krayem, H. (1997). The Lebanese civil war and the Taif Agreement. In P. Salem (Ed.), *Conflict resolution in the Arab World: Selected essays* (pp. 411–35). Beirut: American University of Beirut.

Kurzman, C. (1996). Structural opportunity and perceived opportunity in social-movement theory: The Iranian revolution of 1979. *American Sociological Review*, *61*(1), 153–70.

Kurzman, C. (2003). The Qum protests and the coming of the Iranian revolution, 1975 and 1978. *Social Science History*, *27*(3), 287–325.

Kurzman, C. (2004). The poststructuralist consensus in social movement theory. In J. Goodwin & J. M. Jasper (Eds.), *Rethinking social movements: Structure, meaning, and emotion*. New York: Rowman & Littlefield Publishers, Inc.

Lalani, A. (2000). *Early Shiite thought: The teachings of Imam Muhammad al-Baqir*. London: I.B.Tauris.

Lambton, A. (1964). A reconsideration of the position of the Marja' al-Taqlid and the religious institution. *Studia Islamica*, *20*, 115–35.

Lambton, A. (1988). Concepts of authority in Persia: Eleventh to nineteenth centuries A.D. *British Institute of Persian Studies*, *26*, 95–103.

Lassner, J. (2010). Whither Shi'ite Islam? Authenticating a Shi'ite future based on reading the Islamic past. *Bustan: The Middle East Book Review*, *1*(1), 3–19.

Latour, B. (1984). The powers of association. *The Sociological Review*, *32*(S1), 264–80.

Litvak, M. (1998). *Shi'i Scholars of nineteenth-century Iraq: The 'ulama' of Najaf and Karbala'*. Cambridge: Cambridge University Press.

Lockhart, L. (1958). *The fall of the Safavi Dynasty and the Afghan occupation of Persia*. Cambridge: Cambridge University Press.

Louër, L. (2008). *Transnational Shia politics: Religious and political networks in the Gulf*. New York: Columbia University Press.

Louër, L. (2012). *Shiism and politics in the Middle East* (J. King, Trans.). London: Hurst.

Madelung, W. (1971). Hishām b. al-Ḥakam. In P. Bearman, T. Bianquis, C. E. Bosworth, E. van Donzel, & W. P. Heinrichs (Eds.), *Encyclopaedia of Islam* (Second ed.). Leiden: Brill.

Madelung, W. (1980). A treatise of the Sharif al-Murtada on the legality of working for the government. *Bulletin of the School of Oriental and African Studies*, *43*(01), 18–31.

Makdisi, U. (1996). Reconstructing the Nation-state: The modernity of sectarianism in Lebanon. *Middle East Report*, *200*, 23–6.

Makdisi, U. (2000). *The culture of sectarianism: Community, history, and violence in nineteenth-century Ottoman Lebanon*. Berkeley: University of California Press.

Makiya, K. (1998). *Republic of fear: The politics of Modern Iraq*. Berkeley: University of California Press.

Maktabi, R. (1999). The Lebanese census of 1932 revisited: Who are the Lebanese? *British Journal of Middle Eastern Studies*, *26*(2), 219–41.

Mallat, C. (1988a). *Aspects of Shi'i Thought from the South of Lebanon: Al–'Irfan, Muhammad Jawad Mughniyyah, Muhammad Mahdi Shamseddin, Muhammad Husain Fadlallah*. Retrieved from Oxford.

Mallat, C. (1988b). Religious militancy in contemporary Iraq: Muhammad Baqer as-Sadr and the Sunni-Shia Paradigm. *Third World Quarterly*, *10*(2), 699–729.

Mallat, C. (1993). *The Renewal of Islamic law: Muhammad Baqer as-Sadr, Najaf, and the Shi'i International*. New York: Cambridge University Press.

Mansour, R., & Jabar, A. F. (2017). *The popular mobilization forces and Iraq's future*. Retrieved from Beirut.

Marcinkowski, C. (2006). *Twelver Shi'ite Islam: Conceptual and practical aspects*. Singapore: Nanyang Technological University.

Marr, P. (2012). *The modern history of Iraq* (3rd ed.). Boulder: Westview Press.

Martin, V. (1993). Religion and State in Khumainī's 'Kashf al-asrār'. *Bulletin of the School of Oriental and African Studies, 56*(1), 34–45.
Martin, V. (2003). *Creating an Islamic State: Khomeini and the making of a New Iran.* London: I. B. Tauris.
Mauriello, R. (2011). *Descendants of the family of the prophet in contemporary history: a case study, the Šī'ī religious establishment of Al-Nağaf (Iraq).* Pisa Roma: Fabrizio Serra.
McAdam, D. (1996). Conceptual origins, current problems, and future directions. In D. McAdam, J. D. McCarthy, & M. N. Zald (Eds.), *Comparative perspectives on social movements: Political opportunities, mobilizing structures, and cultural framings.* New York: Cambridge University Press.
McAdam, D., McCarthy, J. D., & Zald, M. N. (1996). *Comparative perspectives on social movements: Political opportunities, mobilizing structures, and cultural framings.* New York: Cambridge University Press.
McAdam, D., Tarrow, S., & Tilly, C. (2001). *Dynamics of contention.* New York: Cambridge University Press.
Mearsheimer, J., & Walt, S. (2003). An unnecessary war. In M. L. Sifry & C. Cerf (Eds.), *The Iraq war reader: history, documents, opinions.* New York: Touchstone.
Mervin, S. (2010). *The Shi'a Worlds and Iran.* London: Saqi Books.
Meyer, D. S., & Minkoff, D. C. (2004). Conceptualizing political opportunity. *Social Forces, 82*(4), 1457–92.
Meyer, D. S., & Staggenborg, S. (1996). Movements, countermovements, and the structure of political opportunity. *American Journal of Sociology, 101*(6), 1628–60.
Mikecz, R. (2012). Interviewing elites addressing methodological issues. *Qualitative inquiry, 18*(6), 482–93.
Milani, M. (1994). *The making of Iran's Islamic revolution: From monarchy to Islamic Republic.* Boulder: Westview press.
Minorsky, V. (1943). *Tadhkirat al-Mulūk: A manual of Safavid administration.* London: Luzac & Co.
Moaddel, M. (1986). The Shi'i Ulama and the State in Iran. *Theory and Society, 15*(4), 519–56.
Moaddel, M. (1992). Shi'i political discourse and class mobilization in the tobacco movement of 1890–1892. Paper presented at the Sociological Forum.
Moin, B. (2009). *Khomeini: Life of the Ayatollah.* London: I. B. Tauris.
Momen, M. (1985). *An introduction to Shia Islam: The history and doctrines of Twelver Shiism.* New Haven: Yale University Press.
Morris, A., & Staggenborg, S. (2004). Leadership in social movements. In David A. Snow, Sarah A. Soule, & H. Kriesi (Eds.), *The blackwell companion to social movements* (pp. 171–96). London: Blackwell Publishing Ltd.
Morris, B. (1987). *The birth of the Palestinian refugee problem, 1947–1949.* Cambridge: Cambridge University Press.
Nakash, Y. (1994). The conversion of Iraq's tribes to Shiism. *International Journal of Middle East Studies, 26*(03), 443–63.
Nakash, Y. (2003a). *The Shi'is of Iraq.* Princeton: Princeton University Press.
Nakash, Y. (2003b). The Shi'ites and the future of Iraq. *Foreign Affairs*(July), *82*(4), 17–26.
Nakash, Y. (2006). *Reaching for power: The Shia in the modern Arab world.* Princeton: Princeton University Press.
Nasr, V. (2004). Regional implications of Shi'a Revival in Iraq. *Washington Quarterly, 27*(3), 5–24.
Nasr, V. (2006a). *The Shia revival: How conflicts within Islam will shape the future* (1st ed.). New York W. W. Norton.

Nasr, V. (2006b). When the Shiites rise. *Foreign Affairs, 85*(4), 58–74.
Newman, A. (1993). The myth of the Clerical Migration to Safawid Iran: Arab Shiite opposition to ʿAlī al-Karakī and Safawid Shiism. *Die Welt des Islams, 33*(1), 66–112.
Newman, A. (2009). *Safavid Iran: Rebirth of a Persian empire*. London: I.B. Tauris.
Nizameddin, T. (2006). The political economy of Lebanon under Rafiq Hariri: An interpretation. *Middle East Journal, 60*(1), 95–114.
Noe, N. (2007). *Voice of Hezbollah: The statements of Sayyed Hassan Nasrallah*. London: Verso.
Noorbakhsh, M. (2008). Shiism and ethnic politics in Iraq. *Middle East Policy Council, 15*(2), 53–65.
Norton, A. R. (1985). Changing actors and leadership among the Shiites of Lebanon. *Annals of the American Academy of Political and Social Science, 482* (Changing Patterns of Power in the Middle East), 109–21.
Norton, A. R. (1986). Shi'ism and social protest in Lebanon. In J. Cole & N. R. Keddie (Eds.), *Shi'ism and social protest*. New Haven: Yale University Press.
Norton, A. R. (1987). *Amal and the Shia: Struggle for the Soul of Lebanon*. Austin: University of Texas Press.
Norton, A. R. (2000). Hizballah and the Israeli withdrawal from Southern Lebanon. *Journal of Palestine Studies, 30*(1), 22–35.
Norton, A. R. (2007). The Shiite 'Threat' revisited. *Current History, 107*(704), 434.
Norton, A. R. (2009). *Hezbollah: A Short History*. Princeton: Princeton University Press.
Ostovar, A. (2016). *Vanguard of the Imam: religion, politics, and Iran's revolutionary guards*. New York: Oxford University Press.
Otterman, S. (2005). Iraq: Grand Ayatollah Ali al-Sistani. Council on Foreign Relations, Washington, DC, 11.
Pahlavi, P. C. (2007). The 33 day war: An example of psychological warfare in the information age. *Canadian Army Journal, 10*(1), 12–24.
Parsi, T. (2007). *Treacherous alliance: The secret dealings of Israel, Iran, and the United States*. New Haven: Yale University Press.
Parsi, T. (2017). *Losing an enemy: Obama, Iran, and the triumph of diplomacy*. New Haven: Yale University Press.
Patel, D. S. (2005). Ayatollahs on the Pareto frontier: The institutional basis of religious authority in Iraq. Working Paper, Stanford University.
Pollack, K. M. (2003). How Saddam misread the United States. In M. L. Sifry & C. Cerf (Eds.), *The Iraq war reader: History, documents, opinions*. New York: Touchstone.
Potter, L. G., & Sick, G. G. (2004). *Iran, Iraq, and the legacies of war*. New York: Palgrave Macmillan.
Puelings, J. (2010). *Fearing a "Shiite Octopus"': Sunni – Shi'a relations and the Implications for Belgium and Europe*. Retrieved from Royal Institute for International Affairs.
Qassem, N. (2005). *Hizbullah: The story from within*. London: Saqi.
Quandt, W. B. (1984). Reagan's Lebanon policy: Trial and error. *Middle East Journal, 38*(2), 237–54.
Rahimi, B. (2004). Ayatollah Ali al-Sistani and the democratization of Post-Saddam Iraq. *Middle East, 8*(4), 12–19.
Rahimi, B. (2008). *The discourse of democracy in Shi'i Islamic Jurisprudence: The two cases of Montazeri and Sistani*. Retrieved from https://cadmus.eui.eu/handle/1814/8223.
Rahimi, B. (2014). Contentious legacies of the Ayatollah. In A. Adib-Moghaddam (Ed.), *A critical introduction to Khomeini*. New York: Cambridge University Press.

Rajaee, F. (1997). *Iranian perspectives on the Iran-Iraq War*. Gainesville: University Press of Florida.
Ramazani, R. (1986). *Revolutionary Iran: Challenge and response in the Middle East* (Vol. 237). Baltimore: Johns Hopkins University Press
Ranstorp, M. (1998). The strategy and tactics of Hizballah's current 'Lebanonization process'. *Mediterranean Politics*, *3*(1), 103–34.
Razoux, P. (2015). *The Iran-Iraq War*. Cambridge, MA: Harvard University Press.
Reisinezhad, A. (2019). *The Shah of Iran, the Iraqi Kurds, and the Lebanese Shia*. Cham: Palgrave Macmillan.
Rizvi, S. (2018). The making of a Marjaʿ: Sīstānī and Shiʿi religious authority in the contemporary age. *Sociology of Islam*, *6*(2), 165–89.
Roemer, H. R. (1986). The Safavid period. In P. Jackson & L. Lockhart (Eds.), *The Cambridge history of Iran* (Vol. 6, pp. 189–350). Cambridge: Cambridge University Press.
Rootes, C. A. (1999). Political opportunity structures: Promise, problems and prospects. *La Lettre de la maison Française d'Oxford*, *10*, 75–97.
Rubin, B. (2006). Iran: The rise of a regional power. *The Middle East Review of International Affairs*, *10*(3), 142–51.
Sachar, H. (1979). *A history of Israel: From the rise of Zionism to our time*. New York: Alfred a Knopf Incorporated.
Sachedina, A. (1994). Activist Shi'ism in Iran, Iraq, and Lebanon. In M. E. Marty & R. S. Appleby (Eds.), *Fundamentalisms observed*. Chicago: University of Chicago Press.
Sachedina, A. (1998). *The just ruler in Shi'ite Islam: The comprehensive authority of the Jurist in Imamite Jurisprudence*. London: Oxford University Press.
Sachedina, A. (2010). Prudential concealment in Shi'ite Islam: A strategy of survival or a principle? *Common Knowledge*, *16*(2), 233–46.
Sadeghi-Boroujerdi, E. (2019). *Revolution and its discontents: Political thought and reform in Iran*. New York: Cambridge University Press.
Salem, P. E. (1991). Two years of living dangerously: General Awn and the unlikely birth of Lebanon's Second Republic. *Beirut Review*, *1*(1), 62–87.
Salibi, K. S. (1961). Lebanon since the Crisis of 1958. *The World Today*, *17*(1), 32–42.
Salibi, K. S. (1966). Lebanon under Fuad Chehab 1958–1964. *Middle Eastern Studies*, *2*(3), 211–26.
Salloukh, B. F., Barakat, R., Al-Habbal, J. S., Khattab, L. W., & Mikaelian, S. (2015). *The politics of sectarianism in postwar Lebanon*. London: Pluto Press.
Savory, R. (1980). *Iran under the Safavids*. Cambridge: Cambridge University Press.
Sayej, C. M. (2018). *Patriotic Ayatollahs: Nationalism in Post-Saddam Iraq*. Ithaca: Cornell University Press.
Schiff, Z. (1983). The green light. *Foreign Policy 50*(1), 73–85.
Schmidt, B. C., & Williams, M. C. (2008). The bush doctrine and the Iraq War: Neoconservatives versus realists. *Security Studies*, *17*(2), 191–220.
Schmidt, S. (2009). The role of religion in politics: The case of Shia-Islamism in Iraq. *Nordic Journal of Religion and Society*, *22*(2), 123–43.
Shanahan, R. (2005). *The Shia of Lebanon: Cans, parties and clerics*. London: I.B.Tauris.
Shawki, N. (2010). Political opportunity structures and the outcomes of transnational campaigns: A comparison of two transnational advocacy networks. *Peace & Change*, *35*(3), 381–411.
Shenton, A. K., & Hayter, S. (2004). Strategies for gaining access to organisations and informants in qualitative studies. *Education for Information*, *22*(3, 4), 223–31.

Sindawi, K. (2007). Hawza instruction and its role in shaping modern shiite identity: The Hawzas of al-Najaf and Qumm as a case study. *Middle Eastern Studies*, *43*(6), 831–56.

Singer, J. D. (1961). The level-of-analysis problem in international relations. *World Politics*, *14*(1), 77–92.

Sluglett, M. F., & Sluglett, P. (1991). The historiography of modern Iraq. *The American Historical Review*, *96*(5), 1408–21.

Sluglett, M. F., & Sluglett, P. (2001). *Iraq Since 1958: From revolution to dictatorship* (3rd ed.). London: I. B. Tauris.

Sluglett, P. (2007). *Britain in Iraq: Contriving King and Country*. London: I.B.Tauris.

Sobelman, D. (2004). *New rules of the Game: Israel and Hizbollah after the Withdrawal from Lebanon*. Tel Aviv: Jaffee Center for Strategic Studies.

Solh, R. (1993). The attitude of the Arab nationalists towards Greater Lebanon during the 1930s. In N. Shehadi & D. Haffar-Mills (Eds.), *Lebanon: A History of Conflict and Consensus* (pp. 149–65). London: I. B. Tauris.

Sourdel, D. (1977). The ʿAbbasid caliphate. In P. M. Holt, A. Lambton, & B. Lewis (Eds.), *The Cambridge History of Islam* (Vol. 1, pp. 104–40). Cambridge: Cambridge University Press.

Suh, D. (2001). How do political opportunities matter for social movements?: Political opportunity, misframing, pseudosuccess, and pseudofailure. *The Sociological Quarterly*, *42*(3), 437–60.

Summitt, A. R. (2004). For a white revolution: John F. Kennedy and the Shah of Iran. *The Middle East Journal*, *58*(4), 560–75.

Tabaar, M. (2018). *Religious statecraft: The politics of Islam in Iran*. New York: Columbia University Press.

Tabatabai, M. H. (1977). *Shi'ite Islam* (H. Nasr, Trans.). Albany: SUNY Press.

Tarrow, S. (1996). States and opportunities: The political structuring of social movements. In D. McAdam, J. D. McCarthy, & M. N. Zald (Eds.), *Comparative perspectives on social movements: Political opportunities, mobilizing structures, and cultural framings*. New York: Cambridge University Press.

Tarrow, S. (2005). *The new transnational activism*. New York: Cambridge University Press.

Tarrow, S. (2011). *Power in movement: Social movements and contentious politics* (3rd ed.). New York: Cambridge University Press.

Terhalle, M. (2007). Are the Shia rising? *Middle East Policy*, *14*(2), 69–83.

Thomas, M. (2005). *The French empire between the wars: Imperialism, politics and society*. Manchester: Manchester University Press.

Tilly, C. (1973). *Revolutions and collective violence*. Center for Research on Social Organization. University of Michigan.

Traboulsi, F. (2007). *A history of modern Lebanon*. Ann Arbor: Pluto Press.

Tripp, C. (2002). *A history of Iraq*. New York: Cambridge University Press.

Troy, J. (2014). *The Catholic Church and International Relations*. Oxford Handbooks Online. Retrieved from https://www.oxfordhandbooks.com/view/10.1093/oxfordhb/9780199935307.001.0001/oxfordhb-9780199935307-e-2.

Visser, R. (2006). *Sistani, the United States and politics in Iraq: From Quietism to Machiavellianism?* Norwegian Institute of International Affairs.

Walbridge, L. S. (2001). *The most learned of the Shi'a: The Institution of the Marja' taqlid*. New York: Oxford University Press.

Walbridge, L. S. (2014). *The thread of Muawiya: The making of a Marja' Taqlid*. Indiana: The Ramsay Press.

Watt, M. (1973). *The formative period of Islamic thought*. Edinburgh: Edinburgh University Press.
Weiss, M. (2008). Institutionalizing Sectarianism: The Lebanese Jaʿfari Court and Shiʿi Society under the French Mandate. *Islamic Law and Society*, *15*(3), 371–407.
Wiley, J. N. (1992). *The Islamic movement of Iraqi Shi'as*. Boulder: Lynne Rienner Publishers.
Wimmer, A. (2003). Democracy and ethno-religious conflict in Iraq. *Survival*, *45*(4), 111–34.
Winslow, C. (1996). *Lebanon: War and politics in a fragmented society*. London: Routledge.
Woodward, B. (2004). *Plan of attack*. London: Simon & Schuster.

Selected Interviews

Alavi Burujirdi, Muhammad Jawad
Amini, Ahmad
Ansari, Hadi
Ansari, Mehdi
Araki, Muhsin
Atrissi, Talal
Bahr al-Ulum, Ibrahim
Besharati, Ali Muhammad
E'temadian, Muhammadreza (d. 2019)
Eftekharzadeh, Hassan
Fahs, Sayyid Ali
Fahs, Sayyid Hani (d. 2014)
Faqih Imani, Sayyid Muhammad
Feirahi, Davood (d. 2020)
Firoozan, Mehdi
Haieri, Sayyid Ali Akbar
Al-Hakim, Sayyid Ali
Al-Hakim, Sayyid Ja'far
Hamdan, Khalil
Hashemi Rafsanjani, Akbar (d. 2017)
Haydous, Samih
al-Husseini, Hussein
Ja'farian, Rasul
Javadi-Amoli, Morteza
Kafayi, Abdolreza
Kamalian, Muhsin
Khafaf, Hamed
Khalil, Khalil
Khoei, Abd al-Saheb
Lahooti, Muhammad
Madadi, Sayyid Ahmad
Madadi, Sayyid Mahmood
Marashi, Hossien
Marandi, Muhammad

Mehdipour, Ali Akbar
Moavenian, Hamed
Mohaghegh Damad, Mostafa
Muhtadi, Muhammad Ali
Musawi Bojnourdi, Muhammad Kazem
Musawi Hawayi, Sayyid Jawad
Musawi, Ibrahim
Nahavandian, Muhammadreza
Nasrallah, Muhammad Deeb
Oun, Adel
Rafighdoost, Muhsin
Rouhani, Sayyid Ali
Rouhani, Sayyid Sadeq
Sadr, Hawra
Sadr, Rabab
Sadr, Sadr al-Din
Saeed Tehrani, Mahmood
Sanad Bahrani, Muhammad
Shahrestani, Sayyid Jawad
Shahroodi, Sayyid Mahmood (d. 2018)
Sharaf al-Din, Sayyid Hussein
Sharara, Abdul Halim
Shirazi, Sayyid Hussein
Shojooni, Ja'far (d. 2016)
Sistani, Sayyid Muhammadreza
Sobhani, Muhammad Taqi
Tabarayian, Safa al-Din
Tabatabai, Sadeq (d. 2015)
Zawawi, Salah

Index

Note: Page numbers in "italic" refer to figures.

Abbasid Caliphate 21, 30, 209 n.2
Abbasids 21–2, 30, 173 nn.10, 15
demise of 32
Sunni 21, 31, 33, 55
Abbas III 176 n.62
Abbas Mirza 42, 43, 177 nn.69, 72, 178 n.74
Abdullah (King of Jordan) 2
Abu Bakr 1, 20, 29
Abu-Nidal 134
activism
comparison with quietism 5–6
in modern Iran *84*
in modern Iraq *109*
in modern Lebanon *149*
myth of 160–3
and mujtahids
in the aftermath of Shi'i Safavid dynasty 40–1
early 31–40
Jihadi 41–3
and Persian Constitutional Revolution 47–56
Shi'i clerical (elite) 4–7
in Iran, Iraq, and Lebanon 12–14
and opportunity structures 7–12, *11*
significance of 1–3, 29–31, 155
tobacco revolt and 43–7
Activism and Quietism in Islam (Cook) 3
Afghan, M. 39
Afghan Ghalzais 39, 40
Aflaq, M. 194 n.62
Afsharids 31, 153
Aga Muhammad Khan Qajar 41, 42
Aghajari, H. 172 n.36
Ahmad Shah Qajar 58, 60, 61, 181–2 n.4, 182 n.17
Akhbāri School 55, 153, 176 n.55, 176–7 n.63
Akhbārism (Islamic Scripturalism) 39
Akhund Khorasani, K. 48, 49, 54, 68, 87, 93, 121, 184 n.42
Ala al-Dowleh, A. 48, 49
Al-Alawi, H. 194 nn.54, 56, 61
Al-Ameli, A. 195 n.80
al-Ardabili, M. 38
al-Asadi, U. S. 171 n.17
al-Assad, H. 124, 125
Al-Badri, A. 90
al-Bakr, A. H. 194 n.61
al-Dawa (journal) 194 n.65
al-Douri, I. 195 n.78
Al-Hakim, M. (Ayatollah) 78, 157, 159
Iran and 188 n.90, 189–90 n.104
Iraq and 86, 96, 97, 99, 101, 107, 110, 192 n.4, 194 nn.47, 62, 195 n.78
Lebanon and 130, 132
political posture of 92–5
al-Hassan, H. 22
al-Hoss, S. 143
Al-Ḥurr Al-Āmili 171 n.23, 176 n.55
Al-Hurriya (journal) 194 n.54
al-Husayn, A. 21
al-Husseini, H. 132, 133, 138
Ali (Shi'i Imam) 18–20, 29, 85, 173 n.15
Ali, M. 21
Ali Ibn Muhammad (Shi'i Imam) 22
Ali Ibn Muhammad al-Samarri 22
Ali Mua'yyid 34
al-Jisr, M. 116
Al-Kailani, A. R. 89–90
al-Karaki 37–8, 174 n.32, 175 nn.33, 36–8, 41
Al-Khafaji, I. 197 n.102
Al-Khatteeb, L. 210 n.16
al-Khoury, B. 117
Al-Kulayni, M. Y. 152, 171 n.21, 172 n.8
Allawi, A. A. 198 n.120
al-Lum'ah al-Dimashqiya (Shahid Awwal) 34
al-Ma'mun 21

al-Nasir 32
al-Nawbakhti, A. 171 n.17
al-Saad, H. P. 199 n.17
al-Sadeq (Shi'i Imam) 21, 171 nn.14–15, 184 n.46
al-Saduq 32, 152, 169 n.40, 173 n.8
al-Salem, H. 171 n.23
al-Samarri, A. 171 n.17
al-Sheybani, Z. 171 n.15
Al-Siraj, A. I. 193 n.44
Al-Tabarsi 171 n.25
al-Tikriti, H. 194 n.62
al-Tusi 85, 152, 171 nn.26, 30, 173 n.8
AMAL (Lebanese Resistance Regiments) 157, 162
  Hezbollah and 135–42
  Lebanon and 128, 131–3, 149–50, 202 n.78, 203 nn.80–1, 206 nn.144, 150, 208 n.190
Amin, A. 202 n.60
Amin al-Sultan, A. 52
Amini Hiravi, S. a.-D. 174 n.30
Amoli, H. 188 n.87
Anglo-Egyptian treaty (1936) 200 n.18
Anglo-Iraqi Treaty (1922) 90
Anglo-Iraqi Treaty (1930) 199 n.18
Anglo-Persian Agreement (1919) 58, 60
Anglo-Russian agreement (1907) 181 n.115
An-Nahar Daily (newspaper) 126
Ansari, M. 25, 26, 43, 158
Aoun, M. 145
April Accord 143, 146–7
Arabism 115
Arab Shi'is, in Iraq 85
Arafat, Y. 124, 135, 140, 144, 206 n.144
Arak 182 n.10
Ardabili, S. 35
Ardebili, A. K. 201 n.39
Arif, A. S. 94
Asaad, K. 131, 138, 202 n.59
Ashtiani, M. H. 45, 46
Assad, H. 144
Astarabadi, M. 175 n.38
Astarabadi, M. A. 39, 176 n.54
Ataturk, K. 62, 155
Azerbaijan 45, 174 n.30

Baalbeck 125, 126, 131, 135, 136, 139, 142
Ba'ath Party (Iraq) 3, 86–7, 92, 156
Bafqi, M. T. 63
Baghdad 172–3 n.8
Bahrain 167 n.7
Bahr al-Ulloum, M. B. (Ayatollah) 88, 107, 108
Bahrani, Y. 177 n.63
Banani, A. 183 n.26
Baqai 186 n.59
Barak, E. 144
Barak, O. 201 n.33
Batatu, H. 192 n.1
Ba'th (Iraq) 99–101, 194 n.61, 196 n.87
Battle of Chaldiran (1514) 36
Bazargan, M. 82–3, 189 n.97, 191 n.127
Begin, M. 134
Behbahani, A. 48
Behbahani, W. 176–7 n.63
Beheshti, M. 160, 201 n.39
Bell, G. 90
Beqaa 123
Berri, N. 133, 135, 137–9, 142, 143, 146, 148, 206 n.143
Beshara, A. 200 n.32
Biḥār al-Anwār (Muhammad Baqir Majlesi) 39
Bolshevik Revolution (1917) 60, 192 n.9
Bristol Hotel Gathering (2004) 144
Britain 115, 181 n.115, 192–3 n.17
Browne, E. G. 180 nn.106, 109, 181 n.115
Budala, H. 187 nn.69, 73
Bullard, R. 167 n.3
Burujirdi (Ayatollah) 10, 16, 28, 66–71, 93, 121, 157
  inheritors of 72
  Iran and 59, 79, 81, 185 n.50, 186 nn.57, 61, 187 nn.69, 76
Burujirdi, Muhammad Javad Alavi (Ayatollah) 8, 170 n.3, 183 n.40, 184 nn.41–2
Bush, G. W. 107, 144

Cairo Accord 203 n.84
Carter, J. 169 n.55
Cedar Revolution 145, 208 n.188
Chalabi, A. 107
Chamoun, C. 119
Chamran, M. 132, 199 n.6, 204 n.99
Chehab, F. 119–20, 122, 200 n.32, 200–1 n.33

Chubin, S.196 n.96
Clinton, B. 107
Compulsory Conscription (Iran) (1926) 62
Cox, P. 58, 89
Curzon, G. 178 n.78

Dagan, M. 209 n.13
Dar al-Tabligh al-Islami 80, 191 n.116
Davani, A. 184 nn.42, 46, 185 n.49, 189 nn.96–7, 191 n.118, 192 n.8
Dawa Party 195 n.69
Debbas, C. 199 n.17
Della Valle, P. 176 n.49
divine legislation (*tashrī*) 18
Dowlat Abadi, Y. 179–80 n.97, 180 n.105
Dress Unification Law 183 n.29
Druze Muslims 119, 120

Eastern Mediterranean Ports 200 n.23
Egypt 119, 192 n.17
Ein al-Dowleh, A. 179 n.95
Emami, J. S. 82
Emami, M. M. 191 n.113
Eslami, G. 196 n.94, 197 n.105
Ettelaat Daily (newspaper) 82

Fadaian-e-Islam (the devotees of Islam) 67–71, 167 n.5, 185 n.57, 186 nn.60, 62, 187 n.69
Fadlallah, M. H. 5, 6, 159, 195 n.69, 205 n.132, 207 n.167
  Lebanon and 131, 136, 137, 140–2, 150
Faisal I 86, 90, 91, 193 n.32
Fal-Asiri, A. A. 44
Falsafi, M. T. 188 n.84
Fatah 124, 133, 135, 204 n.100
Fatah Ali Shah 42
Fatemi 186 n.59
fatwa 46, 161, 186 n.61, 201 n.49, 210 n.16
  Iraq and 87, 89, 90, 192 n.8, 195 n.73
Feuvrier, J. 179 n.89
Feyzieh crackdown (Iran) 74, 80
Fisk, R. 202 n.74, 208 n.184
France 115, 143, 207 n.179
Frangieh, S. 125
Freedom Movement of Iran 189 n.97
Friday Prayer, significance of 38, 175 n.36
Fromkin, D. 193 n.17
Fundamental Law of Iran 50, 77, 91

Gaddafi 130, 133
Gass, N. 185 n.54
Gemayel, A. 137, 138, 146, 206 n.143
Genghis 32, 33
Ghazan 34
Gilani, Z. 35
Goerge, L. 203 n.94
Golpayegani, M. R. (Ayatollah) 72, 79, 80, 130, 187 n.77, 188 n.87, 191 nn.113, 119
Golshayian 185 n.54
Gouraud (General) 115
governing council (Majlis al-Siyadah) 95
Gowharshad crackdown (Iran) 65
Grapes of Wrath' operation 143
Guardianship of the Jurist (Wilayat e Faqih) 4, 6, 57, 135, 168 n.32, 181 n.2
  modernized 78–9
  performative theory and 78–9

Habib 135
Habubi, Sayyid Muhammad Said 93
Hadiths 23
Hairi, Abd al-Hussein 183 n.38
Hairi, A. H. (Ayatollah) 59–65, 71, 72, 75, 81, 157, 182 n.10, 183 n.33
Hairi, M. 188 n.87, 189 n.96
Hakamizadeh, A. 184 n.44
Halperin, S. 200 nn.28–9
Hamas 146, 208 n.198
Hamoudi, H. A. 4–5
Hanafis 24
Harb, R. 136
Hariri, R. 143–5, 207 n.179
Hariri, S. 145, 146
Hashemi, M. 140
Hashemite Monarchy, abolition of 86
Hassan 20
Hassan Ibn Ali (Shiʿi Imam) 22, 90, 171 n.25
hefz beyzat al-Islam (protecting the citadel of Islam (and/or the faith)) 168 n.36
Herz al-Din, M. 182 n.17
Hezbollah 2, 13, 162
  AMAL and 137–42

establishment of 134–7
Lebanon and 145–7, 150, 205 nn.125–6, 207 nn.168, 175, 208 nn.186, 190, 209 n.208
Hilli (Allameh) 24, 34, 39, 152, 173 n.15
Hilli, Sadid al-Din 173 n.15
Hilu, C. 119, 123
Hobeika, E. 206 n.143
Hourani, A. 198 n.1
Hujjati Kermani, A. 202 n.60
Hulagu 33, 173 n.10
Husayn 20–1
Husseini Hairi, K. 194 n.65, 195 n.73

Ibn al-Jawzi, A. 173 n.8
Ibn Alqami 32, 33, 173 n.10
Ibn Ja'far, M. 21
Ibn Tawus, A. 32, 33, 173 n.14
Ibn Uthman, M. 171 n.17
Ibn Yaqteen, A. 30
ijtihad 33, 54–5, 152, 196 n.95, 201 n.49
corollaries, to Shiʿi jurisprudence 24
etymology of 24
of mujtahids xi, 6, 9, 12
opposition to 39
Ilkhanids 30, 32, 34, 152
Imamate, significance of 17, 19–21
Imami, H. 68, 185 n.57
infallible Imams 7, 17, 23, 168 n.37, 170 n.9, 175 n.36
Occultation era and 18
on prerequisites for the laity 24
responsibilities of 20, 22
Iran 13, 57–60, 87, 143, 207 n.178, 209 n.13
Burujirdi's inheritors and 72
establishment of Islamic Republic of 81–3
interregnum era and clerical activism in 66–7
Khomeini's political posture and 75–8
and mujtahid
and national movement 67–71
solidarity and power in 79–81
1963 uprising and 72–5
revolutionary Shiʿism in Lebanon and 131–4
rise of Pahlavi and mujtahids of 60–6
Iranian mujtahids and Iraqi politics 87–8
Iran–Iraq war 101–3, 110
Iraq 2–3, 15–16, 26, 44, 119, 197 n.107
Al-Hakim's political posture and 92–5
Baʿthist, and Khoei's' political posture 99–101
Iran–Iraq war and 101–3, 110
mujtahids' solidarity power in 105–7
1991 Uprising and 103–5
1920 Uprising in 88–91
ottoman to independent 87–8
Sadr and Shiʿi activism in 96–9
Shiʿi clerical political activism and 12–14
Shiʿi political movements in 91–2
significance of 85–7
Sistani and post-Saddam 107–9
Iraqi, M. 186 n.62
Iraqi Revolt (1920) 14
Iraq Liberation Act (1998) 107
Iraq War (2003) 2, 13
Isfahan 31, 39, 40, 45, 158
Isfahani, Abu al-Hasan (Ayatollah) 62, 67, 93
Isfahani, Munir al-Din. 45
Islamic Action Organisation 103, 107
Islamic Dawa Party (Hizb al-Dawa al-Islamiyya) (Iraq) 96, 97, 107
Islamic government, significance of 19, 190 n.108, 195 n.80, 204 n.105
Iran and 66, 68, 77–9, 81
Iraq and 100, 104
Lebanon and 133, 137
Islamic Government, The (Khomeini) 78
Islamic Resistance Party 136
Islamic Revival Society, The' 88
Islamist/activist Shiʿi clerics 4
Ismail 30–1, 35, 36, 40, 174 n.25, 175 n.38
Ismail III 41
Ismailis 32, 33, 174 n.24
Israel 13, 133, 139, 143
Hezbollah and 146–7

Jabal Amil 34, 36–8, 121, 174 nn.26, 31. *See also* Lebanon
Jafarian, R. 173 nn.10, 19, 23, 175 n.36, 191 nn.116, 207 n.167
Ja'far Ibn Muhammad (Shiʿi Imam). *See* al-Sadeq (Shiʿi Imam)

Ja'fari School of Jurisprudence 116
Japan 179 n.93
Jazaeri, M. J. 88
Jihadi mujtahids 41–3
Jilani, M. *See* Qummi, Mirza
Jordan 119
Jumblatt, W. 145, 206 n.143, 208 n.190
jurisprudence 15, 75, 97, 156, 168 n.36, 181 n.2
  clerical authority and 19, 24–5, 170 n.12, 171 nn.26, 30
  Ja'fari School of 116
  Lebanon and 120, 150, 201 n.49
  political activism and 37, 39, 53
  for tribes 198 n.120

Kamarei, H. K. 65, 182 n.5
Kani, A. 178 n.79
Karami, O. 144, 145
Karami, R. 119
Karbala 85, 86
Karbalayi, H. 178 n.82
Kasaba, R. 200 n.23
Kashani, A. (Ayatollah) 67, 83, 184 n.47, 185 nn.48–50, 186 nn.57, 63, 187 nn.65, 68–9
  Iran and 68–70
Kashani, M. 184 n.47
Kashani, M. M. 176 n.55
Kashif al-Ghita, J. 42
Kashmiri, M. A. 177 nn.71–2
Kasravi, A. 52, 68, 180 nn.107–8, 181 nn.114, 118, 184 nn.44, 46
Kechichian, J. A. 167 n.7
Kemal, M. 61
Kermani, N. 179 n.97
Khalesi, M. (Ayatollah) 89–91, 193 n.32
Khalesizadeh, Muhammad 183 n.38
Khamenei, A. (Ayatollah) ix, 12, 159, 160
Khātoonābādi, M. 177 n.67
Khawnsari, A. 190 n.110
Khawnsari, M. B. 174 n.32, 176 n.54
Khawnsari, M. T. 182 n.5, 184 n.47
Khawrazmid 33
Khoei, A. (Ayatollah) 3–5
  Iran and 188 n.90, 191 n.119
  Iraq and 87, 95, 97, 104, 105, 110, 195 n.76, 196 nn.94–5, 197 n.105
  Lebanon and 130, 132
  Middle East future and 157, 159
  political posture of 99–101
Khoei, A. S. 195 n.76
Khomeini, M. 79, 81, 191 n.119
Khomeini, R. (Ayatollah) 4, 6, 28, 54, 181 n.2, 204 n.101
  death of 141
  in exile 77, 81, 82, 101, 130
  Iran and 57, 59–60, 65, 78–9, 183 nn.30, 40, 184 n.44, 187–8 n.77, 188 n.87, 189 nn.97, 100, 102, 189–90 n.104, 190 nn.104, 108, 110, 112, 191 nn.116, 127
  Iran–Iraq war and 102–3
  Iraq and 98, 195 n.80, 196 n.86, 197 n.104
  Islamic Republic establishment and 81–3
  Lebanon and 120, 131, 134, 139, 140
  Middle East future and 157, 159, 160
  1963 uprising and 72–5
  political posture of 75–8
  Sadr and 127
  Shariatmadari and 81
Khorasan 34, 36, 37, 174 n.30
Khosroshahi, H. 186 n.60
Khourshah, R. D. 33
Khwandamir, M. 174 n.25
Kohlberg, E. 33, 173 n.14
König, F. 120
Kufa 95
Kuwait, invasion of 103, 110, 197 n.107

Lahoud, E. 143, 144, 146, 207 n.180, 208 n.184
laity
  Imam's companions as references for 21
  Imams on prerequisites for 24
  relationship with Zai'm 115
  Shi'i clerical elite and 23–4, 54
  Shi'i Marja' and 26
  significance of 18
Lambton, A. 172 n.41, 187 n.75
Lebanon x, xi, 2–5, 12–16, 34, 36, 162, 194 n.64
  birth of revolutionary Shi'ism in 131–4

independent 116–18
mujtahids of 113, 134–7, 198 nn.1, 3, 199 n.8, 199 n.17, 200 nn.18, 33, 201 n.37, 201 n.49, 202 nn.60, 74, 78, 203 n.86, 98, 204 nn.100, 108, 206 nn.133, 143, 207 n.179, 208 nn.188, 190
and solidarity 141–2
Nasrallah and 142–6
republic of 118–20
Sadr's perceptions and postures and 120–30
Shiʿi, as second-class citizens 114–16
Shiʿi political activism clash in 137–41
33-days war and 146–8
legal opinions (*ifta/qadha*) 11, 23, 78, 151, 160, 171 n.18
Le Monde (newspaper) 130
liberal Shiʿi clergy 5
Libya 103
limited monarchy 47, 53

Madadi, A. 196 n.95
Mahdi, S. 22, 92
Mahmood, M. 177 n.65
Majlesi, A. 209 n.4
Majlesi, M. B. 39, 171 nn.19, 24, 176 n.55
Majlis 62, 95, 180 n.107, 181 n.114
Major migration 179 n.96
Makki, H. 185 n.54, 186 nn.58–9, 63
Maktab-e Islam (magazine) 80, 191 n.118
Maktabi, R. 199 n.16
Malkam Khan 48
Mamluk Dynasty 114
Mansour, H. 75
Maraji' Tholath 59
Marashi Najafi, S. (Ayatollah) 79, 80, 130, 187 n.77, 189 n.96, 190 nn.111, 190–1 n.112, 191 n.119
Marja'iyya
formation and consolidation of office of 25–7
significance of 19, 21, 72, 80, 93, 96, 98, 104–6, 108, 110, 158, 159, 172 n.36, 188 n.77, 195 n.74, 197 n.113
Maronites 162, 198 n.3, 199 nn.8, 17, 200 n.18, 203 n.81
Lebanon and 115–20, 124, 128, 137–9, 145
Mas'alah fi al-Amal ma'a al-Sultan (al-Murtada) 32
Mashahd 41, 64
Mashruteh Mashrue' 51
Maudhuwya 98
Mearsheimer, J. 197 n.107
Mehdipour, A. A. 189 n.102
Mesopotamia Campaign 87–8, 109
Middle East. *See also individual entries*
future of
contemporary situation and 154–7
quietism versus activism' myth and 160–3
significance of 151–4
transnational mujtahids and 158–60
modern, demystifying Shiʿi clerical role in politics of 15–16
Mikati, N. 145
Milani (Ayatollah) 130
Minor Autocracy period 53
minor migration 179 n.96
Minor Occultation 169 n.40
Minorsky, V. 36, 176 n.56
Mir-Lowhi, M. *See* Navvab Safavi
Modarres, Hassan 61, 179 n.92, 181 n.4
Mohaghegh Damad, M. 188 n.87, 190 n.110
Muhammad Ali Shah Qajar 50–3
Muhammad Shah Qajar 178 n.76
Mohit Mafi, H. 180 n.100
Mohtashamipour, A. A. 135
Mongol Ilkhanids. *See* Ilkhanids
Montazeri, H. A. 6, 140
Montazeri, M. A. 133
Mosaddeq, M. 69, 70, 185 n.56, 186 nn.57, 58, 62, 187 nn.65, 68–9
Motahhari, M. 201 n.39
Mount Lebanon 115
Movement of the Deprived (Harakat al-Mahrumin) 125
Muawiyah 20, 21
Mufid 39
Mughniyah, Imad Fayez 205 n.125

Muhammad Ibn Ali (Shiʿi Imam) 21
Mujtahid, M. M. 178 n.75
mujtahids (qualified Shiʿi cleric) x
activism of
in modern Iran *84*
in modern Iraq *109*
in modern Lebanon *149*
in aftermath of Shiʿi Safavid dynasty 40–1
early 31–40
ijtihad of xi, 6, 9, 12
of Iran
and Iraqi politics 87–8
and rise of Pahlavi 60–6
Iranian national movement and 67–71
Jihadi 41–3
of Lebanon 134–7
1920 Uprising in Iraq and active 88–91
Persian Constitutional Revolution and 47–56
political activism, in modern Iran *84*
qadha of 11
Shiʿi Usuli 8, 55
significance of 10
solidarity power
in Iran 79–81
in Iraq 105–7
in Lebanon 141–2
transnational 158–60
Mullabashi, M. 40
Musa Sadr (Imam) 96, 191 n.118, 194 n.64
Lebanon and 113–14, 120, 131–3, 148–50, 201 nn.39, 49, 202 nn.52, 60, 203 n.94
Middle East future and 157, 159, 162
perceptions and postures of 120–30
Musawi, A. 142, 150
Musawi, H. 135
Musawi, R. *See* Khomeini (Ayatollah)
Mustawfi, A. 182 n.15

Nader Shah 40–1, 43, 55, 85, 158
Naʿini, M. H. 53, 62, 90, 91
Najaf 51–3, 60, 78, 85–7, 104
Najafi, J. *See* Kashif al-Ghita
Najafi, M. 182 n.20
Najafi, M. H. 25, 171 n.30, 178 n.76
Najafi Ghoochani, M. H. 192 n.7
Najafi Isfahani, Aqa Muhammad Taqi 182 n.20
Najafi Isfahani, Aqa Nur Allah 45, 62–3
Najaf seminary 3, 4, 13, 25, 26, 171 n.26, 188 n.90
criticism of normative view of 5
Iran and 59, 66, 72, 78
Iraq and 91, 95, 100, 106, 109, 110, 194 n.47, 195 n.73
Lebanon and 121, 148
Middle East future and 152, 156–7
Najaf Uprising (1918) 88
Naraqi, A. 177 n.67
Naser al-Din Shah Qajar 44–6, 178 n.77, 179 n.83
end of 47
Nasirean Ethics (*Akhlāq-e Nāṣerī*) (Tusi) 33
Nasr, V. 2, 109
Nasrallah, H. 13, 114, 147, 148, 150, 159, 206 n.133
political posture of 142–6
Nasser 119
National Front 185 n.56
National Iraqi Alliance 198 n.135
National Pact (Mithaq al-Watani) (Lebanon) 113, 119
significance of 117
Navvab Safavi, M. 68–70, 83, 167 n.5, 184 nn.44, 46, 185 n.49, 186 n.59
Nejati, G. 187 n.65
1991 Uprising and Iraq 103–5, 197 nn.110, 113, 115
1920 Uprising, in Iraq 88–91
non-litigious affairs (*al-Umour al-Hesbiah*) 6
Noori, F. 48–53, 58, 180 nn.106–7, 111, 184 n.42
execution of 53–4
Nu'mani, M. R. 195 n.78

Occultation era x, xi, 1, 4, 5, 6, 8, 22, 31, 57, 160
infallible Imam and 18
Shiʿi clerical authority and 23–5
Olmert, E. 13, 146, 147
Ostaglu, M. Q. K. 176 n.47
Our Economy' (*Iqtisaduna*) (Sadr) 97

Our Mission' (*Resalatuna*) (Sadr) 96
Our Philosophy' (*Falsafatuna*) (Sadr) 97

Pakradouni, K. 128
Palestinian Liberation Organization (PLO) 124, 127, 133, 204 n.100
Palestinian refugees 119
  in Lebanon 127–8, 138
Parsi, T. 205 n.129, 207 nn.161, 178
Persia 31, 34–6, 40, 183 n.27. *See also* Iran
  Russia and 42–3
Persian Constitutional Revolution 12, 14–16, 153–4, 179 n.96, 182 n.20, 192 n.7
  Iran and 57, 58, 60, 66, 67, 69, 71, 83, 184 n.42, 188 n.90
  Iraq and 85, 87
  political activism and 31, 41, 43, 47–56
Personal Status Law (Iraq) 93, 94
Peter the Great (Russia) 41–2
Phoenicians 114
political activism. *See* activism
political Maronite 118
political opportunity structure 30, 32, 92, 94–5, 98
  concept of 8–9
  contemporary Middle East and 154–7
  open and closed 9, 11
  outcomes of 11–12
  significance of 13–14
  Zai'm-laity relationship and 115
political quietism. *See* quietism
politics, significance of 27–8
pragmatic quietism 3
Progressive Socialist Party (PSP) 138
Prophet Muhammad 17–19, 23
  roles of 19

Qajars 31, 42, 153, 158, 177 n.65
  establishment of 41
Qanatabadi, S. 185 n.48
Qasim, A. K. 92–4, 195 n.72
Qassem, N. 208 n.186
Qatifi, Ibrahim 175 n.33
Qavam, A. 70, 187 n.65
quietism
  comparison with activism 5–6
    myth of 160–3
  definition of 4
  significance of 1–3, 29, 155
quietist Shiʿi clerics 4–5
Qum 49, 62, 63, 82, 179 n.96, 180 n.105
  Maraji' of 80
Qummi, A. 171 n.15
Qummi, H. 64–5, 67
Qummi, Mirza 177 n.67
Qummi, Muhammad. *See* al-Saduq
Qum seminary 3, 6, 10, 120, 156, 157
  Iran and 59, 60, 64, 66, 69, 73, 74, 81, 183 nn.30, 40, 184 nn.41, 42, 187 n.77, 190 nn.110, 112
  Iraq and 86, 105, 110
Quran 23, 25, 168 n.35, 170 nn.1, 4–6, 9, 172 n.4

Rabin, Y. 134, 143
Rafsanjani, H. 15, 140, 188 n.77
Rahimlou, Y. 173 n.18
Rahman, A. 94
Razmara, H. A. 69
Reagan, R. 138, 205 n.129
religio-political pluralism 5
republicanism 61–2
Reuter, P. 178 n.78
Revolutionary Council (Iran) 82–3
Reza Khan. *See* Reza Shah
Reza Shah 59–61, 183 nn.30, 33, 184 n.44
  abdication of 65, 66
  Aqa Nur Allah and 62–3
  modernization reforms of 63–4, 183 n.26
  Qummi and 64–5
  on republicanism 61–2
Rikabi, F. 196 n.87
Roemer, H. R. 176 n.62
Rumlu, H. B. 37
Russia 42–3, 179 n.91, 181 n.115
Russo-Persian wars 41–3

Sa'dun, A. 90–1
Saad, M. 126
Sabzevar 34, 174 n.30
Saddam Hussein 99, 100, 102–3, 106, 107, 111, 133–4, 140

Sadr, M. 90
Sadr, M. B. (Ayatollah) 4, 6, 131, 142
  death of 99, 196 n.86
  Iraq and 86, 95, 105, 107, 110, 194 nn.54, 63–4, 195 nn.69, 73, 76, 78, 80–1, 196 n.82
  Khomeini on 196 n.86
  Shiʿi activism and mission in Iraq and 96–9
Sadr, M. M. S. (Ayatollah) 106, 198 n.120
Sadr, R. 121
Sadr, S. 65, 182 n.5
Safavids 173–4 n.24, 175 n.41
  fall of 39, 55, 153, 158, 172 n.40
  mujtahids in the aftermath of 40–1
  relationship with Shiʿi clergy 36–7
  rise of 30–1, 35, 55, 85, 121, 153, 173 n.22, 175 n.36
Safi Golpayegani, A. 187 n.73
Sahabi, Y. 189 n.97
Salam, S. 135
Salman the Persian 85
Samarra 86
Sarbadars of Sabzevar 34
Sarkis, E. 135
Saudi Arabia 167 n.7
SAVAK 74, 82, 122–3, 191 n.119, 202 n.52
semi-quietist Shiʿi clerics 5
Sepehr, M. T. 177 nn.67, 69–70
Shaaban, S. 205 n.123
Shah, Muhammad Reza 59, 65, 68–73, 82, 155, 157, 184 n.41
  1963 uprising and 73–5
Shahabadi, M. A. 189 n.94
Shah Abbas 39, 176 nn.47, 49–50
Shahid al-Thāni 38, 174 n.26
Shahid Awwal 34, 37, 174 n.31
Shah Sultan Hussein 39
Shah Tahmasb 31, 37, 175 nn.38, 41
Shah Tahmasb II 40, 176 n.62
Shalit, G. 146
Shams al-Din, M. M. 132, 137, 140, 141, 149, 204 n.105
Sharaf al-Din, A. 121, 201 n.42
Shariat-Sangelaji, R. 184 n.44
Shariat Isfahani, F. (Ayatollah) 89–91
Shariatmadari, K. (Ayatollah) 72, 79–81, 130
  Iran and 187 n.77, 188 n.87, 189 nn.96, 102, 191 nn.116, 118, 191 n.119
Sharif al-Murtada 24, 32
Sharif Razi, M. 184 n.47
Sharon, A. 134
Shiʿi Buyids 24, 30, 32, 55
Shiʿi clerical authority
  early Shiʿi political doctrines and 19–23
  formation and consolidation of office of Marja'iyya and 25–7
  Occultation era and 23–5
  significance of 17–19
Shiʿi community as outcast, in Lebanon 116–18
Shiʿi Crescent 2–3, 167 n.11
Shiʿi revival, in Iraq 2–3
Shiraz 41, 44, 45, 123, 179 n.83
Shirazi, M. M. H. 45–6, 61, 158, 178 n.82
Shirazi, M. S. 178 n.74
Shirazi, M. T. (Ayatollah) 88–9
Siniora, F. 13, 145
Sistani, A. (Ayatollah) ix, 4–7, 12, 15, 148, 210 n.17
  Iraq and 87, 100, 105–7, 111
  Middle East future and 159, 161–2
  post-Saddam Iraq and 107–9
Six-Day War 124
Soleimani, Q. 12
Solh, R. 117
Sudan 192 n.17
Sufi orders 35
Sufi Safavid order 173 n.23
Sunni Islamic Unification Movement 205 n.123
Sunnis 3, 13, 14, 170 n.3, 171 n.26
  Abbasids 21, 31, 33, 55
  clerical authority and 18, 19, 24, 26
  Iraq and 2, 85–7, 90, 94–6, 108, 192 nn.1–2, 193 n.43, 198 n.135
  Lebanon and 114–21, 124, 126, 135, 137, 138, 148, 198 n.1, 199 n.6, 200 n.18, 202 n.60, 205 n.123, 209 n.208
  Middle East future and 152, 153, 156, 161, 162

political activism and 30–40, 173 nn.10, 14, 19, 174 n.26, 175 n.36
Supplementary Fundamental Law 50, 182 n.17
Supreme Council for Islamic Revolution in Iraq (SCIRI) 103, 107
Supreme Islamic Shiʿi Council (SISC) 128, 131–3, 135, 202 n.59, 204 n.102
Syria 103, 206 n.143
Lebanon and 114, 115, 119, 138, 141, 143, 145
Syrian Baʿath Party 144

Tabatabai, M. 43, 48, 177 nn.71–2, 180 n.111
Tabatabai, M. H. 170 n.9, 187 n.75, 188 n.87
Tabatabai, S. 132
Tabriz 36, 45, 179 n.83, 180 n.108
Tabrizi, M. J. 45
Talbot, G. 44, 178 n.79
Taleqani, M. 189 n.97
Tanbīh al-ummah wa-tanzīh al-millah (Naʿini) 53
Taqizadeh, H. 50
Taqlid
concept of 25–6
Marja' 26–7
Tarrow, S. 8, 154
Tehran 49–54
Tehrani, A. B. 178 n.76
Tehrani, M. 184 n.46
Teymouri, I. 179 n.90
33-days war 146–8
Tikrit 194 n.61
Timurid dynasty 35
Tobacco Protest (1891–2) 31, 43–7, 178 n.82, 179 n.92
transnationalism 43–7
Treaty of Finckenstein (1807) 177 n.65
Treaty of Gulistan (1813) 42, 177 n.69
Treaty of Tilsit 177 n.65
Treaty of Turkmenchay (1828) 43, 55, 58
Treaty of Zahab (1639) 85
Trump, D. 12
Truthful Pledge 147
Tudeh Party (Iran) 66, 68–70
Tueni, G. 126
Tufaily, S. 139–42, 150, 207 n.168
Turkaman, I. B. 39
Turkey 61, 78
Tusi, N. 32–3, 37, 39, 152, 173 n.10
Twelver Shiʿism 167 n.2
Tyre 121, 122, 136

Ulama Association (Jamaʿat al-Ulama) 92, 93, 96, 97
Uljeitu 34, 152
Umar Ibn al-Khattab 20, 172 n.8
Umayyads 21
UN Security Council Resolution (UNSCR) 425 145
UN Security Council Resolution (UNSCR) 1559 144, 146
UN Security Council Resolution (UNSCR) 1701 147
Usuli School 8, 25, 39, 55, 152, 160, 168 n.34, 176 n.63
Uthman Ibn Affan 20, 29

Vosuq al-Dowleh, H. 58

Walt, S. 197 n.107
Weir, B. 205 n.129
Wilson, A. 88
World Liberation Movement (WLM) 133

Yazdi, K. 49
Yazdi, M. K. (Ayatollah) 87, 88, 192 n.8
Yazid 21

Za'imism 115, 118
Zahediyeh Sufi order 35
Zand, Karim Khan 41, 176 n.62
Zand, Lotf Ali 41
Zand dynasty 41
Zanjani, A. 188 n.87
Zu'ama, of Lebanon 115, 117, 119, 124, 126, 128, 199 nn.4, 6

www.ingramcontent.com/pod-product-compliance
Lightning Source LLC
Chambersburg PA
CBHW062137300426
44115CB00012BA/1960
* 9 7 8 0 7 5 5 6 4 4 8 7 2 *